RE-MAKING LOVE

Also by Barbara Ehrenreich

The Hearts of Men: *American Dreams and the Flight from Commitment*

By Barbara Ehrenreich and Deirdre English

For Her Own Good: *150 Years of Advice to Women*
Witches, Midwives, and Nurses: *A History of Women Healers*
Complaints and Disorders: *The Sexual Politics of Sickness*

RE-MAKING LOVE

LOVE

The Feminization of Sex

Barbara Ehrenreich,
Elizabeth Hess,
Gloria Jacobs

ANCHOR PRESS/DOUBLEDAY
GARDEN CITY, NEW YORK
1986

Library of Congress Cataloging-in-Publication Data

Ehrenreich, Barbara.
Re-making love.

Bibliography: p. 217.
Includes index.
1. Women—United States—Sexual behavior.
2. Sex customs—United States.   3. Feminism—United
States.   4. Sex (Psychology)   I. Hess, Elizabeth.
II. Jacobs, Gloria.   III. Title.
   HQ29.E35   1986   306.7′088042   86–2074
        ISBN 0-385-18498-0

To our children—Alexa, Gideon, Kate,
Rosa, and Benjy—
and to the memory of Betty Ann Colhoun.

Contents

ACKNOWLEDGMENTS

This book was written during a time of exciting new debate on issues of sexuality; the debate has brought argument *and* fresh energy to a discussion that had grown moribund. All of this new work, even when not cited directly in our book, has challenged us and helped to clarify our thinking. Writers such as Dennis Altman, Kate Ellis, Jeffrey Escoffier, Lynne Segal, Christine Stansell, Ann Snitow, Sharon Thompson, Carol Vance, and Ellen Willis have expanded the parameters of the debate and reasserted the importance of sexual liberation within the broader context of women's liberation.

The original idea for this book developed out of an article we wrote for *Ms.* in 1980, and we would like to thank our many friends there for their encouragement and advice.

The numerous women and men who spoke to us about the intimate details of their lives must feel that their reputations are in our hands. We'd like to thank them for their time and their trust in us. In return we have altered their names and some background information to protect their anonymity.

We would like also to thank all the people who offered varied kinds of help, ranging from hours of discussion and shared reading material to typing assistance, computer hookups or a free room to work in. These include Dick Colhoun, Marilyn Gaizband, Lindy Hess, Deborah Huntington, Karen Judd, Mimi Keck, Ellen Keniston, Nancy Lewis Peck, Virginia Reath, Ruth Russell, Brenda Steinberg, Fannie Steinberg, and Stephanie Urdang. John Russell, Harriet Bernstein, and Susan Butler were our extremely able research assistants. In addition, Barbara Ehrenreich thanks the Institute for Policy Studies in Washington, D.C., and the New York Institute for Humanities for providing good fellowship as well as more concrete forms of support.

To our agent, Charlotte Sheedy, and our editor, Loretta Barrett: Both wondered what they were getting into when they took on three authors to do one book. Both knew when to stand back and let us find our way and when to step in with advice and encouragement. We are deeply grateful to each for their deft touch and supportive friendship.

Finally we want to thank Peter Biskind, Jon Steinberg, and Gary Stevenson, who provided sympathetic companionship throughout the many versions of this book. Yes, they changed the diapers, made the dinners, and read and commented on various drafts. Most important, they never considered such support beyond the call of duty.

RE-MAKING LOVE

Introduction

For most Americans, the "sexual revolution" is what Gay Talese found when he set out on his quest to see what middle-aged, middle-class men had been missing all these years: wife-swapping clubs, massage parlors, Hugh Hefner's harem of bunnies, *Screw*. It was a sexual marketplace that dominated and marginalized women; and if this was all there was to the sexual revolution, then its critics have been right to see it as little more than a male fling and a setback for women. The dark side of the gaudy new industry of pornography and commoditized sex for men has been, as feminists have noted, the exploitation of women as "sex workers" (models, masseuses, etc.) and the deepening objectification of *all* women as potential instruments of male pleasure.

But the sexual revolution that Talese found is only half the story, or less. There has been another, hidden sexual revolution that the male commentators and even the feminist critics have for the most part failed to acknowledge: This is a *women's* sexual revolution, and the changes it has brought about in our lives and expectations go far deeper than anything in the superficial spectacle of sexuality we have come to identify as "the" sexual revolution.

In fact, if either sex has gone through a change in sexual attitudes and behavior that deserves to be called revolutionary, it is women, and not men at all. This fact should be widely known, because it leaps out from all the polls and surveys that count for data in these matters. Put briefly, men changed their sexual behavior very little in the decades from the fifties to the eighties. They "fooled around," got married, and often fooled around some more, much as their fathers and perhaps their grandfathers had before them. Women, however, have gone from a pattern of virginity before marriage and monogamy thereafter to a pattern that much more resembles men's: Between the mid-sixties and the mid-seventies, the number of women reporting premarital sexual experience went from a daring minority to a respectable majority; and the proportion of married women reporting active sex lives "on the side" is, in some estimates, close to half. The symbolic importance of female chastity is rapidly disappearing.

It is not only that women came to have more sex, and with a greater variety of partners, but they were having it on their own terms, and enjoying it as enthusiastically as men are said to. As recently as the 1950s, America's greatest acknowledged sexual problem—or as we would now say, "dysfunction"—was female frigidity. Some experts estimated that over half of American women were completely nonorgasmic, or "frigid," and volumes of speculation were devoted to the sources of this unfortunate condition. But in 1975, a *Redbook* survey found that 81 percent of the 100,000 female respondents were orgasmic "all or most of the time."

When a *Cosmopolitan* survey resulted in similar results five years later, writer Linda Wolfe characterized American women, at least those who respond to magazine surveys, as "the most sexually experienced and experimental group of women in Western history."

The statistics on women's sexual revolution may be surprising and unfamiliar, but other evidence of it has become as much a part of the American cultural landscape as shopping malls and video-rental shops. We no longer, for example, expect books offering advice on sex to be the remote, authoritarian works of male physicians. More likely today they are written by women, and based on the experiences of women. Nor do we expect women's sexuality to be simply passive and decorative in its public manifestations. Even in the staid and married suburbs, women flock to male strip joints, provide a market for the new, "couple-oriented" pornographic videotapes, and organize Tupperware-style "home parties" where the offerings are sexual paraphernalia rather than plastic containers. And in media fiction, we no longer find the images of women divided between teasing virgins and sexless matrons: Whether on the prime-time soaps or in the latest teen film, women are likely to be portrayed as sexually assertive, if not downright predatory.

So it is surprising, even somewhat mysterious, that *women's* sexual revolution has been so little heralded, discussed, or even noted. Despite all the evidence as to which sex really changed, the phrase "the sexual revolution" is still more likely to conjure up the image of Hugh Hefner rather than, say, the work of Shere Hite, or to put us in mind of the Times Square smut shops than the expanding sexual marketplace for

women only. One could think of the predictable feminist explanations for why women's sexual revolution,
and only women's, has been so effectively "hidden from
history." This would not be the first time men have
claimed innovations that were originally wrought by
women. Nor would it be the first time men have evaded
a feminine innovation they found vaguely troubling—
or perhaps even overtly disturbing.

But feminists, for the most part, have not been eager
to claim women's sexual revolution either. When they
have acknowledged the change at all, they have tended
to be ambivalent about its meaning for women: To have
more sex, even better sex with men may be liberating
or it may represent no great gain—especially if the men
themselves have evolved so little from the era when
their word for sex was "scoring." But on the whole,
feminists, much like everyone else, have been content
to let "the" sexual revolution mean men's sexual
revolution—and to concentrate on women's roles as
bystanders or victims, not as instigators.

This book is about women's sexual revolution—its
origins in a culture that was repressive not only to sexuality in all its forms but to women as citizens; its connections, often frayed and tattered, to women's better
known, feminist revolution; its evolution from the optimistic sixties to the much more guarded and conservative eighties. Our focus is on the cultural mainstream—
not the avant-garde and not the brave members of sexual minority groups, most prominently gays and lesbians, who did so much to broaden the American concept
of sexuality. Rather, we are concerned here with the
changes as they occurred in the most obvious places,
the most visible parts of American mass culture, where

strangely, for all their "obviousness," they have been most thoroughly ignored.

Our emphasis, too, is on the cultural implications of women's sexual revolution rather than the raw, demographic indicators of deeper change. It will take another Kinsey to sort through, systematize, and verify the disparate sex surveys of the last two decades. We are less concerned with "how much" than with "what" happened, and—perhaps even more important—how Americans understood and interpreted the change to themselves. Thus, one of our major focuses is on how sex itself changed in the process of women's sexual revolution. It is not that women simply had more sex than they had had in the past, but they began to transform the notion of heterosexual sex itself: from the irreducible "act" of intercourse to a more open-ended and varied kind of encounter. At the same time, the social meaning of sex changed too: from a condensed drama of female passivity and surrender to an interaction between potentially equal persons.

One of our deepest motivating concerns is the relationship between sexual liberation and the larger goals of women articulated by the feminist movement of the past two decades. Feminist ideas, including lesbian feminist ideas, were centrally important to the emergence of women's sexual revolution—even as it has been experienced by women who would never call themselves feminists and who have no sympathy for the gay and lesbian movements. Yet the women's sexual revolution has gone its own way and found itself in settings that are indifferent to feminist concerns and, in some cases, actually hostile to them. The result is, to us, an odd and disturbing separation of goals: Women have won a new range of sexual rights—to pleasure, to fantasy and variety—but we have not yet achieved our full *human* rights. This disjuncture between feminism and women's sexual revolution affects both movements, as we shall see, in ways that are strange and even painful to relate.

The roots of women's sexual revolution lie in a set of circumstances that arose with the waning of the fifties: Middle-class women were beginning to experience the malaise so brilliantly documented by Betty Friedan in *The Feminine Mystique,* and much of their private dissatisfaction centered on marital sex, which fell short of being a glowing payoff for a life of submersion in domestic detail. At the same time, new opportunities were opening up for women. As jobs for women proliferated, young single women crowded into the major cities, and began to enlarge the gap between girlhood and marriage, filling it with careers, romances, and—what was distinctly new—casual sexual adventures. Even very young women were finding, in the burgeoning teen-centered consumer culture, a space of their own between childhood and womanhood. It was these new "spaces"—a teen culture dominated by the heavy beat of rock 'n' roll and a singles culture populated by young, urban adults—that incubated women's sexual revolution.

We begin, perhaps surprisingly, with "Beatlemania," that huge outbreak of teenage female libido that so confounded adults at the time. The experts called it "female hysteria," but it contained the germs of a more serious rebellion against the rules that defined a teenage girl's sexuality as something to be bartered for an early engagement ring. Rock 'n' roll offered a new vision of sexuality (female as well as male) that was distinctly undomesticated; and it offered an unprecedented vision of men, not as beaux or breadwinners but as sex objects for *women*.

In Chapter 2, we move on to the full-scale beginnings of women's sexual revolution, as young, single women began to challenge both the practice and the social interpretation of heterosexual sex. Masters and Johnson have received most of the credit for the new understanding of female sexuality that emerged in the 1960s, but they were, in a way, only providing a scientific rationale for a new social reality that women were creating for themselves. In Chapter 3, we follow the subsequent transformation in the way American culture thought of sex: from a two-stage encounter divided into "foreplay" and intercourse to a far more complex and varied set of possibilities. With sex redefined, the sexual relationship began to be reimagined—not as a spontaneous burst of (mostly male) passion but as an arena for negotiation where women were no longer the automatic losers.

Chapter 4 examines the growing sexual marketplace for women, and the way that the consumer culture has served to perpetuate and proselytize for the women's sexual revolution. Novelty is key to the growth of the sexual marketplace, and it actually encourages practices that were once considered to be marginal and perverted, such as sadomasochism. Nothing could be further from the earlier feminist notions of sexual liberation, yet in one form or another S/M has been assimilated into America's mainstream sexual culture, and not only in its "hard-core," male-oriented expressions. Even stranger, perhaps, is the development we trace in

Chapter 5, the penetration of women's sexual revolution into the otherwise closed-minded culture of right-wing Christian fundamentalism. In this culture, an unacknowledged kind of sadomasochism is the rule for male-female relationships, yet some covertly feminist notions of sex itself are gaining ground.

While we were researching and writing this book, a backlash against "the" sexual revolution was growing in volume and intensity. The voices raised to denounce the sexual revolution or declare it dead never specify, of course, *whose* revolution is in question. But it seems to us that what inflames the new rhetoric of sexual conservatism must be women's behavior, which *has* changed, rather than men's, which has barely changed at all. Two or three years ago, the critics of sexual revolution focused on what they saw as a loss of "romance" and "meaning," as sex became more casual and less attached to the old consequences—marriage and maternity. Today, arguments for "the death of sex" have gained more force, though not always more scientific credibility, by focusing on the danger of AIDS and other venereal diseases. In Chapter 6, we trace the backlash and show how it represents a revival, not only of repressive notions about sexuality but of traditional, sexist notions of women's role in society. We will also find that even as the backlash spreads in the media, more women—from blue- and pink-collar workers to executives—are waging the sexual revolution in their own lives.

We ourselves see much to celebrate in women's sexual revolution but also much to reassess and rethink. To us, the greatest problem with this sexual revolution is not that it took away the meaning of sex; if anything, sex has been overly burdened with oppressive "meanings," and especially for women. Nor is it even the threat of disease; historically, sex has always carried risks for women, not the least of which is unwanted pregnancy. Rather, the problem is that women's sexual liberation has become unraveled from the larger theme of women's liberation. For women, sexual equality with men has become a concrete possibility, while economic and social parity remains elusive. We believe it is this fact, beyond all others, that has shaped the possibilities and politics of women's sexual liberation.

To follow and understand this sexual revolution, we ask you to set aside, at least temporarily, both feminist and conservative dogmas about what is good and bad or right and wrong when it comes to sex. The suburban woman who gets her thrills from watching male strippers is paying, with her admission price, to invert the usual relationship between men and women, consumer and object. The born-again Christian woman who imagines her sex life as a service to Jesus has gained purchase to yet another realm of erotic possibilities. At a different end of the cultural spectrum, a practitioner of ritualistic sadomasochism confronts social inequality by encapsulating it in a drama of domination and submission. Desire takes strange paths through a landscape of inequality; we need to be able to follow them, at least in spirit, before we judge.

1

Beatlemania

Girls Just Want to Have Fun

> . . . witness the birth of eve—she is rising she
> was sleeping she is fading in a naked field
> sweating the precious blood of nodding
> blooms . . . in the eye of the arena she bends
> in half in service—the anarchy that exudes
> from the pores of her guitar are the cries of the
> people wailing in the rushes . . . a riot of ray/
> dios . . .
>
> Patti Smith, "Notice," in Babel

The news footage shows police lines straining against
crowds of hundreds of young women. The police look
grim; the girls' faces are twisted with desperation or, in
some cases, shining with what seems to be an inner
light. The air is dusty from a thousand running and
scuffling feet. There are shouted orders to disperse, answered by a rising volume of chants and wild shrieks.
The young women surge forth; the police line
breaks . . .

Looking at the photos or watching the news clips
today, anyone would guess that this was the sixties—a

demonstration—or maybe the early seventies—the beginning of the women's liberation movement. Until you look closer and see that the girls are not wearing sixties-issue jeans and T-shirts but bermuda shorts, high-necked, preppie blouses, and disheveled but unmistakably bouffant hairdos. This is not 1968 but 1964, and the girls are chanting, as they surge against the police line, "I love Ringo."

Yet, if it was not the "movement," or a clear-cut protest of any kind, Beatlemania was the first mass outburst of the sixties to feature women—in this case girls, who would not reach full adulthood until the seventies and the emergence of a genuinely political movement for women's liberation. The screaming ten- to fourteen-year-old fans of 1964 did not riot *for* anything, except the chance to remain in the proximity of their idols and hence to remain screaming. But they did have plenty to riot against, or at least to overcome through the act of rioting: In a highly sexualized society (one sociologist found that the number of explicitly sexual references in the mass media had doubled between 1950 and 1960), teen and preteen girls were expected to be not only "good" and "pure" but to be the enforcers of purity within their teen society—drawing the line for overeager boys and ostracizing girls who failed in this responsibility. To abandon control—to scream, faint, dash about in mobs—was, in form if not in conscious intent, to protest the sexual repressiveness, the rigid double standard of female teen culture. It was the first and most dramatic uprising of *women's* sexual revolution.

Beatlemania, in most accounts, stands isolated in history as a mere craze—quirky and hard to explain. There had been hysteria over male stars before, but

nothing on this scale. In its peak years—1964 and 1965
—Beatlemania struck with the force, if not the conviction, of a social movement. It began in England with a
report that fans had mobbed the popular but not yet
immortal group after a concert at the London Palla-
dium on October 13, 1963. Whether there was in fact a
mob or merely a scuffle involving no more than eight
girls is not clear, but the report acted as a call to may-
hem. Eleven days later a huge and excited crowd of
girls greeted the Beatles (returning from a Swedish
tour) at Heathrow Airport. In early November, 400
Carlisle girls fought the police for four hours while trying to get tickets for a Beatles concert; nine people
were hospitalized after the crowd surged forward and
broke through shop windows. In London and Birming-
ham the police could not guarantee the Beatles safe
escort through the hordes of fans. In Dublin the police
chief judged that the Beatles' first visit: was "all right
until the mania degenerated into barbarism."[1] And on
the eve of the group's first U.S. tour, *Life* reported, "A
Beatle who ventures out unguarded into the streets
runs the very real peril of being dismembered or
crushed to death by his fans."[2]

When the Beatles arrived in the United States, which
was still ostensibly sobered by the assassination of President Kennedy two months before, the fans knew what
to do. Television had spread the word from England:
The approach of the Beatles is a license to riot. At least
4,000 girls (some estimates run as high as 10,000)
greeted them at Kennedy Airport, and hundreds more
laid siege to the Plaza Hotel, keeping the stars virtual
prisoners. A record 73 million Americans watched the
Beatles on "The Ed Sullivan Show" on February 9,

1964, the night "when there wasn't a hubcap stolen anywhere in America." American Beatlemania soon reached the proportions of religious idolatry. During the Beatles' twenty-three-city tour that August, local promoters were required to provide a minimum of 100 security guards to hold back the crowds. Some cities tried to ban Beatle-bearing craft from their runways; otherwise it took heavy deployments of local police to protect the Beatles from their fans and the fans from the crush. In one city, someone got hold of the hotel pillowcases that had purportedly been used by the Beatles, cut them into 160,000 tiny squares, mounted them on certificates, and sold them for $1 apiece. The group packed Carnegie Hall, Washington's Coliseum and, a year later, New York's 55,600-seat Shea Stadium, and in no setting, at any time, was their music audible above the frenzied screams of the audience. In 1966, just under three years after the start of Beatlemania, the Beatles gave their last concert—the first musical celebrities to be driven from the stage by their own fans.

In its intensity, as well as its scale, Beatlemania surpassed all previous outbreaks of star-centered hysteria. Young women had swooned over Frank Sinatra in the forties and screamed for Elvis Presley in the immediate pre-Beatle years, but the Fab Four inspired an extremity of feeling usually reserved for football games or natural disasters. These baby boomers far outnumbered the generation that, thanks to the censors, had only been able to see Presley's upper torso on "The Ed Sullivan Show." Seeing (whole) Beatles on Sullivan was exciting, but not enough. Watching the band on television was a thrill—particularly the close-ups—but the real goal was to leave home and meet the Beatles. The ap-

propriate reaction to contact with them—such as occupying the same auditorium or city block—was to sob
uncontrollably while screaming, "I'm gonna die, I'm
gonna die," or, more optimistically, the name of a favorite Beatle, until the onset of either unconsciousness or
laryngitis. Girls peed in their pants, fainted, or simply
collapsed from the emotional strain. When not in the
vicinity of the Beatles—and only a small proportion of
fans ever got within shrieking distance of their idols—
girls exchanged Beatle magazines or cards, and gathered to speculate obsessively on the details and nuances
of Beatle life. One woman, who now administers a
Washington, D.C.–based public interest group, recalls
long discussions with other thirteen-year-olds in Orlando, Maine:

> I especially liked talking about the Beatles
> with other girls. Someone would say, "What do
> you think Paul had for breakfast?" "Do you
> think he sleeps with a different girl every
> night?" Or, "Is John really the leader?" "Is
> George really more sensitive?" And like that
> for hours.

This fan reached the zenith of junior high school popularity after becoming the only girl in town to travel to a
Beatles' concert in Boston: "My mother had made a
new dress for me to wear [to the concert] and when I
got back, the other girls wanted to cut it up and auction
off the pieces."

To adults, Beatlemania was an affliction, an "epidemic," and the Beatles themselves were only the carriers, or even "foreign germs." At risk were all ten- to
fourteen-year-old girls, or at least all white girls; blacks

were disdainful of the Beatles' initially derivative and unpolished sound. There appeared to be no cure except for age, and the media pundits were fond of reassuring adults that the girls who had screamed for Frank Sinatra had grown up to be responsible, settled housewives. If there was a shortcut to recovery, it certainly wasn't easy. A group of Los Angeles girls organized a detox effort called "Beatlesaniacs, Ltd.," offering "group therapy for those living near active chapters, and withdrawal literature for those going it alone at far-flung outposts." Among the rules for recovery were: "Do not mention the word Beatles (or beetles)," "Do not mention the word England," "Do not speak with an English accent," and "Do not speak English."³ In other words, Beatlemania was as inevitable as acne and gum-chewing, and adults would just have to weather it out.

But why was it happening? And why in particular to an America that prided itself on its post-McCarthy maturity, its prosperity, and its clear position as the number one world power? True, there were social problems that not even *Reader's Digest* could afford to be smug about—racial segregation, for example, and the newly discovered poverty of "the other America." But these were things that an energetic President could easily handle—or so most people believed at the time—and if "the Negro problem," as it was called, generated overt unrest, it was seen as having a corrective function and limited duration. Notwithstanding an attempted revival by presidential candidate Barry Goldwater, "extremism" was out of style in any area of expression. In colleges, "coolness" implied a detached and rational appreciation of the status quo, and it was de rigueur among all but the avant-garde who joined the Freedom

Rides or signed up for the Peace Corps. No one, not even Marxist philosopher Herbert Marcuse, could imagine a reason for widespread discontent among the middle class or for strivings that could not be satisfied with a department store charge account—much less for "mania."

In the media, adult experts fairly stumbled over each other to offer the most reassuring explanations. The New York *Times Magazine* offered a "psychological, anthropological," half tongue-in-cheek account, titled "Why the Girls Scream, Weep, Flip." Drawing on the work of the German sociologist Theodor Adorno, *Times* writer David Dempsey argued that the girls weren't really out of line at all; they were merely "conforming." Adorno had diagnosed the 1940s jitterbug fans as "rhythmic obedients," who were "expressing their desire to obey." They needed to subsume themselves into the mass, "to become transformed into an insect." Hence, "jitter*bug*," and as Dempsey triumphantly added: "Beatles, too, are a type of bug . . . and to 'beatle,' as to jitter, is to lose one's identity in an automatized, insectlike activity, in other words, to obey." If Beatlemania was more frenzied than the outbursts of obedience inspired by Sinatra or Fabian, it was simply because the music was "more frantic," and in some animal way, more compelling. It is generally admitted "that jungle rhythms influence the 'beat' of much contemporary dance activity," he wrote, blithely endorsing the stock racist response to rock 'n' roll. Atavistic, "aboriginal" instincts impelled the girls to scream, weep, and flip, whether they liked it or not: "It is probably no coincidence that the Beatles, who provoke the most violent response among teen-agers, resemble in manner the witch doctors who put their spells on hundreds of shuffling and stamping natives."[4]

Not everyone saw the resemblance between Beatlemanic girls and "natives" in a reassuring light however. *Variety* speculated that Beatlemania might be "a phenomenon closely linked to the current wave of racial rioting."[5] It was hard to miss the element of defiance in Beatlemania. If Beatlemania was conformity, it was conformity to an imperative that overruled adult mores and even adult laws. In the mass experience of Beatlemania, as for example at a concert or an airport, a girl who might never have contemplated shoplifting could assault a policeman with her fists, squirm under police barricades, and otherwise invite a disorderly conduct charge. Shy, subdued girls could go berserk. "Perky," ponytailed girls of the type favored by early sixties sitcoms could dissolve in histrionics. In quieter contemplation of their idols, girls could see defiance in the Beatles or project it onto them. *Newsweek* quoted Pat Hagan, "a pretty, 14-year-old Girl Scout, nurse's aide, and daughter of a Chicago lawyer . . . who previously dug 'West Side Story,' Emily Dickinson, Robert Frost, and Elizabeth Barrett Browning: 'They're tough,' she said of the Beatles. 'Tough is like when you don't conform. . . . You're tumultuous when you're young, and each generation has to have its idols.' "[6] America's favorite sociologist, David Riesman, concurred, describing Beatlemania as "a form of protest against the adult world."[7]

There was another element of Beatlemania that was hard to miss but not always easy for adults to acknowledge. As any casual student of Freud would have noted, at least part of the fans' energy was sexual. Freud's initial breakthrough had been the insight that the epidemic female "hysteria" of the late nineteenth century —which took the form of fits, convulsions, tics, and what we would now call neuroses—was the product of sexual repression. In 1964, though, confronted with massed thousands of "hysterics," psychologists approached this diagnosis warily. After all, despite everything Freud had had to say about childhood sexuality, most Americans did not like to believe that twelve-year-old girls had any sexual feelings to repress. And no normal girl—or full-grown woman, for that matter— was supposed to have the libidinal voltage required for three hours of screaming, sobbing, incontinent, acute-phase Beatlemania. In an article in *Science News Letter* titled "Beatles Reaction Puzzles Even Psychologists," one unidentified psychologist offered a carefully phrased, hygienic explanation: Adolescents are "going through a strenuous period of emotional and physical growth," which leads to a "need for expressiveness, especially in girls." Boys have sports as an outlet; girls have only the screaming and swooning afforded by Beatlemania, which could be seen as "a release of sexual energy."[8]

For the girls who participated in Beatlemania, sex was an obvious part of the excitement. One of the most common responses to reporters' queries on the sources of Beatlemania was, "Because they're sexy." And this explanation was in itself a small act of defiance. It was rebellious (especially for the very young fans) to lay claim to sexual feelings. It was even more rebellious to lay claim to the *active,* desiring side of a sexual attraction: The Beatles were the objects; the girls were their pursuers. The Beatles were sexy; the girls were the ones who perceived them as sexy and acknowledged the force of an ungovernable, if somewhat disembodied, lust. To assert an active, powerful sexuality by the tens of thousands and to do so in a way calculated to attract maximum attention was more than rebellious. It was, in its own unformulated, dizzy way, revolutionary.

SEX AND THE TEENAGE GIRL

In the years and months immediately preceding U.S. Beatlemania, the girls who were to initiate a sexual revolution looked, from a critical adult vantage point, like sleepwalkers on a perpetual shopping trip. Betty Friedan noted in her 1963 classic, *The Feminine Mystique,* "a new vacant sleepwalking, playing-a-part quality of youngsters who do what they are supposed to do, what the other kids do, but do not seem to feel alive or real in doing it."[9] But for girls, conformity meant more than surrendering, comatose, to the banal drift of junior high or high school life. To be popular with boys and girls—to be universally attractive and still have an unblemished "reputation"—a girl had to be crafty, cool, and careful. The payoff for all this effort was to end up exactly like Mom—as a housewife.

In October 1963, the month Beatlemania first broke out in England and three months before it arrived in America, *Life* presented a troubling picture of teenage girl culture. The focus was Jill Dinwiddie, seventeen, popular, "healthy, athletic, getting A grades," to all appearances wealthy, and at the same time, strangely vacant. The pictures of this teenage paragon and her friends would have done justice to John Lennon's first take on American youth:

> When we got here you were all walkin' around in fuckin' Bermuda shorts with Boston crewcuts and stuff on your teeth. . . . The chicks looked like 1940's horses. There was no conception of dress or any of that jazz. We just thought what an ugly race, what an ugly race.[10]

Jill herself, the "queen bee of the high school," is strikingly sexless: short hair in a tightly controlled style (the kind achieved with flat metal clips), button-down shirts done up to the neck, shapeless skirts with matching cardigans, and a stance that evokes the intense posture-consciousness of prefeminist girls' phys ed. Her philosophy is no less engaging: "We have to be like everybody else to be accepted. Aren't most adults that way? We learn in high school to stay in the middle."[11]

"The middle," for girls coming of age in the early sixties, was a narrow and carefully defined terrain. The omnipresent David Riesman, whom *Life* called in to comment on Jill and her crowd, observed, "Given a standard definition of what is feminine and successful, they must conform to it. The range is narrow, the models they may follow few." The goal, which Riesman didn't need to spell out, was marriage and motherhood, and the route to it led along a straight and narrow path between the twin dangers of being "cheap" or being too puritanical, and hence unpopular. A girl had to learn to offer enough, sexually, to get dates, and at the same time to withhold enough to maintain a boy's interest through the long preliminaries from dating and going steady to engagement and finally marriage. None of this was easy, and for girls like Jill the pedagogical burden of high school was a four-year lesson in how to use sex instrumentally: doling out just enough to be popular with boys and never enough to lose the esteem of the "right kind of kids." Commenting on *Life*'s story on Jill, a University of California sociologist observed:

> It seems that half the time of our adolescent girls is spent trying to meet their new responsibilities to be sexy, glamorous and attractive, while the other half is spent meeting their old responsibility to be virtuous by holding off the advances which testify to their success.

Advice books to teenagers fussed anxiously over the question of "where to draw the line," as did most teenage girls themselves. Officially everyone—girls and advice-givers—agreed that the line fell short of intercourse, though by the sixties even this venerable prohibition required some sort of justification, and the advice-givers strained to impress upon their young readers the calamitous results of premarital sex. First there was the obvious danger of pregnancy, an apparently inescapable danger since no book addressed to teens dared offer birth control information. Even worse, some writers suggested, were the psychological effects of intercourse: It would destroy a budding relationship and possibly poison any future marriage. According to a contemporary textbook titled, *Adolescent Development and Adjustment,* intercourse often caused a man to lose interest ("He may come to believe she is totally promiscuous"), while it was likely to reduce a woman to slavish dependence ("Sometimes a woman focuses her life around the man with whom she first has intercourse").[12] The girl who survived premarital intercourse and went on to marry someone else would find marriage clouded with awkwardness and distrust. Dr. Arthur Cain warned in *Young People and Sex* that the husband of a sexually experienced woman might be consumed with worry about whether his performance matched that of her previous partners. "To make matters worse," he wrote, "it may be that one's sex partner is not as exciting and satisfying as one's previous illicit lover."[13] In short, the price of premarital experience was likely to be postnuptial disappointment. And, since marriage was a girl's peak achievement, an anticlimactic wedding night would be a lasting source of grief.

Intercourse was obviously out of the question, so young girls faced the still familiar problem of where to draw the line on a scale of lesser sexual acts, including (in descending order of niceness): kissing, necking, and petting, this last being divided into "light" (through clothes and/or above the waist) and "heavy" (with clothes undone and/or below the waist). Here the experts were no longer unanimous. Pat Boone, already a spokesman for the Christian right, drew the line at kissing in his popular 1958 book, *'Twixt Twelve and Twenty*. No prude, he announced that "kissing is here to stay and I'm glad of it!" But, he warned, "Kissing is not a game. Believe me! . . . Kissing for fun is like playing with a beautiful candle in a roomful of dynamite!"[14] (The explosive consequences might have been guessed from the centerpiece photos showing Pat dining out with his teen bride, Shirley; then, as if moments later, in a maternity ward with her; and, in the next picture, surrounded by "the four little Boones.") Another pop-singer-turned-adviser, Connie Francis, saw nothing wrong with kissing (unless it begins to "dominate your life"), nor with its extended form, necking, but drew the line at petting:

> Necking and petting—let's get this straight— are two different things. Petting, according to most definitions, is specifically intended to arouse sexual desires and as far as I'm concerned, petting is out for teenagers.[15]

In practice, most teenagers expected to escalate through the scale of sexual possibilities as a relationship progressed, with the big question being: How much, how soon? In their 1963 critique of American teen culture, *Teen-Age Tyranny,* Grace and Fred Hechinger bewailed the cold instrumentality that shaped the conventional answers. A girl's "favors," they wrote, had become "currency to bargain for desirable dates which, in turn, are legal tender in the exchange of popularity." For example, in answer to the frequently asked question, "Should I let him kiss me good night on the first date?" they reported that:

> A standard caution in teen-age advice literature is that, if the boy "gets" his kiss on the first date, he may assume that many other boys have been just as easily compensated. In other words, the rule book advises mainly that the [girl's] popularity assets should be protected against deflation.[16]

It went without saying that it was the girl's responsibility to apply the brakes as a relationship approached

the slippery slope leading from kissing toward intercourse. This was not because girls were expected to be
immune from temptation. Connie Francis acknowledged that "It's not easy to be moral, especially where
your feelings for a boy are involved. It never is, because
you have to fight to keep your normal physical impulses
in line." But it was the girl who had the most to lose, not
least of all the respect of the boy she might too generously have indulged. "When she gives in completely to
a boy's advances," Francis warned, "the element of respect goes right out the window." Good girls never
"gave in," never abandoned themselves to impulse or
emotion, and never, of course, initiated a new escalation on the scale of physical intimacy. In the financial
metaphor that dominated teen sex etiquette, good girls
"saved themselves" for marriage; bad girls were
"cheap."

According to a 1962 Gallup Poll commissioned by
Ladies' Home Journal, most young women (at least in
the *Journal*'s relatively affluent sample) enthusiastically
accepted the traditional feminine role and the sexual
double standard that went with it:

> Almost all our young women between 16 and
> 21 expect to be married by 22. Most want 4
> children, many want . . . to work until chil-
> dren come; afterward, a resounding no! They
> feel a special responsibility for sex *because*
> they are women. An 18-year-old student in
> California said, "The standard for men—sow-
> ing wild oats—results in sown oats. And where
> does this leave the woman?" . . . Another

student: "A man will go as far as a woman will let him. The girl has to set the standard."[17]

Implicit in this was a matrimonial strategy based on months of sexual teasing (setting the standard), until the frustrated young man broke down and proposed. Girls had to "hold out" because, as one *Journal* respondent put it, "Virginity is one of the greatest things a woman can give to her husband." As for what *he* would give to her, in addition to four or five children, the young women were vividly descriptive:

> . . . I want a split-level brick with four bed-rooms with French Provincial cherrywood fur-niture.
> . . . I'd like a built-in oven and range, count-ers only 34 inches high with Formica on them.
> . . . I would like a lot of finished wood for warmth and beauty.
> . . . My living room would be long with a high ceiling of exposed beams. I would have a large fireplace on one wall, with a lot of copper and brass around. . . . My kitchen would be very like old Virginian ones—fireplace and oven.

So single-mindedly did young women appear to be bent on domesticity that when Beatlemania did arrive, some experts thought the screaming girls must be auditioning for the maternity ward: "The girls are subconsciously preparing for motherhood. Their frenzied screams are a rehearsal for that moment. Even the jelly babies [the candies favored by the early Beatles and hurled at them by fans] are symbolic."[18] Women were asexual, or at least capable of mentally bypassing sex and heading straight from courtship to reveries of Formica counters and cherrywood furniture, from the soda shop to the hardware store.

But the vision of a suburban split-level, which had guided a generation of girls chastely through high school, was beginning to lose its luster. Betty Friedan had surveyed the "successful" women of her age—educated, upper-middle-class housewives—and found them reduced to infantile neuroticism by the isolation and futility of their lives. If feminism was still a few years off, at least the "feminine mystique" had entered the vocabulary, and even Jill Dinwiddie must have read the quotation from journalist Shana Alexander that appeared in the same issue of *Life* that featured Jill. "It's a marvelous life, this life in a man's world," Alexander said. "I'd climb the walls if I had to live the feminine mystique." The media that had once romanticized togetherness turned their attention to "the crack in the picture window"—wife swapping, alcoholism, divorce, and teenage anomie. A certain cynicism was creeping into the American view of marriage. In the novels of John Updike and Philip Roth, the hero didn't get the girl, he got away. When a Long Island prostitution ring, in which housewives hustled with their husbands' consent, was exposed in the winter of 1963, a Fifth Avenue saleswoman commented: "I see all this beautiful stuff I'll never have, and I wonder if it's worth it to be good. What's the difference, one man every night or a different man?"[19]

So when sociologist Bennet Berger commented in *Life* that "there is nobody better equipped than Jill to live in a society of all-electric kitchens, wall-to-wall carpeting, dishwashers, garbage disposals [and] color TV," this could no longer be taken as unalloyed praise. Jill herself seemed to sense that all the tension and teasing anticipation of the teen years was not worth the payoff. After she was elected, by an overwhelming majority, to the cheerleading team, "an uneasy, faraway look clouded her face." "I guess there's nothing left to do in high school," she said. "I've made song leader both years, and that was all I really wanted." For girls, high school was all there was to public life, the only place you could ever hope to run for office or experience the quasi fame of popularity. After that came marriage—most likely to one of the crew-cut boys you'd made out with —then isolation and invisibility.

Part of the appeal of the male star—whether it was James Dean or Elvis Presley or Paul McCartney—was that you would *never* marry him; the romance would never end in the tedium of marriage. Many girls expressed their adulation in conventional, monogamous terms, for example, picking their favorite Beatle and writing him a serious letter of proposal, or carrying placards saying, "John, Divorce Cynthia." But it was inconceivable that any fan would actually marry a Beatle or sleep with him (sexually active "groupies" were still a few years off) or even hold his hand. Adulation of the male star was a way to express sexual yearnings that would normally be pressed into the service of popularity or simply repressed. The star could be loved noninstrumentally, for his own sake, and with complete abandon. To publicly advertise this hopeless love was to protest the calculated, pragmatic sexual repression of teenage life.

THE ECONOMICS OF MASS HYSTERIA

Sexual repression had been a feature of middle-class teen life for centuries. If there was a significant factor that made mass protest possible in the late fifties (Elvis) and the early sixties (the Beatles), it was the growth and maturation of a teen market: for distinctly teen clothes, magazines, entertainment, and accessories. Consciousness of the teen years as a life-cycle phase set off between late childhood on the one hand and young adulthood on the other only goes back to the early twentieth century, when the influential psychologist G. Stanley Hall published his mammoth work *Adolescence*. (The word "teenager" did not enter mass usage until the 1940s.) Postwar affluence sharpened the demarcations around the teen years: Fewer teens than ever worked or left school to help support their families, making teenhood more distinct from adulthood as a time of unemployment and leisure. And more teens than ever had money to spend, so that from a marketing viewpoint, teens were potentially much more interesting than children, who could only influence family spending but did little spending themselves. Grace and Fred Hechinger reported that in 1959 the average teen spent $555 on "goods and services not including the necessities normally supplied by their parents," and noted, for perspective, that in the same year schoolteachers in Mississippi were earning just over $3,000. "No matter what other segments of American society—parents, teachers, sociologists, psychologists, or policemen—may deplore the power of teenagers," they observed, "the American business community has no cause for complaint."[20]

If advertisers and marketing men manipulated teens as consumers, they also, inadvertently, solidified teen culture against the adult world. Marketing strategies that recognized the importance of teens as precocious consumers also recognized the importance of heightening their self-awareness of themselves *as teens.* Girls especially became aware of themselves as occupying a world of fashion of their own—not just bigger children's clothes or slimmer women's clothes. You were not a big girl or a junior woman, but a "teen," and in that notion lay the germs of an oppositional identity. Defined by its own products and advertising slogans, teenhood became more than a prelude to adulthood; it was a status to be proud of—emotionally and sexually complete unto itself.

Rock 'n' roll was the most potent commodity to enter the teen consumer subculture. Rock was originally a black musical form with no particular age identification, and it took white performers like Buddy Holly and Elvis Presley to make rock 'n' roll accessible to young white kids with generous allowances to spend. On the white side of the deeply segregated music market, rock became a distinctly teenage product. Its "jungle beat" was disconcerting or hateful to white adults; its lyrics celebrated the special teen world of fashion ("Blue Suede Shoes"), feeling ("Teenager in Love"), and passive opposition ("Don't know nothin' 'bout his-to-ry"). By the late fifties, rock 'n' roll was the organizing principle and premier theme of teen consumer culture: You watched the Dick Clark show not only to hear the hits but to see what the kids were wearing; you collected not only the top singles but the novelty items that advertised the stars; you cultivated the looks and personality that would make you a "teen angel." And if you were still too young for all this, in the late fifties you yearned to grow up to be—not a woman and a housewife, but a teenager.

Rock 'n' roll made mass hysteria almost inevitable: It announced and ratified teen sexuality and then amplified teen sexual frustration almost beyond endurance. Conversely, mass hysteria helped make rock 'n' roll. In his biography of Elvis Presley, Albert Goldman describes how Elvis's manager, Colonel Tom Parker, whipped mid-fifties girl audiences into a frenzy before the appearance of the star: As many as a dozen acts would precede Elvis—acrobats, comics, gospel singers, a little girl playing a xylophone—until the audience, "driven half mad by sheer frustration, began chanting rhythmically, '*We want Elvis, we want Elvis!*' " When the star was at last announced:

> Five thousand shrill female voices come in on cue. The screeching reaches the intensity of a jet engine. When Elvis comes striding out onstage with his butchy walk, the screams suddenly escalate. They switch to hyperspace. Now, you may as well be stone deaf for all the music you'll hear.[21]

The newspapers would duly report that "the fans went wild."

Hysteria was critical to the marketing of the Beatles. First there were the reports of near riots in England. Then came a calculated publicity tease that made Colonel Parker's manipulations look oafish by contrast: Five million posters and stickers announcing "The Beatles Are Coming" were distributed nationwide. Disc jock-

eys were blitzed with promo material and Beatle interview tapes (with blank spaces for the DJ to fill in the
questions, as if it were a real interview) and enlisted in a
mass "countdown" to the day of the Beatles' arrival in
the United States. As Beatle chronicler Nicholas Schaffner reports:

> Come break of "Beatle Day," the quartet had
> taken over even the disc-jockey patter that
> punctuated their hit songs. From WMCA and
> WINS through W-A-Beatle-C, it was "thirty
> Beatle degrees," "eight-thirty Beatle time"
> . . . [and] "four hours and fifty minutes to
> go."[22]

By the time the Beatles materialized, on "The Ed Sullivan Show" in February 1964, the anticipation was un-
bearable. A woman who was a fourteen-year-old in Du-
luth at the time told us, "Looking back, it seems so
commercial to me, and so degrading that millions of us
would just scream on cue for these four guys the media
dangled out in front of us. But at the time it was something intensely personal for me and, I guess, a million
other girls. The Beatles seemed to be speaking directly
to us and, in a funny way, *for us.*"

By the time the Beatles hit America, teens and
preteens had already learned to look to their unique
consumer subculture for meaning and validation. If this
was manipulation—and no culture so strenuously and
shamelessly exploits its children as consumers—it was
also subversion. *Bad* kids became juvenile delinquents,
smoked reefers, or got pregnant. Good kids embraced
the paraphernalia, the lore, and the disciplined fandom
of rock 'n' roll. (Of course, bad kids did their thing to a

rock beat too: the first movie to use a rock 'n' roll sound-track was "Blackboard Jungle," in 1955, cementing the suspected link between "jungle rhythms" and teen rebellion.) For girls, fandom offered a way not only to sublimate romantic and sexual yearnings but to carve out subversive versions of heterosexuality. Not just anyone could be hyped as a suitable object for hysteria: It *mattered* that Elvis was a grown-up greaser, and that the Beatles let their hair grow over their ears.

THE EROTICS OF THE STAR-FAN RELATIONSHIP

In real life, i.e. in junior high or high school, the ideal boyfriend was someone like Tab Hunter or Ricky Nelson. He was "all boy," meaning you wouldn't get home from a date without a friendly scuffle, but he was also clean-cut, meaning middle class, patriotic, and respectful of the fact that good girls waited until marriage. He wasn't moody and sensitive (like James Dean in *Giant* or *Rebel Without a Cause),* he was realistic (meaning that he understood that his destiny was to earn a living for someone like yourself). The stars who inspired the greatest mass adulation were none of these things, and their very remoteness from the pragmatic ideal was what made them accessible to fantasy.

Elvis was visibly lower class and symbolically black (as the bearer of black music to white youth). He represented an unassimilated white underclass that had been forgotten by mainstream suburban America—or, more accurately, he represented a middle-class caricature of

poor whites. He was *sleazy*. And, as his biographer
Goldman argues, therein lay his charm:

> What did the girls see that drove them out of
> their minds? It sure as hell wasn't the All-
> American Boy. . . . Elvis was the flip side of
> [the] conventional male image. His fish-belly
> white complexion, so different from the
> "healthy tan" of the beach boys; his brooding
> Latin eyes, heavily shaded with mascara . . .
> the thick, twisted lips; the long, greasy hair.
> . . . God! what a freak the boy must have
> looked to those little girls . . . and what a
> turn-on! Typical comments were: "I like him
> because he looks so mean" . . . "He's been in
> and out of jail."[23]

Elvis stood for a dangerous principle of masculinity that
had been expunged from the white-collar, split-level
world of fandom: a hood who had no place in the
calculus of dating, going steady, and getting married.
At the same time, the fact that he was lower class
evened out the gender difference in power. He acted
arrogant, but he was really vulnerable, and would be
back behind the stick shift of a Mack truck if you, the
fans, hadn't redeemed him with your love. His very
sleaziness, then, was a tribute to the collective power of
the teen and preteen girls who worshipped him. He
was obnoxious to adults—a Cincinnati used-car dealer
once offered to smash fifty Presley records in the presence of every purchaser—not only because of who he
was but because he was a reminder of the emerging
power and sexuality of young girls.

Compared to Elvis, the Beatles were almost respectable. They wore suits; they did not thrust their bodies about suggestively; and to most Americans, who couldn't tell a blue-collar, Liverpudlian accent from Oxbridge English, they might have been upper class. What was both shocking and deeply appealing about the Beatles was that they were, while not exactly effeminate, at least not easily classifiable in the rigid gender distinctions of middle-class American life. Twenty years later we are so accustomed to shoulder-length male tresses and rock stars of ambiguous sexuality that the Beatles of 1964 look clean-cut. But when the Beatles arrived at crew-cut, precounterculture America, their long hair attracted more commentary than their music. Boy fans rushed to buy Beatle wigs and cartoons showing well-known male figures decked with Beatle hair were a source of great merriment. *Playboy*, in an interview, grilled the Beatles on the subject of homosexuality, which it was only natural for gender-locked adults to suspect. As Paul McCartney later observed:

> There they were in America, all getting house-trained for adulthood with their indisputable principle of life: short hair equals men; long hair equals women. Well, we got rid of that small convention for them. And a few others, too.[24]

What did it mean that American girls would go for these sexually suspect young men, and in numbers far greater than an unambiguous stud like Elvis could command? Dr. Joyce Brothers thought the Beatles' appeal rested on the girls' innocence:

The Beatles display a few mannerisms which
almost seem a shade on the feminine side, such
as the tossing of their long manes of hair. . . .
These are exactly the mannerisms which very
young female fans (in the 10-to-14 age group)
appear to go wildest over.[25]

The reason? "Very young 'women' are still a little
frightened of the idea of sex. Therefore they feel safer
worshipping idols who don't seem too masculine, or too
much the 'he man.' "

What Brothers and most adult commentators
couldn't imagine was that the Beatles' androgyny was
itself sexy. "The idea of sex" as intercourse, with the
possibility of pregnancy or a ruined reputation, was
indeed frightening. But the Beatles construed sex more
generously and playfully, lifting it out of the rigid scenario of mid-century American gender roles, and it was
this that made them wildly sexy. Or to put it the other
way around, the appeal lay in the vision of sexuality that
the Beatles held out to a generation of American girls:
They seemed to offer sexuality that was guileless, ebul-
lient, and fun—like the Beatles themselves and everything they did (or were shown doing in their films *Help*
and *A Hard Day's Night*). Theirs was a vision of sexuality freed from the shadow of gender inequality because
the group mocked the gender distinctions that bifur-
cated the American landscape into "his" and "hers." To
Americans who believed fervently that sexuality
hinged on *la différence,* the Beatlemaniacs said, No,
blur the lines and expand the possibilities.

At the same time, the attraction of the Beatles bypassed sex and went straight to the issue of power. Our

informant from Orlando, Maine, said of her Beatlemanic phase:

> It didn't feel sexual, as I would now define that.
> It felt more about wanting freedom. I didn't
> want to grow up and be a wife and it seemed to
> me that the Beatles had the kind of freedom I
> wanted: No rules, they could spend two days
> lying in bed; they ran around on motorbikes,
> ate from room service. . . . I didn't want to
> sleep with Paul McCartney, I was too young.
> But I wanted to be like them, something larger
> than life.

Another woman, who was thirteen when the Beatles
arrived in her home city of Los Angeles and was working for the telephone company in Denver when we
interviewed her, said:

> Now that I've thought about it, I think I identi-
> fied with them, rather than as an object of
> them. I mean I liked their independence and
> sexuality and wanted those things for myself.
> . . . Girls didn't get to be that way when I was
> a teenager—we got to be the limp, passive ob-
> ject of some guy's fleeting sexual interest. We
> were so stifled, and they made us meek, giggly
> creatures think, oh, if only *I* could act that way,
> and be strong, sexy, and doing what you want.

If girls could not be, or ever hope to be, superstars and
madcap adventurers themselves, they could at least
idolize the men who were.

There was the more immediate satisfaction of knowing, subconsciously, that the Beatles were who they

were because girls like oneself had made them that. As with Elvis, fans knew of the Beatles' lowly origins and knew they had risen from working-class obscurity to world fame on the acoustical power of thousands of shrieking fans. Adulation created stars, and stardom, in turn, justified adulation. Questioned about their hysteria, some girls answered simply, "Because they're the Beatles." That is, because they're who I happen to like. And the louder you screamed, the less likely anyone would forget the power of the fans. When the screams drowned out the music, as they invariably did, then it was the fans, and not the band, who were the show.

In the decade that followed Beatlemania, the girls who had inhabited the magical, obsessive world of fandom would edge closer and closer to center stage. Sublimation would give way to more literal, and sometimes sordid, forms of fixation: By the late sixties, the most zealous fans, no longer content to shriek and sob in virginal frustration, would become groupies and "go all the way" with any accessible rock musician. One briefly notorious group of girl fans, the Chicago Plaster Casters, distinguished itself by making plaster molds of rock stars' penises, thus memorializing, among others, Jimi Hendrix. At the end of the decade Janis Joplin, who had been a lonely, unpopular teenager in the fifties, shot to stardom before dying of a drug and alcohol overdose. Joplin, before her decline and her split from Big Brother, was in a class by herself. There were no other female singers during the sixties who reached her pinnacle of success. Her extraordinary power in the male world of rock 'n' roll lay not only in her talent but in her femaleness. While she did not meet conventional standards of beauty, she was nevertheless sexy and powerful; both genders could worship her on the stage for their own reasons. Janis offered women the possibility of identifying with, rather than objectifying, the star. "It was seeing Janis Joplin," wrote Ellen Willis, "that made me resolve, once and for all, not to get my hair straightened." Her "metamorphosis from the ugly duckling of Port Arthur to the peacock of Haight Ashbury"[26] gave teenage girls a new optimistic fantasy.

While Janis was all woman, she was also one of the boys. Among male rock stars, the faintly androgynous affect of the Beatles was quickly eclipsed by the frank bisexuality of performers like Alice Cooper and David Bowie, and then the more outrageous antimasculinity of eighties stars Boy George and Michael Jackson. The latter provoked screams again and mobs, this time of interracial crowds of girls, going down in age to eight and nine, but never on the convulsive scale of Beatlemania. By the eighties, female singers like Grace Jones and Annie Lenox were denying gender too, and the loyalty and masochism once requisite for female lyrics gave way to new songs of cynicism, aggression, exultation. But between the vicarious pleasure of Beatlemania and Cyndi Lauper's forthright assertion in 1984 that "girls just want to have fun," there would be an enormous change in the sexual possibilities open to women and girls—a change large enough to qualify as a "revolution."

2

Up from the Valley
of the Dolls

The Origins of the Sexual
Revolution

Anne Welles's personal sexual revolution was indistinguishable from her rebellion, in an unconsciously feminist fashion, against the rigid sex roles of small-town America. Anne was the heroine of Jacqueline Susann's 1966 best-seller, *Valley of the Dolls,* and for Anne, like Susann herself, the big city—in both cases, New York— promised freedom and inexhaustible adventure:

> She would *never* go back to Lawrenceville!
> . . . She had escaped. Escaped from marriage to some solid Lawrenceville boy, from the solid, orderly life of Lawrenceville. The same orderly life her mother had lived. And her mother's mother. In the same orderly kind of a house. A house that a good New England fam-

ily had lived in generation after generation, its
inhabitants smothered with orderly, unused
emotions, emotions stifled beneath the creaky
iron armor called "manners."[1]

In no small part, it was the sexlessness of life in Law-
renceville that drove Anne to a cramped apartment
and an uncertain secretarial career in New York. She
recalls asking her mother, "When a man takes you in his
arms and kisses you, it should be wonderful, shouldn't
it? Wasn't it ever wonderful with Daddy?" To which her
mother replies stiffly, "Unfortunately, kissing isn't all a
man expects after marriage."

In 1966–67 the media began to talk about "the sexual
revolution," and the sexual playfulness of the emerging
counterculture was only one element of the change.
Novels like *Valley of the Dolls,* which seemed at the
time to border on pornography, were themselves a sign
of the "revolution." *Human Sexual Response,* by Dr.
William Masters and Virginia Johnson, also published in
1966, was to become one of its major ideological
manifestos. The women's liberation movement and the
mass spread of feminist consciousness were still two or
three years ahead, but the designation of a sexual
"revolution" implied a change that went beyond manners and mores to fundamental relationships of power.
Women's sexual revolution grew out of the same frustrations and emerging opportunities that inspired the
feminist movement and, like it, initially represented
the aspirations of the "new woman"—urban, single, educated—who had to overcome both the puritanism of
small-town America and the smothering conformity of
suburban married life.

By the early sixties, thousands of young women, like the fictional Anne Welles, were rejecting the lockstep sequence that led from college or high school graduation directly to marriage and maternity. They expected to spend a few years on their own, working and dating, and not just as a way of passing time until "Mr. Right" arrived. Being single had its own rewards, especially in a city packed with other young people and far from parental oversight. While the teens and preteens were still shrieking over the Beatles—and anticipating a more adventurous sexuality—young women in their twenties were already carving out a new kind of sexual identity. Sex had been defined as an adjunct to marriage, as a means to getting married, and as proof of a "mature acceptance of the female role." But for women who were trying out new roles, even on a temporary basis, the old rules and definitions would not do.

The birth control pill, which first became commercially available in 1960, contributed to women's sexual revolution but by no means *caused* it. The causes of the sexual revolution were more sociological than technological: Without a concentration of young, single women in the cities, there would have been no sexual revolution. But without the pill, there would still have been the diaphragm; and for many young women who came of age in the prepill years, that first diaphragm, discreetly packed in purse or college book bag, was both the symbol and the instrument of sexual liberation. The pill was more convenient—though, as women were to discover later in the decade, it was also far more hazardous than the diaphragm. But its real function was, in a sense, to legitimize a sexual revolution already in progress: The existence and widespread marketing of a technology for presumably effortless contraception was evidence that millions of women (almost 6 million by 1965), single as well as married, were "doing it"—and, apparently with the blessings of the medical profession, getting away with it too.

THE CRISIS OF MARRIED LOVE

The sexual revolution reflected not only the opportunities opening up to the "new," single women, but the discontent of the married majority. The only officially acceptable setting for an active sex life was still the bedroom—in a house, preferably a new suburban split-level, not a makeshift apartment. Outside of a small avant-garde, most young women still expected their single years to culminate in marriage, which, ideally, would be a source not only of financial security but of companionship and sexual fulfillment. But by the early sixties, it was clear that all was not well even within the "ideal" marriages of well-adjusted, educated, middle-class women. To Betty Friedan, who remains our best chronicler of such women's frustrations on the eve of the feminist revival, it seemed that a sexual revolution, of a fairly nasty and unrewarding type, had already taken place by the early sixties. The housewives she surveyed for *The Feminine Mystique* seemed to be pouring the energies that might have gone into careers or other "larger human purposes" into a vacant and obsessive search for sexual fulfillment. "The mounting sex-hunger of American women has been documented ad nauseam," she wrote, and was reflected in the salaciousness of best-sellers addressed to women *(Peyton*

Place was the most egregious example), and what she saw as a "joyless" preoccupation with sexual technique.[2]

The changes Friedan perceived had less to do with actual sexual practice than with the way women thought about sex and the emotional intensity they brought to the subject. She attributed the new way of thinking about sex in large part to the Kinsey reports, both what they reported "and the way they reported it"—which was dryly, and with masses of statistics, as if sex had nothing to do with human feelings. Like most critics of Kinsey (and later, of Masters and Johnson), she believed that a purely scientific approach to human sexuality was necessarily depersonalizing and possibly an invitation to licentiousness. The Kinsey reports (one on male sexuality, in 1948, and one on female sexuality, in 1953) "reduced [sexuality] to its narrowest physiological limits." In particular, Friedan observed, they treated "sexuality as a status-seeking game in which the goal was the greatest number of 'outlets,' [or] orgasms."[3]

In fact, the "discourse" on sexuality—the collective way of thinking and talking about it—had been shifting decisively throughout the post–World War II period. The vague references to sexual "satisfaction" or "fulfillment" that had characterized sexological writing earlier in the century were being replaced by a one-word description of a physiological event—"orgasm." In part, the new emphasis on the orgasm as the touchstone of sexual experience came from the émigré psychoanalyst Wilhelm Reich, who attributed the orgasm with a mystical, redemptive power to heal and inspire. His influence, however, was largely limited to an intellectual avant-garde. Most Americans learned to think of sex in terms of orgasms from Kinsey, and his interest in them was far more prosaic than Reich's. A scientist, Alfred Kinsey was determined to make his study of sex quantitatively precise; and that meant he needed some way to measure the amorphous notion of sexual experience. He needed something to *count,* and what he chose to count was orgasms.

The Kinsey reports were sensational for their revelations about the sheer volume of extramarital and often deviant sex in pre–sexual-revolution America. But it was his methodology, rather than his findings, that had a lasting effect on how Americans think about sex. His focus on the orgasm count—as opposed to, say, the number of "affairs" or "acts of penetration"—carried with it the implicit notion that all routes to orgasm are somehow equivalent or at least equally worthy of note. Sex, as studied by Kinsey and his colleagues, did not necessarily include love, heterosexual attraction, or even any human interaction. It included homosexual sex, masturbation, and even bestiality—all of which were horrifyingly deviant but which nonetheless showed up in the bottom line, the orgasm count. The latent message, which did not achieve widespread acceptance for decades, was that if we were to be objective about sex, we would have to learn to be a little less judgmental about how it was defined.

Another message, which was much more readily absorbed even in the fifties, was that men and women were not so different sexually after all. In *Sexual Behavior in the Human Female,* Kinsey and his colleagues asserted that in spite of the widespread and oft-repeated emphasis on the supposed differences between female and male sexuality, we fail to find any anatomic or physiological basis for such differences.[4]

In particular, "orgasm is a phenomenon which appears to be essentially the same in the human female and male." These conclusions contradicted the dominant, Freudian theories of female sexuality that still prevailed in most popularly available information and advice, but they were hard to ignore. If sexology was a science, and if the orgasm was its principle "unit of measurement," then surely women's orgasms had to "count" as much as men's.

The Kinsey reports encouraged women to take a more hardheaded—the critics said "selfish"—view of sex. Vaguer descriptions of sexual pleasure, like "satisfaction" or "fulfillment," could easily be confused with intangible feelings of love and affection. But orgasm was a definite event; it could happen quite independently of any human feeling. Thus sex was not just an extension of love but a separate realm within which a marriage could either falter or succeed. Within this realm, there was little ambiguity: While a woman might be aware of more or less "satisfaction," she could actually count orgasms. If American women were beginning to think of sex as a "status-seeking game," as Friedan worried, there was now a way to tally the score.

In popular, as well as expert opinion, American women did not measure up very well. Physicians believed that over 50 percent of American women were "frigid"[5] a condition which had expanded to include not only those who were totally unresponsive but those who failed to have orgasms. In medical literature, frigidity emerged in the fifties as a major health problem, the presumptive cause of a range of gynecological disorders from menstrual pain to infertility. To the average female, "frigidity" was a judgment freighted with a variety of resentments: that American women dominated their men (an inexhaustible theme in popular magazines); that American men were being "emasculated" by everything from the corporate work world to the suburban barbecue (a major motif of fifties' sociology); that the average wife was in fact a sexless creature compared to the cone-breasted Hollywood ideal of femininity. No wonder, then, that Friedan's informants seemed so joylessly preoccupied with their sexual status —their self-worth was at stake. In *Valley of the Dolls*, Anne's first tentative sexual encounter leads to agonizing introspection:

> Something was wrong with her. Why should
> she feel this cold distaste at a man's kiss? . . .
> She was deep in her own thoughts as they
> drove home. She knew the awful truth now.
> She was frigid. That awful word the girls in
> school used to whisper about. Some girls were
> born that way—they never reached a climax
> or felt any real passion. And she was one of
> them.

Anne's problem, however, was uncomplicated: She had not yet truly fallen in love. With the right man, the dapper and unreliable Lyon, she is finally able to report that "it happened," admitting, "I was beginning to worry about myself." Reassuringly he tells her, "Not at all—it's very rare for a girl to actually feel anything or reach a climax in the beginning." In response, "she kissed his face eagerly. 'I function, Lyon—I'm a woman!' "[6]

In the Freud-tinged sexual theories that most women were likely to encounter in magazine advice columns, orgasm—that is, vaginal orgasm during intercourse—was an important proof of womanhood. But, frustratingly, there seemed to be nothing a woman could actually *do* to achieve one. The available sex manuals—or "marriage manuals" as they were then known—stressed both the necessity of achieving orgasm and its total dependence on male effort. (It did not matter to the advice-givers that Kinsey and his research colleagues had publicized alternative routes to female orgasm, such as masturbation and lesbian sex. In the Freudian view, those were "immature" and deviant forms of female sexuality.) In the most widely read manual of the fifties, *Ideal Marriage: Its Physiology and Technique,* by the Dutch physician Th. H. Van de Velde (the book was originally published in the United States in 1930 and went through thirty-two reprints between 1941 and 1957), orgasm was described as a physiological requirement—at least for any woman who had set out on the path to coitus. According to Van de Velde, failure to relieve the "congestion" created in the first stages of sexual arousal would lead immediately to "nervous anger, fatigue, malaise, and pain" and, over time, to a variety of gynecological disorders, including painful and irregular menstruation and "vague or definite localized or wandering pains." Thus there were sound medical reasons why men had to strive to satisfy their wives, for as he warned repeatedly, and in italics:

Every considerable erotic stimulation of their
wives that does not terminate in orgasm, on
the woman's part, represents an injury, and
repeated injuries of this kind lead to perma-
nent—or very obstinate—damage to both
body and soul.[7]

It was Van de Velde's zealous insistence on female orgasm (not merely "pleasure" but orgasm) that en-
deared him to female readers and no doubt contributed
to what Betty Friedan deplored as the "mounting sex
hunger" of American women.

But in the sex act described by Van de Velde and his
numerous, easy-to-read imitators in the fifties, women
were barely participants, much less full "partners." The
man was to set the pace, introduce innovations, and
decide when foreplay would end and the real business
of penetration would begin; the woman had only to
respond. Van de Velde did not even think women were
a worthwhile audience for his fund of knowledge, and
addressed *Ideal Marriage* to physicians and "married
men," explaining that the latter "are naturally educa-
tors and initiators of their wives in sexual matters."[8]
Nor could women be useful sources of information, for
example on the experience of orgasm, since "only few
women are at present capable of observing and recording their own sensations, and then subsequently of ana-
lyzing them." Officially, then, women were barred
from the discourse on sex. They had nothing to say and
no reason to be told anything, and whatever they felt
was the product of male effort. When women's role in
the sex act had to be explicated, Van de Velde and his
successors drew on Balzac's musical analogy: "Woman

is a harp who only yields her secrets of melody to the master who knows how to handle her."[9]

As to how a man was to achieve this degree of virtuosity, the pre–sexual-revolution manuals were either vague or misleading. At times, for example, Van de Velde acknowledged the importance of clitoral stimulation (without, however, offering much advice on how to accomplish it), and at times he wrote as if the female orgasm would be triggered automatically by the "refreshing" flow of the male ejaculation. Another popular advice book, *A Marriage Manual* by Drs. Hannah and Abraham Stone (but written in the third person singular, "Doctor"), advised manual stimulation of the clitoris only as a last-ditch effort, to be undertaken after "normal sexual union" had failed to produce a female orgasm.* And, having gone this far, the Stones felt constrained to have their imaginary interlocutor (a frequent character in sex manuals) inquire, "Wouldn't such a practice be a perversion, Doctor?"[10]

Van de Velde believed that male dominance in sex was completely "natural," but not so natural that couples did not have to be warned against more egalitarian modes of expression. Thus he found it necessary to caution against having the woman too frequently on top during intercourse, a position he felt encouraged "the

---

* Writing years later, but still untouched by any sexual revolution, Dr. David Reuben undertook to define the male responsibility for female orgasm in scientifically quantitative terms:

> No woman deserves to be labeled sexually frigid unless her sexual partner provides her with at least enough mechanical stimulation to trigger the orgasmic response.
>
> *How much stimulation is that?* For the average couple, about eight minutes of actual intercourse or seventy-five to eighty pelvic thrusts.[11]

complete passivity of the man and the exclusive activity
of his partner." This, he wrote, "is directly contrary to
the natural relationship of the sexes, and must bring
unfavorable consequences if it becomes habitual." In
another place he tells us that "on purely aesthetic
grounds," male passivity in sex "is out of the question
for men of white Western races in modern civilization."[12]

In fact, for Van de Velde, it was not enough to establish the aesthetic superiority of male leadership in sex;
he seemed driven to suppress all signs, however involuntary, of female initiative. Female *movements* during
coitus (the notion was strange enough to italicize) were
contraindicated on the ground that "with too vigorous
[female] motion, the intromittent organ slips out of the
vagina"—a most embarrassing sidetrack. Female initiative in "genital kissing" was discouraged for reasons of
"delicacy" and "discretion." Female sounds were another potential problem, and provided the basis for a
bizarre argument against rear-entry positions, which
might otherwise have been assumed to guarantee male
"mastery":

> The piston-like backwards and forwards mo-
> tion of the phallus may occasionally force some
> of the air out of the vaginal cavity again, to the
> accompaniment of unpleasantly suggestive
> and quite audible whistling sounds. Even
> when the air leaves the vagina again on the
> assumption of a more normal position after
> intercourse . . . the process is only too audi-
> ble and extraordinarily repulsive in its effect.[13]

Here the ancient fear of the "toothed vagina" has been extended to the repulsive possibility of a talking vagina —genitalia which might appear to have a life of their own, independent of a woman's "natural" reticence and submissiveness.

So much did the sex act depend on male agency and female passivity that Van de Velde and his contemporaries rarely referred to the participants as "partners"—a usage which became widespread only in the sixties. In their misogynist classic of 1947, *Modern Woman: The Lost Sex*, which was influential well into the fifties, Ferdinand Lundberg and Marynia Farnham had pointed out to any residual "female egalitarians" that

> for the male, sex involves an objective act of
> his doing but for the female it does not . . .
> her role is passive. It is not as easy as rolling off
> a log for her. It is easier. It is as easy as being
> the log itself.[14]

If there was widespread female frigidity, it was because modern woman suffered from "morbidly intense ego-strivings"; "rivalrous" feelings toward the male prevented her from attaining the passivity of a truly feminine woman, i.e., of a harp or a log.

So, almost necessarily, the area of maximum sexual preoccupation—the female orgasm—became a combat zone in the battle of the sexes. If the orgasm count was low, and everyone believed there was a national deficit of female orgasms, the blame could be apportioned either way. The man might be inadequate in his "performance" (though, with the weight or blame shifting toward women, specific male shortcomings, like premature ejaculation, were not yet major focuses of anxiety). More likely, in the prevailing judgment, the woman was frigid, or, in some deep way, withholding and resistant. Marriage, especially the ingrown, isolated marriage of the suburbs, provided a lifetime forum for mutual recrimination and resentment that could be deflected from the bedroom to the breakfast nook and back again.

On the eve of the sexual revolution, and prior to a developed feminist analysis of sexuality, there was no elucidation of America's orgasm impasse outside of psychoanalytic thought. In his introduction to the 1966 anthology *Psychoanalysis and Female Sexuality*, the prolific psychoanalytic commentator Hendrik M. Ruitenbeek offered an analysis that was curiously modern, even covertly feminist, in its focus on women's inferior social status. Along with Marie Bonaparte, Helene Deutsch, and other Freudian analysts of women's condition, he believed that true or mature female sexuality was passive and vaginally centered. Active, clitoral sexuality was immature and represented a refusal to accept the lack of a penis and "the male organic and psychical elements" that go with it. Thus, to grow up along psychoanalytically acceptable lines, "the active little girl must change into a far more passive creature." However, all kinds of complex changes, which Ruitenbeek associated with women's relative emancipation, had made "the female movement to passivity . . . more difficult in our time." In a remarkably perceptive passage, he explained how frigidity, or the failure to achieve fully passive, vaginal orgasm, was actually a "rebellion":

In a world where male activity sets the standards of worth—and analysts point out that
both physiologically and psychologically, male
sexual performance is an achievement—female experience in sex as in other aspects of
life takes on the character of a peculiarly ambiguous struggle against male domination.[15]

The struggle was "ambiguous" because, in the Freudian scheme, there seemed to be no way to win.
Ruitenbeek acknowledged that even psychoanalytically adjusted women might fall apart:

Some women submit; they do not rebel; they
do not become aggressive and therefore a
threat to the men in their lives, but their inability to enjoy their assigned role or to react
against it leads to feelings of despair and to a
kind of disintegration of the self.[16]

The woman who did have the spunk to "react," one
way or another, was no less pathetic. There was no way
to escape the passivity imposed by nature—without becoming a lesbian or other deviant, as Bonaparte cau-
tioned in her contribution to Ruitenbeek's anthology.
And there was obviously no way to "achieve" passivity
by actively striving for it. All that Ruitenbeek could
advise was that women scale down their expectations to
more diffuse satisfactions than orgasm:

In my opinion, too many contemporary
women tend to forget that satisfactory sexual
experience entails something more than orgasm. Now as in the past, a woman can know
sexual gratification by satisfying the compo-

nent drives of her ego: awareness that she is desirable, ability to excite the man sexually, childbearing, and the aim-deflected pleasures of affection and tenderness.[17]

The "aim," Ruitenbeek implied, was still penetration and vaginal orgasm, but the contemporary woman might have to settle for cuddling.

SEX AND THE BIG CITY

If sex was stymied in the suburbs, a new terrain for erotic experience was opening up, by the early sixties, in the emerging "singles culture" of the cities. The cities had always lured young men and women from the monotony of rural life. By the mid-twentieth century, big cities were drawing young women from small cities; Jacqueline Susann "escaped" from Philadelphia to New York and the chance of an acting career in the late thirties. With the growth of corporate bureaucracies in the fifties, it was no longer only the daring or exceptional young woman who headed for the skylines after college or high school; thousands upon thousands of women were drawn in by the expansion of secretarial and clerical office jobs. In New York's Upper East Side, which was to become the first singles "ghetto," a real-estate boom in high-rise apartments and renovated tenements matched the in-migration of hopeful secretaries, stewardesses, editorial assistants, and would-be models and actresses marking time as receptionists or waitresses. Three or four "girls" might share a two bedroom apartment for three hundred dollars a month,

losing some roommates to marriage, others to discour-
agement (there was usually a hometown to return to for
the girl who failed to make her way), while all the time
gaining new recruits from college campuses and small
Mid-western cities.

The young middle-class woman who arrived in New
York in the late fifties or early sixties probably expected
to marry and retire to the suburbs in a few years, for the
experts still agreed that "motherhood is the defining
feature of a woman's life," but in the meantime she had
sexual advantages—and possibilities—she would never
regain as a housewife. First, she made her own money,
so she was not required to "work" on a relationship out
of sheer financial need. Like the fictional Anne Welles,
she did not have to brood forever over a sexual disappointment; she could move on to a more satisfying partner. Second, she inhabited a social world that was infi-
nitely richer in heterosexual contacts than the
unisexual married women's world of shopping centers
and playgrounds. There was the office—a work world
which was mostly female and certainly male-dominated, but which offered opportunities for fantasy and
flirtation. And there was the public space of streets,
bars, even bookstores and buses, where a woman could
move anonymously from one encounter with a potential partner to the next. As historian John d'Emilio has
argued, the postwar cities—especially New York and
San Francisco—provided the setting for the creation of
a gay culture.[18] And for young, single, heterosexual
women in the fifties and sixties, the city held forth an
entirely new vision of female sexual possibility—and
the first setting for a sexual revolution.

Other settings, too, fostered a rapid change in women's sexual expectations. On college campuses—which, like big city apartment complexes, offered a modicum of independence and a large population of young, single people—numerous studies documented a rapid decline, during the sixties, of the number of women who held on to their virginity until graduation. And although the sexual revolution was seen by many blacks as a white affair, *Ebony* noted in 1966 that it seemed to be having a profound effect on the young, middle-class black woman, who was "freed . . . from many inhibitions imposed on her by a now outdated puritanical outlook on sex . . . [and] like her white sister, has gained a new perspective on herself." *Ebony* attributed the change in part to the civil-rights movement, which had helped black women overcome the twin stereotypes of the Jezebel and the sexless Mammy and achieve "awareness of her true sexual self."[19] Whatever the sources, or the setting, a generation of young, mostly middle-class women were undertaking a sexual revolution or, at the very least, were being swept along by it.

The first spokeswoman for the revolution was a woman whom many feminists would be loath to claim as one of their own, but of the two best-sellers on women's condition—Helen Gurley Brown's *Sex and the Single Girl,* published in 1962, and *The Feminine Mystique,* published a year later—Brown's was in many ways the more radical. Friedan documented the discontents of middle-class housewives and proposed a "new life plan for women," which would include both motherhood and a career. Brown went further and announced that marriage was unnecessary and that a new life was already possible, the life of the single, urban, working "girl." Brown's book was a gushy guide to self-improvement, in the style she later immortalized in *Cosmopolitan,* while Friedan's was first-rate journalism. But it was *Sex and the Single Girl* that disposed of what Friedan called the feminine mystique in a few brief, confident sentences. "You may marry or you may not," she told her readers:

> In today's world that is no longer the big question for women. Those who glom onto men so that they can collapse with relief, spend the rest of their days shining up their status symbol and figure they never have to reach, stretch, learn, grow, face dragons or make a living again are the ones to be pitied. They, in my opinion, are the unfulfilled ones.[20]

Recall that Brown wrote this at a time when the *Ladies' Home Journal* still found most of its young readers looking ahead, not only to marriage but to the details of their future kitchen decor. Even the "new" urban, single women Brown addressed were still hoping, for the most part, that their stint in the city would culminate in an engagement and retreat to the married suburbs. Brown was way ahead of her time; the skirt-suited, full-time career woman, for example, would not emerge as a feminine role model until well into the seventies. But Brown was not so far ahead as to neglect the frustrations—and aspirations—of millions of very conventional and nonradical American women. Her book *Sex and the Single Girl* was a best-seller at a time when "feminism" did not even exist in the American political vocabulary, and when most middle-class women could imagine few options other than marriage and full-time motherhood.

Sex and the Single Girl argued simultaneously for women's financial independence and sexual liberation —a heavy burden, one might think, for such a light-hearted, chatty book. For Brown, though, the two goals were almost indistinguishable: Sex justified the need for financial independence, because the single working woman could spend money on the clothes and cosmetics and apartment accessories that would make her sexy; in fact, it was Brown's impression that she had more to spend "than any but a wealthily married few." Singleness itself was essential to sexiness, and not only because of the variety and availability it implied. Friedan found that housewives were bored; Brown announced that they were also boring, unattractive, and no match for the sexual challenge of the single girl:

> There is a more important truth that maga-
> zines never deal with, that single women are
> too brainwashed to admit, that married men
> *and* single men endorse in a body, and that is
> that the single woman, far from being a crea-
> ture to be pitied and patronized, is emerging
> as the newest glamour girl of our times.[21]

What made the single woman sexually superior to women who had married? How could the erstwhile spinster meet the psychoanalytic criteria for feminine fulfillment? "She is engaging because she lives by her wits," Brown explained. "She supports herself." In contrast to the married woman, "she is not a parasite, a dependent, a scrounger, a sponger or a bum."

If single women were sexy, they also had a right to

sex, and perhaps the most important thing about *Sex and the Single Girl* was that it legitimized the sexual possibilities opening up to young, urban working women. Brown offered no new moral perspective on premarital sex, which was still viewed as a social problem and symptom of eroding values; she simply stated that it was happening, at least in cities large enough to accommodate the new breed of woman. Responding to articles in *Reader's Digest* and the *Ladies' Home Journal* advising single women to either marry or say no, Brown reported:

> I don't know about girls in Pleasantville and Philadelphia, where these magazines are published, but I do know that in Los Angeles, where I live, there is something else a girl can say and frequently does when a man "insists." And that is "yes." . . . Nice girls *do* have affairs, and they do not necessarily die of them![22]

This was, for many women in 1962, a major news item, almost as if a cure had been found for a fatal illness: "Nice" girls, meaning middle-class girls in pink- or white-collar jobs, not "sluts" or "whores," were having affairs and they were surviving. Sometimes, Brown acknowledged, they did get hurt and suffered, but happily "quite a few 'nice' single girls have affairs and do not suffer at all!" So extramarital sex did not have to mean ruin, as *Reader's Digest* warned, or be a sign of sickly obsession, as Friedan feared. Brown's single girl was not "using" sex to fill a void, as did some of the slatternly matrons described by Friedan; she had plenty of other things on her mind, like, Brown suggested, "retailing, advertising, motion pictures, exporting, shipbuilding." For a vibrant, self-determining single woman, sex was not a dangerous emotional morass but something to seek because you felt The Urge. With revolutionary simplicity, Brown explained that the number one reason for a single woman to start an affair was because "her body wants to."[23]

Within a few years after the publication of *Sex and the Single Girl,* the single, sexually acquisitive way of life for women would no longer require book-length vindication. By 1964, there were enough single girls (and envious married women) to warrant Helen Gurley Brown's transformation of the failing, family-oriented magazine *Cosmopolitan* into the *Cosmo* we know today. The first singles bars (Maxwell's Plum, P. J. Clarke's, T.G.I. Friday's) opened in Manhattan's Upper East Side, and new words entered the American vocabulary: "relationship," to accommodate both marriage and "affairs" (at the same time "affair," with its permanent image of marginalization, became archaic); "lifestyle," to accommodate singleness as well as marriage (and eventually homosexuality as another "alternative"); and "singles" itself as an adjective which might pertain to a neighborhood or a lifestyle. The commercialization of singles' needs—through bars, resorts, magazines, etc.—helped create a singles culture and identity which, over time, had less and less reason to feel defensive in the face of the married majority. In a 1969 book, *The Single Girl's Book: Making It in the Big City,* which could be taken for a pallid sequel to *Sex and the Single Girl,* Stanlee Miller Coy assumed that young women just want to know where the singles action is (in Chicago; the Near North Side, Old Town, and the Prairie Shores high-rise complex; in Boston; Beacon Hill,

Back Bay; and so forth through "those seven cities" offering outposts of singles culture). In New York, the new culture had long since achieved a critical mass, and "you can singles bar-hop up and down Third, Second, and First avenues on the Upper East Side, seeing thousands of singles."[24]

As the sixties wore on, the limitations of the new urban singles culture would become more and more apparent, even to its devotees. It was an all-white culture, largely untouched by the movements of the sixties, upper-middle-class in ambition, and conservative in all ways but sexual. The gap, for example, between New York's Upper East Side singles enclave and the center of Harlem's night life on 125th Street might have been forty miles instead of forty blocks, and the Lower East Side, which briefly supported a hippie culture second only to Haight-Ashbury's in San Francisco, might have been a foreign country, invisible from the subways rushing upscale singles from their apartments uptown to their jobs in the financial district. Within the singles scene, there was a gradual disenchantment with the ritual of sodden pickups, one-night stands, and the "meat-market" atmosphere of the bars. More sophisticated singles of both sexes began to settle in new territory (quickly gentrifying it, however, to their own tastes), to meet in therapy groups or events advertised in *The Village Voice*, and to look for opportunities for psychological "growth experiences" in their sexual encounters. But the singles culture, even at its most crass and preppie-conformist, nurtured women's sexual revolution: It *was* the mainstream, and in it casual sex was normal, acceptable, and in no way compromising to a woman's marital or career aspirations.

Unless, of course, she got pregnant; and in the sixties, with abortion still illegal, an accidental pregnancy was at best a costly and traumatic mishap. Though illegal, abortion was not unavailable, but an illegal abortion was likely to be exorbitantly expensive, horribly unsafe, or both. The birth control pill, which was a more reliable contraceptive than the diaphragm, reduced the chance of an unwanted pregnancy and gave many women the illusion of sexual invulnerability. But the pill was neither a necessary nor sufficient cause of women's sexual revolution: When the hazards of the pill became widely known in the late sixties, thanks in large part to Barbara Seaman's book *The Doctors' Case Against the Pill,* young women did not abandon the sexual revolution—they campaigned to legitimize abortion.

MASTERS & JOHNSON AND THE NEW SEXUAL MATERIALISM

The opportunities for more sex and sex with more men did not, at first, change the nature of the sexual experience itself for women. A single cosmopolite, no less than the long-term housewife, still faced the social definition of sex as intercourse and orgasm as the more or less spontaneous proof of womanhood. One woman, a college roommate of one of the authors, reports that as a young woman in Los Angeles in the early sixties, she had "about a dozen" lovers in three years, but

> my feeling for quite a while was that sex was
> no big deal. I had a girlfriend who claimed to

have ecstatic orgasms every time she went to bed with a man, so I naturally figured there was something wrong with me. . . . But with twenty years of hindsight I realize that it was just bad sex. The most sophisticated man I knew got all his information from D. H. Lawrence and Henry Miller, and the others had no information at all. Either way it was something that usually happened in the dark, that took fifteen minutes or less, and left me wanting to turn on the lights and read a book. It was not something I thought a lot about until I had to get an abortion in 1965, which cost over $500, and then I thought: Was it really worth it?

Sex and the Single Girl had said almost nothing about sex itself, and left the mysteries of the orgasm to the psychiatrists. Under the heading "You're Frigid," Brown advised:

If after some experience you are still unable to enjoy making love, *and this bothers you,* psychiatric consultation may be in order.[25] (Emphasis added.)

Sex was still in the dark, and any problems that arose were in the minds of women, hence in the terrain of psychiatry.

It took the successors of Kinsey, William Masters and Virginia Johnson to turn on the lights and restore the human body—especially the female body—to the discourse on sexuality. What they established—about the female capacity for orgasm and the centrality of the clitoris to female sexuality—is by now well enough known. Less well known today is that none of this should have been news, even in 1966, when *The Human Sexual Response* was first published. Up until and for some time after Masters and Johnson's media triumph in the late sixties, most psychiatrists and psychoanalysts clung to Freud's theory of the female progression from immature clitoral sexuality to normal, mature vaginal sexuality, and postulated an exclusively vaginal orgasm for the successfully adjusted woman. But a wealth of contradictory evidence had been available for decades. There was the fact that the vagina has almost no nerve endings, while the clitoris is far more richly nerve-endowed than any part of the male sexual apparatus. There was Kinsey's documentation of the extent of female masturbation and lesbianism, practices which may have been "immature" by psychoanalytic standards but were apparently orgasmic. Reviewing the evidence, psychiatrist Judd Marmor had concluded in 1954 that clitoral sexuality persisted in adult women and that there was probably no such thing as a purely vaginal orgasm. By 1960, even the redoubtable Freudian Dr. Helene Deutsch publicly conceded her doubts about the existence of a psychoanalytically correct vaginal orgasm.[26] So if it was a surprise when the two St. Louis sex investigators revealed the intensity of clitoral sexuality and its role in female orgasm, it was only because of the psychiatric establishment's dogged adherence to the vaginal orgasm as prescribed by Freud.

Masters and Johnson employed a careful public relations strategy, designed both to keep them in the limelight and to maintain their aura of academic detachment. They offered scientific briefings for the press, but would not appear on television talk shows. They wrote an advice column for *Playboy,* but would not stoop to debate their critics. Between 1966 and 1970, articles about and occasionally by Masters and Johnson appeared in almost every mass circulation magazine, from *Redbook* to the *Saturday Review;* their book and a popularization by Ruth and Edward Brecher had become best-sellers. But it was not only skillful PR that made Masters and Johnson a household word, or, more accurately, an infallible bedroom reference. Their findings arrived at a time when expert theories of female sexuality ran increasingly counter to women's social experience. In psychoanalytic theory, female sexuality was an exercise in passivity, as complementary to male sexual activism as vagina to penis, and female orgasm was a magnificent surrender, symbolic of woman's acceptance of her subsidiary role in life. So for women, the official "meaning" of sex—the message emerging from all the sensations, positions, etc.—was powerlessness, and intercourse was an act of submission redeemed only by the certainty of a man's love. But if you were not married, or were tired of marriage, if you were self-supporting and adventurous, capable of sleeping with strangers or even social "inferiors," then sex had to "mean" something other than a submission to cosmic necessity. Masters and Johnson potentially offered a new social meaning for sex, one that was more consistent with women's emerging sense of independence.

The most common, and loudest, response to Masters and Johnson was that they had stripped sex of any meaning at all. The experiments, for many critics, were more shocking than the results. In a laboratory, Masters and Johnson had followed seven hundred volunteers (divided roughly evenly by gender) through various stages of arousal and orgasm, charting changes in the appearance of the genitalia, body motions, skin conductivity, etc. Some of the subjects were observed during heterosexual intercourse; others were studied while masturbating, either by hand or with artificial assistance. You had to wonder, the critics insisted, what kind of mind could have devised such an experiment, or, worse, what kind of person could be so depraved as to volunteer for it. Then, with the ad hominems out of the way, but before getting to the actual findings, there was the disturbing fact that there was anything to observe at all: that sex could occur in a laboratory, under the scrutiny of technicians, between strangers, or between people and vibrators, in a tangle of wires leading to monitoring machines. Liberal sociologist Kenneth Keniston complained that Masters and Johnson "repeatedly reduce human sexuality to physical responses," though, of course, only physical responses are accessible to quantitative measurement. Psychoanalyst Natalie Shainess railed that Masters and Johnson had released "a pipeline of pornographic sewage . . . into the vital heart of our life," corrupted youth, cheapened and "thingified sex," "trivialized it . . . [and] trampled on the ultimate mystery of life."[27] If sex were no longer the "ultimate mystery," it could mean anything —or nothing—like any sensation or any tracing on a laboratory recording device.

Finally, there were the findings themselves: that women actually had greater orgasmic capacity than men and were capable of multiple orgasms; that women have only one discernible kind of orgasm; and that it was more intense when self-induced by clitoral stimulation than when achieved through heterosexual intercourse. The implication was clear: Women did not need men for orgasmic sex. In fact, as Dr. Masters himself suggested, the presence of a partner could be a "distraction" to a woman on her way to orgasm. In an article in *Commentary*, Dr. Leslie Farber gleefully mocked Masters and Johnson for introducing the specter of the sexually self-sufficient woman:

> Her lust would lie to hand, ready to be invoked and consummated in sickness or in health, in coitus or "automanipulation," in homosexuality or heterosexuality, in exasperation or calm, hesitancy or certainty, playfulness or despair. . . . In other words, her sexuality would be wholly subject to her will.[28]

FEMINISM AND SEXUAL REVOLUTION

It was Dr. Farber's genius to anticipate almost precisely the feminist interpretation of Masters and Johnson. A psychoanalyst, he had written with the smug security of a man who knows feminism only as a diagnostic category. In the forties, Lundberg and Farnham, still eager to reduce women's sexual initiative to that of a log, had echoed the prevailing opinion on feminism. They described it only in the past tense, judging it to be "at its core a deep illness." "It was out of the disturbed libidinal organization of women" that accompanied "modern life," they wrote, "that the ideology of feminism arose."[29] Friedan had done her best to rehabilitate the term, but it was only in the late sixties, on the crest of the radical movements for peace and civil rights, that large numbers of women dared to flout the Freudian stigma attached to feminism and declare themselves a radical movement of women and for women. One of the earliest and most radical initiatives of these new "radical feminists," as they called themselves, was in the still confused and contradictory area of sexuality.

In taking up the issue of sex, the radical feminists opened up entirely new terrain to political purview, and in the process, redefined "politics" itself. To the earlier, and now older, feminists like Friedan and the National Organization for Women, which she had organized in 1966, women's rights were to be achieved in the public realm of jobs, legislation, and conventional pressure-group politics. The "private realm"—which only the radicals conceptualized as an equal sphere of female activity—was at best uninteresting, and at worst a swamp of trivial and personal preoccupations. But to the younger radicals, every repressed corner of private life and daily experience—from housework to sexuality and childbearing—was a valid arena for political action. Consciousness-raising groups encouraged women to trust their subjective experience, even when it contradicted male judgment or expert opinion. Sex—the area of secrecy and self-doubt and of maximum competition between women—was opened up to informal analysis and sharing. Did you worry that you might be frigid? Fake orgasms to please a boyfriend? Secretly prefer masturbation, or wonder about lesbianism? So, it turned out, did almost everyone else, and not every woman could be as frigid or sexually warped as the marriage manuals and therapists insisted. It did not take long for women, buoyed with the confidence of the new movement, to trace the links connecting women's widespread sexual anxiety to their feelings of worthlessness and self-hate, and hence to the social oppression of women as a group.

Masters and Johnson's work was already widely known by 1968, the year the women's liberation movement announced its emergence. There is no way to know whether the early feminists would have dared to defy Freudian sexual dogma on the strength of subjective experience alone. Mainly by chance (though Virginia Johnson was in her own way a feminist), they did not have to: Here was a body of objective, and by most standards, respectably scientific findings on which to rest the case for a radically new, feminist interpretation of sexuality. The critics of Masters and Johnson had feared that sexual reductionism would lead to sexual nihilism. Reduced to anatomy and sensation, sex would lose its old meanings—love, commitment, and the established sex roles—and come to mean nothing at all. Feminism offered sex (as revealed by Masters and Johnson) an entirely new set of meanings. Sex did not have to be a microdrama of male dominance and female passivity; it was, properly understood and acted on, an affirmation of women's strength and independence.

"Think clitoris," concluded Alix Shulman in her 1971 essay "Organs and Orgasms," for if the vagina was the stronghold of Freudian, male-dominated sexuality, the clitoris was the first beachhead of feminist sexuality.[30] Some feminists, like Germaine Greer, criticized the early, exclusive championing of the clitoris, and later feminist work would expand the genital erotogenic area to include the entire vulva and perianal region.

But the first task of feminist sex rebels was to resurrect the long repressed—and sometimes even surgically excised—clitoris. It was visible proof of women's sexual autonomy from men, the possibility Dr. Farber had glimpsed and psychoanalytic theory had done so much to discredit. With Masters and Johnson's "discovery" of the clitoris and its central role in orgasm, it was possible to think of heterosexuality and even intercourse itself as an "institution," rather than a physiological necessity. In the 1970 essay "The Myth of the Vaginal Orgasm," Anne Koedt easily swept aside the old sexual dogma and spelled out the implications of clitorally-centered sexuality: If only for "strictly anatomical reasons," women might just as well seek pleasure from other women as from men. Koedt's classic essay was no less than a declaration of sexual independence; women could now be sexual, fully orgasmic beings not only outside of marriage but apart from men, who, she acknowledged, now had good reason to "fear that they will become sexually expendable."[31]

Feminists also seized on Masters and Johnson's other major finding—that women's orgasmic capacity far exceeded that of men. Dr. Mary Jane Sherfey's work, popularized in Barbara Seaman's *Free and Female*, argued that women, not men, were the sexually aggressive, orgasmically potent sex, capable of "having orgasms indefinitely if physical exhaustion did not intervene." Frigidity had been a social artifact of the vaginally centered sex men preferred; the clitorally aware woman was sexually voracious to the point of being a threat to the social order. Women's true sexual drive, Sherfey wrote, was "too strong, too susceptible to the fluctuating extremes of an impelling, aggressive eroticism to withstand the disciplined requirements of a settled family life."[32]

The feminist reclamation of sex made women's liberation, at least for a brief few years in the early seventies, as much a movement for sexual liberation. Clearly, women had been deprived, sexually stunted in service to the vaginal and phallocratic sex imposed by men. They needed more sex, but they needed sex in a variety that went far beyond the traditional in-and-out, man-on-top, intercourse. Clitoral sex, Alix Shulman pointed out, demanded a wider range of options, including oral sex, lesbian sex, and positions for intercourse that were more favorable to clitoral stimulation. All the old prohibitions and taboos would have to give way to the needs of the sexually liberated woman. Masturbation, for example, had been found by Masters and Johnson to produce the most intense orgasms in women, so feminists reclaimed it from the status of a "filthy habit" to a legitimate sexual alternative. At the high point of the fusion of feminism and sexual revolution, feminist conferences routinely offered workshops and conscious-ness-raising sessions on sexuality in general, genital and body awareness, and techniques of masturbation. Betty Dodson, a popular advocate of masturbation and leader of "bodysex" workshops, expressed the new feminist optimism about sex in a 1972 article in *Ms.:*

> Exploring my sexual potential has taken me on many paths of learning and change. Re-claiming my body as a source of strength and pleasure has given me power over my own life and the freedom to design my sex life cre-atively, just like painting a picture. Self-sexual-

ity, along with heterosexuality, homosexuality,
bisexuality, and group sexuality is simply all
part of human sexual behavior.[33]

But there was controversy from the beginning over
the status of sexuality in the fledgling women's movement. Betty Friedan and others in the leadership of the
National Organization for Women feared that the radical feminists' sexual heterodoxy—especially the encouragement of lesbianism—would marginalize the
movement from the mainstream, which still consisted
of married, presumably sexually orthodox, housewives.
Others worried that sex was a detour leading to individual self-improvement and away from political involvement; certainly orgasms, now that the anatomy had
been clarified, were easier to achieve than equality. But
on the whole, feminism was strengthened by its appro-
priation of the sexual revolution. Sex *was* a major preoccupation for thousands of mainstream women locked in
the orgasm impasse created by Freudian dogma, and
for many of them, the feminist solution had the force of
revelation. Books celebrating female sexuality—including *Our Bodies, Ourselves,* Seaman's *Free and Female*
and many others—offered an instant boost in self-confi-
dence as well as a lasting message about the dignity and
value of women's experience. Instead of narrowing the
movement to a subculture of politicized, urban women,
sexual liberation contributed to the populist outreach
that eventually brought the movement itself into the
mainstream of American culture and politics. And,
what is perhaps no less important, the sexual liberation-
ist thrust of the movement protected it from the well-
worn psychoanalytic slur linking feminism to frigidity

and sundry deeper derangements of the libido. You could say, and many men did at first, that women became feminists because they were frustrated, or were too unattractive to find husbands. But you could *not* say, "All they need is a good lay." Feminists were doing very well in that department, thank you, and what they most emphatically did not want was a man's idea of quick and easy sex.

What feminism did for women's sexual revolution is a longer story, and one which we will see played out in succeeding chapters. Helen Gurley Brown's sexual revolution had stopped at the bedroom door, leaving any disappointments that lay behind it to the psychiatrists. Feminism opened the door, aired the room, and advanced the revolution into the smallest gesture and caress. Men's needs and women's needs were not automatically compatible, and the liberated woman had much more to say to a man than "Yes." As the psychoanalysts had suspected, heterosexual sex was a battleground in the war between the sexes. But victory was not what the psychoanalysts recommended: Real winners were conscious participants, fighting for what they wanted. If the battle seemed to men to rob sex of its "mystery," if the clitoris seemed like a demanding intruder, there was still no turning back. Feminism had used the sexual reductionism of Kinsey and Masters and Johnson to create a program of sexual reform, and too bad for the retrograde male who felt, like Norman Mailer,

> a hate for the legions of the vaginally frigid,
> out there now all the pent-up buzzing of a hive
> of bees, souped-up pent-up voltage of a clitoris
> ready to spring![34]

3
The Battle for Orgasm Equity
The Heterosexual Crisis of the Seventies

For men, the point of sexual revolution was, above all, more sex. If there was a problem, it was scarcity; and if there was a solution, it was greater quantity and availability. *Playboy*, which for most men represented *the* sexual revolution until women launched their own demands, rarely hinted at any qualitative transformation of sex itself. The centerfold models were selected to look as much as possible like the girl next door or down the hall in the typing pool; and the message, at the simplest level, was that she was much more available than you might have thought. Norman Mailer, for all his hostility, was one of the first to see that women had more in mind than "more." Women's sexual revolution meant that heterosexuality itself was about to be redefined.

As women's heightened expectations began to spread from the urban singles culture to the suburbs, the media responded with a sense of crisis. The divorce rate was rising precipitously, and it was clear that one of the biggest trouble spots was in the bedroom. For example, in 1972 *Life* singled out as a "typical" American couple David and Lynn Maxwell, who had been married for twelve years, had two children, and were now on the verge of divorce. In a feature article, the Maxwells went public with a list of problems, not the least of which was sex. Lynn asserted she could no longer sleep with David until she achieved more freedom in other areas of her life. "Before we were married David and I had a great sex life," Lynn said. "After we were married sex was one more obligation . . . making love was a very empty thing, and afterwards I would get so depressed."[1] Both had gone out and found alternative sexual partners. At least for Lynn, sex now signified everything that was wrong with their marriage.

David was angry that he was losing his traditional wife and baffled by what Lynn wanted from him. "A major friction which had readied David for his affair," *Life* reported, was Lynn's increasing involvement with women's liberation. David lived in fear that Lynn would actually become "confident and self-reliant," transforming not only their sex life but all their domestic affairs.

As women's sexual revolution spread to thousands of other "typical" American couples, the ancient, male question "What do women want?" began to take on distinctly sexual overtones. Did they want affection or technique, more cuddling and conversation or more decisive climaxes? And if women got what they

wanted, what was in it for men? In the literature of
male angst that has flowed prolifically since the beginnings of women's liberation, men tried out a variety of
responses. Herb Goldberg, psychologist and men's liberation spokesman, tried to refocus attention on what
he saw as the neglected penis, even claiming that men,
when suitably aroused, were as capable as women of
multiple orgasms. At the other extreme, the male lover
of a well-known radical feminist announced that he
now managed to have sex without erections, which
seemed to him to be an atavistic reminder of male
domination. A more typical response is represented by
a recent book billed as a "survival guide" for men,
which finds the aftermath of sexual revolution "frightening," and complains that "bedroom conversations focus on the female orgasm and performance evaluation
[of the male]; the tender pillow talk is gone."[2]

A large part of the problem for men like David Maxwell was just that: There was so much *talk* about sex.
Before the advent of women's sexual revolution, a man
didn't have to worry that his wife would confide her
sexual dissatisfactions to the press; in fact, he probably
didn't suspect that there were any dissatisfactions to
confide. Sex was part of a wife's responsibility; and if, as
was frequently the case, it wasn't all that rewarding for
her, any marriage counselor would have pointed out
that bad sex was certainly not a justification for ending a
marriage. In the paradoxical advice of the psychiatrists,
women simply had to work harder to overcome their
inability to relax and enjoy it. Prior to feminism and
women's sexual revolution, wives kept silent about
their sexual disappointments because they did not want
to incriminate *themselves*.

There was a deeper problem. If men didn't know what was expected of them—or at least claimed to have no idea—it was because the heterosexual "act" itself was in the process of fundamental revision. Sex had meant intercourse, plus whatever preliminaries were required, by civility or affection, to achieve it. Now women were reporting that intercourse was incidental to their enjoyment; feminist writer Germaine Greer defined it as "masturbation in women's vaginas"—an embarrassing denouement for the premier event of the heterosexual relationship. Obviously homosexuals had done without vaginal intercourse, and, with the emergence of the gay liberation movement in 1969, it was apparent that gay sex was not—as had been commonly believed—a fumbling, pathetic substitute for the "real thing." So if heterosexual sex was not the spontaneous union of two physically complementary bodies, what *was* it?

But at the very moment, historically speaking, that the question could be raised, there were no longer any clear authorities to provide the answer. Women's sexual revolution, reinforced by the scientific rediscovery of clitoral sexuality, was rapidly discrediting the old medical authorities who had presided over sexual matters for at least a century. In the seventies there were no experts, or rather there were suddenly thousands of experts, each with a particular notion of how heterosexuality might be salvaged and reconstructed. The battle of the sexes, which had focused until now on the causes of female frigidity, now shifted to the question of "technique," or, more generally, *what was to be done.*

DEMEDICALIZED SEX

Before the sexual revolution, the public discourse on sex was dominated by the medical profession. Medical doctors—gynecologists and psychiatrists—wrote the popular guides to sex, chastely called "marriage manuals"; they appeared in magazines to answer anxious readers' questions; and they convened in academic gatherings to discuss sex, its failures (such as frigidity and impotence), and deviant forms. The medicalization of sex assured that there must be such a thing as "healthy sex", but by definition—and by way of defining it—healthy sex was ringed by its less than healthy, pathological variations. Doctors and the audience for their opinions were concerned with where to draw the line and how, if possible, to "treat" those who fell outside of it—the too avid, too slow, too specialized, too polymorphously promiscuous.

Any sex manual is inevitably a definition of sex: To describe "how to" is to define what there is to be done. The classic medical advice book *Ideal Marriage* stood out, not only for the largesse of physiological detail it provided but because it consciously, and painstakingly, undertook the problem of definition. Van de Velde offered what he believed was the "most exact and complete definition of normal sexual intercourse":

> That intercourse that comes between two sexually mature individuals of opposite sexes; which excludes cruelty and the use of artificial means for producing voluptuous sensations; which aims directly or indirectly at the consummation of sexual satisfaction, and which, having achieved a certain degree of stimula-

tion, concludes with the ejaculation—or emission—of semen into the vagina, at the nearly simultaneous culmination of sensation—or orgasm—of both partners.[3]

This definition, which was faithfully cited in later sex manuals such as Dr. Eustace Chesser's best-selling *Love Without Fear*, established not only what was normal or, more accurately, "ideal" but what the sex "act" was: preliminaries leading to vaginal penetration and ejaculation or, simply put; foreplay and intercourse. There could be many variations along the way. Van de Velde, for example, recommended the "genital kiss," a tentative version of oral sex, though how this was to be achieved he declined to explain, saying only that the technique could be "constructed" from a knowledge of "the kiss in general" and "the special structure of the female organs." For the most part, however, the road was straight and narrow. To meander off course or to fail to reach the destination ("nearly simultaneous . . . orgasm") was to jeopardize one's marriage, sanity, and physical health.

While the medical account of sex turned women into passive objects of male attention, it also gave them a powerful new way of perceiving their own sexual experiences. To Van de Velde, sex was a straight path leading to orgasm for both partners. This single-minded emphasis on the orgasm as the irreducible unit of sexual pleasure meant that if women had the right to pleasure within marriage, they also had the means to assess whether that right was being fulfilled. More to the point, if frigidity was as widespread as doctors suspected, women had a way of expressing the precise measure of their discontent. So it was ironic that the medical view of sex, which all but abolished women as active, conscious participants, also helped inspire the assertive new orgasm acquisitiveness that Betty Friedan noted, disapprovingly, among American women on the eve of the sexual revolution.

Medicine began to lose its authority over sex just as the sexual revolution began. For one thing, medicine had always deferred to psychoanalytic theory in matters of sex—hence the orgasm as an affirmation of adult married life, potential motherhood, and, in advanced versions of the theory, female masochism. But in the mass culture, psychoanalytic theory was now being forced aside by a more cheerful, open-ended outlook on the human condition. Humanistic (soon to be "popular") psychology valued "growth" itself above any presumed end point, such as marriage or parenthood. Instead of being a ratification of "marital adjustment" and female conformity, healthy sex could now be understood as a means to personal growth, hence by its nature not restricted to one position or sequence of acts, or even to one partner. In the postmedical vision of healthy sex offered by popular psychology, a varied and abundant sex life was the prerogative of any questing individual and, it was available, potentially, to anyone who was open to "growth".

Equally important to undermining medical authority was women's own changing experience of sex. The single most irrefutable measure we have of a "sexual revolution"—the vast increase in women's extra- and premarital experiences that occurred in the sixties and seventies—meant that tens of thousands of women were no longer viewing sex simply as a means of push-

ing a relationship closer to marriage but as a realm of
experimentation and pleasure to be indulged in for its
own sake. To young women in the mid-sixties, the shock
troops of sexual revolution, the medical representation
of sex as the touchstone of "marital adjustment" could
only seem arcane, if not faintly repulsive. No wonder
that the first feminist sallies into sexology—*The Hite
Report* and *Our Bodies, Ourselves*—took women's own
experience as the relevant data. In the seventies, more
and more sex books would be authored, not by M.D.s
and other "experts" but by ordinary people using everyday language.

With the medical monolith—foreplay plus intercourse—out of the way, the new "experts" began to
redefine sex as a variety of options from which the
savvy couple could pick and choose. The most significant "innovation" to enter the sexual mainstream in
the seventies was oral sex—a possibility the medical
sexologists had barely hinted at. Oral sex, of course, had
always existed. Daring teenagers in the fifties tried
"69"; and John Updike's 1960 best-seller, *Rabbit Run*,
featured a shocking (though by today's standards, somewhat sketchy) incident of fellatio. Oral sex gained
prominence in the seventies in part because of the increasing awareness of gay and lesbian sexual practices
but also because it seemed to offer a solution to the
crisis of heterosexual sex. Unlike intercourse, oral sex
isolated the most sexually responsive organs—the clitoris and the penis—and dispensed with the relatively
inert vagina. And unlike intercourse, oral sex seemed to
offer the possibility of making heterosexual sex more
reciprocal and egalitarian: Either partner could do it,
and either could, presumably, enjoy it. For women,

particularly "frigid" women, oral sex made orgasm possible, even probable.

But oral sex was not automatically reciprocal or even mutually pleasurable. In the sexual discourse of the seventies—which included not only sex manuals but surveys, confessional literature, and a new genre of couple-oriented pornography—oral sex was a contested zone. Men fantasized about unlimited fellatio; and, to judge from the pornography directed to them, were even beginning to prefer fellatio to vaginal penetration. Women—or women influenced by the new feminist views of sex—were looking to cunnilingus as the obvious way to satisfy clitoral sexuality. Who would get which, and in what amount, would become a subject for negotiation, debate, and no small amount of tension.

THE RISE OF ORAL SEX

"Now don't turn up your nose and make that ugly face" scolded J in *The Sensuous Woman.* "Oral sex is, for most people who give it a try, delicious."[4] In 1969 some readers were shocked—even appalled—by the frankness of this new sex manual. Oral sex was still not discussed openly and many people associated it with venereal disease. The outrageous and mysterious J reassured women that "kissing a man's penis [is] a lot more sanitary than kissing him on the mouth." Joan Terry Garrity was born in Minneapolis and moved to New York in 1960, where she worked for ten years as a book promoter. She used a pen name for her graphic best-seller because the average woman was not supposed to be voraciously interested in sex. (Garrity confessed much later to *People* that when her publisher revealed her true identity, she was primarily concerned about her mother's response to the book.) J displayed her knowledge of male genitalia and was proud of her expertise. Her enthusiasm helped sell nine million copies, and *The Sensuous Woman* is still in print.

The success of this manual was due to J's radical departure from mainstream sexual technique—and from popular ideas about women's attitude toward sex. Instead of a reverential attitude toward the male apparatus, she was breezy, witty, iconoclastic. All this from an "ordinary" person—a woman no less—without a medical degree. *The Sensuous Woman* had no scientific pretense nor any information culled from the medical profession to justify its personal perspective. This was straight talk for women, unfettered by academic jargon, geared to those who were just entering the sexual arena or needed a refresher course to update their technique. Sex was defined primarily as a physical, rather than an emotional, act that could be performed by any two people, regardless of whether they were married to each other. J offered some basic skills that anyone could learn easily enough and, unlike male experts, she conveyed her appreciation for the opposite sex: She liked men, and found no particular deep meaning in sex—other than pleasure.

Garrity described her own pet techniques in a language that middle-class housewives could easily understand. She personalized her methods by assigning them names that made sex sound as ordinary as cleaning house: "The Hoover requires using your mouth like a vacuum cleaner." Fellatio, performed in a number of original styles, dominates Garrity's sexual act. For instance, "The Butterfly Flic," another one of her creations, required locating the corona and carefully using "your tongue [to] flip it lightly back and forth . . . like you were strumming a banjo." Immersing herself in parts of the anatomy that her male peers ironically had left unattended, J recommended sucking on testicles—and even more: "When your man reaches that final peak, he could decide to come in your mouth. Did I shock you again? Yes, this is another completely normal sex act." On the brighter side, she informed her readers, "It's also pretty hard to get pregnant this way."

J's practical attitude toward sex and her everyday language turned her predecessors into dinosaurs by comparison. But like the majority of manuals prior to *The Sensuous Woman*, this one was also extremely phallocentric. She assumed women were typically nonorgasmic, and that this condition could be lived with—for better or worse. A chapter called "Orgasm—Yours, Not His" is devoted to faking orgasms: "To avoid disappointing him and spoiling his plateau of excitement and sexiness . . . fake that orgasm! Throw in a few extra wriggles and a yelp or two along the way to match his passion—but be careful not to ham it up too much."

Although J had never been swept away by the feminist rebellion, she was arming the troops for the sexual revolution. Garrity wasn't interested in questions of gender or sex roles; nevertheless she defined sex as an arena that women could control, where they could explore a number of different options. Even married women who were sexually frustrated were free to sleep with other men (affairs with their husbands' friends were more advisable than picking up men on the streets). J's realm of sexual possibilities included swapping and orgies ("If you go don't wear a good dress") and even anal sex ("Cheer up," she comforted her stunned readers, "this is an optional").

In *The Sensuous Woman* sexual variety outside the boundaries of traditional monogamy is considered fairly mundane, indicating a growing female wanderlust. But J knew that fellatio was still a problem for women, single or married, who were beginning to broaden their sexual horizons. For men, fellatio was fast, could be performed almost anywhere, and required no birth control. For women, there was no automatic appeal. They not only had to get used to the idea, but fellatio was a difficult physical proposition. One woman in particular, Linda Lovelace, the star of the porn film *Deep Throat*, exemplified this female dilemma. By working to overcome the gag reflex, she became renowned for her dubious skill. The film articulated contemporary problems with oral sex (obviously from the male point of view) and picked up a cult following: *Deep Throat* became a vehicle for the mass (male) fantasy of oral sex.

Even though this was a typical porn film (characterized primarily by a low budget, inexperienced actors, and a minimal story line that interrupts long sex scenes), it was one of the first "couples" or "crossover" films to engage a mixed audience of men and women. Lovelace became a cult figure because of her sexual dexterity, bringing pornography out of its male ghetto. In the film, she plays a visiting nurse who cures men's "illnesses" with a miraculous throat that seems to have no end. One of the many climaxes in the film occurs when a doctor discovers why Lovelace gets so much pleasure from her work. As he pokes around inside her mouth he discovers that instead of tonsils, she has a clitoris in her throat. "It's not so bad," the doctor reassures Lovelace as she bursts into tears. "You should be glad you have a clitoris at all."

In a sense the doctor was right. The average woman in a porn film (let alone real life) had no clitoris: It was rarely given any screen time and was never the source of any kind of sexual excitement. Geared to the male spectator, these films were not interested in pleasure from a woman's point of view, and oral sex was never a reciprocal act. But in *Deep Throat* the clitoris is the center of attention, the key to a woman's sexuality—and, as usual, extremely difficult to find.

In real life, however, Lovelace wasn't getting any pleasure and what she was swallowing was largely her own pride. In *Ordeal*, her autobiography, she tells the story of her marriage to porn pimp Chuck Traynor, whom she credits as her fellatio mentor. At his instigation, Lovelace practiced opening up her throat during oral sex—bypassing her tonsils—until this expertise became her trademark. According to Lovelace, one of Traynor's favorite pastimes was to put her into a trance and give her posthypnotic tasks to perform. One evening after putting her under he ordered her to wake up, perform fellatio and simultaneously have an orgasm. Lovelace put on such a good act that Traynor used the evening's entertainment as the basis for *Deep Throat*.

Lovelace eventually got up the courage to leave Traynor, who, she explained, had forced her to be a slave to his sexual and economic interests. She eventually changed her name, remarried, and discovered God, all to the media's delight. But Traynor's brutality never showed up on film, and even if it had, *Deep Throat* might still have become a classic. For men, it was wishful thinking to rediscover the clitoris in the throat. But by the early seventies there was more than enough evidence that the significance of this small, elusive organ could no longer be underestimated: The clitoris wasn't a figment of the female—or feminist— imagination. *Deep Throat* accurately expressed the male anxiety about integrating the clitoris into sexual practice. Men, it seemed, longed for the clitoris to be a moveable feast.

ORGASM EQUITY

By 1975 a *Playboy* study found that 90 percent of married women under twenty-five had integrated fellatio into their regular sexual agenda. Even *Redbook,* whose readers were supposedly more interested in interior decorating and cooking than sex, discovered that of 100,000 women surveyed that same year, 85 percent of them indulged in fellatio.[5] "While a certain feminist fringe may have found a target in the male genitalia, by far the vast majority of us like penises," wrote Chris Weygandt in *Oui.* Arguing against the feminist notion that women had to become much less subservient to the phallus—at least in bed—Weygandt scoffed at the idea that women's sensibilities "were offended at the mention of oral sex."

But when a *Oui* survey in 1980 asked women who *didn't* like fellatio, "Is the prime difference in your attitude that he doesn't reciprocate?" 75 percent replied yes.[6] "My ex-husband was wild about blow-jobs," wrote one of the women, "but he hated going down on me. So what was the point of giving him special treatment? He didn't make it worth my while."[7] For heterosexual women, making sex reciprocal required a major transformation of the sexual act. But oral sex was still a better battlefield than traditional intercourse—if only because it was, after all, potentially reciprocal.

During the seventies even mainstream porn magazines were beginning to discover the clitoris. "Stimulating a woman's genitals with a penis is like trying to cut a diamond with a chain saw," wrote the author of a letter to one such publication.[8] Yet in the early seventies, both Kinsey and Morton Hunt, the author of *Sexual Behavior in the 1970's,* found that on the average only 56 percent of men surveyed found cunnilingus desirable. A typical woman reader wrote to one porn magazine as late as 1980 to complain that a third of the men she was meeting "wouldn't do it for a million bucks" and another third "act like they're doing me this big favor." The figures went up to 74 percent toward the end of the decade, but that statistic seemed too high when compared to the revelations of *The Hite Report.* In 1976 Shere Hite's study indicated that only 42 percent of the women she surveyed were reaching orgasm through oral stimulation of the clitoris. But the number could have been greater with a change of male perspective: "Most oral stimulation was done for arousal, not orgasm. All too often cunnilingus was offered by the partner for very short intervals."[9]

But *The Hite Report* went further than simply arguing that women wanted more oral sex. For the first time, a volume of female voices statistically turned women's right to good sex into a political issue. The question of how to have sex could not be reduced to technique. "If we make it easy and pleasurable for men to have an orgasm, and don't have one ourselves, aren't we just 'servicing' men?" Hite asked her readers. She demonstrated statistically that more women were able to orgasm on their own than with men, who mostly encouraged them to be passive and obedient in bed. "If we *know* how to have orgasms, but are unable to make this a part of the sexual relationship with another person, then we are not in control of *choosing* whether or not we have an orgasm." Hite's analysis concluded that women, when it came to sex, were "powerless."

This feminist analysis of heterosexual relations immediately provided more grist for the sexual revolution. And when it was published in 1976, Hite's controversial study was backed up by the liberal medical establishment. Citing Masters and Johnson, Kinsey, Seymour Fisher,[10] Helen Kaplan,[11] and a burgeoning movement of sexologists, the evidence was conclusive that frigidity was not a female problem: Many heterosexuals were unable—or unwilling—to have good sex. "It is difficult to believe that the millions of otherwise responsive women who do not have coital orgasms," Kaplan asserted, "are all 'sick.'" Women weren't sick, Hite passionately argued and scientifically demonstrated. They were oppressed by men, whose definition of intercourse left them cold. When one woman in *The Hite Report* was asked whether her partners were even aware of her orgasms she answered: "Usually not. Sometimes they ask, and sometimes they assume I [have one] or else they couldn't care less."

The Hite Report put pressure on men who couldn't "care less." Hite's study was a call to action for women to openly demand orgasmic sex. Many of the women in her book clearly articulated what was wrong with sex down to the last anatomical detail. Women, it seemed, could speak about sex, and now it was time for them to speak to men. Hite stripped the orgasm of its layers of patriarchal illusions, and powerfully enhanced a woman's ability to negotiate in bed.

THE JOY OF SEX

If there is a single metaphor for the reconstructed heterosexuality of the seventies, it would be a bartering session. Since all pleasures were not mutual or simultaneous, equity would have to be achieved through a conscious process of give and take. The ideal setting would be a long-term relationship, with plenty of time for negotiation and reassessment. If this seemed like a cold and unromantic approach—especially to men—it was still the only practical way for women to assert their needs. In the imagination, though, it transformed sex from a magical communion to the kind of social interaction one might experience in the business world or, for that matter, a garage sale.

The Joy of Sex, published in 1972, could be described as the ultimate postmedical sex manual. There was no longer one definition of sex, only an array of options to choose from—like goods in a department store or dishes in a lavish buffet. The author, Alex Comfort, was a doctor, but that was almost incidental to his sexological pursuits. Although he became a household name in America only at the age of fifty-four, he was already well known in his native England as an "anarcho-pacificist philosopher." An antiwar activist who refused to serve in World War II, a Cambridge scholar, poet, novelist, husband, father, and gerontologist, Comfort was not the kind of man one would have expected to write a best-seller on sex. Yet in England his long-standing interest in these matters was public. A nudist and member of the Diogenes naturalist club, Comfort sought out situations where he could observe sexual behavior. After moving from England to Santa Barbara in the early seventies, he frequented the Sandstone Retreat in Topanga Canyon. This fifteen-acre estate was a commune for those interested in "liberated" sexual encounters. There were rules that governed membership to the club, but sexual freedom was the highest priority. "Often the nude biologist Dr. Alex Comfort," reports Gay Talese in *Thy Neighbor's Wife*, "brandishing a cigar, traipsed through the room between prone bodies with the professional air of a lepidopterist strolling through the fields waving a butterfly net." Comfort "brought a bedside manner to an orgy," and unlike other professionals, he even participated: "After he had deposited his cigar in a safe place—he would join a friendly clutch of bodies and contribute to the merriment."[12]

Comfort preferred the immediacy of actual human behavior to lab work. Hugh Kenner speculated in the New York *Times* that this might have had something to do with the fact that his scientific curiosity had led him to experiment with gunpowder at the age of fourteen and blow away most of his left hand. This disaster didn't prevent him from getting a Ph.D. in biochemistry, or completing ten books by the age of twenty-four. For the most part, however, he remained outside of the lab. By

American medical standards, this was a radical practice. To Comfort, the problem with medical experts—and their manuals—was their obsession with everything other than what people actually *do* in bed. He blamed his peers for treating the average person like a sexual cripple who used a manual as a crutch, rather than a guide to creative possibilities.

The Joy of Sex was more of a "manifesto," to use Comfort's term, than a medical tract, and it implicitly took the medical profession to task. Instead of narrowing the definition of sex to determine normalcy, Comfort offered an encyclopedia of sexual acts that gave credibility to any form of experimentation. *Joy* mocked the experts who had made sex taboo, and people guilt-stricken for enjoying themselves. "There is nothing to be afraid of and never was," he concluded in *More Joy,* his sequel. "We [the experts] manufacture our own nonsense."

Joy was written for men and women, whom Comfort assumed were equal players in sex, although at times his masculine bias showed through. Structuring the manual like a cookbook was an ingenious way to illustrate his notion that people may have very different kinds of tastes, but, it was to be hoped, they all had a sense of humor. Variety, for Comfort, was the spice of life: "Being stuck rigidly with one sexual technique usually means anxiety," he wrote in his introduction. In Comfort's opinion, sexual intercourse was vastly overrated by his peers, who organized their manuals around one position in which the penis could most successfully penetrate the vagina. *Joy* was filled with sexual techniques ranging from the mundane to the exotic. His intent was to help people heighten their sexual experiences by exploring a variety of techniques, rather than perfecting only one. Comfort did not ask his readers to search for one monumental, ever-elusive orgasm. Instead he encouraged both men and women to go out and explore a new limitless sexual landscape which his book described in graphic detail—without setting up any rules or regulations. Reading *Joy* was the closest thing to an uncensored tour of a sexual paraphernalia shop.

The book implicitly redefined heterosexuality as a pluralist institution that could accommodate those who chose the monogamous heterosexual path—which Comfort acknowledged as the main highway and often the safest route—and those who detoured through bisexuality, which he considered perfectly normal. "In threesomes and group experiences, which are getting more acceptable socially," Comfort told his readers, " 'bisexual' opportunities are inevitable." Even more unusual in a mainstream sex manual, Comfort theorized: "All people are bisexual. . . . If it worries you don't do it, but it isn't bad magic, poisonous or odd."[13]

There was no "correct" way to have sex in *Joy*, which included some extremely idiosyncratic techniques. In a section called "Sauces and Pickles" he covered obscure practices like "femoral intercourse," a technique used to maintain a woman's virginity without contraception: "The woman presses her thighs together and the penis goes between them with the shaft between her labia. This gives the woman special sensations—sometimes keener than penetration—so it's well worth trying." Comfort included technical information for virgins on the one hand and sophisticated sadomasochists on the other. The use of chains was on the menu for heterosex-

uals: "Women like both the coldness and the symbol-
ism," he opined, "while men can spend hours locking
and unlocking them," along with "discipline," the code
word "for beating each other." Erogenous zones covered the body from top to bottom, including "big toes."
For those who were curious, Comfort recommended
pornography, leather, sexual substitutes, and more. Essentially anything was worth a try between consenting
adults.

What distinguished this poet/scientist from his predecessors was not only his encyclopedic scope but the
illustrations he used to accompany his text. While the
jacket of the book was snow white, the inside title page
had a drawing of a naked man and woman rolling into
position for oral sex; on the following page, they are
casually enjoying cunnilingus. (At the time one male
reviewer attacked Comfort for having fallen prey to
clitoral emphasis and downplaying fellatio.) Readers
became familiar with this nameless, imaginary couple,
who popped up on almost every page, trying out dozens of techniques. They were symbolic representations
of the sexually liberated generation; the man sported a
scruffy beard; the woman, armpit hair. Relaxed and
uninhibited, these erotic illustrations were a long way
from the anatomical drawings in conventional manuals
that highlighted one part of the body or another—without giving away the whole picture. In a separate color
signature titled "The Art of Making Love," the *Joy of
Sex* couple is carefully drawn in sequence, going
through all the motions.

In addition to these illustrations, Comfort used art to
make a connection between sex and the imagination.
In a most surprising section, he included a series of full

color, erotic Japanese prints. These were pictures that could potentially turn his readers on or, at the very least, stir the imagination. It was an intellectual's peep show that managed to parody the entire genre of sex manuals. Manuals of course were rarely illustrated at all, to keep them fit for the library shelf. Some future authors found it so difficult to compete that they resorted, like Dr. Ron Pion in *The Last Sexual Manual,* to recommending that heterosexual couples buy two copies of *Joy*—his and hers—go through and rate each sexual technique, and then trade copies. At the time it seemed that Comfort had written the last word on sex —it was difficult to imagine going any further.

SEXUAL FANTASIES: THE MENU EXPANDS

"Admittedly the reader will at times have to fight off shock, prurient interest and distaste," wrote J in an introduction to *My Secret Garden.* "This is no coffee-table book."[14] In 1973, one year after *The Joy of Sex,* Nancy Friday's first sex manual was advertised as a "milestone in sex education." While Comfort was promoting the notion of heterosexual variation, Friday was out doing fieldwork on women's sexual fantasy lives. The result was a range of sexual possibilities that went well beyond Comfort's generous menu. *Publishers Weekly* commented that Friday was "astonishingly outspoken, even in a period of unusual sexual frankness." But men had been frank about their fantasies—not women. Friday's work was shocking because women had remained outside this aspect of the public discourse on sex.

My Secret Garden was filled with hundreds of wild fantasies illustrating how easily women could imagine themselves with aggressive sexual lives. Friday stressed that an active imagination didn't necessarily signify sexual problems; many women fantasized during masturbation, or while they were having perfectly adequate sex. No one, it seemed, wanted to act their fantasies out in real life—that would come later. But to the distress of many readers, the female libido was shown to be remarkably similar to that of the male; women were interested in adulterous affairs, incest, prostitution, voyeurism, S/M, rape—even sex with animals. By traditional standards, this was the landscape of *male* sexual lust.

The book was riddled with complaints about husbands who were either unwilling or unable to satisfy their wives. Consequently some women fantasized about sex with each other: "My husband doesn't know about my secret desire to sleep with another woman," a middle-aged woman confessed. Friday devoted an entire section of *My Secret Garden* to such fantasies involving "Other Women." Most of her subjects had never had a lesbian experience, yet they relied primarily on same-sex fantasies while having sex with men or masturbating. "I enjoy a full sex life with my husband. Sometimes, however, I do have lesbian fantasies. . . . I am not a lesbian in any way—I enjoy men too much— but when it's necessary for me to masturbate . . . While my boyfriend is making love to me I often fantasize about my best friend. . . . Does this mean I'm a latent homosexual?"

Most modern experts might have answered yes, but if Friday's book was prophetic in any way, it signaled the homosexualization of heterosexual sex. The similarities between these once distinct groups were now becoming visible in sexual fantasies and popular notions of sexual practice. The newfound appreciation of oral sex was not so new to the lesbian community. And, as monogamous relations broke down, single women were no longer necessarily looking for a permanent male date. The homosexual delight in sex as a defiant expression of liberation was catching on with heterosexual women.

My Secret Garden was so successful that Friday wrote two more fantasy collections. Like a feminist version of Hugh Hefner, she developed a market for a particular style of female porn. Although it was quite distinct from the male genre—written by and for women—much of the language was the same. "I would be joining the very army of inhibitors if I latinized my writing and drew a sharp line between my text and the four-letter-word language of fantasy itself." No one could accuse Friday of exploiting one sex to benefit the other, yet her books, like other forms of mass-market pornography, could as easily be used for masturbation as sexual edification.

Collections of women's personal experiences such as *The Hite Report* and *My Secret Garden* were now the vanguard of the genre. Friday was not predominantly interested in changing the social or sexual relations between men and women, but she, like Hite, gave the female subject ample room to speak. For women, it was the first time that a mass market was developing to actually solicit, digest, and eventually serve up their sexual desires to be transformed back into practice.

Comfort, Friday, Hite, et al. signaled the death of the medical profession's monopoly on sex. Any expert unable to shake the Freudian search for the exemplary vaginal orgasm seemed as rigid as the missionary position. Sex had been redefined as a social interaction rather than a hazardous undertaking that could only be discussed lying down on the couch. It was no longer a diagnostic test for female illness but a potentially orgasmic activity in which everyone had equal rights.

Now that the consensus around the definition of sex had crumbled, there was no one sex manual dominating the market as Van de Velde's had. The democratization of information made room for a cacophony of voices. Anyone who had anything to say on the subject regardless of credentials or ideological perspective found room to speak. In general, manuals that exclusively promoted monogamous sex were in the minority and most authors turned their attention toward the long-neglected female orgasm. That orgasm was now the subject of great debate, open to many different interpretations. Some authors treated it with spiritual reverence, others as an ordinary biological function—as mundane as digesting food.

Feminist psychiatrist Lonnie Barbach attempted to unravel the mysteries of achieving an orgasm by teaching women how to satisfy themselves. A self-described expert on masturbation, she advised nonorgasmic women to educate themselves in her techniques rather than count on male partners to lead the way to ecstasy. Barbach pointed out that even for heterosexual couples, the penis wasn't necessary for a female orgasm. (Neither, of course, was the vagina always useful to men.) "If the old thrusting in and out would do it," one of her patients at long last realized, "it would have happened by now."[15] In Barbach's manual *For Yourself,* the first step for women was spending some time alone to learn about their bodies. By 1975, masturbation wasn't news. Regardless, the word was considered too dangerous for prime time. Barbach had trouble promoting her book, as she was prevented from describing exactly what it was about.

Five years later when she published her sequel, *For Each Other*, masturbation was a household word. The average manual now included a section on female masturbation, offering a creative array of equipment that ranged from cucumbers to Coke bottles. But these techniques obviously didn't solve many of the problems between heterosexuals. Eva Margolies went so far as to suggest in *Sensual Pleasure* that sex with some men was essentially hopeless—no matter how well women knew their own bodies: "A small, but significant minority of men are only interested in their own pleasure." Margolies used to think that women should stay in their place and "grit their teeth," but during the sexual revolution she had a change of heart: "I've come to believe that such behavior is inexcusable, and unless you feel your physical well-being is in jeopardy, I suggest you get dressed and head straight for the door."[16] If a man was selfish, changing his personality structure was a job for the psychoanalytic profession, not a lover. The guiding principle throughout *Sensual Pleasure* was that sex had to be defined as a balance of power: "It's not fair to expect something of your partner without being willing to reciprocate." She had no illusions about mutual orgasms: Men and women would have to patiently take their turns.

SEPARATE BUT EQUAL

This new notion of separate but equal orgasms was displacing the old obsession with coming together. The experts had consumed themselves with methods to hold men back or speed women along. But getting into a rhythm to reach a simultaneous plateau was proved to be physiologically difficult. Sex was becoming more like jogging: It was better at one's own pace.

On the one hand, the female libido that had been revealed to the public at large had great similarities to its male counterpart. Yet, when it came to the pursuit of sexual desire, men and women were physically far apart. It wasn't simply a problem of mutual timing, but more basic than that, the mutual dependence of the penis and vagina was no longer the key for women, or even men, to sensual pleasure. Men and women, it seemed, had different styles and sexual tastes that could actually interfere with sexual relations. Whereas once heterosexuality had been thought of as "natural," almost automatic, men and women had discovered that their distinct sexual needs could actually get in the way of good sex. It was unrealistic to expect that either sex knew instinctively how to satisfy the other. Ending up in bed with a new partner was often a whole new exploration, rather than a familiar routine. "For the first time in my life," Ben, a thirty-five-year-old artist in New York, confessed, "I took a woman who obviously wanted to sleep with me home from a party to my loft. But she wanted me to perform certain acts in a particular way that I wasn't prepared for. I was so stunned, neither of us enjoyed the sexual experience and she went home in the middle of the night. I couldn't handle it."

How to Make Love to a Man by Alexandra Penny, expressed, more than any other manual, the growing physical alienation between heterosexuals. It was so difficult for men and women to satisfy each other simultaneously that Penny advised them to take turns, not during the same evening but alternately, with the woman giving the man whatever he wants one night and the man reciprocating on a separate occasion. Rather than refashion sex by bartering and trading sexual pleasures, Penny told her readers to get everything they want on *their* night. She advised women to take over the responsibility for sex, to conceptualize it ahead of time and aggressively go out and seduce the objects of their desires. The total experience required a major investment in the tools of the trade—makeup, new hair styles, sexy clothes, and gadgets—in order to pull off a professional act. This was theatrical sex, so tightly scripted that there was little room for spontaneous heterosexual impulses to destroy a scene.

The Penny method of making love to a man would have confounded Van de Velde. Her approach to sex acknowledged mounting heterosexual antagonisms based on the distinct sexual preferences of men and women. In the wake of women's sexual revolution, there was nothing "natural" about heterosexual sex, at least nothing more natural than masturbation, homosexual love, or any other "option." The old romantic model of sex as an experience of abandonment and self-loss would not work for a heterosexual world in which men and women stood so far apart in understanding each other's sexual needs. Sex was now something a woman went into with her eyes open—figuratively at least—her intellect alert, and her skills honed. There was no reason a determined heterosexual woman should not find as much pleasure as she was capable of experiencing. But she had to negotiate, to bargain, and, if necessary, to shop around.

If it still didn't work, other options were opening up —ones which would have less and less to do with the initial feminist impulse that inspired women's sexual revolution. The crisis in heterosexuality had introduced new metaphors for sex that drew on the world of market relationships: Sex as a system of bartering, sex as consumerism. In the next phase of the sexual revolution, the metaphors would become reality. Women's sexual revolution would be drawn into the commercial marketplace; and women would be able to purchase the means to sexual pleasure as impersonally as they might expand their wardrobes.

4

The Lust Frontier
From Tupperware to Sadomasochism

On a muggy summer evening in a suburb of Washington, D.C., Jane Cooper kicked her husband and kids out of the house. Thanks to the 90-degree weather and Indiana Jones, they were far from unhappy spending the evening in an air-conditioned theater. Cooper didn't really mind the heat. It added some body to her limp brown hair and with a little suntan she could easily dispense with a layer of makeup. In the summer Cooper felt more relaxed. It was unusually quiet in her kitchen now as she emptied the ice into a container and refilled the trays at the sink. Tonight she was hosting a special event—a party for women only.

The doorbell rang and Cooper's stomach tightened. The guest of honor this evening was a door-to-door saleswoman with a trunkful of sexual paraphernalia, and the other guests were a group of Cooper's closest friends. In this neighborhood, vibrators in the bedroom were already as common as blenders in the kitchen, and Cooper's friends were interested in taking the next step: a private introduction to a broad range of sexual objects—from erotic lingerie to ankle restraints.

Women like Jane Cooper were lured into the sexual consumer market by offers of monumental orgasms requiring very little effort from either partner: creams promising to turn women into "savagely erotic and uninhibited" creatures; french ticklers guaranteeing "feverishly hot sex in seconds." If Jane's friends were searching for a new sexual thrill, they could browse through catalogs filled with Vice Spice Pills, Sta-Erect Sheaths, adult videos, and Emotion Lotions, to name only a few of the items. By making so many erotic products available, the consumer culture was encouraging her to play around, or at the very least to experiment with the purchase of an erotic product.

Home parties, as they are innocuously called in this small industry, are a popular way for women both to purchase sexual paraphernalia and bring an expert on sex into their living rooms. Tupperware-style parties where sexual aids are sold rather than plastic containers are no longer rare. Several businesses—some of which are owned by women—are now scattered across the country. Compared to shopping in a sex paraphernalia shop, a party offers a less commercial, more social context for imagining new sexual frontiers. For Cooper, organizing this party felt similar to doing community work. She was used to orchestrating block parties and car pools, but this was much more exciting—even a little secretive. Over the past few years "The Phil Donahue Show" and its parade of swingers, sadomasochists, male prostitutes, and other sexual mavericks had monopolized the conversation at many neighborhood events. Now they were after a live show.

Not so long ago the most common, and in most places the only sexual aid available to women was a vibrator packaged as an electric massager for a stiff neck. As long as the sole source of information on sex was the medical and pseudo-medical experts, and as long as they promoted intercourse as the only legitimate form of sex, sexual paraphernalia were nowhere to be found because they were simply unnecessary. There was nothing compelling to market, buy, or sell. But when sex became more varied than intercourse, new products emerged to complement an expanding list of sexual practices. Suddenly vibrators were not alone in the classified sections of pulp magazines but were accompanied by magic creams and edible nighties.

As women transformed sexual practices to meet their needs, they were quickly targeted as a new consumer class for the sex industry. There was nothing novel about dildos or the ancient Japanese tradition of ben-wa balls. What was new was the proliferation of objects and information for sale carefully aimed at women as the prime audience. In this consumer arena female sexuality functioned differently than it had previously in mainstream society: It was clearly unattached to reproduction, motherhood, monogamy—even heterosexuality. Women, whether gay or straight, married or single, all had something in common in this arena: The pursuit of pleasure—at a reasonable price.

Jane Cooper was surprised at how quickly her friends discovered that sexual paraphernalia were not obscene but playful and provocative—fruit-flavored creams and lotions were best-sellers. When a variety of vibrators were laid out on the coffee table, a discussion began on the idiosyncrasies of clitoral stimulation. Some women demanded strokes before intercourse, some during. One woman explained that her husband had to climax first for her to enjoy manual, oral, or any kind of sex. There was no formula offered that evening for "good" sex. In a sexual arena that promoted diversity, the "expert" had been replaced by a pluralist market, and purchasing power, rather than psychiatric insight or pseudo-medical information, was the key to an exciting sex life.

Indeed any object purchased and integrated into the sexual act brings with it a new sexual consciousness. The diaphragm, the first object that many women had to slip into their sex routines, was initially awkward. But experts advised eroticizing the process, turning the placement of birth control devices into sexual play. Sexual paraphernalia initially piggybacked on a birth control market offering flavored condoms and vaginal creams. But the range of products quickly outgrew their functional relationship to reproduction. Novelty itself held out the possibility of transforming the sexual experience—for better or worse—particularly for women whose monogamous sex lives had grown stale and routine over the years.

Feminism had helped to develop this new sexual arena by promoting masturbation and vibrators as keys to women's sexual independence. But it took American free enterprise to transform the search for sexual novelty into a small industry. In 1971, when two men opened a shop in New York City to sell water beds—clearly to enhance sex—business was slow. When the Pleasure Chest, as they called the store, added "amorous and prurient paraphernalia: lotions, cock rings, handcuffs, and dildos" according to a history printed in their catalog, business suddenly took off.[1] Today the Pleasure Chest is a multimillion-dollar operation with stores in seven major cities, a home-party division, and a huge mail-order department that sells hundreds of items.

The financial success of the chain was only made possible by diversifying its products to attract female consumers, who initially accounted for no more than 10 percent of sales. When the New York store originally experimented with a female window display in 1975, it was nervously greeted with a few giggles, according to Stan Farwell, who has been in the business for more than ten years. But the real goal was to turn women into serious consumers rather than window-shoppers, and this required some new interior decoration. "Pornographic" images of penetration were taken off the walls; the floors were carpeted and the store was bathed in pink lights. After six years and an active marketing strategy, 30 percent of the clientele was female.

"The changes were due to women's demands," said Farwell, which in part was true. Women—single or married, gay or straight—were more than happy to turn dildos and lotions into best-sellers. Today, the mail-order department receives about 500 orders a day for one item alone, a natural lubricant called "Foreplay," which rivals Baskin and Robbins in its variety of flavors. By 1983 more than half the customers shopping in the Pleasure Chest were women.

SEX IN THE MARKETPLACE

There had always been a sexual marketplace for men, offering pornography, prostitutes, strippers, go-go dancers, and more exotic possibilities for the connoisseur. The extension of the commercial sex industry to include women as consumers is, from a strictly egalitarian point of view, long overdue. As a setting for learning about sex, the marketplace offers some clear advantages over friends, medical experts, or even the more liberated manuals. The marketplace is impersonal; if there is a demand for something, it will sooner or later turn up, no matter how offensive it may be to some people's tastes. And the marketplace is democratic; its potential pleasures are not limited to the beautiful or fit, but to any woman who can shop.

In fact in some ways the market is especially congenial to women, given women's legacy of being made to feel sexually inadequate. The woman who consults a sex expert—even one of the more permissive radio personalities—or who goes to a bookstore to buy the latest published promise of "Great Sex!" is admitting she may not be sophisticated enough, experienced enough, or possibly *good* enough. But the woman who can enter the marketplace and shop for new sexual possibilities is in the familiar position of judging whether the merchandise is good enough for *her.* One of the reasons for the popularity of parties like Jane Cooper's is that they transpose the still anxiety-ridden subject of sex into one of the most comfortable and familiar settings of female domestic culture. Seated around a living room, comparing wares and experiences, the women are in charge—

only the products and the possibilities they represent are being judged.

The marketplace for sexual products, images, and even new forms of pornography for the female consumer has spread the sexual revolution to women who would never have attended a feminist conference on sexuality or perhaps even have read one of the new sex manuals. Home parties might seem laughable or peculiar to an urban sexual sophisticate, but to a woman in, say, suburban Ohio, they may be a major source of sexual information—packaged in a uniquely palatable form. For example, we were surprised to meet a young woman who is working her way through graduate school in psychology by giving home parties in rural Missouri. Weren't her wares a little racy for the Bible Belt, we asked. No, she insisted. "I get mothers and daughters, sisters—almost whole families—coming out to the parties together. There is a real fascination and the way we meet, in someone's home, is a very safe environment for finding out what you might want to know. And it's fun, too; it can get pretty raucous sometimes."

But if the sexual marketplace is impersonal, nonjudgmental, and pluralistic, it still has its own built-in biases. These biases are covert—invisible in a snapshot impression—and they have more to do with the nature of markets than the nature of sex. The market for consumer goods of any kind is ever-changing, quick to absorb each new novelty and abandon the old. We are barraged with fads—Smurf figures and designer jeans one year, videogames and oversize T-shirts the next. The minute we are jaded with one product or motif, the next one arrives; and each, of course, is temporarily a necessity. Without novelty and variety, short-term "necessities" and quick-turnover "classics," our consumer culture would go into decline and, so too, no doubt, would our particular variety of capitalism.

Even the nascent marketplace for sexual products both requires and generates variety. If sex were still what it had been in the marriage manuals of the fifties, there would be little or nothing to market. Even the now-staid and familiar vibrator would have no place in a sexual culture that denied the validity and autonomy of clitoral sexuality; flavored ointments would have no function in a culture that officially disapproved of oral sex. Sex itself had to undergo the diversification of the sexual revolution before it lent itself to being packaged and marketed in a form that women could consume.

Once sexual possibilities have been commoditized as products and aids, the search for novelty takes on a life of its own. If flavored creams are exiting one year, they will be old hat the next; what is daring the first time is soon routine. So if parties like Cooper's or stores like the Pleasure Chest are to draw their customers back, something new must be found to market. It is not a sign of moral breakdown or "excessive" permissiveness that the sexuality visible in the consumer culture seems always to be outreaching old limits: This is the dynamic of the market, and in sex as well as fashion or entertainment, it pushes always and inexorably toward new frontiers.

Thus the sexual marketplace both democratizes and *institutionalizes* the sexual revolution. Practices that were once pioneered by a few brave souls become, through the marketplace, the potential property of anyone. The variety once enjoyed by an avant-garde or

urban elite becomes available through mail-order catalogs to a housewife in Iowa. The perverse becomes the
commonplace. And as soon as it does, the market must
reach further into forbidden areas for the next novelty,
the next marketable sensation. In this way, the sexual
revolution begins to take on a dynamic of its own, without conscious iconoclasm or risk-taking on anyone's
part, driven along by the impersonal energy of the marketplace.

PORNOGRAPHY—FOR WOMEN?

The most visible—and perhaps the most innocuous—
form of the new female sexual consumerism is the male
strip joint, which by the mid-seventies had almost surpassed bowling as the most popular way to spend "ladies' night out." Male strip joints offer an experience of
complete role reversal and a chance for grown women
to shriek like teenagers and be as bawdy—at least verbally—as middle-aged swingers. If the role reversal allows the release of certain covert hostility to men—as
some shocked male observers have guessed—it doesn't
seem to bother the typical male performer. When a
Washington *Post* reporter asked Michael Rapp, a
dancer from Chippendales, a well-known club on the
East and West coasts, what his parents thought of his
line of work, he affectionately replied, "My mother
comes to watch and my father wishes he could do it."[2]
For women who enjoy the shows and use them to celebrate everything from engagements to promotions, it's
clear that sexual entertainment doesn't have to involve
sexual exploitation. Ironically, they have been more

than willing to learn how to objectify the opposite sex. Strip joints offer groups of women a night out on the town without their husbands—some of whom thoroughly approve of the phenomenon: "I encourage my wife to go out with her friends to the clubs," a man told his less liberated peers in a men's magazine. "When she comes home at night we always have incredible sex."

By late 1985, male strippers had become an acceptable, almost routine part of female consumer culture. In the film *Twice in a Lifetime,* a shy, middle-aged woman who has been abandoned by her husband for another woman is taken out by her daughters to a male strip joint to celebrate her birthday, her new hair style, and her recovery from heartbreak. It is impossible not to be moved as the heroine, played by Ellen Burstyn, emerges from her depression and begins to gasp and giggle along with her daughters at the display of wriggling male pelvises. The impact of the scene is distinctly feminist: Men are not such a big deal after all. In fact, reduced to bikini shorts while dancing around to a disco beat, they're fun to watch, and a little silly, too.

There is a similar message at the "male entertainer" parties set at a Long Island health and diet spa for women. On occasional Thursday evenings, rum and Diet Coke is served after the last aerobics class, and the forty or so participants, still wearing their sweaty leotards, sit in a semicircle on the floor while the male entertainer struts and strips. It is a neat symbolic revenge for the women, who have spent the last hour confronting their own, never quite adequate bodies. In the real world, these women know they will be judged by their thick thighs or sagging bellies; in fact, a poster on the wall shows a collage of gorgeous female torsos, with the legend, "This is your competition." But on party night at the spa, it is the male who must exert himself, who must entertain and be judged.

The male stripper could be seen as a diminished version of the male rock star: Like the star, he is something for women to consume collectively; almost all the pleasure is in the group experience. No one, after all, goes to a male strip joint alone, without a contingent of friends to giggle and shriek with, just as a solitary fan is not likely to experience the transports of hysteria. But with the stripper, women have more obvious kinds of collective power than they do as a crowd of fans. The stripper is of course not a celebrity. He has no name or only a first name; he usually shares the stage with one or two other strippers; even the music, which was the excuse for the star's performance, has been reduced to a beat to drive the male pelvis. And what is perhaps most important—it is up to the women to tip the stripper. In a parody of male behavior, women clutch at his bikini and pull it open to tuck a folded bill inside. Thus is the phallus—the awesome centerpiece of fifties sexuality—demystified in the sexual marketplace.

Male strippers were only one sign of the growing female market for sexual imagery. By the late seventies, another formerly male sexual commodity—pornography—was being revamped for a female market. Ideally, viewing sex in all its varieties could be thrilling, even educational, for either sex. For women this was a novel activity, since images created for them, rather than men, were all too rare. But traditional pornography had objectified women to such an extent that from the point of view of the female spectator the content was either distasteful or excruciatingly dull. In particular, the women depicted in films were usually devoid of personality, and used mostly as physical receptacles for showers of sperm. This was a medium for men to enjoy with men, not with women, whose point of view had never even been a consideration.

In Hollywood, the film industry began to recognize the new female sexual consumerism of the late seventies with a succession of "hunks," actors who were often short on talent but long on muscle and sex appeal. Men were redesigned as sex symbols, a category previously reserved for the 36-26-34 female. Richard Gere, who played a rapist in *Looking for Mr. Goodbar,* turned up as the ideal male sexual commodity in *American Gigolo,* where his torso was seductively uncovered. In that film, he plays a high-class prostitute who takes particular pride in his ability to give women extraordinary orgasms. In *An Officer and a Gentleman,* which was notable for its steamy sex scenes, Gere's naked body actually flashed across the screen—unusual for an R-rated film. Gere hit the cover of *Newsweek* in 1983, as Hollywood's male idols became a national preoccupation for women. Another hunk, John Travolta, who danced to stardom in *Saturday Night Fever,* confessed in *Rolling Stone* that his biggest problem was getting a woman to treat him "as a person rather than a stud." Nevertheless, his ideal date had a "big sexual appetite" and needed no "coaching."[3]

The traditional porn-movie industry has also been turning its sights on the female market. "Combat-zone" theaters are making a stab at respectability by cleaning up their floors and their language: "Pornography" is passé and "erotica" is in. According to Ron Sullivan, the Eastern vice president of the Adult Film Association of

America, the key to bringing women in is "running erotic films in clean and well-lighted theaters complete with soft drinks and popcorn." But the rise of cable television, which allows anyone to watch X-rated films in the privacy of their homes, is unquestionably the best way to reach a female audience. By 1982 there were roughly 3 million videocassette recorders plugged into televisions across the country, and 22 million households were wired for cable TV; a selection of 200 adult entertainment stations was available in different parts of the country, which the industry claimed accounted for more than half the cable market.

By the mid-seventies, "crossover" films that had escaped the porn ghetto, like *Behind The Green Door* or *Deep Throat,* were becoming more visible. In 1982 *Roommates,* a typical crossover film, was so successful in New York City that it ran in a legitimate theater and received serious reviews. "I can't say *Roommates* is sexually progressive," wrote Carrie Rickey in *The Village Voice.*[4] But what made it worthy of note at all was the film's atypical attitude toward both sexes: Rickey called *Roommates* a "virulent man-hating document." It wasn't exactly for the raincoat crowd. The protagonists were women—not men—and many of the heterosexual sex scenes were shot from the female's vantage point. The film tells the story of three women who have active but very unsatisfactory sex lives. As they search for long-term (more traditional) relationships that offer recreational rather than abusive sex, we watch them wade through a selection of callous, women-hating, manipulative men. The message is that most men are evil, and that women have to search long and hard for any kind of decent sex at all.

"Erotica for women isn't flooding the market" wrote Jean Callahan in *Playgirl*, "but it's on its way."[5] In an interview with Callahan, Richard Pachenco, a popular male actor in the X-rated market, explained the conscious changes that producers were attempting in order to attract a female audience: "Instead of seven out of seven sex scenes being brutal and exploitative, only one will be. The sex is more real. You'll still see arbitrary fucking scenes—it's a shotgun blast meant to attract everyone." Pachenco is best-known for his award-winning performance in *Nothing to Hide* (porn "Oscars" are given out by the Adult Film Association of America), where he plays a character who is made to look foolish—almost retarded—because he doesn't want to rape and exploit the opposite sex. But eventually he meets a virgin whom he hotly pursues all the way to the altar—a rare narrative development for a porn film. "As more people [i.e. women] watch these films at home," Pachenco predicts, "they'll get better. The bedroom is the environment in which adult films will become adult, instead of portraying a male sexuality arrested at the age of 13."

Meanwhile, the pornographic press was also reaching out to a female market. Like cable TV, it had the potential to reach masses of women in relative privacy. *Penthouse* eventually gave birth to *Forum,* a porn publication that included articles oriented toward women. The same size as *Reader's Digest* and *TV Guide, Forum* could easily be purchased in drugstores or supermarkets and slipped into a purse. Unlike men's "skin" magazines, *Forum* didn't feature nude pinups of women as sex objects but more often matched articles with softer, "erotic" illustrations. *Forum* refused to tell us whether their circulation is going up or down, but in October 1985 their print run was 598,000.

Small format porn magazines seeking a couples audience multiplied on the stands. While *Forum* includes nonfiction articles on sexually related topics along with letters from readers, *Penthouse* also offers its readers a more lurid magazine called *Variations*. Devoted exclusively to first-person narratives describing almost every sexual experience imaginable, *Variations* is raunchy. The editor, V. K. McCarty, who is referred to in the industry as "the grandmother of kinky sex," insists that all the letters are genuine. Unlike the more discreet *Forum*, *Variations* offers photographs of men and women in all sorts of strenuous poses, but McCarty believes the magazine is something "any American housewife would find palatable." As women began to show up in their rising circulation figures, the business department told editorial to "soften the graphicness of the sexuality." McCarty took "bare nipples off the cover" and dropped "incest and bestiality" from the magazine's pluralist menu of sexual dishes.

Perhaps surprisingly, S/M was one form of sex that *Variations* didn't have to drop in order to broaden its circulation. The editor herself was a notorious "dominatrice," a female expert in sexual dominance, who had told all in a 1982 article in *Penthouse* called "S/M for Beginners." A year earlier, *Variations* had already devoted an issue exclusively to the subject; it included articles on bondage, female domination, female submission, humiliation, the gay leather scene, branding and more. It contained detailed descriptions of almost everything anyone ever wanted to know about S/M, ostensibly from the mouths of typical married women:

> My husband and I have been married seven
> years. We have two small children and live a
> middle-class life in California. . . . The first
> time we actually tried B&D [bondage and dis-
> cipline] I tied my husband spread eagle on the
> bed and strapped him in a few times with one
> of his belts. It wasn't much, really, but I'll
> never forget how exciting it was to see for the
> first time, my husband helplessly bound, na-
> ked and under my control. Now . . . we have
> an interesting assortment of collars, whips,
> cock rings and other "tools of the trade."

Women counseled one another not to accept automatically the masochist's role unless by choice: "At first it
was difficult for me to get into the S/M scene because I
hate to be tied up," a frustrated female sadist wrote to
the magazine. "After a talk with my husband, however,
I found out that he had no objection to bondage. . . .
Today, in the dominant role, I have come to love our
S/M sessions." Dominant women even get rewards outside the boundaries of sex: "[Thanks to S/M] I've come
to enjoy being the complete boss," explained an anony-
mous reader, "and I leave lots of housework for Ned to
do!"

S/M ENTERS THE MAINSTREAM

The crowd at Jane Cooper's house had unanimously
negative responses to certain objects; they all found a
baby's pacifier in the shape of a penis repulsive—even
perverse. But its inclusion in the display didn't discour-

age anyone from participating in the party. In fact it was comforting to be able to draw the line somewhere by rejecting some products in order to heartily endorse others.

As the wine flowed, Cooper's guests examined Passion Flowers, Rub-Her Bands, Lick-Ness Monsters, erection and nipple creams, anal intruders, satin sheets, and Orgy Butter. When it seemed as if every imaginable item was out of the closet, the expert asked if anyone was interested in S/M toys. "If you're not," she seductively added, "it may be because you haven't seen what I have to offer." Despite a few groans, as the group anticipated the sting of her whip, everyone was curious about this part of the show. Instead of torture equipment, however, they were confronted with soft black leather ropes that are used to tie a lover down in bed. As the ropes were cautiously passed around, some women asked questions about bondage. But not everyone was a total novice.

"We were roughhousing one night after a lot of brandy," began Jill McLoughlin, as the crowd at Cooper's house quieted down. "Tom was on top of me, holding my arms down with each hand, while I had him in a scissors grip with my legs. He suddenly reached for a pair of stockings and managed to tie my arms to the bedposts. Then he pinned down my legs. We were laughing, biting each other—like kids—it was all very playful, very spontaneous. But I found myself tied down, unable to free my hands or legs. The last thing I was was angry or scared. My strongest desire at that moment was to surrender—give in totally to the sexual experience. I was in a frenzy and Tom was thrilled, not having gotten me as excited since our premarital days of heavy petting. Sex once again felt almost taboo." Jill and her husband had not repeated the experience, but for her it was a night to remember.

After two women purchase leather ropes ($34 a pair), it's time to go home. To Jane and her friends, S/M is no longer beyond the pale; it's something they expect to see—at least in attenuated form—in mainstream magazines, rock videos, and the fashion world. In 1977 when *Vogue* first published Chris Von Wangeheim's infamous photographs of Dobermans snapping at a model's ankles, most readers were shocked. Likewise, appalled critics questioned the use of S/M as a background for Geoffrey Beene's "metallic sandals" and "sliding necklines." This was pornography disguised as chic, high-fashion photography. The protest only underlined the power of the images, which seem to have affected American culture like a long-lasting aphrodisiac. On some level the connection between women's captivity, submission, and high fashion made sense, and S/M began to be a recurrent, if usually covert theme in fashion and advertising for women.

By 1981 S/M was no longer covert. In *Self,* Michael Korda, the editor in chief of Simon & Schuster, ascribed to the work of Helmut Newton, perhaps the most well-known photographer to create a context for S/M in high fashion, an "elegance with a flair for startling, sadistic sexuality."[6] Any reader who picked up this issue could have turned to the centerfold and mistakenly thought he or she had purchased a porn magazine: A double-spread color photo of a half-naked woman screaming in ecstasy as she receives a hard spank from a fully dressed man. Korda's article, "Love Bites and Slaps: What to Make of Them, When to Play the Fantasy Game, When to Draw the Line," described and endorsed the escalation of aggression in heterosexual sex.

Coming from Korda, the surgeon general of publishing, this was strong medicine for those who felt they had unhealthy sex lives. Pain, he argued, helped to intensify sexual pleasure. The caption accompanying the centerfold provided most of the evidence: "A sudden affectionate swat on the rear—one of love's traditional plays—usually elicits a response of shocked pleasure." For Korda, S/M was not only an accepted form of sex, it was even glamorous. He speculated that in a consensual situation, S/M was an opportunity for "a return, however momentary, to the animal self within each of us." Korda made S/M sound like an exotic drink that wasn't appropriate every night, but that could on occasion hold out the possibility of a new kind of sexual peak. Like homosexuality or marijuana, it took some time to get used to the idea, but S/M was easily packaged as a safe heterosexual sport.

There was actually nothing new about S/M, other than its visibility in the mass culture. Historians believe that S/M has been practiced since the Renaissance, although the medical community has only begun, with some anxiety, to explore the phenomenon. In a 1972 study of 141 suburban, married housewives, Dr. E. Hariton found that 49 percent of the women had submissive sexual fantasies.[7] Masters and Johnson completed a comparative study of the sexual fantasies of heterosexuals and homosexuals in 1979, in which they found that "forced sexual encounters" were prevalent fantasies for men and women, regardless of their sexuality.[8] Commenting on the study to the New York

Times, Bernard Apfelbaum, director of the Berkeley Sex Therapy Group, said, "It's important to look at the content of a sex fantasy during lovemaking for what it suggests about what's missing in the sexual encounter."[9] While the study did not indicate that men or women, regardless of their sexual preference, wanted to bring their fantasies to life, it did reveal that for many people, S/M was a typical erotic fantasy theme.

Statistically, too, there is evidence that S/M is entering "normal" sexual practice. As early as 1953, the Kinsey Institute found "sizable portions of their samples" had been involved in light S/M such as biting or slapping. More recently, in a study of a "self-defined" S/M group of 225 men and women, Dr. Charles Moser of the Institute for Advanced Study of Human Sexuality found "no evidence to suggest that the psychological functioning of the S/M self-identified individual was impaired." The majority of his sample rejected the notion that S/M was "inborn" (an animal instinct as Korda has suggested) or a "mental illness," and more than 45 percent found " 'straight sex' as satisfying as, or more satisfying than S/M," indicating that this population was not obsessively limited to one kind of sex.[10]

But it was the sexual marketplace, more than anything else, that brought S/M into the mainstream of sexual options. The market demands novelty, and by the eighties oral sex was no longer novel. It had been described meticulously in sex manuals, portrayed in the new "couples" porn, and promoted implicitly by the flavored cremes and ointments. Movie scenes suggestive of oral sex, or scenes of couples seemingly on the brink of oral sex, had become so routine that they barely warranted a PG rating. Little references to oral sex, like the bumper sticker recommending that one "Sit on a Happy Face," were hard to avoid and no longer shocking. The sexual marketplace needed a new frontier and by the eighties the only imaginable remaining novelty—perhaps even the last frontier—was sadomasochism.

S/M is not only the latest sexual novelty, it is perhaps the ultimately commercial form of sex. First, it lends itself to a more gripping form of imagery and presentation than any other activity can. In pornography based on oral sex, the creative challenge was to wrap some sort of plot around the various episodes of fellatio and cunnilingus. Oral sex is only an act, but S/M is itself a *drama*. There is no single act that defines it, only a drawn-out sequence of events that may in themselves not even be overtly sexual. The thrill is in the buildup; the "foreplay" is the play itself. So even in one of the most primitive and familiar forms of commercialized sex—the vignette presented as a letter to the editor of a porn magazine—S/M has much greater possibilities than any particular sexual practice. Anything else needs some crude narrative buildup: "She entered the room. I could see she was wearing nothing under the trench coat . . ." S/M, appropriately ritualized, contains its own narrative.

S/M has another, equally powerful, commercial quality: It is innately fetishistic; it *requires* paraphernalia. More familiar sexual practices might be enhanced with oils or cremes or eroticized birth control devices, but basically the human body is adequate for their performance. Hands, mouths, genitals, are "equipment" enough, and anything else—to touch, smell, or read as an adjunct to sex—is an aesthetic sidelight to the main event. The commercial possibilities are inherently limited.

Not so with S/M, which depends on an inventory of devices—whips, chains, ropes, even outlandish costumes. The gear is not just an optional enhancement, it is essential to the act—if not to the very imagining of it. Perhaps Van de Velde, the classic sex expert of the pre-sexual-revolution era, understood this when he defined "normal sex" as excluding "cruelty and the use of artificial means." The cruelty, even in its more harmless, ritualized forms, is hard to imagine without the devices; and the devices are hard to look at without imagining cruelty or at least the simulation of cruelty. If it is to be anything beyond routine brutality, S/M requires its collection of evocative objects. And if it is to be fresh and interesting time after time, its performance requires new objects—more horrifying bondage gear, more fetishistic outfits—to center the drama on. S/M almost requires a sexual marketplace, impersonally promoting the "objects" of desire. From a strictly capitalist viewpoint, it is the ideal sexual practice.

S/M owes its entrance into the sexual mainstream to its paraphernalia: The symbols and gear precede the actual practice into the homes and imaginations of millions. Thus a rock video on television can convey the possibility of S/M without being in any way overtly pornographic—simply through the images and gear. For example, a 1984 video by the popular group Duran Duran showed nothing suggestive of sex (we are tempted to say "normal" sex), but contained almost subliminal images of female figures in chains. Even the twelve-year-old viewers could understand that the reference was to "S and M," rather than to sex as we ordinarily understand it. Similarly it is the paraphernalia that brought S/M into the forefront of possibilities for the women gathered at Jane Cooper's home party. Introduced in the form of commodities, with prices and even sizes, S/M was no longer bizarre and disgusting—just something else for the curious consumer to try.

Certainly, women like Jane Cooper seem to be perfectly capable of experimenting with S/M without radically transforming their entire sex lives or becoming in any other way eccentric. While Cooper was the first woman on her block to host a home party, she is hardly viewed as a sexual maverick. Neither are any of her friends—secretaries, computer technicians, clerks, bank tellers—who are for the most part happily married women. For those of them who were having S/M fantasies, the home party provided evidence that they weren't alone, and no longer had to feel guilty. The consumer culture was offering them validation by selling items that could bring their fantasies to life. S/M had become visible.

THE DAUGHTERS OF DE SADE

While some women were experimenting with bondage or spanking, others were involved in a more extreme, ritualized form of S/M. For them S/M ironically provided the answer to a difficult question: How can men and women—gay or straight—play fair in bed? S/M could be a carefully constructed sexual ritual offering an enormous amount of control to both participants. For heterosexual women who desired more control over the sexual act—a common enough request—S/M offered a method of binding each partner to play by a set of mutually agreed on rules. The element of power —and powerlessness—inherent in the traditional heterosexual experience is the core of the S/M ritual. Dominance and submission, two roles most often played out in bed, are complementary elements in an S/M drama. For some men and women it is desirable to define these roles in order for each person to choose their favorite part.

Unlike the days before the sexual revolution, heterosexual S/M does not automatically assign roles based on traditional notions of gender. Men don't have to lead; or women, follow. Either sex can be dominant or submissive. "Leadership"—who does what first, when, and why—has always been an issue, particularly for heterosexuals battling for equality in bed. But for sadists and masochists, power is not exclusively located in the person directing the scene. To S/M devotees, there is no social value or inherent investment in either of these roles—which are mutually dependent and freely chosen.

The imagination is what shapes an S/M scene to meet the individual desires of both players. The top and bottom (as the sadist and masochist are called, respectively) often begin by familiarizing each other with their sexual fantasies; they choose one that is mutually pleasing to act out and then determine what equipment will be used and the limits of the scene. Often the bottom is given a code word that can be used to stop any particular act, while preserving the illusion that the sex is nonconsensual. While the roles of top and bottom remain rigid, it takes a great deal of communication prior to having any sex to determine the content of an S/M scene.

Given the openness—and confusion—over sex during the seventies, part of the appeal of S/M for some of its devotees was the rigid structure that it provided. If heterosexual women had difficulty getting men to perform, or even explaining what they wanted, here was one form of sex that could do away with the confusion surrounding the issue of equality in bed. Instead of kicking power relations out of the bedroom, as many feminists had recommended, sadists and masochists prefer to eroticize domination and submission. The issue of power, its use and abuse, creates the erotic content in a scene. The illusion that sex is not consensual empowers the top and turns the bottom on. Costumes are used to reinforce the notion that each partner is giving a performance and to authenticate the particular fantasy. In its most exaggerated form S/M is tragicomic theater: power here equals powerlessness.

"The successful S/M act can be compared to the successful production of a drama composed by two or more authors," said Terry Kolb, co-founder of the Till Eulenspiegel Society. "A great deal of intuition, ability to improvise, and cooperation is needed." This S/M society in New York City (named after a masochistic character in German folklore who preferred to climb up hills rather than down) began in 1976 and had three hundred dues-paying members by 1984. The purpose of the group is to support and educate the S/M community. "I was the only woman when we first started T.E.S.," secretary-treasurer Goldie told us (she does not use her own name in S/M circles to protect her job). "Now one third of the members are women." The

group offers Monday night lectures "on things like water sports, the history of S/M, or the perils of masochism." They are open to the public for a three-dollar
admission ticket.

The majority of members in T.E.S., according to
Goldie, are heterosexual submissives. "Most of the men
are submissive, while among the women it's about half
and half." Inside the S/M culture no one is surprised
that men prefer to be dominated by women. "If I had a
dollar for every man who asked me to switch, I'd be
rich!" reported Goldie, who has been a masochist for
the past thirteen years. In the S/M configuration, the
sadist is burdened with the responsibility for directing a
scene, turning sex into little more than a spectator
sport. The top must continually watch and gauge the
level of the bottom's sexual enjoyment in order to make
sure that no one gets hurt. While it is taboo to go beyond the predetermined limits of a scene, an experienced top stays close to the edge.

Insiders consistently report that masochists—male
and female—make up the majority of the S/M population. "It's a lot of work to be a good dominant," explains
Goldie. "You have to set the scene and all that. People
are lazy. It's easier just to be done to." Dominance,
once an honorable, male tradition, is now not a particularly desirable role to either sex. Dominants are so
much in demand that a new category called "masochist
servers" has developed to meet the need. These are
people who, though not usually dominant, are occasionally willing to perform certain acts. Apart from any
deeper psychological reason, masochism seems to be
more attractive because it's more rewarding. Paradoxi-
cally, the passive masochist is always the center of at-

tention, the consumer in an S/M scene: The sadist is only catering to his or her desires.

In theory S/M was a logical next step for the sexual revolution. The crisis in heterosexual relations in the seventies left many women thinking there was no way to reconstruct the sexual act as long as women remained powerless in the dominant culture. While feminism promoted mutuality and better communication, in practice men and women were still at odds in bed. S/M was one way to bring men and women back together again by offering them a form of self-conscious, carefully negotiated sex. Power could be rationed, doled out according to who wanted more—and who wanted less: "Submission" could be redefined as a crucial element in sex, and stripped of its automatic ties to the female gender. S/M gave equal license to both men and women to explore their weaknesses and their strengths.

In the formality and premeditation it required, S/M was almost a parody of the heterosexual interaction recommended by the liberated sex manuals of the seventies. The new, nonmedical sex advisers no longer assumed that the sexual act was bound to be mutually pleasurable. Some things would please one partner, while the other partner might need an entirely different set of stimuli. All they could hope to do was negotiate a fair enough exchange—a little of this for a little of that. S/M went beyond whispered negotiations to a more conscious recognition of the partners' different needs and of the impossibility of fulfilling them with perfect simultaneity. If heterosexuals in general were learning that good sex took work, practitioners of S/M had taken the further step of turning sex into a *project*.

But in other ways S/M was a repudiation of the sexual revolution. Not only was it overtly anti-egalitarian, but it ruled out spontaneity and any casual promiscuity. A woman would have to genuinely trust a man before allowing him to use handcuffs or leather straps; and a man, too, would be well advised to know something about a woman he wished to be dominated by. S/M was not for people who enjoyed making love spontaneously in the dark, or for people looking for a casual one-night stand. The process of gathering equipment, working out a fantasy, and then acting it out turns sex into an elaborate set of activities that most people simply don't have time for. Particularly for devotees rather than occasional explorers, S/M demands enormous attention and concentration—even an obsessive devotion to sex.

On the whole, the feminist movement is divided on the issue of S/M. Some see sexual variations, including S/M, as progressive openings within a culture that fails to support individuals who break the monogamous heterosexual standard. For Pat Califia, a self-described lesbian feminist sadomasochist and founder of an S/M society on the West Coast, S/M has an ideological function. It is a way of using sex to demonstrate real—in this case, female—sexual power: "S/M is not about pain," she argues, "but about power."[11]

Yet for many women who are practicing light S/M in its less ritualized, less extreme form, S/M is probably not so much an empowering force as it is simply a novelty, tantamount to experimenting with a new haircut. The process of buying the accessories and making preparations may be half—or much more than half— the fun. Not only the devotee but the curious novice has to invest in uniforms, equipment, instructions, and more, very much like someone beginning a new sport. At Patty's Place in Miami, a store similar to the Pleasure Chest, the most popular items are ankle and wrist restraints. According to the owner, the clientele sees nothing horrifying about the S/M equipment sold. "S/M is something new to try," she told a *Time* reporter, "like redecorating your bedroom."[12]

S/M is in many ways a product of the modern sexual marketplace, but elements of the ritual had been integrated into sexual practice long before Alex Comfort put "Discipline" and "Chains" on the table of contents page of *The Joy of Sex.* Sex for women has traditionally involved a form of role playing considered so natural that it was unconsciously integrated into the sexual act. "Faking it," for example, is the most familiar element of dramatic ritual in conventional, prerevolutionary sex— which was itself a ritual in which men were required to dominate and women to remain submissive. Strange as ritualistic S/M may seem, power plays and role playing are hardly unfamiliar terms of endearment.

For some women, S/M may have been an improvement on the old, unconscious variety of sadomasochism promoted by the marriage manuals of the fifties. At least with S/M, a woman had a chance to be a consumer in her own right, rather than being the passive instrument of male urges. She might even be able to dictate the terms of her sexual encounters. And as with any other new technique, S/M could be used to solidify the bonds of a monogamous relationship, just as the more daring could use it to make a conscious statement about relationships of power. In either case, it provided an expression for the fantasies of erotic domination and violence that seem to figure so prominently in the dreams (and nightmares) of both sexes, according to experts ranging from Masters and Johnson to Nancy Friday. For some women, S/M may simply have been a way of taking the guilt out of sex—as if, in the form of S/M, the sex itself had become punishment enough.

Still, S/M was a bizarre side trail for a sexual revolution that had begun in women's emerging drive for equality and independence. The pioneers of women's sexual revolution, whether or not they called themselves feminists, had insisted on a more self-determined, assertive form of female sexuality than the arbiters of "normal" heterosexuality allowed them. But the feminist aspirations that had originally inspired the sexual revolution had no control over its commercialized forms. In the sexual marketplace, ideals and causes have no place; novelty is all that counts—even when the novelty seems to subvert women's original impulse to sexual liberation. Of course, independent career women as well as unadventurous housewives could experiment with S/M without changing anything else about their lives or self-images. But S/M was still an admission that equality might not work—at least in sex —and that we might as well make the best of inequality, even in its most contrived and ritualized form.

S/M was not, however, the strangest denouement of the sexual revolution. In S/M, inequality is sexualized out of the context of everyday life and relationships. There is no relation between wanting to be a top in S/M dramas and being domineering and authoritarian in daily life, or between being a bottom and being a masochist in relation to a spouse or friends. By sequestering off sex into a realm of conscious ritual, S/M could still be consistent, in an odd way, with feminism or any other egalitarian belief system. But this is not true of the next setting into which we follow the sexual revolution: In the world of Christian fundamentalism, masochism is the prescribed role for women, and yet there, too, women's sexual revolution has been inexorably gaining ground.

5
Fundamentalist Sex
Hitting Below the Bible Belt

The women filling the auditorium were well-dressed, their hair meticulously arranged, their makeup carefully detailed. A hint of past, better times surrounded them, a whiff of the fifties in the tight control of their look. They were there to learn how to maintain that image: The theme of the seminar they were attending was "How to Be Beautiful Inside and Out." The workshop was part of a larger conference sponsored by the Christian Women's National Concerns, one group in the proliferating network of Christian right organizations. According to sociologist Joanne Young Nawn, an observer at the session, undergarments, those objects of beauty that are neither inside nor out, occupied a large part of the discussion. The need for a good bra was emphasized, since the sight of an erect nipple can apparently induce a man to uncontrolled lust. The audience was told that light, silky bras are too suggestive, especially during brisk cold weather, which makes the nipple stand out.[1]

To Nawn, the workshop was a "downright prurient" lesson in the embarrassingly detailed requirements for women who act as guardians of morality. Sitting on their pedestal of feminine modesty, they are expected to be totally womanly—sweet, passive, nurturing—yet at the same time they are held responsible for the lewd reactions of every passing male.

According to the sex experts of the religious new right, women must take responsibility for the way men treat them because men can't control themselves. The male is a victim of what one conservative Christian book calls the "Y chromosome factor," something in the male genes that makes "sexual arousal . . . much more quickly stimulated through eye contact." According to the authors, fundamentalist therapist George Rekers and his equally conservative colleague, minister Michael Braun, once they are stimulated, men cannot be expected to rein in their urges. Women must no longer tempt them by wearing, "even to public worship . . . clothing that would have been considered the attire of a prostitute fifty years ago." Such dress creates a "problem" which can be solved if "Christian women will . . . accept the fact that they will be hopelessly out of style." But there is a silver lining for a woman who wears the proper attire. She has the privilege of providing "a feminine mystique that ennobles a man."[2]

Detailed fashion commentary may seem inappropriate coming from spiritual leaders, but the assumptions of the Christian right are theocratic: All aspects of one's life are theoretically subject to religious law. Yet, in the last decade, the sexual revolution has penetrated even the self-enclosed world of right-wing fundamentalism.

And the Christian right is fighting desperately to keep out—or to co-opt—the challenge.

Until very recently, Protestant fundamentalism occupied a peculiar backwater of American culture. Beaten back in the Scopes trial in 1927 (where, though Thomas Scopes was found guilty of teaching evolution, in spirit the agnostic rationalism of Clarence Darrow prevailed), fundamentalism retreated to rural and small-town America—especially the Southern Bible Belt. While mainstream Protestantism became increasingly secular in outlook—and spiritually undemanding —fundamentalists withdrew into a rigidly patriarchal and puritanical subculture of their own. But the sixties politicized fundamentalist leaders like the Rev. Jerry Falwell, who emerged in the seventies determined to enter the mainstream culture and combat the "Satanic forces" represented by feminism, the civil rights movement, gay liberation, and atheism. By the mid-seventies, fundamentalist leaders like Falwell and Pat Robertson of TV's evangelical "700 Club" had joined with more secular political right-wing leaders like Richard Viguerie, Howard Phillips, and others, to build a powerful network of fund-raising and lobbying organizations, political action committees, and publications. This network constitutes what is known as the Christian right, which ranges ideologically from Billy Graham on what might be called the liberal wing to—on the far, far right —paramilitary groups that urge white Christians to take up arms for the coming confrontation with Jews, nonwhites, and atheists. On this spectrum, Falwell and Robertson represent the mainstream of the Christian right.

While not all fundamentalists became political conservatives, any more than all conservatives became true believers, the Christian right (which designates its own enterprises and beliefs simply as "Christian") has emerged as a major political and social force in America. Its leaders see nothing wrong with mixing religion and politics. "The idea that religion and politics don't mix was invented by the devil to keep Christians from running their own country," Falwell has said.[3] It is this ambition to run America as a "Christian republic" that alarms less theocratically oriented Americans. But there is no denying that the Christian right has struck a responsive chord with a considerable segment of the American public. By the mid-eighties, 40 percent of adult Americans were calling themselves born-again Christians, and another 20 percent counted themselves as evangelical Protestants. Some twelve to twenty million people were tuning in to the huge Christian broadcasting empire.[4]

The message put out by these media gospels, whether overtly political or not, is deeply authoritarian, and the ultimate source of authority is the Bible. Hardcore fundamentalists stand their ground on the principles of biblical inerrancy: If it's in the Bible, it's the law, no matter how times have changed in nearly two thousand years. Yet new ideas representing a unique interpretation of the Bible, if not a departure from it, have found their way into the fundamentalist world. Feminism was far too radical for most fundamentalist women, but the women's sexual revolution, which appeared without fanfare or formal organization and exerted its influence first in the privacy of the bedroom, infiltrated even this corner of conservative America.

Within fundamentalist ideology, it is automatically

assumed that women will marry. Like men, they are said to be governed by genetic programs, primarily those that create the need for marriage and maternity. "I was created to be the wife of Bailey Smith and the mother of his children," explains Sandy Elliff Smith, whose husband served two terms as president of the Southern Baptist Convention in the early eighties. (Smith is known for his comment that "God Almighty does not hear the prayers of a Jew.")

There is nothing wrong, however, with using a little innocent deception to advance God's marital designs. "There aren't many things more upsetting to the male ego than a female super-brain," advises one book for single Christian women. "If you're blessed with an unusual set of brains, use them, won't you, to keep from showing them too much?"

Once married, fundamentalist couples base their relationship on Ephesians 5:22–28:

> Wives, submit yourselves unto your own husbands, as unto the Lord. For the husband is the head of the wife, even as Christ is the head of the church; and he is the savior of the body. Therefore, as the church is subject unto Christ, so let the wives be to their own husbands in everything. Husbands, love your wives, even as Christ also loved the church, and gave himself for it.

This can be and has been interpreted in different ways by different people. A small group of women within the evangelical* movement see in the passage a message of

---

* Evangelicals, according to one view, generally "tolerate a somewhat broader range of Bible interpretation and cultural outlook," while for histo-

"mutual submission" between husband and wife, a sharing of power, a willingness to compromise. Fundamentalist interpretations emphasize the submission of the woman to her supposedly loving husband, but some hard-liners, by coupling Ephesians with a passage from I Timothy, infer that in principle all men have authority over all women:

> Let the woman learn in silence with all subjection. But I suffer not a woman to teach, nor to usurp authority over the man, but to be in silence. For Adam was first formed, then Eve. And Adam was not deceived, but the woman being deceived was in the transgression. (11:14)

Rekers and Braun interpret Timothy to mean that women are incapable of an active role in life by divine intention. According to them, Paul (the author of the letters to Timothy and the Ephesians) was going back to the creation story in order to draw

> upon principles of proper leadership that are expressed in human sexuality. . . . God does not act arbitrarily. God doesn't flip a cosmic coin in eternity and say, "Heads, I'll make man first." There was a plan to it. And when, under the pressure of satanic assault, that order of leadership was reversed and Eve initiated action, the result was catastrophic. . . . It is no wonder that Satan assaulted Eve first; she was woman, made by God to be ever so sensitive to

rian George Marsden, "a Fundamentalist is an Evangelical who is angry about something."[5]

spiritual input. She was made to respond, and
Satan lured her to take independent initiative.[6]

THE "SECOND COMING"

One would think there was no hope for a sexual revolution given such doctrinaire, misogynist notions. But
some fundamentalist women have proved themselves
neither as docile as they are expected to be nor as
ashamed of their "original sin" as their men might like
them to be. They have learned to fight with the weapons on hand, receiving advice on guerrilla warfare from
an unlikely source. In the early seventies, a born-again
Christian housewife in Florida began to push the idea
that if wives would act like homemaking Playboy Bunnies, they might gain a power advantage over their
indifferent or domineering husbands. Her name was
Marabel Morgan and her discovery of what women
could do to transform their marriages won her millions
of followers (and millions of dollars).

Morgan developed her principles of total womanhood after a typical argument with her husband, a
wealthy lawyer named Charles. One evening he informed her that they were having dinner with business
associates the following night. When Marabel pointed
out that she had made other plans for the evening,
Charlie said in "an icy voice, 'From now on, when I plan
for us to go somewhere, I will tell you twenty minutes
ahead of time. You'll have time to get ready and we'll do
without all this arguing.' "[7]

Rather than throwing dinner in his face, Morgan submitted. Like the chastised child he considered her, she went to her room, but instead of sulking, she came up with a plan. "I'd tried to change Charlie, and that hadn't worked. Now I would have to change me." On the face of it, Morgan's newfound strategy was antithetical to feminism, yet it provided her with an area of initiative and control in an otherwise dependent life. While the scheme was centered on Charlie, and utilized the most traditional of society's expectations of what men wanted, there was little accommodation for Charlie in the actual plan; he was the object.

Morgan's program involved what theologian Martin Marty has called a "costume fetish [that] would dazzle Krafft-Ebing."[8] In her books *Total Woman* and *Total Joy,* she advocated that wives dress up as cowgirls and pirates (miniskirted versions), spies (with nothing on under the trench coat), elves, pixies, and strippers (with tea-bag tassles for those who couldn't afford costumes). Dressing as gorillas suited Morgan's piquant sense of sexual play as well. Men were not completely left out of the fun either. Morgan described one husband who came home as a scuba diver, changing in the men's room of the local gas station before arriving goggled and tanked at the door. Sex was to be inventive and unexpected. Wives were encouraged to have intercourse under the dining room table, on diving boards, trampolines, and bales of hay. Even the mundane bedroom was to be jazzed up with candles, edible massage lotions, and perfume-sprayed sheets.

All this was aimed at making the husband feel he was king of his home and master of a one-woman harem. "It is only when a wife surrenders her life to her husband, reveres and worships him, and is willing to serve him, that she becomes really beautiful to him . . . she becomes a priceless jewel, the glory of femininity, his queen!" Throughout the latter half of the seventies, millions bought this message through Morgan's books and Total Woman seminars. *Total Woman,* her first book, sold more than half a million copies in hardcover and had a first paperback print run of two million. The seminars, often sponsored by churches, cost about fifteen dollars, well within the range of the many lower-middle-class women who sought her help. Churches were quick to support Total Woman programs because, as Marty has pointed out, Morgan and her disciples were "massively evangelical," expecting "an imminent and literal Second Coming."

Morgan was born again, she says, after dropping out of Ohio State University and becoming a beautician. "There with the water running," she has written, "I was born again. I had asked Him to take me before, but I had never got any answers. This time I asked Him to take me and he took me. There was no bolt of lightning. Only peace. I was tickled to death."[9]

Despite Marty's tongue-in-cheek comments, many religious leaders took Morgan very seriously. The number of books sold were testimony to the need women felt to be "totaled," as the critics put it, by Morgan. Beyond that was the dawning recognition in the seventies that women and their sexuality could no longer be smothered under the sheets. Arguments on the merits of Morgan's ideas flew thick and fast in the popular and religious press, with the majority of commentators calling for an end to Total Womanhood.

Many religious observers were shocked by its message. "What hypocrisy," wrote liberal evangelical John Scanzoni of Morgan's advice that Total Women greet their husbands dressed only in an apron and black stockings, "telling a wife she is subject to her husband and then encouraging her to use sex to manipulate him." Jim Wallis, who represents the left wing of evangelical thought, complained that "evangelical wives and single women can now look like Hollywood starlets and feel good about it."[10] And journalist Joyce Maynard wrote, "The image of women presented in *Total Woman* is an ultimately demeaning one, and it demeans men as well; it represents women as weak and empty-headed complainers, obsessed with material possessions. I do not like to think what would happen to a Total Woman if her husband died." Probably no worse than would happen to her fundamentalist sister who had never paraded nude before her husband: all fundamentalist women are considered equally helpless, while Total Women at least have the benefit of "a book which simply reassures them," as Maynard wrote, "that sex is not sinful."[11]

Despite Scanzoni's misgivings, *Total Woman* was not primarily about manipulating men. It provided women with a frequently successful way to manipulate *themselves* out of an untenable situation. Morgan was overtly advocating submission, but she was decidedly subversive between the lines. In her books and interviews she displayed a spunkiness, an independent streak that belied her message. She publicly hinted that after working so hard to shake up a traditional marriage, it's a little difficult to go back to being suitably passive. "I rarely have to compromise," she once gloated, a surprising comment in any marriage. To Scanzoni and Wallis, Mor-

gan may seem manipulative, but in a sense her idea that
women should get something in return for their efforts,
rather than merely submitting or sacrificing, is a decidedly feminist idea. If we are to service men and their
homes, Morgan implicitly argued, why not get paid?
Morgan received a new refrigerator-freezer soon after
initiating her Total Woman techniques. Other rewards
were flowers, perfume, lingerie, and jewelry. Soon
enough, of course, she could afford these on her own.

But the biggest and best prize was a new sex life. In
Total Joy, Morgan sounded as if she'd read either *The
Sensuous Woman* or *Our Bodies, Ourselves,* both
banned in most Christian bookstores. Women were encouraged to enjoy not only the playfulness and unself-
consciousness of sexuality, they were told to get pleasure for themselves. "Have him apply rhythmic
pressure [to the clitoris] and don't give up,"[12] she advised. While her instruction wasn't very explicit, coming as she did out of a cultural milieu that had tried its
hardest to ignore the social upheavals of the sixties, this
was definitely revolutionary. Instead of a docile, possibly frigid wife for whom the vagina was the only thinka-
ble sexual organ, Morgan held up the vision of a woman
doing who knows what in her daily bubble bath.

In addition to a new sex life, Morgan tempted women
who had been raised in the isolated fundamentalist tradition with a taste of the wider world. "I want to do
something. I don't know what. Someday I wish I could
travel," a Total Woman told Joyce Maynard while relaxing in her bubble bath with a glass of wine, preparing for her husband. "You have to understand, things
were very different when I was dating. Today, all these
kids living together and not married. . . . All these

new things. Orgies and couples that switch off and girls having careers and living with their boyfriends. It's not for me. But you wonder about it." As the bubbles disappear in her bath, the woman murmurs, "I have my own checking account. It, you know, makes you feel more human. . . . Still, if I were doing it all over again, I wouldn't get married quite so soon."[13]

Morgan's message, whether salvation for unhappy housewives or merely a spark for a tired marriage, was a sharp break from traditional fundamentalism, which claimed, according to Christian commentator Lewis Smedes, "Sexuality is nature's strongest competitor for . . . loyalty to Christ. 'You cannot love God and sex.' " Given the choice (most fundamentalists assumed there was none), they'd have to give up sexual pleasure and concentrate on God instead. Morgan, operating out of the newly changed mores of the sixties and seventies, tried to turn the forbidden into something "as pure as cottage cheese," but with a little spice added. "Costumes provide variety without him ever leaving home," she wrote, promising men (and women) the same exotic thrill a secret affair might give.

Morgan's genius lay in eliminating the hang-ups that made sex inaccessible, while retaining the taboos that made it exciting. Traditional fundamentalist revivalism had drawn much of its dynamism from repressed sexuality. Anarchist Emma Goldman wrote of being nauseated by the "vulgar manner, . . . coarse suggestiveness, erotic flagellations and disgusting lasciviousness" of the early twentieth-century evangelist Billy Sunday. In Goldman's view, the "atmosphere of lewd mouthings and sexual contortions . . . goaded his audience to salacious hysteria."[14] For a sexual rebel herself, she seems to have had little sympathy for those who found their sexual expression where and how they could.

The steamy character of revival meetings has carried over to the present day, although less overtly "lewd" even by our more relaxed standards: The All-American pretty girls who sing their way through meetings, the beauty queens from Anita Bryant to Wonder Woman Lynda Carter who espouse fundamentalism, are an integral part of the television gospel scene and serve a purpose similar to the beautiful model selling cars in commercials. Morgan built on the subliminal erotic appeal of evangelism, moving the sexy girl into the home, giving the man a reason to come home at night and the woman a reason to welcome him.

Despite the criticism from some of her more liberal coreligionists, Morgan's impact on fundamentalist culture was profound. In the late seventies, books on sexuality suddenly began to appear on the shelves of Christian bookstores. These books were written by preachers and important fundamentalist leaders and usually coauthored with their wives—few men seemed willing to handle X-rated material alone. Many of the leaders no doubt recognized in Morgan's sometimes belligerent tones the same note of dissatisfaction they were hearing from the women in their own communities. There was an obvious market for Morgan's sexy, eccentric religion.

The response was a sudden proliferation of Christian sex books and manuals. As Jeffrey Hadden, coauthor of *Prime Time Preachers: The Rising Power of Televangelism,* put it, the new attitude seemed to be "if God gave you the plumbing, you might as well enjoy it." Some book titles, like *Tough and Tender, Celebration in the*

Bedroom, Intended for Pleasure, sounded as if they had been lifted from porn shops and blue-movie marquees, while others took a more homely and simple approach. In *Do Yourself a Favor: Love Your Wife,* Pastor H. Page Williams of Cairo, Georgia, offers the "talking cure" for sexual troubles:

> It is in talking with your wife that you let her take off your clothes, so to speak. She "talks off" your shirt of self-righteousness, your pants of self-sufficiency, your undershorts of self-pity. This is what stimulates her sexually.[15]

Some books contain surprisingly explicit examples from the Bible and real life on how to achieve a richer sex life. Reverend Tim LaHaye, for instance, advocated rereading the Song of Solomon for information on clitoral stimulation. LaHaye has long been a member of the national board of the Moral Majority, and in 1985, while working as a lobbyist for "traditional values" in Washington, he was described as "one of the shrillest of the Fundamentalist idealogues."[16] But LaHaye, writing with his wife, Beverly, was encouraging rather than shrill when it came to sex. The LaHayes provided specific positions: "the wife lying on her back with her knees bent and feet pulled up to her hips and her husband lying on her right side." This is the position described in the Song of Solomon, said the LaHayes, quoting verses 2:6 and, here, 8:3, "Let his left hand be under my head and his right hand embrace me." Following the interpretation of a Christian sexologist, they take this to be the best position for a man to "fondle" or "stimulate" a woman—i.e., masturbate her rather than rely on intercourse. They emphasized the centrality of

clitoral orgasms, described the physical changes a
woman goes through as she approaches orgasm, and
advocated mutual masturbation rather than intercourse on the first night together (the wedding night, of
course) because it "increases the possibility for both to
experience orgasm."[17]

"Everywhere we go to speak . . . the one question
we can count on is, 'What about oral sex?' " wrote religious therapists Clifford and Joyce Penner, the authors
of *The Gift of Sex.* And according to the LaHayes, they
were, at one time, receiving a question about oral sex
almost every week: "Husbands tend to desire this experience more than wives, but recently, because of the
many sex books on the market, there seems to be increasing curiosity on the part of women." The Penners,
fairly liberal, approved of oral sex. The LaHayes were
much more cautious. They pointed out that many people felt guilty about it, that venereal diseases, especially
herpes, could be spread this way, and "some girls find it
harder to reach orgasm in marriage by the conventional method after they have had the premarital experience of oral sex."[18] (It is not clear whether the marital
experience of oral sex has the same devious effect.) Ar-
kansas doctor and religious leader Ed Wheat and his
wife Gaye admitted in their book *Intended for Pleasure*
that the Bible doesn't forbid oral sex, but the practice
"definitely limits the amount of loving verbal communication that the husband and wife can have as they
make love."[19]

While most of their peers were ambivalent about oral
sex, the Reverend Charles and Martha Shedd, wed for
nearly forty years when they published their book, *Celebration in the Bedroom,* had moved beyond oral to

anal sex. The Shedds have been full of truly evangelical
zeal over their newfound sex lives. They told a national
audience on the Phil Donahue show that God had instructed them to "have more time . . . to celebrate in
the bedroom," necessitating a move from their large
congregation in Houston to a smaller, less time-con-
suming church. And later in the same show, they dismayed the LaHayes, also Donahue's guests, by admitting to a "whole drawerful" of vibrators, which were
also "inspired" by God.

Whether explicitly or by suggestion, these books indicated (and continued to do so in the eighties) that submission, the cornerstone of fundamentalist thinking on
women, was out when it came to sex. But only when it
came to sex. Reciprocal pleasure was important, at least
in this area of Christian life. Even here, sex was a commodity of sorts, just as it had become in the rest of
American culture. Men were told if they wanted to
keep a woman contented and in the home they would
have to change their sexual practice. "Every wife has
the right to be loved to orgasm," insisted the LaHayes,
repeating Morgan's message that sex is the reward for
being a good wife. Once men were "selfish lovers. . . .
Sexual pleasure from the 'little woman' was assumed to
be their divine right. . . . Such men were (and some
still are) sexual illiterates." Today, said the LaHayes, the
"modern" Christian man must educate himself to "tai-
lor his affectionate passions to her emotional needs."[20]
In what amounted to a virtual parody of seventies ideas
about sexual give and take, the Charlie Morgans of the
fundamentalist world were being asked not only to provide their wives with new couches and refrigerators
but to take care of their physical needs as well.

Have orgasms and bubble baths and wine created a sexual revolution among fundamentalists? Is a newly discovered zeal for mutually satisfactory sex capable of transforming a way of life based on literal interpretations of the Bible, strict adherence to authority, and the submission of women? In many ways, today's pro-sex Christian leaders seem to have merely absorbed the messages of the women's sexual revolution into their authoritarian culture. Certainly there are some areas where fundamentalists don't even pretend to be interested in change. Premarital sex still amounts to spiritual destruction. In *Your Half of the Apple: God and the Single Girl*, Gini Andrews wrote that premarital sex

> tears living fibers apart . . . when you get up and put your clothes on and go home (or he does), you are not the same as you were. There's been a real mingling of life itself, and because God intended this to be a permanent, one-for-life arrangement, you are damaged when you try to treat it as something casual.[21]

To avoid the damage, Christian women were advised to pray with their dates before setting out for the latest movie or disco, and to avoid dark corners. At Jerry Falwell's Liberty University as recently as 1981, there was little point in praying before going out. Students were required to obtain written permission from the dean to go on dates, and only double dates were allowed. An interracial date had to be approved in writing by both sets of parents. Going out to a disco was grounds for suspension. To encourage students to obey these rules, uniformed guards with American-flag patches on their shoulders stood watch over a bridge that was the only exit from campus.[22]

When single men and women fail to live up to fundamentalism's regulations, the lapse appears to have greater consequences for women. According to the LaHayes, "Many a married woman suffers today from guilt and shame caused by indulging in [sexual intimacy] before meeting her husband. . . . We know of cases where couples had to leave their home churches after marriage because the wife couldn't face the man she was previously so intimate with before breaking the engagement."[23]

Men, apparently, suffer no such shame and can remain in their home church with impunity. Not surprisingly, many Christian women end up believing that being single is a punishment to be endured for as short a time as possible. "It's terrible to be single," says TV star Lynda Carter, who surely has had her choice of interesting men to date. "You're dating different people, and you don't know who to believe and who not to believe. You're constantly insecure without a mate or a real friend."[24]

FUNDAMENTALIST S/M

Despite the appearance of change, much remains the same in the fundamentalist world, proof that even the most feminist aspects of the women's sexual revolution can be co-opted by male authority. For the long term, the impact of a more modern, feminist—or feminoid— sexual ideology remains to be seen. New attitudes may be taking root that will someday be a powerful influence on the lives of fundamentalist women. For the short term, the changes are mainly superficial. Fundamentalist women have hardly moved forward, despite Marabel Morgan and the proliferation of sex books. Little can touch the bonds that hold most of these women in place because the prerequisites for independence—education, careers, worldly experience—are not there. The traditional fundamentalist family tends to treat women as servants, moral misfits, or virgin goddesses—anything but equals. For many couples, sex is still something done by a man to his partner in the dark. While Marabel Morgan is pushing Saran Wrap party clothes for at-home wear, many women are still changing into their nighties in the bathroom and crawling into bed in the dark, to do whatever an inexpert and insensitive husband demands.

Not that sex is *always* a perfunctory duty. Repression, as the Victorian era showed, can offer up its own rich lode of sexual imagery, which relies on being unacknowledged and illicit for titillation. As Morgan proved, roles play an important and acceptable part in fundamentalist sexuality. In role playing, it is not just important to have—and be put in—one's place, but all participants must know exactly what that place is. Fundamentalists like to define exactly what men and women are, using the old standbys about men being "aggressive, dominant, logical, independent, active, ambitious, and task-oriented," while women are "submissive, intuitive, dependent, nurturant, supportive, patient, and person-oriented."[25]

Such concrete definitions can force a woman to flee into the more flexible world of the imagination. For fundamentalists, the sultry femme fatale can also be the

Lilith side of Eve, who was created to be the good girl, "God's helpmate for man," as Dr. Wheat says. While the dogma may call for a quiet unassuming woman, the Biblical message of her evil heritage is part of woman's sexual secret; a reason to be despised, objectified, and desired—particularly in a darkened bedroom. In real life the seductress has too much autonomy to be a fundamentalist woman.

Another fantasy, more accessible to the light of day, emphasizes the submission and helplessness of women. During the seventies one Christian sex expert even endorsed teaching women how to act out the exciting game of "little girl." Helen Andelin, founder of Fascinating Womanhood, which was almost as popular among Christian women as the Total Woman program, recommended that her followers, when settling an argument with their husbands, "stomp your foot. . . . Or, beat your fists on your husband's chest, pouting: 'You hairy beast. . . . How can a great big man like you pick on a poor little helpless girl? I'll tell your mother on you.'" For fashion pointers, Andelin sent her "domestic goddesses" to the little girls' department of their local stores to see what the prepubescent crowd was wearing. While Total Women were shopping for sexy negligees, Fascinating Women were searching—not all that successfully, if you were a full-figured gal—for what would be kinky stuff in any other context: Mary Janes and anklets, gingham and ruffled dresses.[26] Morgan at least restricted her fetishes to the sexual act. Andelin's consumed a woman's life; she dared not step out of character and ruin the image by appearing intelligent, competent, or the least bit independent. Fascinating Womanhood was a life sentence.

Women's helplessness, their submission to their role if not their man, could be dangerous. Despite the promise that the submission of the wife will be matched by the kindness of the husband, fundamentalist imagery sometimes vies with that classic of sadomasochism, *The Story of O*. Bev LaHaye has called on wives to adopt the attitude of Jesus Christ: "The willingness to be humbled, to be obedient unto death, and to be submissive." LaHaye's instructions to the "spirit-filled" wife could match the rules O was presented with upon entering the chateau where she was to be held in bondage by its male caretakers. Compare these two quotes.

LaHaye:
As the woman humbles herself (dies to self) and submits to her husband (serves him), she begins to find herself within that relationship. A servant is one who gets excited about making somebody else successful. . . . You can live fully by dying to yourself and submitting to your husband.[27]

O:
You are here to serve your masters . . . you will drop whatever you are doing and ready yourself for what is really your one and only duty: to lend yourself . . . you are totally dedicated to something outside yourself.[28]

The tone might just be silly if it weren't for the seriousness fundamentalists have attached to wifely submission. If the line between normal and perverse sex is as thin as experts in the fifties thought, fundamentalist women are walking on a razor's edge: They are expected to submit and ultimately *enjoy* their degradation. The idea of pleasure never occurs to O, old-fashioned masochist that she is, but Bev LaHaye promises *excitement* in the service of a total master. Yet she offers no recourse for the times when a master's whims take a malicious turn. Andelin's naughty little girl getting spanked, Bev LaHaye's "excited" servant are both symbols of women's brutalization in right-wing Christian culture. There are few alternatives for the woman who doesn't conform. Rekers and Braun claim there are times when a wife can refuse to submit to her husband, as in "the sad story of a Christian wife whose non-Christian husband encouraged her to extend her sexual favors to a business associate in order to help the husband close a big deal."[29] That example leaves quite a bit of room for abusing the principle of wifely submission. Even the books dedicated to helping men treat their wives better assume that women need to be dominated. "When you bully your wife and push her around and overpower her with cursing and anger, you are really sick. You have a sick marriage," warned Pastor H. Page Williams. But he was not surprised some men fell into this pattern. "The reason this is such a big temptation is because a woman wants to be ruled. Her great desire is to be subject to her husband, because God has ordained it so . . . that's the curse of a woman . . . her desire to be ruled leaves her wide open to be abused." His solution? A call for absolute, but enlightened monarchy—the man must be a "good king" in his castle.[30]

Some fundamentalist ministers show no sympathy for women, despite what they may see and hear in their offices. "Wife-beating is on the rise because men are no longer leaders in their homes," one minister told an interviewer. "I tell the women they must go back home and be more submissive. I know this works, because the women don't come back." University of Texas sociologist Anson Shupe described one woman he interviewed whose second husband had been beating her for four years. When she finally got up the courage to see her minister about the problem, he told her the abuse was her "payment" for divorcing her first husband.[31]

Except for a small group of evangelical feminists, there is surprisingly little outcry from within fundamentalism against the principle of absolute male rule. According to evangelical feminist Virginia Mollenkott, Jesus was a feminist, calling on the early Christians to treat each other, man and woman alike, with greater kindness than their culture had previously shown. "Jesus was calling for mutual submission" in the context of that era, she says. But she and others like her are fighting an uphill battle in the face of many women's conviction that submission is something they can live with and adapt to. In *Who Will Save the Children,* a documentary film by Vicki Costello, Mary Morris, young and fresh-faced, sits with her minister and her husband, describing not only why she is opposed to the Equal Rights Amendment but why, thanks to the new direction fundamentalism has taken, she no longer needs the ERA: "You don't have to be a doormat anymore. That's not what submission means. It means we're equal but we each have certain things we do better than the other. Like diapers. I change diapers better than he does."

Even women committed to the idea of submission have their way out when they need one. Women who could never dream of making a Total Woman's demands on their man can still get through the long day of

washing clothes, making beds, cleaning up after everyone—and through an equally long night of joyless sexual relations—by pushing God's presence in their lives
to the ultimate, but perhaps obvious, end point. They
dream of a love affair with Christ.

Gini Andrews, for example, calls on single women to
dedicate their lives to Christ and not some male's sex
drive: "Which is freedom: being the love-slave of the
Lord Jesus Christ who went through physical, mental,
and spiritual anguish beyond your wildest imaginings
to buy you back from Satan's camp, or being slave to a
human being's sex drives—yours and/or his?"[32] Other
women turn to God for relief from an unhappy marriage. "I prefer to snuggle up under Jesus' love in bed,"
one woman told sociologist Nawn. Or they may resort
to the more encompassing fantasy of yet another
woman who imagined her husband fading from her
life. "A lovely young wife," as Ed Wheat described her,
she said that it was

> often difficult dressing to go out for the eve-
> ning with her husband because she knew in
> advance that he would not treat her the way
> she longed to be treated. So she developed the
> habit of thinking of the Lord Jesus as her
> friend and escort for the evening. "It helped
> me tremendously," she said. "I looked my best
> for Him, I behaved myself for Him, and I was
> constantly aware of His steadying presence
> with me!"[33]

A Boston area wife told radio producer Aimee Sands,
"I like a man who knows he's a man. Somebody that can
be tender when it's necessary. Somebody that can tell

you to cut it out when you're being foolish. There are not many men around today. Jesus Christ is real to me. No other man satisfies."[34] Fundamentalism has given some women a place for their passions, by letting them turn on to someone who can't push them around the way a mere mortal can.

This is not just a fantasy that women conjure up in private, nor are they expected to feel embarrassed about it. Ministers themselves often set the stage for the dream, referring to sexual intimacy that "could never be complete without the three persons—man, woman and God." The Wheats, offering yet another interpretation of the Song of Solomon, explain a mysterious voice in the bedroom King Solomon shares with his lover as "God Himself . . . the only One [who] could be with the couple at this most intimate time." Andrews advised single women to get in the habit of going on dates with God or even taking him shopping: "Ask Him to help you find the right dress, or the new car, or even the gloves you had in mind. You may be surprised at what good taste He has and find you've spent far less money than you'd feared."[35]

As an outlet for unexpressed frustrations, this fantasy of a love affair with Jesus is both a part of religious doctrine and beyond it. Nawn, in her analysis of the Christian right, has pointed out that fundamentalism has "put God the man back into religion." God is depicted as a physical participant in fundamentalist life, not an ethereal, divine presence. Compared to the actual men who run the lives of the women on the Christian right, God is a psychological amulet, a more loving consciousness than that provided by many conservative fundamentalist husbands.

Jesus may make it possible to survive one's marriage to a good king, bad king, or a violent one, but the underlying theme of the relationship is still sadomasochism. The spokesmen of the Christian right don't call it that, for pointing out its correspondence to a known sexual "variation"—in itself a highly secular notion—would open up the prospect of alternative sexual and social themes. But the ritualized partnership, the role playing, the overwhelming concern with power and authority, match the sadomasochistic game—with a critical difference. This is no game; it doesn't end when the sexual encounter is over; there are no rules allowing the woman to end the scene. Better orgasms and more sensitive partners can't make a difference because they are bought at too high a price: accepting a slave mentality not just for a finite sexual encounter but for an entire life.

Ironically, while feminist ideas about sex have been moving into fundamentalist culture, fundamentalist ideas about monogamy have been moving into the mainstream. Fundamentalists may be trying to work new sexual techniques into patriarchal marriages, but sex outside of marriage remains the work of the devil. Most religious conservatives regard extramarital sex as a kind of mark of Cain branding women's psyches with the "searing knowledge that something unique was lost along the way."[36] But we can also see in the ranting against this extramarital experience the fear that male authority might be undermined. When Bev LaHaye comments that men can distinguish between sex and emotional commitment but women cannot, she is really saying women *must not* make this distinction. When women are not dependent on one man to fulfill

their needs, men have lost control over them. The fear
of women's sexual independence has become a major
theme of the eighties, one that indicates not only the
growing strength of the Christian right, but the powerful, lingering influence of sexism in American culture.

6

The Politics of Promiscuity

The Rise of the Sexual Counterrevolution

Ellen, at thirty-four, has made what she considers a "nice little life" for herself. She works for the local telephone company and has managed to buy a small house on the outskirts of Santa Fe. She has what used to be called All-American good looks—straight, gleaming hair, and clear blue eyes. She is single, has had numerous boyfriends, and is currently seeing one man, whom she has been dating for the last two years. By her own description she is a "cowgirl," with a rough and ready attitude toward sex. Her present relationship is just one more phase in her continuing sexual exploration. The late sixties, when she made her first discoveries of her sexuality, were, she says, "one of the most intense periods of my life. I had learned nothing about sex at home and was constantly randy as a teenager. It was a relief to let my needs explode. I had a chance to discover what I liked sexually, who I liked. I made a lot of demands on men too; I chose them for their sexiness or sensuality. Amazing discovery that I could do that."

Ellen's enthusiasm is typical of the generation of women who came of age sexually at a time when repression was coming undone. Their newfound sexual freedom brought the added benefit of a healthy confidence in their bodies—and in their ability to live, at least part of the time, without being seriously involved with a man. Even if they were heterosexuals, other women might still offer the warmth and emotional intimacy that was previously expected of a sexual relationship. They could also, if they chose, experiment with bisexuality or eliminate men from their lives altogether. Such women were realistic: Casual sex was neither heaven nor hell, but it was an important part of their sexual experience.

Nevertheless, by the early eighties a backlash was brewing against what was pejoratively called female "promiscuity." The media began to metamorphize the modern woman, who had been practicing her sexual negotiating skills throughout the seventies, into an old-fashioned girl looking for moonlight, flowers, and commitment. Women who didn't fit this new stereotype were portrayed as hopelessly misdirected. Instead of thinking only about sex, suggested Mike Morgenstern in his 1984 book *How to Make Love to a Woman,* they ought to be considering a "return to traditional sex roles and the warmth these can bring." Despite the enthusiasm women brought to the sexual revolution, this new revisionism inevitably began to feed on their doubts, undermining the positive feelings of many who had enjoyed the freedom of casual sex.

Given the extent of the changes women's sexual revolution had brought to heterosexuality in one brief generation, it is not surprising that some people were confused. As one woman plaintively told a reporter for *New York* magazine in 1984:

> When I was growing up, my mother told me it was important to be a good wife and mother. I was sent off to college to find a man. And then Gloria Steinem said, "No, you want more than marriage, more than motherhood." So I rejected my parents' values. . . . I threw myself into my career. I looked totally androgynous. Is it any wonder my relationships got all screwed up?[1]

This woman was expressing the dilemma of anyone caught in the midst of a revolution—political or cultural. The old verities disappear; choices have to be made where none were demanded before. Freedom may be exhilarating, or it may just bring on a bad case of anxiety—or both. Men probably felt more insecure than women, since their position of strength was being called into question. One male respondent theorized in *The Hite Report on Male Sexuality:*

> The "sexual" revolution, then, is a threat to [men] because it reduces their dominance. If a woman happens to "offer herself" . . . to a man more often because of the "revolution," he's even more threatened than before because the offering is not dominance.[2]

Under the circumstances, a backlash may have been inevitable. But this backlash was ignoring, and in some cases actively denying, the very real statistics and testimony that pointed to women's increasing enjoyment of sexual independence. Ellen was typical of the millions of women who were exploring sex and eager to talk about it. "Sex is an important part of my life," she says. "I'm not willing to do without it if there's no permanent man in my life. I take for granted the pleasure I get. Of course, it's not always easy to find a man to provide that. But I've picked guys up everywhere. I'm more cautious now, but I once spent several months with a guy who was sitting at the table next to me in a restaurant. It was really just sex, but we had a good time for a while."

According to surveys in several major magazines, by the late seventies a majority of women of all ages had accepted with pleasure progressive attitudes toward sex. *Redbook*'s editors were amazed, and awash in responses, after they published their questionnaire on sex in 1975. Almost 100,000 women, overwhelmingly white, married, and middle-class, wrote in and their comments left the surprised editors exclaiming, "Women are becoming increasingly active sexually and are less likely to accept an unsatisfactory sex life as part of the price to be paid for marriage." The study also found that a "considerable number" of *Redbook*'s readers were having affairs while happily married to men they loved, and nine out of ten of the young women who responded were engaging in intercourse before they married.[3]

As statistics, these women were remarkably on target with a survey five years later of *Cosmopolitan* readers, who were supposedly a much more sexually aggressive crowd. *"Cosmo* girls," too, had rushed in, eager to discuss their varied and active sex lives. Helen Gurley Brown described her fears that the survey would never be answered, since it required that "the reader not only . . . answer seventy-nine questions, scissor the pages out, put them in an envelope and address it, but add her *own* postage." Yet soon after the questionnaire ran in the magazine's January 1980 issue, Brown had herself photographed "sitting on a stack of questionnaires that reached nine-feet high. After eight weeks, when we finally stopped counting, more than 106,000 *Cosmo* readers had filled in and mailed their sex-survey questionnaires to us . . . this was the biggest response to *any* magazine survey in history and surely the largest sex survey ever conducted." Many of *Cosmo*'s readers were as sexually satisfied as *Redbook*'s (they reported that, on average, they had had nine lovers) and a little more brazen to boot, in keeping with their favorite magazine's image: "I have lovers because sex feels good," said one, and another claimed, "I have lovers because what else is there in life that's so much fun as turning on a new man, interesting him, conquering him?"[4]

Another round of surveys in 1983 by *Playboy, Family Circle* and *Ladies' Home Journal* concentrated on wives, depicting them as "sexually enthusiastic, confident, romantic and satisfied." One criterion: the number of married women having extramarital affairs. From Kinsey's broad estimate that 6 to 26 percent of married women were having affairs, the statistics jumped in the early 1980s to anywhere from 21 all the way to 43 percent, depending on the magazine conducting the study. Among *Playboy*'s readers, young married wives were "fooling around" more than their husbands.[5]

Some women were downright raunchy in surveys where, thanks to anonymity, they could tell all: "At this point, unless he's well hung, I just wouldn't be interested in him. I know this must sound a little obscene, but it's important to be honest about what you need," said a twenty-nine-year-old stockbroker in *Savvy*'s 1985 "Sex and Success" poll of female executives. A real estate broker said: "I've bedded down with some of the men to whom I was showing apartments. . . . I'd say to them, 'This is the kitchen, this is the living room, and here's the bedroom. Want to try it out?' "[6] At the other end of the spectrum, a more soberly presented 1985 survey by the Roper organization found that eight out of ten women thought single women should have the same sexual freedoms men did—up from six out of ten in 1970.

Women's sexual revolution had a great many committed converts, but men were lagging behind. In the Roper poll 43 percent of the men surveyed wanted a traditional marriage, "in which the husband was the sole provider and the wife ran the house."[7] The traditional man seemed to have equally conservative sexual views. Many surveys still showed a large majority of men who did not think women should engage in premarital sex or have extramarital affairs. As one female veteran of the New York singles scene said, "It's the same old 1950s rules of the game. . . . I've found a lot of fear of my own sexuality. Beneath the rhetoric lie the same old attitudes."

THE DEATH OF SEX?

At the end of 1982, *Esquire* ran a cover story titled "The End of Sex."[8] The article was illustrated with a photograph of a funeral wreath of dying roses laid over a tombstone which read, "The Sexual Revolution, R.I.P." Sex, as we have just seen, was far from dead. But a certain notion of sex—loving, nurturing, long-term sex —was gone, wrote George Leonard. He announced "the trivialization of the erotic climaxes in the practice of 'recreational sex' in which sexual intercourse becomes a mere sport, divorced not only from love and creation, but also from empathy, compassion, morality, responsibility, and sometimes even common politeness."

Was Leonard bemoaning the death of sex after all, or the birth—already over a decade old—of female sexual autonomy? He implied that women were making it too easy: "Recreational sex palls not so much from its immorality as from its dullness. The plot can be summed up, Hollywood style, in three sentences: Boy meets girl. Boy gets girl. They part." Many of the women reading that article had experienced enough of heterosexuality, whether pre– or post–sexual revolution, to know that recreational sex had always been part of the traditional male repertoire. Whether in 1950 or 1980, casual sex had always been *the* macho symbol, and very few men were complaining as long as they controlled the action.

Men like Leonard were responding to the little-discussed fact that the true heart of the sexual revolution was a change in women's behavior, not men's. "There hasn't been a change in male sexual patterns in the twentieth century," historian Vern Bullough told *Time* in 1984. As that article pointed out, "Studies tend to agree that changes in male premarital sexual behavior since the '30s have been rather modest. Premarital sex rates for women more than doubled between the 1930s and 1971, and sharply rose again to a new peak in 1976."[9]

In the early seventies many young men had taken to the sexual revolution with seeming delight; a whole new pool of sexual partners was now available. Their pattern of sexual activity hadn't changed, but the object of men's casual attractions was now more likely to be the girl next door than some woman of "dubious" reputation. In the fifties, sleeping with a "nice girl" was like walking through a china shop: "You break it, you buy it" held true in both cases, and "shotgun" marriages were common. But by the late seventies, marriage was no longer an obvious conclusion to sexual relations. For one thing, a man could not assume that the woman he was sleeping with was monogamously involved with him. The new premises seemed so difficult for some men to accept that they stumbled all over their ambivalent feelings when they talked about sex. "I know it's a contradiction, thinking it would be nice to marry a woman who is a virgin, yet I want a woman who knows how to enjoy a good time in bed. This doesn't mean I want a woman who has been promiscuous. I'm flattered when a woman comes on to me, but I wonder if she's not just a little too forward," a computer programmer told sex educator Carol Cassell, the author of the 1984 book *Swept Away: Why Women Fear Their Own Sexuality.*[10]

Where women had once participated wholeheartedly, some were now having second thoughts when confronted with male ambivalence—and sexism. Despite all the talk of the sensitive, feminist "new man," too many women claimed to be meeting men who simply could not let them participate with equal control in a sexual relationship. "You have no idea what it's like out there," a woman bus driver in Philadelphia says. Married and divorced, she's been happy to "date around and sleep around." But, she says, "Sometimes they treat me like just another woman who 'puts out' for them. Or they think *I* want commitment and to some men that justifies treating a woman like dirt." It seemed that the kind of man who insists on lighting a lady's cigarette or opening the door for her wasn't ready for a woman who would open the door to new sexual experiences. As British author Wendy Holloway points out, men had more to lose when women used sex, rather than emotional ties, as a criterion for a relationship. "Men can represent themselves according to a set of assumptions in which they are not in need of . . . anything that would make them vulnerable." But, she adds, the invulnerable man often relies on a woman to provide the emotional warmth that eludes him. Women who insist that sex need not involve a love affair are thwarting men's ability to decide when they want access to intimacy.[11]

The relationship between sex and intimacy was confusing for both sexes. Substantial numbers of women, such as this respondent to the *Cosmo* survey, still felt guilty about sex:

> There are nights I say goodbye to a lover to whom I've just given the greatest ecstasies in bed, and I think to myself, Here I am in my

dangerous Greenwich Village apartment, with
its fire escapes and dingy staircases. Maybe
someone will break in and rape me during the
night. Or kill me. Will this guy I'm saying
goodbye to ever wonder about me in the
morning?

For other women, economic insecurity was still a strong
incentive to see sex as the gateway to marriage. As
another *Cosmo* reader said:

In the past a man used to have to offer a relationship in order to get sex. Tat for tit. But
now, since so many women give sex so freely,
the men offer nothing—and we women must
accept this, even if we don't like it. Throughout the centuries women have gotten the
short end of the stick. We're still getting it.[12]

There was more at stake here than just a misunderstanding between the sexes. Women's sexual liberation
had touched social bedrock, threatening ideas about
gender, dependence, family, and marriage. Some people didn't like to be touched there.

The increasing ambivalence of both men and women
coincided with the rightward political drift of the eighties. Under Ronald Reagan the United States Congress
voted funds for "chastity centers," a concept more acceptable to conservatives than family planning or sex
education. The new conservatism brought back the
idea that women were responsible for sexual activity
and therefore to blame when a pregnancy ensued. In
this climate attacks on abortion became both rhetori-
cally and physically violent. Between 1982 and 1985

there were over a hundred bombings and other violent attacks on abortion clinics around the country. With the threats to abortion rights and the growing dangers from sex-related diseases, the message to women was that the risks associated with sex—casual or committed—were escalating unacceptably.

The conservative political atmosphere reinforced the anxieties of men and women who were struggling to assimilate the sexual revolution, and the media were quick to pick up on the new mood of hesitation and nostalgia. By the mid-eighties, the nearly unanimous message presented by the mainstream media was that women were fed up with casual sex. There were few criticisms of men; this was a campaign against women and their sex lives.

THE MEDIA FIGHTS CASUAL SEX

A successful TV executive is quoted in a 1984 article in *New York* magazine on being single in the city: "Maybe I'm a victim of arrested development," says the woman, thirty-two, "but I don't feel old enough to be married. Right now I just want to concentrate on my career and enjoy my life."[13] Her comments, typical of many working women, are followed by those of a psychotherapist specializing in adolescent psychology:

> Two earmarks of adolescence are the beliefs that time is limitless and choices are unnecessary. Many singles in their thirties have adopted that same attitude. In the past, there were certain developmental tasks, like mar-

riage and child-rearing, that signaled one's
adulthood. But in today's urban culture, it's
acceptable to postpone those tasks as long as
possible.

Patricia Morrisroe, the writer of this article, never
questions the strange idea that a woman who maintains
a career and supports herself is not mature. In the same
article a thirty-six-year-old financial analyst in search of
a wife says that "somebody over thirty is a definite
negative." He would also "prefer a virgin. 'Why not?' "
he asks. But there are no therapists in evidence to comment on *his* immaturity.

The article, which is really on the terrors of being
single, is illustrated with bleak drawings of the unmarried life. One shows a woman snuggling up to her pillow in an otherwise empty bed. In another, a business-
suited woman in glasses grabs for but misses a tossed
bridal bouquet. The piece, titled "Forever Single,"
ends with the message that singles had better learn to
compromise in their search for companionship.

In the same vein, when "NBC Reports" ran the documentary "Second Thoughts on Being Single," early in
1984, it implied that women's primary goals are love
and security: They need to get married, while men try
to avoid marriage. The program began with the statement that women of the "baby-boom generation" are
"fed up with modern American men, and modern morality." They want to get married, they want a family,
and, said one of the program's experts, sociologist Pepper Schwartz, they won't get those things if they're
sexually active, because "men [don't] like them to be
very sexually experienced." In case some women might

resent men's dictating the range of their sexual experience, Schwartz also insisted that women really weren't meant for casual sex:

> I don't know many women and I haven't studied many women who think of sex as something they could do and never see the identity of the man they had it with. . . . [There are] many men who, as soon as they've had their sex, would like to say "goodbye, that was great; we both enjoyed it, and I don't want to know you." That is a thought that is pretty foreign to most women.[14]

The program showed attractive, educated women with good jobs who seemed hopelessly lost at singles gatherings; others were working out every day—not for pleasure but for vanity, in the hope of simulating the body of a teenager. Then there were women mooning over other people's babies, proof positive to the viewer that they needed a man and a family. A long parade of academic experts was called upon to show that women were naturally monogamous, or if they weren't, had better be. Tired clichés emanated from experts like Dr. Nancy Moore Clatworthy of Ohio State University, who said, "The farmer used to say that a man certainly wouldn't buy the cow if he could milk the cow through the fence."

Boys and girls have always had very different play patterns, said a psychiatrist, implying that it was therefore no surprise if their sexual proclivities also differed dramatically: "Little boys tend to play organized games like baseball . . . little girls tend to play . . . in pairs." And if some would argue that those differences were

mainly due to socialization, Dr. Donald Symons of the
University of California at Santa Barbara was called in
to present his belief that sexual behavior is biologically
determined. Man's prehistoric role, Symons told narra-
tor Jack Reynolds, was "to impregnate as many healthy
looking females as possible." Women, on the other
hand, had nothing to gain from "random copulation"
and faced "enormous risks by becoming pregnant."
Evolution, he said, had made them congenitally monogamous.

These experts all assumed that women hated casual
sex, but they offered no explanation for why so many
women were engaged in it. In fact, several women on
the program explained that the problem wasn't the sex,
it was the attitudes of the men they were sleeping with.
"I've lost lots of guys because I didn't go to bed with
them," explains one single. But, says another, "If you go
ahead and give in to your desires . . . and you do go to
bed with him, then lots of times you really will lose the
man because they, without even realizing it, feel like
you've been too quick and too easy, and if you're that
way with them, God knows how many other people
you're like that [with]." The only solution, according to
one woman, was to become a "born-again prude." If
there were women who were still willing to fight with
men over their right to sexual freedom, NBC never
found them.

More surprising than *New York*'s profile of a group of
neurotic singles or NBC's born-again prudes was the
new tone of *Cosmopolitan*, the bedside companion of
many practicing singles. Once symbolized by the
tough, sultry woman on the back page of national newspapers who might have been saying, "I can't tell Tom,

Dick or Harry apart. Who cares? I guess you could call me that *Cosmo* girl," the magazine now ran stories such as "Why We Don't Like No-Strings Sex" and "Go Slow: Make Love the Old-Fashioned Way." One article, titled "Sketches from the Single Life: Intimate Glimpses of Five Unmarried Women," read like a fundamentalist tract on the wages of sin. Sex and the single girl? The *Cosmo* girl was going to have to pay a price.

> Anne awakes with a start. She's thrown off the covers and is shivering slightly. The landlord cuts the heat at midnight, and without glancing at the clock, she knows it's later than two. That's when the old lady on the fifth floor starts howling. She's into ghostly moans now— aargh, aargh . . . Home . . . where roaches waltz insolently over the dish drainer . . . and where breakfast is a baloney sandwich and dinner a bowl of cornflakes.[15]

What has brought on this misery? As far as we can tell, it seems to be penance for the days

> when she was by herself so much that she'd sometimes take a man home just for the company. (Morning light on the unlovely skin of a stranger; her body pulling away from his, as if from a disease.)

Anne has just one man she sleeps with now, but things aren't much better. Paul, her lover, wants to spend only weekends together, grouses at her, and is wary of commitment. The vignette about Anne ends on a forlorn note. She will give up this hopeless love affair and buy a puppy for companionship, temporarily alone again in her building where "the old lady's moaning is soon to commence." The consequences of the single life seem to be loneliness and near-insanity.

The other four women's lives aren't any better. One is unemployed, longing for her one true love, who refused to stand by her when she lost her job: "Girls these days operate at a terrible disadvantage. Nancy's pretty and charming and can cook and knows she needs to have a career. But that's not nearly enough to get a really good guy." Another, Nina, "opens sludgy eyes to a steamy July day . . . it gives her a headache!" As far as her current romance with a live-in lover, the best she can say is [I've] "known worse relationships, that's for sure." Most of the time she'd just as soon not have sex with him, for there's no "surging passion." Through Nina, the article presents a textbook example of the wages of guilt. Coming from *Cosmopolitan*, these morality tales were surprising. Some of the magazine's more sexually sophisticated readers, who had once counted on it to reinforce their lifestyles, must have felt as though they had stumbled onto an issue of *Reader's Digest*—circa 1950.

SEX RADICALS SEARCHING FOR LOVE

Another serious blow to mainstream acceptance of casual sex came when two women, famous as sexual mavericks themselves—if only in their writing—executed their own about-faces. Erica Jong, who had delighted many female readers with her breezy, picaresque approach to sex in *Fear of Flying*, was, ten years later, not so sure that women had benefited from the sexual revolution. Her 1984 book, *Parachutes and Kisses,* brought Isadora Wing, her alter ego and heroine of *Fear of Flying,* up to date sexually, and while it documented the frequency and variety of Isadora's sexual encounters, the pleasure of the hunt had definitely given way to the search for true love. Passion was no longer an end in itself. Jong began her book with Isadora's musings on the sexual balance sheet a decade after the revolution: "The world has certainly changed. For one thing there is more oral sex. For another, more impotence. For a third, sex is ubiquitous and yet also somehow devoid of its full charge of mystery."[16]

One could argue that Isadora Wing's cynicism arises from her poor choice in lovers. In *Fear of Flying* the assortment of husbands and lovers included a psychotic who tried to kill her; a conductor "who never bathed, had stringy hair, and was a complete failure at wiping his ass"; a psychiatrist who refused to kiss or speak to her when making love ("each orgasm seemed to be made of ice"); and Adrian Goodlove, mostly impotent, dirty and given to farting in public. No wonder she was now looking for romance.

Wing is, after all, a fictional character. Yet Erica Jong had clearly given some thought to the drawbacks of the sexual revolution. "Many women discovered," she commented in an article surveying the influence of the birth control pill, "that the freedom to say yes to everyone and anyone was really another form of slavery. Repeated, meaningless, one-night stands without commitment did not satisfy their hunger for love and connection, and so the so-called sexual revolution was really more a media myth than a reality." The author who had once celebrated the joys to be found when women chose and experimented with lovers now called sexual liberation a "pseudo event."[17]

Another equally influential woman was on the same trail. Germaine Greer, one of the more glamorous exponents of early feminism, had been the perfect media spokeswoman for some very radical sexual ideas. But after years of espousing sexual freedom, Greer reverted to a philosophy suspiciously like that of the fundamentalist right. In 1984, during an interview following the publication of her new book, *Sex and Destiny,* she told a reporter that by exchanging "fidelity" for "promiscuity," women had traded one form of restriction for another: "The sexual revolution never happened. Permissiveness happened and that's no better than repressiveness."[18] But in *The Female Eunuch* she had asked women, as a "revolutionary measure," to refuse "to commit themselves with pledges of utter monogamy and doglike devotion." She had called for the destruction of "the polarity of masculine-feminine." To achieve this, "individual women [must] agree to be outcasts, eccentrics, perverts, and whatever the powers-that-be choose to call them."[19]

Now, in *Sex and Destiny,* she changed her mind. She recounted with obvious embarrassment how, in the early sixties, she had foisted her feminism on the people of Rossano Calabro, a small Italian village where she had gone to write her doctoral dissertation. She flouted local rules on women's behavior by traveling into town on her bike alone, refusing to lower her eyes when she spoke to men, and wearing a bikini to the beach. Rather than admitting that she might have moderated her stance to accommodate an alien culture, Greer now seemed to regret the spirit of independence that had inspired her actions.

She claimed to have realized her mistake while still working in Rossano Calabro. One day she had an "awakening," in which she suddenly noticed the sexuality of her one friend in the village, sixteen-year-old Rosetta. "Sex was in the air that Rosetta breathed: she was ripe and the ripeness was all. . . . Rosetta . . . had more confidence in her female sexual power than I would ever have." Rosetta, the product of a local "morality . . . much sterner than anything the fat priest preached in the marquis's rose-pink chapel," had never even spoken to the young man she was pledged to marry (although Greer had caught her secretly eyeing his crotch). Yet her sexuality left Greer so envious that she was transformed, she says, knocked, like Saul on the road to Tarsus, right off her seat. "I gave my bicycle away to a little boy, and I took another little boy as my chaperone whenever I went out. I lengthened my skirts and kept my eyes down if a man came towards me, and I wore an old bathrobe to the beach."[20]

But Greer was not simply another woman lost to some fantasy of femininity (as though she could re-create Rosetta's blossoming adolescent sexual awareness through copying the forms of female repression). She had, after all, written *The Female Eunuch* several years after her revelation in Rossano Calabro about women's proper role. In that book all her feminist anger had been presented with clarity and wit. Yet a decade later she was glorifying women's sexual repression.

Soon after the publication of *Sex and Destiny*, Greer told a reporter that she regretted waiting to have a child: "Like many women, I chose not to have a child when I could have. Then when I thought I could fit one into my life I found out I couldn't conceive." Critic Linda Gordon believes this is at the heart of Greer's revisionism. A book "about fertility . . . written by a woman suffering from infertility . . . elicited my sympathy," wrote Gordon in *The Nation.*[21] But, she continued, Greer is "generalizing on the basis of what seems to be her personal response"—and forgetting, one might add, that millions of women, including herself, have fought for the idea that their sexuality is not linked absolutely and eternally to their reproductive capacity.

IT HITS THE SPOT

While women were trying to sort out the mixed messages they were receiving from the media about their sexuality, the medical profession once again entered the public dialogue on sex. Science, in the form of the pill and Masters and Johnson, had helped validate the sexual revolution. Now the same authority was used to debunk the pleasures of variety. Psychologists who had once taken up the cause of sexual freedom and experimentation now adopted a more cautionary stance. Despite some popular exceptions like Dr. Ruth Westheimer, known as Grandma Freud to her legions of fans, liberal ideology was being swamped by the tide of experts welcoming a return to "traditionalism . . . the fad of the future," as one commentator termed the new sexual conservatism. Media therapists, offering advice on radio and TV shows or in newspaper columns that reached millions of Americans, had a strong influence on this trend. Dr. Toni Grant, once described as the most "glamorous" practitioner of public therapy, responded to what she viewed as a mismatch between female and male sexual attitudes by claiming women wanted only love and marriage:

> Uninformed people have misled us to believe we could separate sex from feelings, but very few of us are able to. The sexual act is a more profound event for women, based on the nature of femininity itself. We want long-term bonding and union with a man.[22]

Pepper Schwartz, the NBC singles expert and co-author with Philip Blumstein of *American Couples*, a book described as "the largest and most comprehensive study of American couples ever undertaken," believes with Dr. Grant that women have their priorities wrong. "A lot of women went out and wanted to be adventurous," she said:

> Over time, they found a number of things . . . they weren't getting married. I think they found that they weren't getting respect and they weren't getting love, and over time, it gets real old to have a long sexual dating experience with someone and then [have them] leave you for someone else.[23]

The idea that love and sex were inseparable for women was not a new one, but it was being presented as if it were scientific revelation. The pressure on women to become monogamous was increasing steadily. All that was needed, it seemed, was a way to restore to the sexual act earlier, simpler pleasures. It had become too varied, too difficult to define and pin down. Science would try to resolve this sexual dilemma.

> I have always had orgasms, but I never had much stimulation when the penis was completely inside my vagina. In fact, sometimes my excitement and arousal would end abruptly when the penis entered me completely. I have always been most excitable when the penis was only one-half or one-third its way into my vagina. Now I know exactly why—at that point it hit my "magic spot."

Most readers might assume this woman is referring to her clitoris. Until the early eighties, she probably would have been: The clitoris was our rediscovered magic spot, although the penis might not have been the best instrument to stimulate it. But now, clitoral sexuality's association with female sexual assertiveness seemed to inspire some sexologists to head back into their labs. Their new "scientific" goal was to relocate the penis, which had been missing in action, and bring it back where it belonged—into the vagina, of course.

To slow down the sexual revolution it was necessary to explode the notion that sexual practice should be wildly experimental. The clitoris was too free an agent; to bridle the female libido, and return the lead to men, intercourse had to be brought back into the act as the main event. A debate long since put to bed—clitoral vs. vaginal orgasm—was reawakened. Although feminist writers such as Anne Koedt and mainstream researchers Masters and Johnson had shown in the sixties that all orgasms originated in the clitoris and depended on clitoral stimulation, whether direct or indirect, the new experts insisted on producing new distinctions between orgasms. It made good copy and, more important, was an attempt to reestablish the role of the medical profession in defining sex.

The story of the G spot began in 1950 when Dr. Ernst Grafenberg, a German gynecologist, published an article in the *International Journal of Sexology*. He pinpointed a previously ignored erotic zone located "on the anterior wall of the vagina along the course of the urethra." His findings languished in obscurity for years. Then, in the late seventies, Alice Ladas, Beverly Whipple, and John Perry, a psychologist, nurse, and minister/sexologist respectively, came upon Grafenberg's research and decided to conduct interviews to see if his claims could be validated. Their subsequent book, *The G Spot,* did not give the impression there was much science to their method.[24] There were no charts or statistics to support conclusions. Instead, the authors of *The G Spot* insisted that a surprising 100 percent of 400 female volunteers, all of whom were examined by a nurse or a doctor, were able to locate their G spot. The book was filled with testimonials from these and other women who insisted that only vaginal orgasms would do.

Ladas, Perry, and Whipple said that the vaginal area of the G spot, when properly stimulated, swells and produces an orgasm that is distinct from—and better than—a clitoral one. They also claimed, without getting too specific, that many women ejaculated a fluid through the urethra during a G-spot orgasm. Their statistics: When they asked "coed audiences" if they had experienced female ejaculation, about 40 percent raised their hands. The authors said the G spot was a "vestigial homologue of the prostate"—hence the fluid.

Just as peculiar as the sudden discovery of an unsuspected bodily fluid were the acrobatics necessary to achieve the new orgasm. *The G Spot* advocates jettisoning the missionary position, which would have automatically classified the "new" orgasm as old. Instead they insisted that "man is designed as a quadruped and therefore the normal position would be intercourse *"a posteriori."* This enabled men the maximum thrust, because, as one of their male interviewees said, "Certain women really want you to pound them."

Women were turned on their faces, in a position suspiciously similar to one used for anal sex. Indeed it seemed that one of the authors' goals in pushing the G-spot theory was to bring the anus into focus, for, they implied, anal sex was what men really wanted to perform on women and to have performed on themselves. Men were capable, the authors said, of the same multiple orgasms as women, if their prostates were given enough strokes. The best way to stimulate the male prostate, said Ladas et al, was to insert a finger into the anus. If there were women too squeamish to give their men multiple orgasms in this fashion, the authors issued a warning: "One of the reasons some men may enjoy homosexual relationships is that they often provide more frequent stimulation of the prostate than heterosexual involvements."

The G Spot also presented the insidious notion that women's clitoral obsessions were driving men to homosexuality. But the male tendency to flee from sexually demanding women could be combatted. According to the promoters of the G spot, foreplay was not a good idea, since any stimulation of the clitoris merely distracted women from locating their vaginal centers of pleasure. Men could simply return to immediate penetration without having to worry about women's orgasms. The newly discovered mass of tissue in the vagina would supposedly take care of that. Without the worry, men would not have to resort to homosexuality for old-fashioned, self-centered sex.

From *The G Spot* it was easy to infer that women who had still not discovered their sunken treasures were suffering from some sort of vaginal amnesia. But thanks to John Perry's electronic perineometer, which could be ordered through the mail, women could perform exercises in their homes to strengthen the muscles that held the penis in place. Help was on the way, as long as women were willing to move backward into the eighties.

But the attempt by *The G Spot* authors to reinstitute traditional sexual intercourse seemed merely crude when compared to the very real fears about Acquired Immune Deficiency Syndrome, which began to appear in the early eighties. Once it became clear that AIDS was not restricted to gay men but could be spread during heterosexual intercourse, the hysteria surrounding the disease was an epidemic in itself.

Sexually transmitted diseases such as syphilis, gonorrhea, and herpes, as well as AIDS, lend themselves to public moralizing. But in this case, the backlash against sexual promiscuity was well established before AIDS became a topic of general concern. When it did, it was all too easy to use the tragic new disease to reinforce the developing sexual conservatism. The early response to AIDS centered around the concept of "safe sex": the use of condoms or spermicidal jellies, a reduction in the number of sexual partners, and elimination of drugs such as amylnitrate that can affect the immune system. But as public health educator Nick Freudenberg noted in 1985, the recommendation of safe sex quickly degenerated to no sex. The director of the National Centers for Disease Control, Dr. James Mason, announced that to control AIDS it was necessary to control sex. One California health official suggested that anyone who fell within the risk group or had had sex with someone in the risk group since 1978 should not exchange body fluids with anyone else. "This proscription," said Freudenberg, "rules out most known forms of sexual activity (including kissing) with another person for hundreds of thousands, possibly millions of people." The real motivation behind the "no sex" message, he continued, was "political and religious, not scientific. It seeks to impose on all of us the notion that sex is moral only within marriage." Once again, "objective" scientific thought was being used to further moral proscriptions.[25]

While most people did not yet advocate extremist "solutions" to AIDS, such as quarantines and ID cards for possible carriers, many began to reevaluate the role of casual sex in their lives. "The day of the one-night stand is over," a tennis instructor told a reporter for the New York *Times* in 1986. "I go to bars now to drink, not pick up women, and if I go out with a woman I don't sleep with her until I check up on her history and her reputation." Women too are displaying a new caution. "The fear [of AIDS] gets in your head and it can have a chilling effect on your libido," a California woman reported in the same article.[26]

Casual sex, of the one-night stand variety was definitely on the wane, but celibacy was not the alternative. Many women admitted to approaching new sexual relationships with some trepidation, yet the complete absence of sexuality in their lives seemed unthinkable. Caution and a new kind of intimacy have taken on greater importance as the public waits to see how and if AIDS will spread beyond the initial high-risk groups. For safety's sake women who engage in casual sex are spending more time getting to know their partner's sexual background and as an added precaution using condoms. For everyone seeking either a permanent partner or a temporary relationship, there are of course no guarantees. Someone who unknowingly slept with a carrier in 1980 might pass on the disease in 1986, even if they were monogamous for most of the intervening years. "It's strictly a roll of the dice," said one single woman. Living with that knowledge hasn't been easy, but many women have made adjustments which they hope will limit their risk and which have improved their sex lives in other ways as well. They say they prefer, for reasons of safety as much as health, to know a man more than one night if they are going to let him into their home and bed, or go to his. They also prefer sharing responsibility for birth control and safety techniques with a man as opposed to having sole responsibility in this area. Thus, after improving the odds to the best of their ability, most men and women are still willing to play the game.

CAN THIS REVOLUTION BE SAVED?

In the midst of reaction, the women's sexual revolution was being reappraised as part of an attempt to make sense of the events of the past two decades. Since the analysis the conservatives were offering was inherently antiwoman, the question of who controlled the direction of the revolution became one of the most critical issues to be debated. But feminism, which had helped initiate the sexual revolution in the first place, was now deeply divided over it. Some women, described as "cultural feminists," advocated an ideology that, in emphasizing women's "natural" traits, ended up glorifying attributes painfully similar to the reactionary clichés the conservatives were pushing. To these feminists, women's sexuality could be described in terms of gentleness, nurturance, and "circularity," as opposed to aggressive penetration. Others—who should perhaps be called the new radical feminists—argued that the women's sexual revolution had to be open to all possibilities or a new tyranny would be created. Any attempt at this stage to define women's sexuality was premature and too limiting.

Australian-born feminist Lynne Segal suggested that we still had a long way to go in the sexual revolution before most women would experience a real change in their lives. "Many of the ideologies surrounding 'sex' have remained *unchanged* over the last hundred years," said Segal. "Whatever the questioning which is going on, and whatever the tolerance for 'deviance,' sexuality is still seen in terms of its reproductive functioning, symbolised by a genital heterosexuality which men initiate and control." By restating the important but easily obscured point that sex with men will always be based on the nature of men's and women's relations —collectively and individually—Segal offered a reminder that love, romance, and marriage could be just as painful in a sexist society as anything a sexual adventurer might experience.[27]

If women could acknowledge that the problem was greater than the particular man they slept with, they could also insist on their right to continue pushing forward the frontiers of female sexuality. Lesbian activist Amber Hollibaugh seemed to be speaking for more than just the gay women she was describing when she called for a new kind of "speak-out," in which women would admit their secret yearnings.

> Who are all the women who don't come gently and don't want to; don't know yet what they like but intend to find out; are the lovers of butch or femme women; who like fucking with men; practice consensual S/M; feel more like faggots than dykes; love dildoes, penetration, costumes; like to sweat, talk dirty, see expressions of need sweep across their lovers' faces; are confused and need to experiment with their own tentative ideas of passion; think gay male porn is hot; are into power?[28]

The media were not telling the story of the women who spoke up and questioned sexual orthodoxy, nor was it looking for the women who had become, essentially, the avant-garde of sexuality. They were women like Diane, who, with her short, bright red hair, flashy clothes, and uproarious laugh, is a mixture of punkette and flash:

> I have what I call the "gang boyfriend motif." I have one boyfriend I've had for eleven years [she's thirty-eight]. He's been married twice in that time, and I know and his wife knows we're both better off not having him full-time. He's my main man. Then I have other boyfriends, usually out of town, who I see fairly regularly. I also have one other boyfriend in town, who I really like a lot. They all add up to one big boyfriend, and all my needs get taken care of. It keeps me out of the bars—that's what I call the "desperado motif."

Her main man once asked her to marry him, but "I knew we couldn't live together. We can love each other and I know we always will. It's more fun this way."

Diane's gang boyfriend is proof that a better man— Mr. Right?—does exist, only it takes ten men to make one. Obviously this is not an option for most women; they literally don't have the time to juggle ten men into their schedules, even if they would like to. Yet Diane represents a small but important cadre of independent women who *are* promoting sexual solutions. These are the women who laughingly call themselves "sport-fuckers"; who, given the choice between promiscuity and repressiveness, as Greer saw it, will choose promiscuity, although they would prefer not to be faced with such absolute choices. These are women like this:

> I love the mystery of something new . . . the physical and emotional possibilities of testing myself and him. The variety *is* the turn-on. All those sex manuals insist that it takes experience with a partner to have good sex.

It is not necessary that these women speak for all of us. But their solutions are more than symbols; their choices are not so extreme that they have no relevance. Those on the frontier of sexual choice keep alive options that might otherwise be buried under a reactionary avalanche. What seems experimental and marginal at one time may become an important option for all women at another time. Shulamith Firestone, for example, was once regarded as a radical feminist whose ideas were provocative (she recommended separating reproduction from sexuality by having all babies born outside the womb) but had little application in the "real world." Yet in 1970, in *The Dialectic of Sex*, her ground-breaking study of the need for feminist revolution, she wrote:

> The most important characteristic to be maintained in any revolution is *flexibility*. I . . . propose . . . a program of multiple options to exist simultaneously . . . some transitional, others far in the future. An individual may choose one "life style" for one decade and prefer another at another period.[29]

As Firestone thought, casual sex should be a choice, not a duty imposed by ideology and not a privilege to be whisked away as soon as the political climate turned conservative. But sometimes even options are not negotiable; women have come too far to surrender the range of possibilities opened up by their sexual revolution.

Conclusion

Victories that we do not claim are never really ours to celebrate or improve on; and women's sexual revolution remains, for the most part, unclaimed. True, the benefits of this revolution are ambiguous: The sexual double standard is still firmly rooted in the minds of men, or at least enough of them to make the practice of heterosexuality a risky, potentially bruising enterprise for women. The benefits are unevenly distributed: Women who are young, economically independent, attractive, are much more likely to have come out as victors than the majority who are "old," "unattractive," overworked, and constrained by family and financial necessity. And the benefits, the achievements, can be rolled back at any time by new threats to women's sexual health and self-determination: Abortion could be made illegal, just as it has already been made financially inaccessible to women in poverty. New sexually transmitted diseases, such as AIDS, which may have the potential to spread to the mainstream heterosexual society, could send us in full retreat to involuntary chastity or monogamy.

But to imagine that there was only "the" sexual

revolution and that it was a victory for men and a joke on women, to see women as victims even of their self-chosen ventures, is not only to falsify the past but to foreclose the future. A victory, no matter how partial and unfinished, is worth little until it has been acknowledged. Otherwise, when it comes to the next leap—in our own lives or in the next generational upsurge of women—there will be no ground, no freshly conquered territory, to stand on. And in the case of women's sexual revolution, we accomplished more than we sometimes allow ourselves to see—certainly more than a mass culture grown jaded with "revolutions" and stylishly cynical about "liberation" is willing to *let* us see.

First, we challenged the old definition of sex as a physical act. Sex, or "normal sex," as defined by the medical experts and accepted by mainstream middle-class culture, was a two-act drama of foreplay and intercourse which culminated in male orgasm and at least a display of female appreciation. We rejected this version of sex as narrow, male-centered, unsatisfying. In its single-mindedness and phallocentrism, this form of sex does imitate rape; it cannot help but remind us of the dangers and ambiguities of heterosexuality. At best, it reminds us simply of work: "sex," as narrowly and traditionally defined, is obsessive, repetitive, and symbolically (if not actually) tied to the work of reproduction.

We insisted on a broader, more playful notion of sex, more compatible with women's broader erotic possibilities, more respectful of women's needs. Our success in redefining sex can be measured not only in the reported proliferation of "variations" (not all of which are women's innovations, of course) or surveys documenting changes in sexual routine and practice, but in expectations: Twenty years ago the woman dissatisfied with sex was made to believe she was lacking something; the woman who selfishly advanced her own pleasure was made to worry about being less than normal. Today, it is the woman whose marriage still confines her to phallo-centered sex who knows she is missing something; and it is the woman who does not know how to negotiate or find her own way to pleasure who wonders if she is different, abnormal.

It is strange that such a major change in what we think about ourselves and expect from others should be so little heralded today. Perhaps we let our sexual revolution be trivialized by a media eager to absorb each novelty and, in the process, make it instantly passé. Sex would not be the first arena of women's initiative to be trivialized as the price of minimal acceptance: Demands for a more equal division of labor in the home were initially dismissed as frivolous—and only grudgingly accepted as just—and the same is true of feminist efforts to make everyday language include both sexes. Or perhaps we sometimes minimalize the sexual revolution because we have forgotten already how bound we were to the old version of sex, how limiting it was, and how unimaginable the alternatives seemed.

In addition to redefining the physical act of sex, women's sexual revolution challenged the old "meaning" of sex as it had been interpreted, most recently, by medicine and psychiatry. By focusing on what can be directly perceived and experienced—sensations, the anatomy of sexual response—we did, as the critics so loudly complained, take some of the "mystery" and "magic" out of sex. This was perhaps coldhearted and unromantic of us, but we had come to understand that the "mystery" was simply a form of obfuscation. The grand and magical meanings—eternal love, romance, and, always, "surrender"—were there in part to distract us from the paucity of pleasure. Draped in mystery and mythic themes, sex itself was an act of sublimation for women: not an immediate pleasure to be appropriated but a symbolic act to be undertaken for ulterior aims—motherhood, emotional and financial security, or simply vanity.

Early feminist writers on sex, Barbara Seaman and Shere Hite among others, insisted, at least implicitly, that sex should have no ultimate meaning other than pleasure, and no great mystery except how to achieve it. They realized that for *women* to insist on pleasure was to assert power, and hence to give an altogether new meaning to sex—as an affirmation of female will and an assertion of female power. The old meaning, which in one form or another was always submission to male power, could be inverted.

These are no small achievements—the re-making and the reinterpreting of sex—and it would be both excessive and inaccurate to claim that women did it all or did it all for the cause of sexual liberation. Women made the changes, but many factors contributed to the possibility of change. Improvements in birth control in the sixties, especially the pill, gave women a sense of freedom and flexibility that the more cumbersome, "on-site" methods had never done. The effect of the pill may have been as much psychological as practical; even those who became disillusioned as a result of the side effects and risks gained the conviction that contraception *could* be safe and unobtrusive, and could, if the technology only existed, be the burden of men as well as women. Legal abortion was also, as its opponents correctly perceive, a powerful factor in women's sexual liberation. The more decisively sex can be uncoupled from reproduction, through abortion and contraception, the more chance women have to approach it lightheartedly and as equal claimants of pleasure.

Gay liberation was another contributing factor, no matter how remote it may have seemed from the lives of many who benefited from women's sexual revolution. Gay men and lesbians held out a vision of sex utterly freed from the old reproductive "work ethic" that haunts heterosexuality: Sex could be sheer play; it could be the celebration of a temporary affinity, or the indulgence of long-standing lovers. Lesbianism in particular defied the old medical notion of sex centered on heterosexual intercourse as the psychic and physiological means to fulfillment. If lesbian love could be impulsive, passionate, and satisfying—even if only among some "other" women one had read or heard of—then heterosexual sex was merely an option, and thus subject to a new standard of comparison. One could ask, in imagination, how interesting and enthusiastic a partner one's lover or husband would be if he were constrained from bringing the male organ into play. One could imagine, even more subversively, what sex might be like without a trace of the heterosexual drama of male power and female subordination.

Perhaps most of all, women's sexual revolution was made possible by women's growing economic independence from men. Independence is not the same as affluence: Women still earn just over sixty cents for each dollar earned by men, and women college graduates still earn less, on the average, than male high school dropouts. But independence, even in straitened and penurious forms, still offers more sexual freedom than affluence gained through marriage and dependence on one man. The young office worker who earns barely enough to rent her own apartment, the married woman who brings in her own share of the family income, even the single mother on welfare, have more sexual options than a "kept" woman, married or not. In fact, one reason for the stigmatization of welfare, and hostility to it, is undoubtedly that it offers women independence from individual men and, hence, a certain measure of potential sexual freedom. Male fears of women's sexual independence are at least partly responsible for the cruelly inadequate level of support available.

The last change, especially, has been a long time in the making. Traditional patriarchy rested on the economic interdependence of each member of the family, usually in an agricultural setting. Survival depended on participation in the common effort and in the hereditary division of labor—men plowing, women weaving and hoeing, and so forth. For a woman outside of the family economic unit there was only danger, destitution, rape. With the rise of the market system and a *social* division of labor—still plotted, of course, along gender lines—women's economic independence became at least a possibility. In a sense, women's sexual revolution began with the first "working girl" who kept part of her wage to buy a ribbon or hat, or who was able to afford a room of her own with a door that could be shut. In the 1960s and 1970s, a majority of women entered the work force and gained, if not exactly "liberation," at least the financial leverage to imagine being sexual actors in their own right.

Yet, having come this far in our sexual revolution—much further than our mothers and certainly our grandmothers could have imagined—we seem to find cause less for celebration than for ambivalence and anxiety. For what we have achieved, the remaking and reinterpretation of sex, is something that women both deeply want and deeply fear.

So powerful is the backlash today, and the official new mood of sexual conservatism, that we have to remind ourselves of how ancient and deep that desire is. It is expressed not only in the risks taken by a few exceptional women who defied sexual norms in the name of their own freedom—Emma Goldman, Victoria Woodhull, and Frances Wright are among the better-known examples—but by the repressed history of women's most incoherent, apolitical upsurges. Mass female adulation of the male androgynous rock star who represents sex freed from ulterior motive and daily necessity predates Beatlemania by many centuries. In the Dionysian cult of ancient Greece, women abandoned their household responsibilities for nights of frenzied dancing and worship of the beautiful young god. The witches of fifteenth- and sixteenth-century Europe were accused of similar excesses centered on Satan (who may have represented a god surviving from pre-Christian religion), and perhaps they did indulge in orgiastic rituals, though we have only the witch-hunters' word for it. Certainly their sexuality was at issue, as well as their daring to *assemble*, by night, in what were believed to be wanton rites.

But for most women in traditional societies, the possibility of noninstrumental sex, sex without the price of lifelong subordination to one man, was something glimpsed only at rare events—village holidays, religious festivals, carnivals. The carnival foreshadowed some of the best features of modern urban life: a public space apart from the hierarchy of the family, and crowds large enough to offer temporary anonymity and the license that went with it. In our time we re-create the carnival—or at least a diminished, modern version of it —in the discotheque, singles bar, or in the colorful, impersonal spectacle of consumer culture. We are drawn, as women have been for ages, to the possibility of celebrating our sexuality without the exclusive intensity of romantic love, without the inevitable disappointment of male-centered sex, and without the punitive consequences.

At the same time, though, women have grounds to fear sexual liberation, even their own. The fear is not irrational or neurotic, for if sex is disconnected from marriage, childbearing and family commitments, women stand to lose their traditional claims on male support. The teasing, instrumental sexuality prescribed for single women before the sexual revolution had a purpose, after all: to "land" a man, and to claim him as one's breadwinner for life. If sex is "free," then so, potentially, are men; and women are left to fend for themselves in an economy that still drastically undervalues women's labor. This was a dilemma that the radical feminists of the late sixties and early seventies, who boldly proclaimed the link between sexual liberation and women's liberation, did not always seem to grasp—

or, if they did, to sympathize with. Perhaps they imagined change coming suddenly and conclusively in all areas at once, so that no woman would have to fear financial ruin—or emotional desolation—if both women and men were free to express their sexuality.

But women *are* more vulnerable than men to the hurts and dislocations of a society that is sexually more free than it is just or caring. Women still bear the risks and costs associated with contraception and abortion. If they become mothers they undertake a disproportionate responsibility for their children—in most cases, *all* the responsibility if their marriage dissolves or if they have not married in the first place. If they do not become mothers early enough they may spend their prime years worrying about whether they ever will; men's lives are not constrained by the same biological deadline. If they are unmarried and on their own for any reason, they will, in most cases, have a hard time supporting themselves in an economy that still views men as the only legitimate breadwinners. And, sadly, women still "depreciate" sexually far faster than men: The gray hairs and wrinkles that lend character to a man's appearance only sabotage a woman's. One result is that divorced men are much more likely to remarry than are their ex-wives, and the gap widens ominously with age.

It was the fear of liberation that helped motivate the antifeminist backlash that began in the 1970s. Women who oppose abortion often cite its potential to free *men* from the obligations of marriage and parenthood. The fear is that if abortion is a woman's choice, then there will be no way to convince men that children are, in part, their responsibility too. Furthermore, sexual free-

dom for some women—any heterosexual women—
seems to threaten the marriages and financial security
of others. In a similar vein, women who opposed the
ERA cited women's vulnerability, especially financial
vulnerability, if the "protected status" of wives were
undermined by egalitarian legislation. (Not that marriage, and the slender possibility of alimony after it,
ever offered reliable, long-term protection from poverty. The male breadwinner could always leave, or simply spend his earnings on his own pleasures.) Better
then, from an antifeminist perspective, to resist change
and seek to retie the knots linking sex, marriage, and
the economic dependence of women on their husbands.

The fears are real; so, too, is the desire for a freer,
sexually happier life. Nor do the fears and the desire
divide neatly into demographically distinct groups of
women. It is not only young, attractive, self-supporting
women who champion sexual freedom; just as it is not
only middle-aged, financially dependent married
women who worry that the same "freedom" could
mean poverty and loneliness for them. In fact, very
often, it is the same woman who feels both the fear and
the desire. We *are* ambivalent; we seem almost to be
stuck.

If there is a way out of the ambivalence, or at least a
way to resolve it into alternatives and choices, it has to
be a *feminist* way. We do not say this in a spirit of
dogmatism but on the basis of our own experience.
Feminism is not a "line" or a rigid set of beliefs. Rather,
it is our only collective way of making sense of things *as
women.* As radical feminist Kathy Sarachild wrote over
a decade ago, feminism is a way of asking, "What's good

for *women?*" Feminists will differ on the answer; some or all will be wrong at least some of the time. But the feminist milieu of discussion, analysis, and respect for individual experience is still the only space we have in which to ask that question.

For the most part, feminism has tended to stand back from the sexual revolution it helped to initiate. This is not only because mainstream feminism has shied away from controversies peripheral to its more central goals of economic and political rights for women. Nor is it only because feminists are, rightly, less concerned with the beneficiaries of social change than its victims, the women exploited by men's most callous versions of sexual liberation. There is another reason. In the last decade and a half, many feminists had arrived at their own judgment not only of the sexual revolution but of heterosexuality itself, and that judgment—without ever being announced or formally debated—has tended to be profoundly negative.

We are talking not about a superficial and unexamined kind of puritanism but about a deeper kind of insight: Feminists came to understand that sex and gender are not so easily separated after all. That is, sex as an act or activity is not so easily disentangled from gender as a social arrangement in which women, from as far back as there is history to tell us, are unequal and inferior. As the Australian socialist-feminist Lynne Segal writes, sex is, above all, "the endorsement of gender." Heterosexual sex, and especially intercourse, is a condensed drama of male domination and female submission. The man "mounts" and penetrates; the woman spreads her legs and "submits"; and these postures seem to ratify, again and again, the ancient authority of men over women.

To put it another way: Heterosexual sex has had many uses, but it has had, over and over, one social meaning, and that is male domination over women. Midcentury psychoanalysts reinforced this meaning with theories of innate female masochism, and their views filtered into a body of sex "expertise" that prescribed sex as a ritual of husbandly domination and wifely submission. Ordinary men reinforce the same meaning every day when they tell their adversaries to "get fucked." This is not just an accidental limitation of the language: Sex, or women's role in it, is understood as a humiliation no man would want to endure.

So no wonder feminists have retreated from the subject of sex as well as the project of sexual liberation. In the late nineteenth century, feminists accepted the social meaning of sex as female subordination and saw it as an ordeal that women would endure only for the sake of motherhood. Contemporary feminists who campaign against pornography do not go so far as to say that sex itself is an ordeal or insult to women, but what else can be meant by their frequent insistence that every *representation* of heterosexual sex—however "softcore"—is an insult to women and an assault on our rights? For if sex is the ratification of male power, then will it not always be a secret refutation of everything feminism stands for? Does feminism have any real option but to be puritanical or, what almost amounts to the same thing, utterly silent on the subject of sex?

But silence is itself defeat. Just as you cannot have sexual liberation without social equality for women, you cannot have equality in every other domain and an unacknowledged ritual of male domination in the bedroom. You cannot have feminist rationality in the light of public discussion and archaic dramas of power and violence in the dark. Sex cannot be left as a lingering biological embarrassment, something we try to put behind us as we campaign for our public rights. Feminism has no choice, then, but to confront sex—to challenge its social meanings—or be undone by it.

In fact, thanks to women's sexual revolution, there has never been a more auspicious moment for feminism to grapple with sex as an opportunity and an issue. We did challenge the narrow, heterosexual definition of sex as the touchstone and standard for sexual experience. And we did call into question the social meaning of sex. Without the ancient consequences of pregnancy and dependence on male support, sex could "mean" anything we wanted, and could just as well symbolize our own widening aspirations as women.

Quite apart from our conscious efforts to re-make and reinterpret sex, sex changed and diversified in ways that implicitly mock the old and presumedly natural meanings. Where, for example, is the great drama of domination and submission when a woman buys masturbation aids from a mail-order catalog? What happens to the meaning of that drama when two women—butch and femme lesbians—can play all the parts? More profoundly, perhaps, S/M—by making domination and submission into a consciously chosen and deliberately scripted ritual—deprives these venerable themes of their "natural" role in heterosexuality. This is not because ritualistic S/M is widely practiced (we have no real idea of how prevalent it is), but because it is now widely *known* as a potential option or variation. As an imaginable option, it provides an ironic commentary on what has traditionally been understood as normal heterosexuality. If roles can be assumed as easily as costumes, and even traded off for variety, then male power is not the majestic theme our bodies are molded to express, inescapably, time after time.

But it is for our own sake as individual women, as well as for the sake of feminism as a political movement, that we need a feminist reevaluation of sexuality. For if we don't want every pleasure and sensation burdened with "meaning," we *do* need to give meaning to our lives, to our collective aspirations, and to the inchoate social change we call the sexual revolution. In the absence of feminist interpretation, we have no way of apprehending any part of this revolution as our own. It becomes someone else's—a victory for men, or for members of sexual "minority groups," or for anyone but the female majority. Or it becomes trivialized as a product of the consumer culture, the counterculture, the pharmaceutical industry—anything rather than being the product of our own desires and efforts.

The consumer culture offers the ultimately meaningless version of sexual revolution. We have seen the importance of the marketplace in institutionalizing the sexual revolution and offering a relatively neutral space within which women can experiment and learn. But the very neutrality of the market on the matter of small choices—do you prefer flavored cream or bondage gear, pornography or more refined erotica?—amounts to a resounding agnosticism on the meaning of our *collective* choices as women. The sexual marketplace offers sexual revolution without revolutionary ideology, innovation without daring, new frontiers without the old risks of exploration. The problem is not that the market makes choices easy, but that it obscures the fact that a more fundamental, social choice is being made at all.

When we participate in a revolution that we do not acknowledge, when we snatch small pleasures out of a context of unchallenged repression, we risk becoming mean-spirited and sly. The result is already apparent in today's mixture of sexual confusion, evasion, and bad faith: Fundamentalists appropriate a more feminist version of sexuality to shore up the patriarchal marriage . . . Male beneficiaries of the sexual revolution declare it over and done with just as they begin to fear that women may be taking their own sexual revolution too far . . . Young women and teenagers claim to disapprove of premarital sex in rising numbers but engage in it anyway, and their denial contributes to the highest rate of teen pregnancy among the industrialized nations . . . Men who have benefited from the sexual double standard join the chorus of voices labeling women who support abortion as selfish or murderous.

This massive bad faith carries real dangers. Hypocrisy can pave the way to new forms of selective repression—of the promiscuous, the "deviant," or those who are merely honest. Denial can open new possibilities for sexual exploitation, as what cannot be spoken cannot easily be protested. And evasion guarantees that sex will slip back into the old morass of mystery, obfuscation, and false and oppressive meanings.

What, finally, are we afraid of when we stand back from our own sexual revolution, when we leave it unannounced, unclaimed, uncelebrated? Ridicule, perhaps, or a loss of dignity, and for women, dignity is still a scarce and precious resource. If we are feminists, we are under pressure—by no means entirely external pressure—to confine ourselves to the "real issues," the urgent matters of economic survival and political power. If we are simply individual women striving for independence and respect, we often find ourselves working hard just to *appear* hardworking and worthy of being taken seriously. We are afraid of seeming silly, afraid of becoming more vulnerable than we already are.

In a society that holds up an increasingly punitive work ethic above any ethic of love or compassion, it is risky indeed to assert *pleasure*—perhaps especially sexual pleasure—as a legitimate social goal. But to remain silent is to concede to a particular political mentality and view of the world. The same mentality that denies a "free lunch" to hungry schoolchildren seeks to restore the reproductive consequences of sexuality. The same mentality that would require mothers on welfare to "work off" their meager benefits would replace family planning and sex education with "chastity centers." Even on the more liberal fringes of politics, talk of "liberation" or of any expanding sense of human possibility can be dismissed as the dated utopianism of a more naive decade.

Yet it is precisely this punitive mood that most challenges us to pick up the lost thread of sexual liberation. If the "real issues" are economic deprivation, the threat of nuclear holocaust, the destruction of the environment, and so forth down the grimly familiar list, then we should perhaps acknowledge that the issue of human pleasure is not, after all, so marginal or secondary. For the "real issues" only reflect our vast, collective separation from the body, from the earth and other life on it, and from the possibility of delight in ourselves and each other. We may have come to the point where we no longer have the luxury—and puritanism can be a perverse kind of luxury—of dividing what is "real" from what is only personal; what is public, from what is most deeply felt. We may finally be obliged, by the very threats we have created for ourselves, to rethink pleasure as a human goal and reclaim it as a human project.

Notes

Chapter 1

1. Frederick Lewis, "Britons Succumb to 'Beatlemania,' " New York *Times Magazine,* December 1, 1963, p. 124.

2. Timothy Green, "They Crown Their Country with a Bowl-Shaped Hairdo," *Life,* January 31, 1964, p. 30.

3. "How to Kick the Beatle Habit," *Life,* August 28, 1964, p.66.

4. David Dempsey, "Why the Girls Scream, Weep, Flip," New York *Times Magazine,* February 23, 1964, p. 15.

5. Quoted in Nicholas Schaffner, *The Beatles Forever* (New York: McGraw-Hill, 1977), p. 16.

6. "George, Paul, Ringo and John," *Newsweek,* February 24, 1964, p. 54.

7. "What the Beatles Prove About Teen-agers," *U.S. News & World Report,* February 24, 1964, p. 88.

8. "Beatles Reaction Puzzles Even Psychologists," *Science News Letter,* February 29, 1964, p. 141.

9. Betty Friedan, *The Feminine Mystique* (New York: W. W. Norton, 1963), p. 282.

10. Quoted in Schaffner, op. cit., p. 15.

11. "Queen Bee of the High School," *Life,* October 11, 1963, p. 68.

12. Lester D. Crow, Ph.D., and Alice Crow, Ph.D., *Adolescent Development and Adjustment* (New York: McGraw-Hill, 1965), pp. 248–49.

13. Dr. Arthur Cain, *Young People and Sex* (New York: The John Day Co., 1967), p. 71.

14. Pat Boone, *'Twixt Twelve and Twenty: Pat Talks to Teenagers* (Englewood Cliffs, N.J.: Prentice-Hall, 1967 edition), p. 60.

15. Connie Francis, *For Every Young Heart* (Englewood Cliffs, N.J.: Prentice-Hall, 1962), p. 138.

16. Grace and Fred M. Hechinger, *Teen-Age Tyranny* (New York: William Morrow and Co., 1963), p. 54.

17. "Shaping the '60s . . . Foreshadowing the '70s," *Ladies' Home Journal,* January 1962, p. 30.

18. Quoted in Philip Norman, *Shout! The Beatles in their Generation* (New York: Simon and Schuster, 1981), p. 200.

19. Samuel Grafton, "The Twisted Age," *Look,* December 15, 1964, p. 36.

20. Hechingers, op. cit., p. 151.

21. Albert Goldman, *Elvis* (New York: McGraw-Hill, 1981), p. 190.

22. Schaffner, op. cit., p. 9.

23. Goldman, op. cit., p. 191.

24. Quoted in Schaffner, op. cit., p. 17.

25. Quoted in Schaffner, op. cit., p. 16.

26. Ellen Willis, *Beginning to See the Light* (New York: Alfred A. Knopf, 1981), p. 63.

Chapter 2

1. Jacqueline Susann, *The Valley of the Dolls* (New York: Bantam, 1966), pp. 2–3.

2. Betty Friedan, *The Feminine Mystique* (New York: W. W. Norton, 1963), p. 261.

3. Ibid., p. 263.

4. Alfred C. Kinsey, Wardell B. Pomeroy, and Clyde E. Martin, *Sexual Behavior in the Human Female* (Philadelphia: W. B. Saunders, 1953), p. 641.

5. Ferdinand Lundberg and Marynia F. Farnham, *Modern Woman: The Lost Sex* (New York: Harper and Bros., 1947), p. 269.

6. Susann, op. cit., p. 174.

7. Th. H. Van de Velde, M.D., *Ideal Marriage: Its Physiology and Technique* (New York: Random House, 1961; first printing, 1930), p. 189.

8. Ibid., p. 7.

9. Ibid., p. 242.

10. Drs. Hannah and Abraham Stone, *A Marriage Manual* (New York: Simon and Schuster, 1968; first printing, 1935), p. 233.

11. Dr. David Reuben, *Any Woman Can!* (New York: McKay, 1971), pp. 19, 31.

12. Van de Velde, op. cit., pp. 201–2.

13. Ibid., p. 235.

14. Lundberg and Farnham, op. cit., p. 275.

15. Hendrik M. Ruitenbeek, ed., *Psychoanalysis and Female Sexuality* (New Haven: College and University Press, 1966), p. 11.

16. Ibid., p. 12.

17. Ibid., p. 14.

18. John D'Emilio, *Sexual Politics, Sexual Communities: The Making of a Homosexual Minority in the United States, 1940–1970* (Chicago: University of Chicago Press, 1983).

19. Kermit Mehlinger, M.D., "The Sexual Revolution," *Ebony,* August 1966, pp. 57–62.

20. Helen Gurley Brown, *Sex and the Single Girl* (New York: Pocket Books, 1962), p. 246.

21. Ibid., p. 4.

22. Ibid., p. 206.

23. Ibid., p. 207.

24. Stanlee Miller Coy, *The Single Girl's Book: Making It in the Big City* (Englewood Cliffs, N.J.: Prentice-Hall, 1969), p. 260.

25. Brown, op. cit., p. 215.

26. See Barbara Seaman, *Free and Female: The Sex Life of the Contemporary Woman* (New York: Coward, McCann & Geoghegan, 1972), p. 63, and Judd Marmor, "Some Considerations Concerning Orgasm in the Female," in Ruitenbeek, op. cit., pp. 198–208.

27. Quoted in Patrick McGrady, "Can the Love Doctors Help Your Sex Life?" *Vogue,* November 1972, p. 144.

28. Dr. Leslie Farber, "I'm Sorry, Dear," *Commentary,* November 1964, p. 47.

29. Lundberg and Farnham, op. cit., p. 29.

30. Alix Shulman, "Organs and Orgasms," in Vivian Gornick and Barbara Moran, eds., *Woman in Sexist Society* (New York: Basic Books, 1971), p. 292.

31. Anne Koedt, "The Myth of the Vaginal Orgasm," in Leslie B. Tanner (ed.) *Voices of Women's Liberation* (New York: New American Library, 1971), p. 39.

32. Quoted in Seaman, op. cit., p. 36.

33. Betty Dodson, "Getting to Know Me," *Ms.*, August 1974, p. 106.

34. Norman Mailer, *Prisoner of Sex* (New York: Little Brown, 1971), p. 77.

Chapter 3

1. Richard Meryman, "Troubled Marriage," *Life*, October 2, 1972, p. 56.

2. Steve Carter, *What Every Man Should Know About the New Woman: A Survival Guide* (New York: McGraw-Hill, 1984), p. 40.

3. Th. H. Van de Velde, M.D., *Ideal Marriage: Its Physiology and Technique* (New York: Random House, 1961), p. 145.

4. J, *The Sensuous Woman* (New York: Dell, 1969), p. 22.

5. Robert J. Levin and Amy Levin, "Sexual Pleasure: The Surprising Preferences of 100,000 Women," *Redbook*, September 1975.

6. Chris Weygandt, "The *Oui* Sex Survey: Fellatio," *Oui*, June 1980, p. 83.

7. Ibid., p. 127.

8. Theodore Fischer, "The *Oui* Sex Survey: Cunnilingus," *Oui*, November 1980, p. 48.

9. Shere Hite, *The Hite Report* (New York: Macmillan, 1976), p. 233.

10. Seymour Fisher, *Understanding The Female Orgasm* (New York: Bantam Books, 1973).

11. Helen Kaplan, *The New Sex Therapy* (New York: Brunner/ Mazel, 1974).

12. Gay Talese, *Thy Neighbor's Wife* (New York: Doubleday, 1980), p. 349.

13. Alex Comfort, *The Joy of Sex* (New York: Simon & Schuster, 1972), p. 225.

14. Nancy Friday, *My Secret Garden* (New York: Pocket Books, 1974), p. xi.

15. Lonnie Garfield Barbach, *For Yourself* (New York: Anchor Press/Doubleday, 1976), p. 9.

16. Eva Margolies, *Sensual Pleasure* (New York: Avon Books, 1981), p. 137.

Chapter 4

1. *The Pleasure Chest Compendium of Amourous & Prurient Paraphernalia* (New York: Pleasure Chest, Ltd., 4th edition, 1979), p. 6.

2. Tony Ko.nheiser, "Oh, Those Calendar Men," Washington *Post,* December 7, 1983, p. B4.

3. Nancy Collins, "Sex and The Single Star," *Rolling Stone,* August 18, 1983, p. 19.

4. Carrie Rickey, "Unholy Trinity," *The Village Voice,* May 25, 1982, p. 52.

5. Jean Callahan, "Video Erotica Comes Home," *Playgirl,* November 1984, p. 78.

6. Michael Korda, "Love Bites and Slaps: What to Make of Them, When to Play the Fantasy Game, When to Draw the Line," *Self,* July 1981, p. 80.

7. Daniel Goleman, "Sexual Fantasies: What Are Their Hidden Meanings?" New York *Times,* February 24, 1984, p. 1.

8. Ibid., p. 1.

9. Ibid., p. 1.

10. Charles Allen Moser, unpublished doctoral dissertation for the Institute for Advanced Study of Human Sexuality, completed August 1979.

11. Pat Califia, "A Secret Side of Lesbian Sexuality," *The Advocate,* December 27, 1979, p. 21.

12. John Leo, "Stomping and Whomping Galore," *Time,* May 4, 1981, p. 73.

Chapter 5

1. Joanne Young Nawn, private conversation, 1982. We would like to thank Ms. Nawn for her telephone discussions on this topic in 1982. All references to her work are part of those discussions.

2. Michael Braun and George Alan Rekers, *The Christian in an Age of Sexual Eclipse* (Wheaton, Ill.: Tyndale House, 1981), pp. 78–79.

3. Quoted in "A Debate on Religious Freedom," Norman Lear and Ronald Reagan. *Harper's,* October 1984, p. 16.

4. Barry Siegel, "Religious Right Grows and Fights," Los Angeles *Times,* May 15, 1985, p. 1; William Greider, "Attack of the Christian Soldiers," *Rolling Stone,* May 9, 1985.

5. "Jerry Falwell's Crusade," by Richard N. Ostling, *Time*, September 2, 1985, p. 50.

6. Braun and Rekers, op. cit., p. 81.

7. Claire Safran, "Can the Total Woman 'Magic' Work for You?" *Redbook*, February 1976, p. 128.

8. Martin E. Marty, "Fundies and Their Fetishes," *Christian Century*, December 8, 1976, p. 11.

9. Erling Jorstad, *Evangelicals in the White House: The Cultural Maturation of Born Again Christianity 1960–1981* (New York: Edwin Mellen Press, 1981), p. 100.

10. Ibid., p. 102–5.

11. Joyce Maynard, "The Liberation of Total Woman," New York *Times Magazine*, September 28, 1975, p. 106.

12. Marabel Morgan, *Total Joy* (Old Tappan, N.J.: Fleming H. Revell, 1976), p. 143.

13. Maynard, op. cit., p. 58.

14. Emma Goldman, *Living My Life*, Volume II (New York: Dover, 1970), p. 555.

15. H. Page Williams, *Do Yourself a Favor: Love Your Wife* (Plainfield, N.J.: Logos, 1973), pp. 101–2.

16. Ostling, op. cit., p. 51.

17. Tim and Beverly LaHaye, *The Act of Marriage: The Beauty of Sexual Love* (Grand Rapids: Zondervan, 1976), see chap. 5, "The Art of Lovemaking."

18. Ibid., pp. 275–78.

19. Kenneth L. Woodward, "The Bible in the Bedroom," *Newsweek*, Feb. 1, 1982, p. 71.

20. Tim and Beverly LaHaye, op. cit., pp. 33–34.

21. Gini Andrews, *Your Half of the Apple: God and the Single Girl* (Grand Rapids: Zondervan, 1972), pp. 83–84.

22. Edward B. Fiske, "College Aims to Be Fundamentalism's Notre Dame," New York *Times*, Sept. 30, 1981, p. 26.

23. Tim and Beverly LaHaye, op. cit., p. 246.

24. Bob Lardine, "Wonder Woman Finds God, Love and a New Career," New York *Daily News*, February 28, 1982, p. 5.

25. W. Peter Blitchington, *Sex Roles and the Christian Family* (Wheaton, Ill.: Tyndale House, 1980), see chap. 3, "God Had a Purpose in Creating Two Sexes."

26. Barbara Grizzuti Harrison, "The Books that Teach Wives to Be Submissive," *McCall's*, June 1975.

27. Beverly LaHaye, *The Spirit-Controlled Woman* (Eugene, Oregon: Harvest House, 1976), p. 73.

28. Pauline Reage, *The Story of O* (New York: Grove Press, 1965), pp. 15–17.

29. Braun and Rekers, op. cit., p. 114.

30. Williams, op. cit., pp. 17–18.

31. Telephone interview with Dr. Anson Shupe, 1982.

32. Andrews, op. cit., p. 90.

33. Ed Wheat, *Intended for Pleasure* (Grand Rapids: Zondervan, 1981), p. 226.

34. Aimee Sands, producer for WGBH radio, Boston, a three-part series *Women on the Right*, 1982.

35. See Braun and Rekers, op. cit., p. 116; Wheat, *Intended for Pleasure*, p. 162; Andrews, op. cit., p. 30.

36. Andrews, op. cit., p. 84.

Chapter 6

1. Patricia Morrisroe, "Forever Single," *New York*, August 20, 1984.

2. Shere Hite, *The Hite Report on Male Sexuality* (New York: Alfred A. Knopf, 1981), p. 405.

3. "Redbook's Sex Questionnaire: What Readers Had to Say," and "The Redbook Report on Premarital and Extramarital Sex: The End of the Double Standard?" *Redbook*, June and October 1975.

4. Linda Wolfe, *The Cosmo Report: Woman and Sex in the '80s* (New York: Bantam, 1982), p. 153.

5. "Sex and the Married Woman," *Time*, January 31, 1983.

6. "Sex and Success: A Savvy Survey," *Savvy*, October 1985.

7. Roper organization poll for Philip Morris Co., conducted March 1985.

8. George Leonard, "The End of Sex," *Esquire*, December 1982.

9. John Leo, "Sex in the '80s: The Revolution Is Over," *Time*, April 9, 1984.

10. Carol Cassell, *Swept Away: Why Women Fear Their Own Sexuality* (New York: Simon & Schuster, 1984), pp. 99–100.

11. Wendy Holloway, "Heterosexual Sex: Power and Desire for the Other," in Sue Cartledge and Joanna Ryan, eds., *Sex and Love:*

New Thoughts on Old Contradictions (London: The Women's Press, 1983).

12. Wolfe, op. cit., pp. 247–48.

13. Morrisroe, op. cit.

14. "Second Thoughts on Being Single," *NBC Reports*, April 25, 1984.

15. Barbara Creatura, "Sketches from the Single Life," *Cosmopolitan*, March 1984, p. 221.

16. Erica Jong, *Parachutes and Kisses* (New York: New American Library, 1984), p. 2.

17. Elizabeth Pearson-Griffiths, "The Pill + 25," Interview with Jong in *US*, June 3, 1985.

18. Justine DeLacy, "Germaine Greer's New Book Stirs a Debate," New York *Times*, March 5, 1984.

19. Germaine Greer, *The Female Eunuch* (New York, McGraw-Hill, 1970), pp. 322–25.

20. Germaine Greer, *Sex and Destiny: The Politics of Human Fertility* (New York: Harper & Row, 1984), pp. 111–13.

21. Linda Gordon, "Bringing Back Baby," *The Nation*, May 26, 1984.

22. Ellen Kessner, "The Delights of Sexual Mystery," *Cosmopolitan*, September 1984.

23. "Second Thoughts on Being Single," op. cit.

24. Alice Kahn Ladas, Beverly Whipple, and John D. Perry, *The G Spot and Other Recent Discoveries About Human Sexuality* (New York: Holt, Rinehart and Winston, 1982).

25. Nick Freudenberg, "AIDS and Health Education," *HealthPAC Bulletin*, Vol. 16, No. 4, July–August 1985, p. 29.

26. Jon Nordheimer, "With AIDS About, Heterosexuals Are Rethinking Casual Sex," New York *Times*, March 22, 1986, p. 7.

27. Lynne Segal, "Sensual Uncertainty, or Why the Clitoris Is Not Enough," in Cartledge and Ryan, eds., *Sex and Love*.

28. Amber Hollibaugh, "Desire for the Future: Radical Hope in Passion and Pleasure," in Carole S. Vance, ed., *Pleasure and Danger: Exploring Female Sexuality* (Boston: Routledge & Kegan Paul, 1984), p. 403.

29. Shulamith Firestone, *The Dialectic of Sex: The Case for Feminist Revolution* (New York: Bantam, 1971), p. 227.

Bibliography

Altman, Dennis, *The Homosexualization of America* (New York: Beacon, 1983).

Andrews, Gini, *Your Half of the Apple: God and the Single Girl* (Grand Rapids: Zondervan, 1972).

Barbach, Lonnie and Levine, Linda, *Shared Intimacies: Women's Sexual Experiences* (New York: Bantam, 1980).

Belz, Carl, *The Story of Rock* (New York: Harper Colophon, 1972).

Blitchington, W. Peter, *Sex Roles and the Christian Family* (Wheaton, Ill.: Tyndale House, 1980).

Blumstein, Philip, and Schwartz, Pepper, *American Couples* (New York: William & Morrow, 1983).

Braun, Michael, and Rekers, George Alan, *The Christian in an Age of Sexual Eclipse: A Defense Without Apology* (Wheaton, Ill.: Tyndale House, 1981).

Cartledge, Sue and Ryan, Joanna, eds., *Sex and Love: New Thoughts on Old Contradictions* (London: The Woman's Press, 1983).

Cassell, Carol, *Swept Away: Why Women Fear Their Own Sexuality* (New York: Simon & Schuster, 1984).

Comfort, Alex, ed., *The Joy of Sex* (New York: Crown Publishers, 1972).

De Beauvoir, Simone, *The Second Sex* (New York: Vintage, 1952).

Dworkin, Andrea, *Pornography: Men Possessing Women* (New York, Perigee, 1981).

Dworkin, Andrea, *Right Wing Women* (New York: Perigee, 1983).

Eisenstein, Zillah R., *Feminism and Sexual Equality: Crisis in Liberal America* (New York: Monthly Review Press, 1984).

Epstein, Barbara Leslie, *The Politics of Domesticity: Women, Evan-*

gelism, and Temperance in Nineteenth-Century America (Middletown, Conn.: Wesleyan University Press, 1981).

Firestone, Shulamith, *The Dialectics of Sex* (New York: Bantam, 1971).

Foucault, Michel, *The History of Sexuality, Vol. 1: An Introduction* (New York: Vintage, 1980).

Friday, Nancy, *My Secret Garden: Women's Sexual Fantasies* (New York: Pocket Books, 1974).

Friday, Nancy, *Men in Love, Men's Sexual Fantasies: The Triumph of Love Over Rage* (New York: Delacorte, 1980).

Friedman, Scarlet, and Sarah, Elizabeth, eds., *On The Problem of Men: Two Feminist Conferences* (London: The Women's Press, 1982).

Gay, Peter, *The Bourgeois Experience: Victoria to Freud, Vol. 1, Education of the Senses* (New York: Oxford University Press, 1984).

Greer, Germaine, *The Female Eunuch* (New York: McGraw-Hill, 1980).

Greer, Germaine, *Sex and Destiny* (New York: Harper & Row, 1984).

Griffin, Susan, *Pornography and Silence* (New York: Harper & Row, 1981).

Hadden, Jeffrey K. and Swann, Charles E., *Prime Time Preachers: The Rising Power of Televangelism* (Reading, Pa.: Addison Wesley, 1981).

Hite, Shere, *The Hite Report on Male Sexuality*, (New York: Alfred A. Knopf, 1981).

Hite, Shere, *The Hite Report* (New York: Macmillan, 1976).

Hunt, Morton, *Sexual Behavior in the Seventies* (Chicago: Playboy Press, 1974).

J, *The Sensuous Woman* (New York: Dell, 1969).

Jong, Erica, *Fear of Flying* (New York: Holt, Rinehart & Winston, 1973).

Jong, Erica, *Parachutes and Kisses* (New York: New American Library, 1984).

Jorstad, Erling, *Evangelicals in the White House: The Cultural Maturation of Born Again Christianity, 1960–1981* (New York: Edwin Mellen Press, 1981).

LaHaye, Tim and Beverly, *The Act of Marriage: The Beauty of Sexual Love* (Grand Rapids, Zondervan, 1976).

LaHaye, Beverly, *The Spirit-Controlled Woman* (Eugene, Oregon: Harvest House, 1976).

LaHaye, Tim, *Understanding the Male Temperament* (Charlotte, N.C.: Commission Press, 1977).

Lederer, Laura, ed., *Take Back The Night: Women on Pornography* (New York: Bantam, 1982).

Marsden, George, *Fundamentalism and American Culture: The Shaping of Twentieth-Century Evangelicalism, 1870–1925,* (New York: Oxford University Press, 1980).

Masters, William H. and Johnson, Virginia E., *Human Sexual Response* (Boston: Little Brown, 1966).

Mollenkott, Virginia R., *Women, Men and the Bible* (Nashville: Abingdon Press, 1977).

Morgan, Marabel, *The Total Woman* (Old Tappan, N.J.: Fleming H. Revell, 1973).

Morgan, Marabel, *Total Joy* (Old Tappan, N.J.: Fleming H. Revell, 1976).

O'Neill, William L., *Coming Apart: An Informal History of America in the 1960's* (Chicago: Quadrangle, 1971).

Paige, Connie, *The Right to Lifers* (New York: Summit, 1983).

Penner, Clifford and Joyce, *The Gift of Sex: A Christian Guide to Sexual Fulfillment* (Waco, Texas: Word Books, 1981).

Reich, Wilhelm, *The Sexual Revolution: Toward a Self-Governing Character Structure,* trans. from the German by Theodore P. Wolfe (New York: Farrar Straus & Giroux, 1962).

Phillips, Eileen, ed., *The Left and the Erotic* (London: Lawrence & Wishart, 1983).

Seaman, Barbara, *Free and Female: The Sex Life of the Contemporary Woman* (New York: Coward, McCann & Geoghegan, 1972).

Shedd, Charlie and Martha, *Celebration in the Bedroom* (Waco, Texas: Word Books, 1979).

Shupe, Anson, and Stacey, William, *Born Again Politics and the Moral Majority: What Shall We Make of Them?* (New York: Edwin Mellen Press, 1982).

Snitow, Ann; Stansell, Christine, and Thompson, Sharon, eds., *The Powers of Desire* (New York: Monthly Review Press, 1983).

Spence, Helen, *The Beatles* (New York: Crescent Books).

Stimpson, Catherine R. and Person, Ethel Spector, *Women: Sex and Sexuality* (Chicago: Chicago University Press, 1984).

Talese, Gay, *Thy Neighbor's Wife* (New York: Dell, 1980).

Vance, Carol S., ed., *Pleasure and Danger: Exploring Female Sexuality* (Boston: Routledge & Keegan Paul, 1984).

Weeks, Jeffrey, *Sexuality and Its Discontents* (London: Routledge & Keegan Paul, 1985).

Wheat, Ed, *Intended for Pleasure* (Grand Rapids: Zondervan, 1980).

Williams, H. Page, *Do Yourself a Favor: Love your Wife* (Plainfield, N.J.: Logos, 1973).

Wolfe, Linda, *The Cosmo Report: Women and Sex in the '80s* (New York: Bantam, 1982).

Young, Perry Dean, *God's Bullies: Power, Politics and Religious Tyranny* (New York: Holt, Rinehart & Winston, 1982).

Index

BRINGING

ADAM

HOME

BRINGING

ADAM

HOME

THE ABDUCTION THAT CHANGED AMERICA

Les Standiford

with Detective Sergeant Joe Matthews

An Imprint of HarperCollinsPublishers

HarperCollins books may be purchased for educational, business, or sales promotional use. For information please write: Special Markets Department, HarperCollins Publishers, 10 East 53rd Street, New York, NY 10022.

FIRST EDITION

Designed by Mary Austin Speaker

Library of Congress Cataloging-in-Publication Data

Standiford, Les.
 Bringing Adam home : the abduction that changed America / Les Standiford with Detective Sergeant Joe Matthews. — First edition.
     p. cm
   ISBN 978-0-06-198390-0
   1. Walsh, Adam. 2. Kidnapping—Florida—Case studies. 3. Murder—Investigation—Florida—Case studies. I. Matthews, Joe, detective sergeant, author. II. Title.
 HV6603.W35S73 2011
 364.15'23092—dc22
                                                                    2010043572

11 12 13 14 15   OV/RRD   10 9 8 7 6 5 4 3 2 1

This book is dedicated to the memory of
Alexander Standiford, 1991–2009;
to Mama Margaret Matthews, 1914–2008;
and, of course, to Adam Walsh, 1974–1981,
as well as all the other sons and daughters
taken long before their time.

After the first death, there is no other.
—DYLAN THOMAS

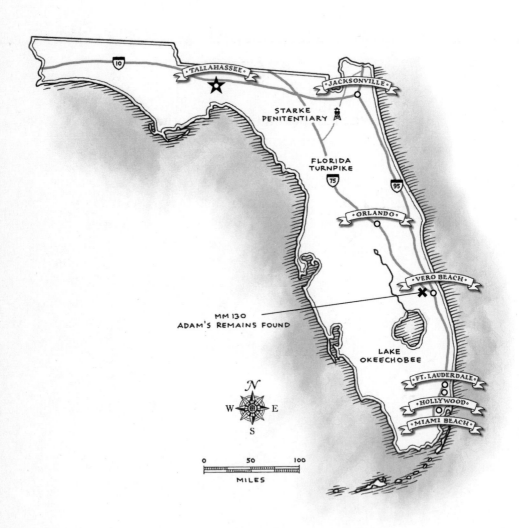

CONTENTS

ACKNOWLEDGMENTS

Sincere thanks are due to Mitchell Kaplan, who saw from the beginning what this endeavor might become; to agent-without-peer Kimberly Witherspoon, who has yet to accept no for an answer; to Jeanne Wilmot, who got it right, right off; and to Dan Halpern and Bill Strachan, who brought this book lovingly into the light.

The authors would also like to offer thanks to Revé and John Walsh, not only for their assistance but for everything they have done on behalf of children and parents everywhere; to Susan Schindehette, who blazed this literary trail, for her advice and encouragement; to the gracious volunteer staff at the Hollywood (Florida) Historical Society; to indefatigable Florida International University reference librarian Adis Beesting; to indispensable adviser Robert Rotstein, Esq.; and to irreplaceable reader Rhoda Zelda Kurzweil.

Particular thanks are also due to any number of individuals within the community of law enforcement and justice, but especially to Joseph Kaplan, attorney for the Miami Beach Fraternal Order of Police, and former Broward County prosecutor Kelly Hancock.

Les adds his own special thanks to Kimberly, Jeremy, and

Hannah Standiford, who believed in and encouraged him and reminded him each day why this story simply must be told. We trust that "Z" would have been proud.

And, from Joe Matthews: How do I begin to thank my wife, Ginny, for her love, dedication, and loyalty? Her encouragement from the moment of Adam's abduction drove me not to give up. Thanks to my children—Joey, Greg, Michael, and Christina— their spouses, and all of my grandchildren for reminding me what is really important. To my brother Peter Matthews for being my big brother, and to my kid sister Mariann Kresge and her son Emir for being very special to me. To my dear friends and colleagues Tom Hunker, Pat Franklin, and Bernie Winer for their advice and support, and to my lifelong friends Tom Panza and Dick Brickman for being there for me always. To my assistant, Mary Alvarez, for having the patience of a saint, and to John and Revé Walsh for their unquestioning trust, which allowed me to give them the justice they so much deserved. And to Hollywood Chief of Police Chad Wagner and Broward County Chief Assistant State Attorney Chuck Morton for their integrity and their desire to put justice first.

CHAPTER ONE

In the Beginning

HOLLYWOOD, FLORIDA—JULY 27, 1981

Shortly after lunch on what seemed an ordinary summer afternoon, a young South Florida housewife set out on a shopping trip with her six-year-old son in tow. It was the sort of outing that millions of other mothers all across the country might have taken on any given day. Her husband, a sales and marketing manager for a local hotel company, had noticed an ad in that morning's newspaper and called home to say that the brass barrel lamps they had been looking for had just gone on sale at the local Sears store. Maybe she ought to run over and take a look.

She was happy to do it—they'd been wanting the lamps, and the chance to save a few dollars seemed too good to pass up. She freshened herself up, dressed her son in shorts, a polo shirt, flip-flops, and his favorite way-big boat captain's hat, and set out for the store.

It was a Monday, typical ninety-degree weather with humidity just as high, but that was July in South Florida for you. Come January, when the rest of the country was in a deep freeze, Floridians would have payback. Besides, traffic in their suburban town of Hollywood was light that early afternoon, and it was less than a two-mile drive to the Sears Mall. As a bonus, the parking space she liked to use—near the receiving dock, on the building's north side, where the whole family could remember it—was open.

Just inside the doors, at the entrance to the toy department, her son spotted a video display with a demo of the new Asteroids game running, and he begged his mother to let him play.

She hesitated, but home furnishings was just a couple of aisles away, and besides, the world had not yet turned upside down. She pointed out to her son where she was going and told him she'd be back in a few minutes to pick him up. She gave her son a kiss, then, and hurried off to see about those lamps.

She would relive the moment a hundred—perhaps a million—times. Had she just said no to him, "Stay with me"; had she simply returned to the game display a minute sooner; had any one of a thousand things happened differently in the slightest— as it is said that the flapping of a butterfly's wings in the Amazon can form a tsunami in a distant time and place—perhaps what occurred might not have occurred at all.

But there is no changing what did happen that day. The mother found a salesperson in home furnishings easily, but there was a bit of a problem: they searched up and down the bright aisles but could find none of the barrel lamps on display. The clerk was happy to check in the back, of course—it would only take a moment. Which turned into something more.

When the clerk finally returned, her downcast expression said it all. The store had not received any of the advertised lamps, but they would be happy to call the moment they came in. The mother quickly gave her name and number and hurried back to where she'd left her son.

She could hear the clamor of spaceships and cannon fire tearing the air as she hurried down the aisle, and smiled at her son's passion for such games. But when she rounded the corner, she stopped short. The game was running, but its stations were deserted, the sounds issuing mechanically from the demo loop. She glanced about, puzzled, hoping she would see her son browsing in the nearby toy department, or ambling toward her from where she had been. But she did not.

She fought the surge of panic that every mother feels when she turns and finds her child suddenly lost from sight. The ripples on the surface of the nearby pond are all menace. The sounds of distant traffic suggest catastrophe and grief and guilt.

But she would not panic foolishly, this mother. She would retrace her steps. She would have the store announce her son's name, and that he should find a clerk and report himself. While store personnel stood ready, she would return to the place she had left her car. He would be waiting there, or he would come to her, or she would find him. She would not panic. She would find her son. Surely, she would find her son.

WASHINGTON, D.C.—FEBRUARY 13, 2006
At a Capitol Hill press conference, a reporter stood to ask a final question of John Walsh, leading proponent for the about-to-be-debated Adam Walsh Child Protection and Safety Act. Walsh, a private citizen, had become perhaps America's most recognizable crime fighter owing to his work as executive producer and host of the long-running television program *America's Most Wanted.* But also, in the wake of the 1981 kidnapping and murder of his son Adam, he and his wife, Revé, had dedicated much of their lives' energies to raising awareness of the problem and the plight of missing children in America.

As a result of the Walshes' work had come the passage of the 1982 Missing Children Act, the establishment of the National Center for Missing and Exploited Children in 1984, and the national AMBER Alert program of 2003. Walsh considered the new bill that was about to go before Congress the capstone of a life's work removing impediments to the recovery of the nearly 800,000 children who are reported missing in the United States each year.

"Mr. Walsh," the reporter began. "You've done much good work on behalf of children and families everywhere, and you've brought any number of heinous criminals to justice with your television show. But I'm wondering if it ever bothers you that you have been unable, in all these years, to find out who killed your own son?"

It was a question asked out of ignorance, the sort of thing that made several in the room wince. Walsh managed to respond without losing his composure, but following the incident, he and Revé contacted longtime associate and *America's Most Wanted* investigator Joe Matthews to set up a meeting that would prove to be momentous. As a veteran homicide detective for the Miami Beach Police Department, Matthews had supervised and conducted more than 20,000 criminal investigations and over 2,000 death and homicide investigations, and had obtained confessions and convictions in a number of high-profile cases, including Miami's infamous Baby Lollipops torture-murder, that of Washington State's spree killer Chad Daniel Roberts, and Canada's University of Waterloo serial rapist Christopher Meyer.

But more important, Matthews, a widely recognized polygraph expert, had been involved in the investigation of Adam Walsh's disappearance and murder from the very beginning, twenty-five years before. His skill and tireless efforts to bring mistakes and overlooked evidence to the attention of those in charge of that still-unresolved investigation had earned him the respect and the friendship of the Walshes over the years, and following his retirement from the Miami Beach force, Matthews had gone to work as a lead investigator for *America's Most Wanted*, where he was quickly credited with solving the program's first cold case investigation, the killing of a former high school wrestling champ by four football players at Lock Haven University, in Pennsylvania.

Matthews was well aware that for all the good work that the Walshes had accomplished over the years, there still existed a

great void in their lives. Adam was gone, and though both they
and he had expended vast resources and energy trying to do
what the authorities had been unable to do, the person responsible had never been brought to justice. And for all the effron-
tery of the reporter's question, it was scarcely the first time it
had been asked: the Walshes had been asking virtually the same
thing of themselves—if only privately—nearly every day for a
quarter century.

On this day, however, Matthews could see that something
different had taken over the Walshes' demeanor. Perhaps it was
the pain of such a jab coming in a context of seeming triumph
with the passage of the Child Protection and Safety Act. Or perhaps the Walshes had simply heard one insensitive question too
many. Whatever, Matthews thought as he waited for the Walshes'
words, he'd walk through fire for John and Revé Walsh.

Normally, it was John who did most of the talking, but on
this day, Revé took over before her husband could get started.

"Joe," she told Matthews in no uncertain terms, "I'm begging
you. I know it's asking a lot, but I want you to go back through
everything we've all tried to show the cops over the years. I want
you to give it one last shot: put everything together and prove
who killed our son, once and for all."

Matthews had made his decision before Revé was finished.
He was honored that she'd even ask, he told her. He was an
investigator through and through, and he had witnessed her
suffering and that of her husband from the beginning of their
ordeal. In truth, he had been aching for much of his adult life
to do the very thing that she had just asked of him. He took her
hands in his and nodded. He would give it his best shot, and he
would start at once.

CHAPTER TWO

Blood of the Lamb

Q: Do you remember if she was a hitchhiker?

A: Yeah, I think she was.

Q: Did she have a name?

A: I wouldn't know.

Q: Didn't you ask her name when you picked her up?

A: I suppose so. I didn't pay much attention to stuff
like that.

—OTTIS TOOLE, TO AN INVESTIGATOR,
JACKSONVILLE COUNTY JAIL, DECEMBER 28, 1983

MIAMI BEACH, FLORIDA—JULY 31, 1981

When veteran Miami Beach PD homicide detective Joe Matthews got the call on Friday from captain of Hollywood detectives
Steve Davis, asking that Matthews assist his department in the
investigation of the disappearance of six-year-old Adam Walsh,
Matthews was more than willing to join in. He was well aware of
the anguish that had gripped the entire South Florida community since the boy had vanished earlier in the week. The reward
offered for Adam's safe return had risen to $100,000, the highest
ever for a missing child in the United States, and the case, which

would be likened to the Lindbergh kidnapping, had attracted the attention of news media, not to mention cops, across the region.

Four days had passed since Adam had gone missing from the Sears store in Hollywood, and though twenty-five officers assigned to the Hollywood PD detective bureau had worked the case full-time, along with assistance from officers from Broward and other South Florida counties, what scant leads they'd uncovered had come to nothing. There was no reason to suspect that Adam had simply run away or wandered off; there were no disaffected family members who might be suspected of abducting him; nor had there been any ransom note or report of anything unusual spotted at the Sears store that day. In short, there had been nothing, and in the days long before AMBER Alerts, children's faces on milk cartons, and national databases that linked police departments in missing children cases, the Hollywood PD was up against a wall.

Furthermore, there was good reason for Captain Davis to contact Matthews. Matthews, thirty-five, had been employed by the City of Miami Beach since 1967, and had quickly risen through the ranks, promoted after only a year and a half as a patrolman to detective for the Criminal Investigations Division. In 1973, shortly after he married his wife, Ginny, he was promoted to the rank of detective sergeant. At about the same time, Matthews—always skilled at interrogation—had enrolled in a state-certified program for polygraph examiners, figuring the training would make him a better cop and, quite frankly, expand his prospects. He and Ginny had plans to start a family, and making do on a cop's salary was always a challenge.

By 1976 Matthews had become the chief polygraph examiner for the Miami Beach Police Department and had started his own state-certified school for polygraph examiners—a sideline that became more and more profitable as word of Matthews's skills as both an investigator and an instructor spread throughout the South Florida law enforcement community. The burly, avuncular Matthews was regarded as a tough but fair cop by his colleagues, and his meticulous style of interviewing subjects prior to the actual polygraph exam itself had proven to be most effective. As he was fond of reminding his students, "How can you know what kind of questions to ask if you don't know the person you are asking them of?"

Among those many students he had trained over the years was Steve Davis, who had even gone on to intern under Matthews at his Southern Institute of Polygraph. And while Davis considered himself an able polygraph examiner, along with others who performed the same duties within the Hollywood police department—many of them also trained by Matthews—in this case he wanted the best. Matthews was not only a top polygraph examiner, he was a highly regarded cop and investigator.

"We need you up here," Davis told Matthews, who needed little convincing. When he had heard the initial news bulletins late on the afternoon that Adam had disappeared, Matthews's initial reaction was one of sadness, mixed with some resignation. He was an experienced police officer, after all, and the world was a hard place. Maybe the Walsh boy had just wandered away and gotten lost. Hopefully, he hadn't fallen into one of the many canals that stitched the narrow habitable strip of South Florida land between the Everglades and the Atlantic. Hopefully, he would turn up safe somewhere.

But shortly after Matthews got home that evening, his feelings began to change. Ginny met him just inside the door, the kids' pj's tucked under her arm, wondering if he'd heard the news. He *had* heard, Matthews assured her.

"My God, Joe," she told him, then. "I was on my way to that same Sears this afternoon. But Joey got sick, and I had to turn around. It could have happened to us, that's what I keep thinking."

Matthews stopped, staring back at her, feeling goose bumps prickle even his thick skin. They lived in the unincorporated area known as Southwest Ranches, then a sparsely populated area of

Broward County a few miles from the fringes of real civilization and the Hollywood store where Adam had gone missing. The houses there sat on lots of an acre or more, and some neighbors still kept horses. The urban centers of Fort Lauderdale and Miami were nearby, and if you wanted a dose of the city, you could easily get it. But out here you could pretend you were still part of an old-time Florida, where foxes and raccoons and possums roamed, and if you were talking about predators, you meant the eagles and hawks and ospreys that still cut the skies overhead.

Matthews glanced into the family room, where his brood—four kids in five years—were raising their usual clamor in front of the TV set while Scooby-Doo hightailed it from a make-believe monster. His oldest son Joey was almost exactly the same age as Adam Walsh, born one day before him, on November 13, 1974. After Joey, there had come two more sons, Greg and Michael, and in 1979, just two weeks before Joey's fifth birthday, their daughter Christina was born. The things you take for granted, he found himself thinking, a wave of dread drifting over him.

It was a feeling that only increased over the course of the week, as reporters continued to chronicle the lack of results in the search for Adam Walsh. By the time Davis called to issue his plea, Matthews was more than primed to help. "Anything I can do," he assured Davis, who immediately put in a call to Emmit Miller, Miami Beach police chief, asking that his former instructor be loaned to HPD to conduct interviews and polygraph examinations.

"We need all the help we can get," an anxious Davis told Chief Miller, and the deal was done.

MIAMI BEACH, FLORIDA—AUGUST 5, 1981

In truth, the Miami Beach that Sergeant Matthews set out from to meet with his Hollywood PD counterparts the following Wednesday bore very little resemblance to the high-octane, pretty-peopled playground of today. Nor had it yet become the drug-fueled, money-laundering center of exotic crime mirrored in *Miami Vice*, where Crockett and Tubbs donned unstructured suits and chased swarthy miscreants in cigarette boats and Ferraris.

There was crime in Miami Beach to be sure, but it was still largely the old-fashioned variety that made its own kind of sense. From the 1930s, mob money had fueled the glittering beachfront resorts where big-name talent performed and movers and shakers cavorted, but much of that was about providing willing customers with what they craved: babes, booze, cards, and dice. Victimless crime, as it used to be called, and hardly a thing that outraged anyone, unless you happened to be standing behind a pulpit on Sunday morning. Besides, by 1981, most of the gambling action had moved on to Las Vegas and other climes, and the Eden Rocs, the Fontainebleaus, and their paler cousins up the Beach were already sliding toward irrelevance.

Residents of Miami Beach, as well as Americans just about anywhere, were aware of a trend toward more disturbing crimes. Truman Capote's depiction of the senseless 1959 murders of a Kansas farm family in his landmark *In Cold Blood* had opened the eyes of a nation to the possibility that dim-witted losers or small-time grifters might morph into homicidal maniacs at a moment's notice. Ten years later would come the stunning Manson Family murders in Los Angeles.

In the wake of the Clutter and Tate/LaBianca killings had come a number of ghouls to command the headlines, including David Berkowitz, the "Son of Sam," who terrorized New York City in 1976 and 1977, killing six persons and wounding seven more in a series of shootings that he said were ordered by a demon who possessed his neighbor's dog. Even more prolific was Ted Bundy, the law student turned killer of coeds and young women, at least thirty of them, including half a dozen in North Florida.

Not only had the nature of evil begun to divorce itself from any semblance of rational explanation, it seemed, but subsequent developments would suggest that the forces of good had lost their power to respond. In 1979, sixty-six Americans were taken hostage in Iran, and the mighty U.S.A., for all its bluster, appeared powerless to do anything about it. A vaunted military rescue operation failed miserably, and only the ouster of yet another president, it seemed, was enough to appease the kidnappers—not until 444 days had passed, and Ronald Reagan had replaced Jimmy Carter, were the last fifty-two hostages released.

There were other signs as well that fault lines had begun to split an orderly world. In December of 1980, apparent lunatic Mark David Chapman pumped four bullets into the back of Beatles singer John Lennon—perhaps the most beloved entertainer of his age—as he strolled arm in arm with Yoko Ono outside his Manhattan apartment. Chapman could offer no reason for the killing beyond the voice inside his head that told him, "Do it, do it, do it."

The attempt on Ronald Reagan's life by John Hinckley Jr. on the following March seemed positively rational in comparison—at least Hinckley claimed that he wanted to impress actress Jodie Foster. Nor did it compare to the events of May 13, 1981, when would-be Turkish assassin Mehmet Ali Ağca shot Pope John Paul II four times as he made an appearance in St. Peter's Square. Theories abound as to why Ağca did what he did—he has been described as everything from an addled opponent of all things capitalist to an agent of the Russian KGB to a brainwashed operative of a Muslim cabal. But what was certain was that someone had actually fired bullets into the body of the pope of the Catholic Church with the intent to kill.

And yet for all the impact such actions may have had upon the underlying psyche of a civilization, it remained in some ways a doggedly innocent age. When in late 1980 Calvin Klein presented CBS-TV with a jeans ad in which fifteen-year-old actress Brooke Shields dared to murmur, "You know what comes between me and my Calvins? Nothing," the network indignantly banned the spot.

And there were other concerns to divert the attention of a nation, as well. The first IBM personal computers were rolling off assembly lines, the wedding of Prince Charles and Diana Spencer was set for July 29, and thirty million tongues were wagging that Luke and Laura from television's *General Hospital* would soon follow suit.

So far as any national obsession with crime went, the burning question in most American minds for most of the previous year was, "Who shot J. R.?" The final episode of the highly successful television series *Dallas* had ended that spring with a cliffhanger in which an unknown assailant fired a bullet into the body of overbearing Texas kingpin J. R. Ewing. More viewers than in all previous television history—an estimated 83 million—watched J. R. go down, and, due to an ensuing Hollywood writers' strike, they would have to wait until late November to learn who pulled the trigger.

As for "ordinary" crime in Miami Beach, there was no short-age of it, not given what had recently taken place in Castro's Cuba, just ninety miles from Florida. In April of 1980, some 11,000 Cubans seeking to escape the clutches of the Communist regime sought refuge on the grounds of the Peruvian embassy in Havana, setting up a clamor that resounded in the world press and had the Cuban émigré community in South Florida seething.

Faced with yet another political and public relations night-mare while also loath to do anything that did not somehow redound to his own benefit, Castro hit on a solution that he con-sidered genius. He would open the nearby port of Mariel, he announced, and allow any Cuban Americans with relatives who wanted to leave the island to come down and pick them up. The response of the Cuban community in South Florida was over-whelming. The ensuing Mariel Boatlift put just about every one of the area's seaworthy craft (and a number that were not) into service shuttling refugees across the narrow Florida Straits.

But the apparent gesture of mercy in fact came with a heavy price. In order to rid himself of undesirables who put a strain on his own social services infrastructure, Castro emptied his jails of criminals of every stripe and his mental institutions of the most deranged, shuffling these individuals into the desperate throngs that filled the docks at Mariel. In the month of May 1980 alone, almost 90,000 Cubans arrived in Miami, many of them without relatives, without education, without prospects . . . and many of them with long histories of violent and criminal acts. It was the beginning of the *Scarface* era in Miami, and the truly despicable of the Marielitos found easy pickings among the frail and the elderly in South Florida, and particularly in Miami Beach, which had long been a haven for retirees.

In fact, the incident that was often talked about when Joe Matthews's name came up among those in the know was one that had taken place at about this time in South Beach, long before it became a glamorous place.

For far less than the cost of a night's lodging in the Delano or the Carlyle today, a retiree in 1981 might have been able to lay down a month's rent for a room in any of the crumbling Art Deco relics that occupied the stretch of Ocean Drive from Fifth to Fifteenth. In those days, the tourists and the players were still staying well northward up the beach, and there were no buxom models or chiseled skateboarders to dodge on South Beach, no plethora of fern-draped sidewalk cafés to choose from, no daisy chain of Maseratis nosed to Lamborghinis nosed to Aston Martins clogging the streets, no $25 valet parking, no pricey boutiques selling furs for pets.

In the de facto retirement village of South Beach, you had your room, and your hot plate, and after some soup for supper, you could walker yourself to the elevator, jigger it down to the lobby, don your plastic nose protector and a pair of those wrap-around sunglasses the size of windshield heat reflectors, and go out to join your fellow pensioners on the hotel porch. You'd sit there in an aluminum chair welded to the next and the next—maybe there'd be room for twenty cheek by jowl on either side of the lobby door—and you'd stare out at the lovely Atlantic through sunglasses dark enough to keep Dracula safe from disintegration, hundreds of you on all those porches up and down Ocean Drive, like members of some strange white-beaked, dark-banded species waiting for the arrival of a ship on the darkening ocean, like you might be ready to step on board that ship and head off somewhere far, far away.

It was to one such establishment—the Shoreham—that Joe Matthews and his team had been called. Matthews was at the time still a young beat cop who had been selected as part of a crime-fighting task force formed by legendary Beach PD chief Rocky Pomerance. An informant in Chicago had passed along a tip that was relayed to the Miami Beach PD that a gang from Chicago that had knocked over some other hotels was headed south and had the Shoreham in its sights as a robbery target. It was the kind of crime that police departments were well equipped to fight, and accordingly a dozen or so cops were hidden on the premises for the first couple of nights: they posed as guests and night clerks, jammed into closets and anterooms, itching for action, but as more and more evenings passed without incident, the size of the detail was trimmed.

Finally, only Matthews and two others were left to the assignment, and as yet more evenings passed uneventfully, his companions gradually became more focused on the nightly card game they set up in one of the anterooms off the lobby and the boozing that went along with it. Matthews was no teetotaler, but he was not a drunk, either. He'd have a drink or two, and play some cards, but invariably he'd be the last man standing by 3:00 or 4:00 a.m., left to keep an eye out on a deserted lobby while the others slept until sunup and time to go home.

He'd almost fallen asleep himself the night things turned all the way around. He heard the lobby door open about 4:15 a.m., and glanced through the curtains of the anteroom where he was stationed to see that three men wearing ski masks and carrying pistols had entered the lobby. Matthews gripped the shoulder of the partner slumped facedown on the table next to him. "Holy shit," he whispered. "They're here. Wake up."

The answer was a muttered curse, followed by a racketing snore. As for the third member of the team, he was fast asleep in another room. Meantime, one of the bandits already had a pistol at the back of the head of the night clerk—an actual civilian who had unluckily returned to the job—and was marching him toward the safe deposit boxes.

History suggested to Matthews what would happen next. The minute the boxes were open, the clerk was likely to be shot. If some bewildered pensioner stumbled onto the scene, whether drawn by the commotion or simply wandering into the lobby thinking he'd found the bathroom down the hall from his room, his fate was likely to be the same.

From the start, in fact, the stakeout team—Matthews among them—had been agreed as to strategy. It was a simpler time in law enforcement. These were bad people they'd been sent to deal with. The thugs would be given a chance to surrender, but if one of them tried anything stupid—and they might well be afforded the chance to—there'd be justice dispensed on the spot. "Whatever it takes" was the task force's watchword. Chief Pomerance had made that much clear.

However, any previous thoughts of strategy were gone from Matthews's mind now. It was him versus three. Even though he'd recently gone through the FBI's SWAT and sniper training academy in Quantico, he knew that a shoot-out would not work in his favor. At the same time, he was not going to hide out in an anteroom and hope that just this once, the gang would be content to empty a safe and leave a potential witness behind unharmed.

Matthews offered up an unspoken prayer, hoisted the shotgun leaning against the wall nearby, and eased silently out the door of the anteroom into the lobby. He carried about 185 pounds on his big-boned five-foot-ten frame, but he wasn't counting on his size to accomplish anything. Instead, he racked a shell into the chamber of the shotgun, a sound that rarely fails to gain a criminal's attention.

"If any of you move, you're dead," he called to the three, the Browning braced at his shoulder. At least *some* of you will be, he was thinking. "Put your guns down, *now*," he added. "And put your hands behind your heads."

Put down your guns and hold up your hands, Matthews heard the mocking echo of his own words in his head. Oh, sure, he thought, preparing himself for the fusillade to come next.

But amazingly, that is exactly what the three men did, and Matthews had handcuffed them all by the time anyone else came to.

It is the kind of story that cops love, and just one more reason why Steve Davis wanted Matthews's help on what was by far the most challenging case his department had ever faced. The Hollywood PD was considered one of the most efficiently run in Broward County, but as the days rolled by without any trace of Adam Walsh, and public scrutiny intensified, it was becoming clear that what was essentially a small-town force (the 1980 population of the city was just over 120,000) was in well over its head.

The department had a new building, a data-crunching computer paid for by federal funds, a Citizens' Crime Watch with more than 4,000 volunteers, and an active, visible chief in Sam D. Martin, proud of such accomplishments as Operation Reindeer, which had been successful in driving down the number of shopping mall robberies at holiday time. But the truth was that Hollywood, Florida, despite its proximity to the glamour towns of South Florida, was an outpost of Mom and Pop America. Drive a couple of miles inland from the beach, and you might as well be cruising the strip mall barrens of Dubuque or Des Moines.

Yet if the place was ordinary, it was becoming clear by the hour that the Adam Walsh case was anything but. According to FBI figures, somewhere between 750,000 and 800,000 children under the age of eighteen are reported missing in the United States each year—an average of more than 2,000 a day. Of these, the vast majority are runaways or young children who wander off and are quickly found. Another 250,000 or so turn out to have been taken by a feuding spouse or family member, or a friend involved in a family dispute. A very few missing children turn out to have met with some tragic accident.

Fewest of all are the victims of what statisticians call "stereotypical" kidnapping, where a child is taken by someone he does not know, or knows only slightly: someone who holds the child overnight, transports him more than fifty miles, demands a ransom or intends to keep the child forever, or—woe upon woe—someone who kills the child.

Only about one hundred children a year are the victims of such a kidnapping, making the odds of losing a child to illness or accident far greater. But parents have been programmed from the beginning of time to cope with the specter of a fatal illness or accident, no matter how tragic. Terrible as such losses are, they at least occur within the bounds of reason.

In contrast, the concept that another human being might have taken one's son or daughter is simply not part of the rational equation of parenthood—or at least it was not in 1981. Yet with every day that passed in the case of Adam's disappearance, the odds increased exponentially that no good end would come.

And still, for all that, and for all the assurances that Steve Davis had given Joe Matthews about how much they needed him on board, it didn't take Matthews long to discover that his association with the Hollywood PD was going to be something other than a honeymoon. Matthews was familiar with the spacious new headquarters building at 3250 Hollywood Boulevard, having been called there several times in the past to lecture on interrogation methods and polygraph examination techniques. But moments after he parked his unmarked Plymouth sedan and entered the building on this go-around, he encountered the first in what would be a long series of challenges to his involvement in the case.

Inside the building, Matthews reported to Lieutenant Dick Hynds, who worked under Steve Davis in supervising the detective bureau. All went smoothly enough at first. Hynds, whom Matthews had never met, was a heavyset old-timer who carried maybe 240 pounds on his six-foot frame—the kind of guy Central Casting would send over if you called and asked for "a cop." The two exchanged a few pleasantries, then Hynds walked him down a corridor to the desk of Detective Jack Hoffman, lead investigator on the Adam Walsh case.

Hynds explained to Hoffman that Matthews had come up from Miami Beach to lend a hand in interviewing and polygraph examinations. Hoffman glanced up impatiently from a report in front of him. He was a heavyset, dark-haired guy with a bushy mustache that accentuated the droop of his lips. He looked like a guy who disapproved of most things on general principle, Matthews thought.

"Why do we need somebody from Miami Beach?" Hoffman asked Hynds brusquely. He hadn't so much as glanced at Matthews. "We've got our own polygraph people."

"This is the guy who *trained* our people," Hynds offered, but Hoffman turned back to his report without a word.

Matthews thought it an unnecessary display of territory marking, but he'd been around a lot of cops. Some guys just seemed to think it necessary to protect their turf. Besides, he knew Hoffman was under considerable pressure, and after all, he'd come up from Miami Beach to help, not start trouble. He shrugged and followed Hynds out of the room without comment.

"Anyway, we want you to start with the father," Hynds told

Matthews as they walked back down the hall, and Matthews nodded. It was natural. Something goes wrong—a spouse is shot, a child goes missing—you begin by looking at the people closest to the situation. Law of averages.

Hynds suggested that they set up the polygraph exam for the day after tomorrow. Meantime, Matthews could familiarize himself with the case files and review what John Walsh seemed to know about his son's disappearance. On Friday, Matthews would go to work on Walsh himself.

HOLLYWOOD, FLORIDA—AUGUST 7, 1981

If they had in fact shown him everything, Matthews concluded after studying the files, then indeed the Hollywood PD did not have much to go on. According to her statement, Revé Walsh had run up and down the aisles of the Sears store for a few minutes after she'd returned and found her son gone, calling for Adam by his nickname, "Cooter, Cooter, where are you?"

Finally, she spotted a store security guard, seventeen-year-old Kathy Shaffer, and rushed to Shaffer to report that she had lost her child. Revé reached into her wallet and pulled out Adam's first-grade picture to show it to Shaffer. "Look, he's even wearing this same shirt," Revé said, pointing at the red-and-white-striped shirt she'd dressed him in that morning. Shaffer studied the photograph for what seemed a maddening amount of time, then finally shook her head.

"We can page him, though," Shaffer told Revé, who glanced at her watch. It was almost 12:45. She and Adam had entered the store almost forty-five minutes ago.

Revé waited nearby while Shaffer made a call, then listened as the announcement crackled over the store's PA system. "Adam Walsh, please report to the information desk. Adam Walsh, your mother is waiting for you."

"It was like I was drowning in a pool and couldn't reach

the edge," Revé would say, trying to describe how unreal her world had suddenly become. "I was trying to reach my child, but he couldn't hear me. I felt so helpless. I kept thinking that if I could just get everything to slow down for a minute, then I could catch my bearings and catch hold of everything. And then I could reach out and pull Adam back."

The announcements were repeated again at 1:00 p.m. and every fifteen minutes thereafter, but Adam did not appear. Revé questioned every store employee she could find, but no one remembered seeing Adam, and worse yet, none seemed too concerned. By 1:55, two hours after Adam's disappearance, Revé was nearing hysteria. Using a Sears phone, she called the Hollywood police to report that her son was missing. Then, fighting back tears, she called her husband John at work and told him what had happened.

By the time John Walsh arrived at the mall, it was almost 3:00 p.m., and a cluster of Hollywood police cruisers were nosed up to the curb outside the garden entrance to the Sears store, their flashers whirling. He parked quickly and ran inside to find a distraught Revé speaking intently with a policeman. When she turned, he saw the desperation in her face. As he put it, "For the first time in my life, I understood what real fear was."

Still, Walsh did his best to calm Revé, and the two of them worked painstakingly to describe their son to the investigating officers, who had already put out word of a child gone missing at the Sears Mall. Local news station WINZ broadcast an announcement of Adam's disappearance, and Miami television stations interrupted programming to run Adam's photograph and a plea for any information. Friends and neighbors were standing by at the Walsh house little more than a mile from the store—they'd call if Adam wandered home.

Police were sympathetic, but there was little that they could do except broadcast the alarm. As the day wore on and the shadows lengthened, one cop pointed out the location of the police station, ironically located just a short walk across the mall's vast parking lot. "We're right over there," he told the Walshes, as if the statement meant something.

As the hours passed and the store began to prepare for closing, the reality of Adam's disappearance heightened for the Walshes. It was almost as if as long as the lights in the aisles burned brightly, Adam might somehow come around the corner of one of the aisles, smiling, with his arms outstretched. He'd just been hiding, nothing bad had happened. But once the store closed, and all was dark, what then?

John rushed home and returned to the lot where Revé waited by the family car. He'd brought blankets and some of Adam's favorite books and toys. Together they made up a little bed in the big backseat of the family car, a converted Checker taxi. Revé folded Adam's favorite blue blanket up to make a pillow. They left the doors unlocked and left a note on the dashboard that could be read through the window: "Adam, stay in the car. Mommy and Daddy are looking for you."

And finally, some time after the lights of Sears had blinked out and the parking lot had emptied except for the hulking shadow of the Checker, the two of them got in John's car and drove home.

Any thought of rest, however, was impossible. Shortly after they'd pulled into the drive and consulted briefly with the family and friends who had gathered, Revé mounted her bicycle and was pedaling up and down the streets of their suburban neighborhood, calling her son's name. She returned to circle the shuttered Sears store, peering through the darkened windows for any sign of Adam, and even made her way up a set of fire stairs to the roof, where she called for him down the building's ventilator shafts.

As Revé searched, John joined with a team of friends and neighbors to form a human chain that swept the nearby Hollywood Golf Course. A group of Crime Watch volunteers organized a walking search of the city, aided by a police helicopter that swept the streets with its spotlight.

At one point late in the night, John Walsh hailed a cruiser driving through his neighborhood. "How's the hunt going?"

The patrolman behind the wheel was a rookie named Mark Smith, who pointed to a photo of Adam pinned to his visor. "We're all looking for him," Smith said. "Don't worry."

But still there was nothing. By morning, the news had hit the local papers, with the local *Hollywood Sun-Tattler* running a front-page banner: "Massive Search Launched for Boy, 6—Adam Walsh Disappeared from Sears Monday Afternoon." A piece in the *Miami News* quoted Hollywood police as saying that while six-year-old Adam Walsh had indeed gone missing, "kidnapping is not suspected." And in fact, there was little concrete reason at that moment to believe that an abduction had taken place. There was no ransom note, no disgruntled parent held at arm's length by divorce, none of the "logical" reasons for a child to be taken.

John Walsh, however, could not shake the feeling that someone who had recently lost a child to some tragic circumstance might have taken his son. Yet even that scenario was preferable to the most logical explanation for many a missing child case in South Florida. The spidery network of drainage canals that intersect the narrow strip of habitable land between the Everglades and the Atlantic—the crackpot work of developers such as Henry Flagler and Napoleon Bonaparte Broward—had claimed more than their fair share of children over the years. It is hard to drive a mile in South Florida without encountering one of the deeply chiseled, rock-walled channels meant to turn the Everglades into homesites, few of them fenced, many of them abutting parks, bike paths, and heavily traveled thoroughfares. If Adam had tumbled into one of those canals . . . well, it was a prospect John Walsh did not want to contemplate.

And despite the efforts of the local police and news media, there was the distressing possibility that Adam and his abductor were long gone from the area. In 1981, there were none of the regional and national alert systems and shared databases that the public and the law enforcement community take for granted today. Despite the fact that hundreds of thousands of children went missing each year, the world had simply not recognized the need for such measures. Most kids "showed up," right? Such disappearances were ordinarily treated by law enforcement as local matters.

But by now it seemed to the Walshes that Adam was not simply going to "show up." And if he had indeed been taken, and his abductor had slipped them outside the local network of cops and media alarum, who would even notice?

To try and cover such bases, the Walshes designed a poster offering a reward of $5,000—no questions asked—for Adam's safe return. It featured a photograph taken only a week before—a gap-toothed little boy in a baseball cap, holding a bat—and assured anyone who might have taken Adam, "Do Not Fear Revenge! We will not prosecute. We only want our son." They printed 150,000 of the posters, and they did a thing unheard of at the time: through friends with connections to Delta Airlines, copies were given to every passenger who passed through the airline's busy Atlanta hub. Copies, including those translated into Spanish, were distributed on every outgoing flight at the Fort Lauderdale airport. Eastern Airlines followed suit, and soon the posters were being issued to their passengers at every airport in the United States.

By Wednesday, forty-eight hours after Adam's disappearance, it seemed almost certain there would be no simple resolution to the case. "Probes Yield No Clues to Missing Boy," the headlines read. "Reward Rises as Police Probe Any, Every Clue."

Fred Barbetta, public information officer for the Hollywood PD, assured reporters that the cops had spared no effort. "We've got the whole Detective Bureau on this one," he told reporters, "the whole patrol, everybody." But then he added a grimmer assessment, one that reflected what many inside the department had come to think: "It's time we hit the waterways hard. If he's in the water, this is when he'd come up." As a result, those same volunteers who'd scoured the streets and combed the parks and playgrounds and golf courses began to walk the banks of the dark canals.

On Thursday, lead detective Hoffman made his first public statement on the case, telling reporters that Adam's disappearance might possibly have been an abduction after all. "This is not the type of child to just walk off," he explained. He'd had considerable discussion with the parents, and they had convinced him that Adam was a well-behaved and happy little boy. "But we don't have any clues whatsoever what the motive would be. It's extremely frustrating," Hoffman added. "We've got no clues, no leads, no evidence and no motives." Hoffman reiterated his department's plea for anyone who might have witnessed anything out of the ordinary that day at the Sears Mall to come forward.

Meanwhile, certainly no one had given up the search. Twenty-two Hollywood police officers had volunteered their unpaid overtime to keep looking for Adam. Influenced by the Hollywood PIO's grisly reminder that gases inside a decomposing body would by now have sent it floating to the surface of the water, the Florida Game and Fresh Water Fish Commission donated one of their helicopters for use in searching area waterways. Seven wildlife officers volunteered their time to conduct a ground search in the nearby Florida Everglades.

Revé, desperate for anything that might help, agreed to undergo hypnosis, in the hopes that she might have blocked some detail, however small, of her activities that Monday. But the account she gave of her activities under hypnosis was depressingly similar to that of her conscious recollections. Her memory of the timing of events matched to the minute, and she had seen nothing out of the ordinary and no one suspicious on her way into the store that day.

Meantime, the press had set up camp outside the Walshes' more-than-modest Hollywood home, eagerly trumpeting any tidbit they picked up off their police frequency scanners. They

had taken to describing John Walsh as a "marketing executive" in their stories, and somehow the converted Checker cab
had become a "custom car." While the reward was bumped
up to $25,000 and ultimately $100,000 through the donations
of friends, the Walshes had begun to fear that they were being
painted as millionaires, the type of people who might be targeted for a colossal ransom.

And then, late on Thursday, came a phone call that finally
gave Hollywood Police some reason to hope. A woman named
Marilyn Pottenberg phoned, explaining that her ten-year-old
son Timothy told her that he had noticed something suspicious
during their visit to the Sears store the afternoon that Adam
Walsh disappeared. She herself had not witnessed it, Mrs. Pottenberg said, but her son told her that he had seen Adam—or
someone who looked like Adam—being pulled into a dark blue
van in the parking lot. Mrs. Pottenberg was not eager to have
her son interviewed by police, because he suffered from severe
migraine headaches. She would have to speak with Timothy's
doctor before she could allow that. She would get back to them.

Though there were certain inconsistencies in the tip, including the suggestion that Timothy had witnessed this event long
after the time that Revé Walsh had raised the alarm for her
missing son, Lieutenant Hynds appeared before reporters on
Saturday, August 1, to announce that his force was following up
on "the first solid lead" they had uncovered to date—and he put
out the call to anyone in the community who might have seen
such a suspicious vehicle.

The local Crime Stoppers staged a reenactment of an Adam
look-alike being snatched through the doors of a blue van by a
white male perpetrator, and the footage was aired on every local
television station. Tips flooded in from everywhere, and hundreds of vans of every shade of blue were stopped and searched
by cops in Palm Beach, Broward, and Dade counties. Florida
highway troopers were doing the same across the entire state.

But by the following Tuesday, eight days after Adam had disappeared, even Lieutenant Hynds was backpedaling. He'd come to have "some misgivings" about the veracity of the Pottenberg tip, he told the press. And, too, he was a bit concerned about inconveniencing innocent citizens, some of whom had been stopped and searched twice.

So this was where *he* had come in, Joe Matthews thought, dropping the last of the case files on his desk. Beyond the "blue van" lead, which seemed about as consequential to him as a sighting of the Loch Ness Monster, precious little had been developed over ten days and thousands of man-hours of police work. Furthermore, during the time that he had spent at Hollywood police headquarters, he'd noticed a few disconcerting things about the way the investigation was being handled in the offices around him.

While Matthews sat at a vacant desk, poring over the files that were rather grudgingly parceled out to him, the phones at other desks were ringing constantly. While some of the detectives seemed organized, others assigned to the case would answer incoming calls randomly, jot information given by tipsters on scraps of paper or napkins or whatever might be handy, then hurry out on unrelated assignments without bothering to log their calls.

Desks were shared, files piled and unpiled, scraps of paper sent fluttering, napkins balled and tossed and swept. To Matthews, it seemed impossibly chaotic. It wasn't that the detectives seemed incompetent or unconcerned—there simply seemed to be no one in charge.

In his own department, all calls pertaining to a specific investigation went through one central logging station, and each lead, however lunatic or promising on the face of it, was assigned to someone for follow-up. After the leads were checked, reports were filed, and someone with authority over the case regularly reviewed the status of each and every inquiry, no matter how unimportant it might appear. Such organization seemed to Matthews the first principle of effective investigation technique, but when he mentioned the seeming disarray to Hoffman, he got only a raised eyebrow in return. If Hoffman had anything to say about it, Matthews wouldn't be there to begin with, he was reminded.

Matthews was hardly surprised at Hoffman's response, but he couldn't have stopped himself from making his point. Ten days gone by and not a scrap of worthwhile information turned up, how could he keep his mouth shut? He even walked down the hallway to repeat his concerns to Lieutenant Hynds. Hynds gave him a look obviously meant to remind Matthews who was in charge. "I'll look into it," he told Matthews.

Matthew got the picture. He'd stick to what he could do, he thought, what he'd been authorized to do. And he would begin with the father of the missing boy.

Matthews had formed no impression as to any involvement that John Walsh might have had in the crime that he'd been called to help investigate. Impressions only got in the way. What Matthews relied upon was his technique.

Before conducting a polygraph exam, any competent expert performs something of a pre-exam interview with a subject, but in Matthews's case those interviews were anything but perfunctory. Though he has thought about the matter, he is not exactly certain where his ability to connect with people comes from, though he does recall that as a child growing up in a devout Catholic household, he'd thought he was going to become a priest. "When it got closer to the time to go away to the seminary, though, I wasn't so sure. My mother knew I was upset and sat me down one day to tell me it was okay if I didn't want to go. I didn't have to be a priest just to please her, she told me." He shrugs. "It was a big relief to me at the time. But sometimes I think being a cop is almost the same thing."

In any event, when his subject on the day of August 7, 1981, sat down in the examining room, Matthews started by asking, "Tell me a little about yourself, John." When Walsh began by telling Matthews where he'd gone to college and what his major had been, Matthews held up a hand. "No, I mean, tell me about how you grew up. About your mother and father. Like if I asked you to rate them on a scale of one to ten, with ten being tops, and why. That kind of thing."

On that day, "that kind of thing" went on for almost seven hours. Prompted by Matthews, Walsh said that if ten were tops, then his father, a hardworking war hero he had idolized, was probably a twelve in his eyes. Walsh and his mother had what he considered a normal relationship. There were typical mother-son issues between them, but he loved her, and she had always been supportive of him. Give her an eight.

Matthews and Walsh did get around to a discussion of college, though it took a while. He was an English major at the University of Buffalo in New York when he met Revé, though he'd been stunned to discover she was still in high school at the time. Even though she was five years younger than he was, he'd found her so poised, and so intelligent. From the moment they met there had been no one else for him, Walsh told Matthews. They'd been married for ten years, since July 1971.

Walsh also told Matthews a story from his days as a pool manager and lifeguard at the Diplomat Hotel out on Hollywood Beach. He was keeping watch at the pool one afternoon when he saw a group of kids rushing toward him from the nearby jetty. Frantic, they told him that one of their friends was in trouble out by the jetty's end, where a massive discharge pipe emptied runoff water into the ocean. They'd been playing near the mouth of the pipe when the tide shifted in and trapped their pal, lodging him in a crevice against the rocks. The boys had tried, but they couldn't get him out. The force of the incoming tide was just too strong.

John ran out to the end of the jetty and scrambled down the

rocks to find matters just as the boys said. Indeed there was a kid lodged between the rocks and the mouth of the pipe, the waters rising inexorably toward his chin. And as if it could be worse, he realized that he knew this child. It was John Monahan Jr., son of the Diplomat's chief executive, trapped there in the rising waters. He'd given the boy a series of scuba lessons earlier that summer.

He managed to get young John calmed somewhat, then tried pulling him out of the crevice by the arms, but it wasn't working. The water was close to the boy's chin when John called to the kids watching from the top of the jetty for help, but they couldn't understand what he wanted.

"You've got to hang on," he said, turning to young Monahan. "I'm coming right back." Then he bounded up the rocks and back to the pool storage shack, where the diving equipment was stored. He kicked the door open, found a tank, mask, and regulator, and raced back along the jetty to Monahan. "We're going to do it just like we did it in the pool a hundred times," he assured the boy, helping him into the gear as the waters rose over his head.

Once the boy had been reassured and was breathing in a passable way, Walsh slipped under the water and put his arms around Monahan's chest. He pushed hard with his feet, levering against the rocks, and suddenly, as if a cork had popped from a bottle, the boy was free.

Needless to say, the incident made John Walsh far more than a trusted employee at the Diplomat. When Walsh and Revé got married, Monahan's father insisted on paying for a honeymoon trip to Europe for the couple, and the Walshes and the Monahans had remained friends ever since.

It was a captivating story, but it was the sort of thing that Matthews encouraged for other reasons. "You get someone talking about emotional things they haven't thought about in ten or twenty years, you establish a good baseline," he says. "When you finally get around to asking about some crime they may or may not have been involved in just the other day, you can judge any little changes in body language, in rate of speech or eagerness to respond and so on, and know you may be onto something."

As for the polygraph instrument itself, Matthews says, "It's not infallible. It's just a tool that helps validate the information that is gathered during the interview. The polygraph can indicate deception, but only a confession establishes guilt."

At the end of his time with Walsh, and following the administration of the polygraph exam itself, Matthews felt he had his unequivocal answer, however. "It is the examiner's opinion that Mr. Walsh was not criminally involved nor has he guilty knowledge as to who is responsible for the abduction of his son Adam."

On the other hand, Matthews did come across one item of interest during his interview, one that would affect the investigation irrevocably. As they talked, Walsh brought up a name that had surfaced nowhere else in the course of the investigation: it was that of Jimmy Campbell, a man Walsh identified as Adam's godfather.

Campbell was a younger man whom Walsh had gotten to know at the Diplomat Hotel in his lifeguarding days. Campbell was a pool boy, a decent, hardworking kid who'd never had much of a home life or any chance for a college education, and Walsh had always liked him and felt sorry for him— "Dudley Do-Right," he nicknamed him. When the Walshes started to move up in the world and he and Revé bought a house, Walsh and his wife invited Campbell to live in one of the spare rooms. He was to help out around the place and get himself into the community college. As long as he stayed in school, he could stay with the Walshes, but if Campbell quit school or flunked out, he'd have to leave. That was the deal. Unfortunately, Jimmy *had* dropped out of school a few months ago, Walsh told Matthews during their interview. And Walsh had been true to his word.

"So where is this Jimmy Campbell now?" Matthews asked, casually enough, after their exam had ended.

"Dudley?" Walsh shrugged, clearly still disappointed with his former ward. "He's out there helping with the search."

Matthews took another look at Hoffman's list of subjects to be examined, which Hynds had passed along. No Jimmy Campbell among them. A guy living in the Walsh house until a few months ago, intimately connected to the family, and he's not on the list? He glanced back at Walsh.

"You got this Campbell's phone number?"

Walsh was puzzled, but he was already reaching into his pocket for his address book. Matthews jotted down the information, and by 9:00 p.m. that evening, Jimmy Campbell was in the examining room at Hollywood PD, and Joe Matthews was hard at work on his next subject.

HOLLYWOOD, FLORIDA—AUGUST 8, 1981

In the wee hours of Saturday morning Matthews finished his work with Jimmy Campbell. He was tired, and what he had learned during his interview with Campbell had wearied him even more. He completed his notes on the examination and took a walk down the hall to Detective Hoffman's desk.

"Yeah?" Hoffman asked in his normal surly fashion when Matthews approached.

"I finished with John Walsh," Matthews said.

"It took you long enough," Hoffman said, with a glance at his watch. "So what's the story?"

Matthews shook his head. "He's clean. No involvement, no guilty knowledge."

Hoffman said nothing, but he seemed anything but pleased. "So who's next?"

"I already did 'next.' A guy named Jimmy Campbell."

Hoffman stared back, surprised. "That name's not on the list."

"I know," Matthews said, and then began to explain why he

had called Campbell in and what he had learned during the interview.

When he finished, Hoffman was beside himself with excitement. "That's it. There's our fucking guy," he said, halfway out of his seat.

Matthews held up his hand. "What are you talking about? You're not even listening to me." He pointed to his notes, where everything of real importance was spelled out:

> The following are the relevant questions asked of Mr. Campbell during his polygraph examination:
>> Concerning Adam's disappearance, do you intend to answer all my questions truthfully?
>> Answer: Yes.
>> Do you know who took Adam?
>> Answer: No.
>> Do you know where Adam is now?
>> Answer: No.
>> Did you conspire with anyone to cause Adam's disappearance?
>> Answer: No.
>> Are you withholding information from the police concerning Adam's disappearance?
>> Answer: No.
>> Do you suspect anyone of taking Adam?
>> Answer: No.
>> Do you know who took Adam?
>> Answer: No.
>> Did you take Adam?
>> Answer: No.

"I worked him every which way. He's not involved," Matthews assured Hoffman.

"Bullshit," Hoffman responded, shaking Matthews's report

between them. "You tell me the guy was living in the house, doing what you say he was, and he's not involved in the crime somehow?"

Matthews sighed. He knew what he'd written down, what Hoffman was so worked up about. In fact, he had realized very early on in his interview with Campbell that the young man was holding something back, and it had not taken Matthews long to draw his secret out.

However, as with John Walsh, Matthews had gone to considerable lengths to determine just who he was dealing with before he got around to any pointed questions concerning the here and now. It was quickly apparent that Jimmy Campbell's childhood had been an unfortunate one: he had never received much affection from his own parents, and he might well have taken that deprivation out on the world in turn, just as many of the miscreants Matthews dealt with on a daily basis had. Instead, Campbell turned out sweet and gentle, one of the rare ones who understood just how important a little kindness could be. It was the less common response to a lousy upbringing, but it happened, just as some abused animals come crawling for affection instead of trying to tear your face off. Sometimes, Matthews thought, you catch a break.

Campbell loved John and Revé for their kindness and generosity, and he loved being with a family who cared about each other and who clearly cared for him. With John often away on business—his company was expanding, with a major resort hotel in the Bahamas under construction, among other things—Jimmy was happy to help out around the house, doing the heavy lifting when John was away, filling in when Adam needed pointers with baseball, doing anything he could do to repay the Walshes and show his appreciation.

No way had he intended this, Campbell explained to Matthews, but over time his affection for Revé had gradually turned to something else. Obviously, she was attractive and smart and warm . . . and quite simply, he fell in love with her. And one night while John was away on an extended trip, well, something happened that shouldn't have.

No way he could have stopped himself, Jimmy admitted. He was way too smitten for that. But however much he was attracted to Revé and however much affection she felt toward him, they realized in the aftermath that what they had done was wrong. Understandable, maybe—everyone is human—but nonetheless it was wrong.

Campbell could hardly live with himself for betraying John, his old friend and benefactor, he told Matthews. No way he could stay on in the Walsh house, that much was certain. And soon he had moved out.

All this Matthews had included in his report, of course, the good, the bad, and the ugly. Unfortunately, however, Jack Hoffman was fixated upon the ugly.

"It's as clear as day," Hoffman told Matthews excitedly, still brandishing the report. "Campbell's banging the wife, Walsh finds out, throws his ass out, and the guy snatches the kid to get back at him."

"Come on, Jack," Matthews protested, but the beleaguered detective was having none of it. Almost two weeks without a thing to go on, and finally this bombshell dropped in his lap.

Hoffman snapped his fingers then, as another thought occurred to him. "Maybe Campbell still had the hots for Mrs. Walsh, and he thought getting rid of the kid would help clear the way."

"You're not listening to me," Matthews said, trying to counter Hoffman's belligerence. "We're not writing a fucking novel here, we're conducting an examination. He's got a solid alibi for the day Adam Walsh went missing. And his polygraph test is absolutely conclusive. He and Revé might have made a *big* mistake. But as to Adam's disappearance, there is no deception. Look at what I'm telling you. *Read.*"

Hoffman shook his head. "He beat the test somehow, that's all. I want a follow-up exam."

Matthews stared back at Hoffman for a moment. He should have been prepared for this. Clearly, Hoffman and the department as a whole were desperate. Earlier, when Matthews had asked Hoffman why the department hadn't announced that they no longer believed in the "blue van" theory, Hoffman had simply shrugged. "Hey, that's all we have to give the public," the detective told him. "We have to keep something out there so they'll stay interested in the case."

Matthews sighed inwardly, trying to put himself in Hoffman's shoes. "Jack," he said patiently, "there is no need for a follow-up examination. There is no doubt here."

Hoffman seemed about to go off at that, but he caught himself and mustered a conciliatory gaze. "Listen," he said. "I'll make a deal with you. You do a follow-up with Campbell, and if he passes, I'll drop him as a suspect. You have my word."

It was a waste of time, Matthews thought, but if it would put the matter to an end, he supposed he could do it. "Okay," he told Hoffman. "I'll call him back in."

"You do that," Hoffman said, satisfied. "Meantime, I'll check out this so-called alibi of his."

Thus, a weary Matthews reluctantly called Campbell, who agreed to appear at Hollywood PD at 10:00 a.m. on Monday for a follow-up exam. And later that Saturday, Hoffman took another detective with him to the Gold Strand Motel on Collins Avenue in far north Dade County, where Campbell had been running a boat rental concession for about seven months.

At the Gold Strand, Hoffman spoke with the hotel manager, Carroll Shannon, who confirmed that Campbell indeed worked there, but as to his whereabouts on the Monday that Adam Walsh disappeared, she had no idea. Maybe they should talk to Louis Munoz, her assistant pool manager. When Hoffman and his partner found Munoz, he remembered the day well. Munoz told them that Jimmy Campbell had arrived at about ten thirty that morning, excited about getting his sailboats cleaned up for a TV commercial that would be filmed at the hotel later in the afternoon. He noticed Jimmy puttering about throughout the day, Munoz said. When Joe Walsh, John's brother, came by looking for Jimmy at around three thirty, he was out on the ocean on one of his boats.

From the Gold Strand, Hoffman and his partner went to Jimmy Campbell's home, where they interviewed him regarding his association with the Walsh family and his whereabouts on July 27, the day Adam disappeared. As he had told Matthews, Campbell explained that he had known John Walsh for nine years and that he had lived with the family for about four years. He did various chores around the place, and sometimes babysat for Adam, whom he had come to love. He took the boy on outings to the beach, the zoo, and baseball games. He'd even served as Adam's T-ball coach this past year.

He'd been at work the day of Adam's disappearance, leaving only briefly to go to the nearby Thunderbird Motel boat concession to see if he could borrow two clean sails for his upcoming shoot, but the person in charge wasn't around, so he returned to the Golden Strand. As to who might have been responsible for Adam's disappearance, Campbell told the detectives that he had not the slightest idea. Hoffman took it all down in the form of notes, for some reason failing to record the interview as he had all the others he had conducted during his investigation. At the end of the interview, Hoffman noted that he asked the subject to voluntarily submit to a polygraph examination, as if Matthews hadn't already conducted one. It would be a long time before the reason for that odd statement—and Hoffman's failure to record his interview—came to light.

HOLLYWOOD, FLORIDA—AUGUST 10, 1981

On Monday, Joe Matthews was back at Hollywood police headquarters bright and early, preparing to reexamine Jimmy Campbell. Matthews was convinced it was a waste of time, but if it might somehow put Hoffman's suspicions concerning Campbell to rest, then he would do it.

When the appointed hour of 10:00 a.m. came and went without Jimmy Campbell's appearance, however, Matthews became concerned. By 11:00, he decided to walk down to Hoffman's desk and let the detective know that Campbell was a no-show. Maybe the kid was scared, he thought. Maybe he'd overslept. But he wasn't involved in Adam's disappearance. That much he was sure of.

Hoffman, however, was not at his desk. When Matthews asked the detective bureau's secretary where Hoffman was, she told him Hoffman was in the interview room. He and his partner Ron Hickman had been grilling a suspect since seven that morning. What suspect? Matthews wondered. He hadn't heard anything about a suspect.

"Some guy named Campbell," was the secretary's answer.

Matthews couldn't believe it. He hurried down to the interrogation room—where the "Interview in Progress" sign had been left unlighted, he noted—and yanked open the door. Some "interview," he was thinking. He had heard Hoffman screaming, "You lying piece of shit," all the way down the hall. Sure enough, inside the room, he found an ashen Jimmy Campbell on the other side of a table from a livid Hoffman and Hickman.

"What the fuck are you guys doing?" Matthews asked.

"We're interviewing a suspect," Hoffman managed. His bravado seemed to have faltered. Even Hickman was avoiding Matthews's gaze.

"The hell you are," Matthews replied. "He's supposed to be with me right now. I can't fucking believe it," and with that he pulled Campbell from the room and back to his own desk. There wasn't even a murmur of protest from Hoffman and Hickman.

"Why are they treating me so rough?" Campbell asked when

they were finally settled. "They seem to think I'm responsible for Adam being missing. They're making all kinds of accusations." Matthews did his best to get Campbell calmed down so that he could be productively examined, all the while thinking that it was just one more screwup on the part of Hoffman. No way on earth could you accuse a suspect of a crime minutes before administering a polygraph exam and expect to get anything usable out of it. Hoffman simply seemed oblivious to standard police procedures.

After a bit of time in Matthews's presence, Campbell finally began to breathe again. "I know I've got to calm down," he told Matthews. "I've got to calm down and convince myself not to let the barbarians get to me." Still, as he confided to Matthews, it was more than difficult to be accused of doing harm to a child whom he loved. "I *do* take it personally. It's very upsetting."

To get Campbell relaxed, Matthews took him out to lunch, then brought him back to the station, where they went back over the events they'd discussed two nights earlier. Finally, early that evening, Matthews deemed Campbell ready, and he began the testing once again.

They were nearing the conclusion of this second exam when the door to the room flew open and Matthews saw an obviously agitated assistant chief of police Leroy Hessler beckoning him outside. Matthews told Campbell to hold on for a moment and went to join Hessler in the hallway.

"We just got a call," Hessler told Matthews, grimly. "They found a severed head in a drainage ditch beside the turnpike up in Indian River County. They think it's the boy's."

He pointed at the door to the interview room where Campbell sat, oblivious. "We know he did it," Hessler said to Matthews. "And I want a confession."

Matthews paid little attention to Hessler's demands, but at the same time he was numbed by the information that Hessler had delivered. Statistics might dictate that fewer than one hundred children are kidnapped and murdered in a year, but reassuring statistics are little comfort when you're one of the exceptions. As for Hessler's cockeyed demands that he extract a confession from Jimmy Campbell come hell or high water, Matthews considered any number of outraged responses, most of which would have accomplished little good.

"I'm in the middle of an examination," he told Hessler finally, turning away. "I'll bring my report down as soon as we're finished in there."

Back inside the room, Matthews apologized to Campbell for the interruption and managed to complete his examination, which indicated once again that his subject—despite everything he had been subjected to—clearly and positively had no idea of what might have happened to Adam Walsh. Matthews thanked Campbell for his cooperation and told him to go on home. He sat alone then for a moment, wondering if it was true—that the water had claimed Adam Walsh after all, if scarcely in a way that anyone might have imagined. Tragedy didn't come any grimmer than that, he thought. Then he went to track down Hoffman.

He found the lead investigator in a back office where a crowd of somber-looking detectives had gathered, along with Assistant Chief Hessler. In the two hours that had passed since Hessler burst into Matthews's examination room, the news had been confirmed. With the Walshes off in New York City to be interviewed about the search for Adam on *Good Morning America*, family friend John Monahan had been summoned by Indian River authorities to see if he could make an identification and confirm what dental records seemed to suggest.

Coincidentally, the canal where the gruesome find had been made bordered an orange grove recently treated by pesticides. The runoff had so drenched the canal with chemicals that nothing was alive to disturb the flesh on the severed head, despite all the time that had passed. There was not a doubt in the witness's mind.

In the back office of the Hollywood PD, about a hundred miles south of where Monahan had made his identification, Hessler turned to Matthews and jabbed a finger angrily. "You don't have the balls to call this Campbell deceptive."

Matthews was astonished. No way on earth had Jimmy Campbell murdered Adam Walsh, then hacked off his head and dumped it in an upstate canal. Every fiber in his cop's body was certain of it.

Jimmy Campbell had nothing to do with the crime and there was no way Matthews would be bullied into saying otherwise. Everyone else in the crowded room was quiet, looking at him expectantly. In other offices down the hall, phones rang, file doors creaked and slammed, voices rose and fell, all the humdrum sounds of daily cop business. In this room, Matthews thought, "ordinary" had lost its meaning, "procedure" had taken a hike.

Finally, Matthews spoke. "I'm nobody's whore," he told Hessler. "I call it the way I see it."

Hessler regarded him for a moment, his face a mask of rage. Matthews wondered for a moment if the man might be about to take a swing at him, but the moment passed, and Hessler turned to take Hoffman by the arm, guiding him quickly out of the room. As the two disappeared down the hallway, Hessler fired his parting shot. "This one you called wrong, Matthews."

CHAPTER THREE

World of Hurt

Q: How many killings would you say you've been
   involved in?
A: I don't know. Maybe a couple hundred.
Q: Would you say more of those were women or more
   were men?
A: A little bit of both.
Q: And you say you did these killings because it gave
   you a high?
A: That's right.
Q: And how long did that feeling last?
A: Maybe a week, maybe a month.
Q: And when the feeling went away?
A: Then you go out and do it again.

—OTTIS TOOLE, WITH TEXAS RANGERS,

MARCH 24, 1984

JACKSONVILLE, FLORIDA—MAY 16, 1981

If Ottis Toole had ever felt much sense of control over his life, the sensation was a fleeting one. He had an IQ of 75, considered the borderline for retardation in the adult population, just above the average intellect of a twelve-year-old child. According to the literature, adults in this category are considered "slow and simple," and while they are capable of gainful employment, supervision must be constant. Such individuals are only marginally capable of coping in an adult world, and in the language of the Stanford-Binet Intelligence Scales, "need help from friends or family to manage life's complications."

In Toole's case, about the only such help he ever received came from his mother, Sarah. He'd been born to her in March 1947, but he'd never known his father. A stepfather named Robert Harley arrived when Toole was ten, but he had never bonded with the man, who had alcohol problems. Perhaps the fact that Toole was "slow" helped keep them apart. Or it could have been the seizures that he had suffered since the day when a neighbor kid chucked a rock against Toole's skull, intending to "kill the retard."

He'd managed to struggle through seven years of special education classes and had even gotten to the point of being able to read and write, and also, to suffer when other kids ridiculed him. He was sexually molested by the husband of a neighbor when he was six, and once, during the several times he ran away from home, was picked up by cops who noticed that he had dressed himself as a girl. Gradually, he came to think of himself as a homosexual, but he wasn't entirely sure. He had intimate relations with women as well, and even tried marriage, thinking it might help "change" him. The experiment hit its first serious obstacle after four days when Toole disappeared, and one of his older sisters informed his new bride that Toole was "queer as a three-dollar bill."

Life had obviously been a continual struggle for Toole, but there was one constant, one source of comfort in his mind, and that was his certainty that his mother loved him. She herself suffered from bouts of mental illness, but when it came to Ottis, the youngest of her nine children, she seemed to understand that she was the only force standing between her son and an unimaginable bleak emptiness.

If indeed it was the love of Sarah Toole that enabled Ottis to cope, it was a tenuous form of coping by any standards. He'd been booked at seventeen for loitering, and for petty larceny the year after. In 1968, at the age of twenty-one, he was arrested for vagrancy and a few months later for prowling. The next year he was again charged with vagrancy. In 1972, he was apprehended while carrying a concealed weapon, a four-inch hunting knife. He'd been arrested for loitering in a bus station in 1975, for lewd and lascivious behavior in an adult theater in 1976, and later that year for public intoxication. In 1977, he was arrested for making obscene phone calls, window-peeping, cross-dressing, and exposing himself in public.

Yet Toole had still managed to weather all this, to make his way through a sad facsimile of life, because—in his mind, at least—he had his mother, and she loved him, right up to the last day of her life, which was May 16, 1981. And that is when things truly began to fall apart.

At the time of his mother's death, Toole, then thirty-four, was living at home with her and his stepfather, Robert Harley, and the three young children of his sister Druscilla: Frieda, Frank, and Sarah Powell. Also living in the home at 708 Day Avenue was Toole's lover, Henry Lee Lucas, forty-five, a slightly built, glass-eyed drifter he had met at a Jacksonville soup kitchen three years earlier. While photographs taken of Lucas around the time depict him as marginally presentable, it is difficult to imagine what he might have found attractive in the gangly, slump-shouldered, gap-toothed Toole, who generally sported several days' growth of grizzled facial hair, his sandy hair thinning and generally unkempt, his clothing characteristically rumpled and rank from days of wear.

Still, indifference to style and hygiene are not always barriers to love, nor to gainful employment. In fact, Toole was working as a laborer for a man named John Reaves, who owned a couple of roofing businesses in Jacksonville. Toole took his mother's death hard, Reaves recalls. He'd go out to the Evergreen Cemetery where she had been buried and lie down on her grave. To Toole, the ground above her coffin seemed inexplicably warm, and he was convinced that at times he could feel it move beneath his body.

Toole, who was becoming more despondent by the day, confided that he began to hear voices suggesting that he should kill himself and "go to rest" with his mother. Sometime he heard the voices in his sleep, and other times he was wide awake. It could have been his mind, he thought. Or it could have been the devil.

Not surprisingly, Toole's appearances at Reaves Roofing company became less and less frequent, and on Friday, June 5, 1981, they ceased altogether. Meantime, Robert Harley reported the theft of several items, including jewelry and furniture, from the house he had shared with Toole's mother. He suspected Toole and Lucas, but he had no idea where the two of them might have gone. Harley was alone in the house now, since Toole's older brother Howard had agreed to take custody of the younger children. And then, on June 23, 1981, while Harley was away, the home at 708 Day Avenue was set ablaze, an apparent case of arson.

Police might have talked to Ottis Toole and Henry Lee Lucas about the thefts and the fire, but the two were nowhere to be found. As it turned out, they had borrowed a Ford pickup truck from Toole's sister-in-law Georgia, telling her they were going to haul a load of scrap iron to the Jacksonville dump. In truth, they were on their way up the East Coast to Maryland, intending to make "a fresh start," and taking with them Ottis's twelve-year-old nephew Frank and his 13-year-old niece Frieda "Becky" Powell.

On July 8, the truck was found abandoned in Wellington, Delaware, and police contacted Georgia, telling her she had thirty days to reclaim it before it would be sold at auction. Georgia quickly filed a report with the Jacksonville sheriff, accusing Ottis Toole and Henry Lee Lucas of the theft of her truck, and on July 22, 1981, after an APB was issued, Maryland state troopers spotted Henry Lee Lucas in the town of Pikesville. Lucas was arrested on charges of unauthorized use of a motor vehicle and taken immediately to jail. The children, who were with him at the time, were placed in the hands of Child Protective Services to be sent back to Florida.

Toole, meantime, was not involved, because he had wandered off from the others during a hard night of drinking the night before in Newport News, Virginia. Convinced that Lucas (an admitted bisexual) had fallen in love with thirteen-year-old Frieda and run off without him, Toole swallowed an overdose of sleeping pills and collapsed on the streets.

When he awakened in the Riverside Hospital in Newport News on July 23, Toole was willing to talk with doctors concerning his depression over the death of his mother, but he denied that he had attempted suicide. He said that he had been drifting around the country, sleeping on the streets, and now wanted only to return to Jacksonville, where there was a job waiting for him with a roofing company. Adjudged no threat to himself or to others, he was discharged from the hospital, and on the afternoon of July 24, Ottis Toole was given a check by the Newport News Salvation Army, made out payable to the Greyhound Bus Company in the amount of $71.93.

Toole walked the two miles from Salvation Army headquarters to the Greyhound station, where he exchanged the check for a one-way ticket to Jacksonville, and at 6:30 p.m. he was on board. It would take somewhere between sixteen and twenty hours for the bus to make its way from Virginia to Florida, and as every mile clicked by, Ottis Toole thought of his mother, and of the lover who had betrayed him, and listened to the voices in his head.

JACKSONVILLE, FLORIDA—JULY 25, 1981

It was around eleven on Saturday morning when Ottis Toole stepped off his bus at the Greyhound terminal in Jacksonville.

Some individuals might have been exhausted by a twenty-hour bus ride across five states, but Toole was not. Compared to sleeping on the seat of a pickup truck carrying four passengers, or on a sidewalk, or in a jail cell, or in a hospital psychiatric ward with lunatics screaming and doctors and nurses poking and prodding, to Toole all those hours in the broad reclining seat of a Greyhound bus was an interlude in paradise.

He stretched, undaunted by the humid blanket of Florida summer heat, and began the seven-mile walk to Reaves Roofing, the company owned by John Reaves Sr. There wouldn't be anyone there on a Saturday morning, but that was fine by Toole. Despite what he'd told the doctors and the people at the Salvation Army in Newport News, he had no intention of going back to work firing up tar pots and hoisting heavy rolls of one-ply asphalt up to scalding rooftops. There were easier ways to make money and better places than Jacksonville to do it in.

It took him about two hours to reach Reaves Roofing. As he expected, the compound was deserted, and his key to the gate still worked. There by the gas pumps, just where it was the last time he'd been in the yard, sat the black-over-white '71 Cadillac he'd purchased back in January from Faye Reaves McNett, the aunt of his boss.

Technically, the car was no longer his, since he'd long since fallen behind on the weekly payments of $25 he'd agreed to make. He'd returned the car to McNett some months ago, but she stored it in the company compound, and Toole, using the spare keys he had for the place and those he had made for the car, had "borrowed" the Caddy on more than one occasion since.

Toole filled the Caddy with gas from the company tanks, locked the gate behind him, and drove the few miles to what was left of his mother's house. He'd forgotten something that day that he'd set the place on fire, but he was fairly certain it was still there.

He kept a number of tools in the Caddy, and it did not take

him long to unearth the coffee tin full of cash that constituted his "bank," buried underneath the still-standing front porch. Toole stuffed $300 worth of bills in his pocket, tossed the can into the charred rubble of the house, and set out on the five-hour drive down I-95 to South Florida.

It was his intention to hit the gay parks up and down Biscayne Boulevard in Miami, where he could fatten his bankroll by anywhere from $20 to $50 a trick, and even more by jack-rolling the defenseless among his clientele. But by the time he passed through Fort Lauderdale, a half hour north of his target, it seemed a bit early for such goings-on.

Still, he thought, there were ways he might amuse himself in the meantime. Accordingly, at the Hollywood Exit, he swung the Cadillac off I-95 and cruised along the boulevard until he spotted a Kmart up ahead. Toole pulled into the crowded lot, nodding with satisfaction at all the cars. He didn't need to buy a single thing, it was true, but there were other attractions at a place like this.

Arlene Mayer remembers that it was about seven in the evening when she and her husband, Wayne, arrived at the Hollywood Kmart. They had their twelve-year-old daughter Heidi in tow and were set on picking up a few things for the house. If Heidi kept her promise to be good, she might get that toy Arlene had been promising.

Wayne had just gotten off work, and since he considered himself too dirty to be seen, he told Arlene that he would just relax in the car while she and Heidi did the shopping. It presented no problem for Arlene. She reminded Heidi that she had better be good, and the two set out for the store.

As they walked past what Arlene remembers as a "large white car," they noticed the driver's door swinging open. He was white, in his mid-thirties, and was odd-looking to both of them, "like a bum." Most distressing was the fact that Arlene could hear his footsteps dogging the two of them all the way across the parking lot. Why had she been so accommodating when Wayne said he wanted to sit tight? she wondered.

As they neared the building, the man hurried past them and approached a bank of pay phones by the entrance. He lifted the receiver of one of the phones and mimed dropping coins into the slot, Arlene recalls, even though it was obvious he had no money in his hand. The two of them were happy to get past this creep and into the safety of the brightly lit store.

They grabbed a shopping cart just inside the entrance, and to appease her daughter, Arlene took them straight to the toy department. "Go ahead and look around," she told Heidi, then pointed to the nearby housewares section. "I'm running right over there for something. You keep the cart. I'll be right back."

Heidi was understandably delighted to be left alone in wonderland. But the moment her mother had disappeared and she turned her cart to head for the section where the dolls were stacked, she stopped short. Blocking the aisle before her was the man who'd followed them through the parking lot. In the bright Kmart lights, he looked like something out of a slasher film. Several days' growth of beard pocked his cheeks, his hair was unkempt, one eye wandered aimlessly, and a lunatic smile exposed a set of yellowing teeth. Heidi could feel the wash of this man's fetid breath and smell his ripe body odor from several feet away.

"Why don't I give you a ride in that shopping cart?" he asked in a tone that was meant to be enticing.

Heidi had the good sense to scream.

Toole was gone long before store security came looking for him. By the time the girl was able to stop crying and make herself understood to her mother, he had ambled away, into the shadows of the parking lot. As soon as things calmed down, he'd get into his Cadillac and drive away, just another departing Kmart shopper.

He would head on down to Miami now and spend the night

as he had intended. And once that was over, he would find a place to park the Caddy, somewhere that he could sleep in peace. And tomorrow or the next day, he could try some shopping again.

That little girl he'd followed into the Kmart was about the same age as his niece Becky Powell, who'd dumped him and ran off with Henry Lee. This one hadn't seemed too fond of him either, but that was okay. There were lots of young ones to talk to, and he knew that, eventually, he would find one who would listen. In these parts, there seemed no end of promising malls.

HOLLYWOOD, FLORIDA—JULY 27, 1981

Bill Mistler, owner of a local pest control company, is certain of what he saw outside the Sears store in Hollywood on the fateful Monday afternoon that the Walsh boy disappeared. Mistler was on his way to Sears to pick up some supplies for a camping trip he'd planned for his family the next day, and while he was waiting for an old lady to work her way into a parking space at the curb by the store entrance, he noticed a white Cadillac with a black top coming toward him from the opposite direction.

The Cadillac, which seemed to have a bunch of long-handled gardening tools in the backseat, stopped in the driving lane opposite, and Mistler watched as an odd-looking man with reddish brown hair and a wandering eye got out and started toward the store.

As Mistler waited, the man, who was wearing a filthy T-shirt, approached a neatly dressed boy of about five who was standing on the sidewalk by the curb. Nearby were a woman and another young boy and girl. Mistler assumed it was a mother and her three children at first, but when the odd-looking guy from the Cadillac bent down and began talking to the younger boy, the mother seemed to take no notice. After a moment, in fact, the woman gathered her two children and walked away.

Mistler looked again at the shabbily dressed man and the little boy. Though it seemed impossible that the two belonged together, the child did not seem afraid. After a moment, the man stood and took the boy's arm and the two walked together toward the Cadillac. The man helped the boy into the front seat through the driver's door, then got in after him.

By this time, another parking space had opened up, and Mistler pulled his truck in. As the Cadillac drove past, Mistler noticed that someone had left quite a dent in the right side of the car's rear bumper. And, to his everlasting dismay, that is the last that he thought of it all for a very long time. He simply did what anyone might have done: he went into the Sears store, did the shopping for his trip, and forgot all about what he had seen.

"I told the little cocksucker I had some candy and toys," Toole confided later. The moment the boy was in the car, he locked all the doors and windows. The boy wondered about that, but Toole explained that it would make them safe. They would just have to drive a ways to where the candy was.

He made a quick right out of the parking lot, and inside ten minutes they were headed north on Florida's Turnpike. He had to stop at a tollbooth to pick up a ticket, and by now the boy was raising all kinds of hell, trying to get the attention of the clerk. Toole gave the clerk a weary smile—"Kids."

As they rolled on out of the toll chute, Toole gave the boy a healthy backhand across the face, which only seemed to set him off further. The kid was really getting on his nerves now, so Toole landed a few more punches to the boy's stomach and face. "I'm pretty sure I knocked that kid out," he remembers. In any case, the car was now quiet.

Toole drove in silence for a while, the Caddy's big V8 chewing up the miles. He'd intended to take the kid slumped on the seat beside him back up to Jacksonville where they could live together and be friends, but obviously, that wasn't going to work. The problem was, what to do next?

Toole was no dummy, after all. This kid was very young, but

he also seemed pretty smart. Smart enough to identify Toole if he just let him go.

All in all, there didn't seem to be much choice. He'd driven quite a ways up the turnpike by the time he made his decision, and the busy sprawl of South Florida was far behind him. The brightly lit malls had disappeared, the glittery beachside hotels that loomed like giant, overdecorated Cadillacs were gone, the whole miragelike tropical landscape that seemed to offer up anything a person might want was vanished like a fever dream.

He was alone with an unconscious little boy on the broad seat beside him, and now they were driving through flatlands that seemed to stretch forever, plains dotted here and there by hardwood hammocks or clusters of palmetto scrub, vistas that might have evoked the Serengeti Plains had there been anyone around to know what Africa was.

Prehistoric. Elemental. A man could distinguish crazy dreams from cold, hard reality in a place like this.

Finally, from the corner of his eye, Toole spotted an unmarked service road leading off the turnpike. He'd overshot the unpaved exit, and had to pull to the side of the turnpike and back up to get to it, but that made it perfect for his purposes. It was a rough road, winding through a thick tangle of Australian pines and Brazilian holly, but the jolting did not wake the boy.

Just as well, Toole thought. He didn't want to have to hurt anyone. When he reached a fork in the road and was sure that they were out of sight of the turnpike, he stopped and switched off the Caddy's engine. He got out and went around to the passenger's door, opened it, and lifted up the unconscious little boy. It was so quiet here that the distant traffic was like a gentle surf, the pinging of the cooling Caddy's hood keeping time. He carried the boy to an open space he had spotted in the forsaken tangle of trees and brush and laid him facedown in the sandy dirt.

Toole walked back to his car and stood surveying his tools,

ignoring the cloud of bloodsucking mosquitoes that had already homed in on him. There was a machete in the backseat that he supposed he could use, and a bayonet that he kept hidden under the front seat. That ought to be enough to manage it. He reached for what he needed, and then he went to do his work.

VERO BEACH, FLORIDA—AUGUST 10, 1981

At 8:45 p.m. on a Monday evening two weeks after Adam Walsh went missing, Indian River County medical examiner Franklin H. Cox received a phone call from the sheriff's office informing him of a gruesome find in a canal near the turnpike about twenty miles west of his office in the town of Vero Beach. Cox was no stranger to the aftermath of violence, for even a sleepy beachside hamlet like Vero Beach has its share of bloody family disputes and garden-variety shootouts at convenience stores, but it is safe to say that the call he received that evening, informing him that fishermen had found the decapitated head of a young boy floating in the water, was the first of its kind.

The severed head was transported to the autopsy room at Indian River Memorial Hospital in Vero Beach, and at 2:00 a.m., Cox met police there to perform a preliminary examination of the remains. Don Coleman and Sid Dubose, homicide detectives from Indian River County, were present, along with three detectives dispatched from Jack Hoffman's team at Hollywood PD, 136 miles to the south.

Cox described his findings in the dispassionate language of his profession, noting "extensive cutting and chopping wounds . . . posteriorly from ear to ear" as well as cuts to the ears and occipital bones. One of the cervical vertebra was exposed at the base of the skull, "transversely sectioned," Cox recorded. There were no ragged tissues anywhere—just the clean, sharp edges that might be expected when a head is cleaved from its body with a heavy weapon.

Cox observed that the eyes in the head were bulging, but that was likely a postmortem phenomenon, a result of the gas that had formed in the decomposing tissues of the brain and sent the organ rising to the surface of the canal. As Cox also took the time to mention, "Extensive putrefaction with a foul-smelling odor [was] present."

Cox completed his work with an examination of the teeth. He found the upper right incisor missing, where a new tooth had been erupting through the gum to take its place. All the other teeth were whole, though there looked to be an amalgam filling in the last left molar, an observation that Cox confirmed with X-rays. With that, Cox concluded his examination. All he could do then was wait.

At about 11:00 a.m. on Tuesday, Lieutenant Dick Hynds, the supervisor of detectives who had introduced Joe Matthews around Hollywood PD less than a week before, arrived in Vero Beach, accompanied by John Monahan, the man whose own son John Walsh had saved that long-ago day at the Diplomat Hotel. Hynds brought with him Adam Walsh's records and X-rays from Hollywood dentist Marshall Berger, which showed an amalgam filling "on the buccal side of the last lower left deciduous molar." The filling was identical to that which Cox had discovered.

If there remained any doubt as to the identity of the remains, Monahan quickly took care of it. He took one look at the face—he *could* be wrong, he told himself—then asked the medical examiner to part the lips. When he saw the missing incisor and the tooth that had been coming in to replace it, his hopes vanished. He closed his eyes briefly, then turned to Hynds and Cox. "That's him," Monahan said. "That's Adam Walsh."

Earlier that morning, John Walsh awakened in his bed at the St. Moritz Hotel in New York City, groping over a still-sleeping Revé for the ringing phone. As he lifted the receiver, he glanced at the bedside clock: 6:00 a.m.

Walsh was so groggy he couldn't even be sure who the caller was, but when he finally made his purpose clear, Walsh snapped awake.

Some remains had been found, the voice on the other end was telling him—it was a cop, wasn't it?—but Walsh was not to be concerned, since the discovery had been made such a distance from Hollywood. They suspected it was a missing ten-year-old boy from the Tampa area. They just needed the name of the Walsh family dentist—they'd get the records and rule out any chance that it was Adam. Meantime, Walsh should not be worried.

Not be worried? Walsh thought, as he gave the caller the information. He hung up the phone, trying to process what he had just heard, trying to decide whether or not to wake Revé and share the news.

As he pondered, the phone rang again, and Walsh snatched it up. This time it was a producer from *Good Morning America*. Word had already reached the network that a severed head had been found in a canal in Florida. The producer wanted to offer the Walshes a chance to cancel their appearance on the show in case the remains turned out to be Adam's.

But Walsh wasn't canceling anything. Despite the dread that he was feeling, he couldn't be certain what this discovery in Florida might mean, and the opportunity to appear on national television to publicize Adam's disappearance was one in a million. He had brought along photographs of other desperate parents' missing children as well; no way could he cancel the appearance.

"What else can I do?" he told the producer, willing away his dread. Even if it was Adam who'd been found, he said, "I still have to give it a shot for all the other kids."

The producer understood. This was the Walshes' call. The car would be at the hotel to pick them up, as scheduled.

By the time Revé woke, Walsh had made the decision to keep the phone calls to himself. No point in worrying her, he told himself. And besides, to talk about the calls only made the possibility that Adam had been harmed seem all the more real.

The interview, with *Good Morning America* coanchor David Hartman, went on for seven full minutes, without a hitch. The Walshes described their plight in touching detail, and Adam's photograph and description were broadcast to millions of viewers around the country. John got the opportunity to work in photos of the other missing children as well. It was the first time that national network news had ever broadcast such a story on the helpless situations parents of missing children often found themselves in, and for all that the Walshes were cheered.

At the end of the piece, however, Hartman asked about the chilling report that remains of a young boy had been discovered in a canal near Vero Beach. Walsh stole a quick look at Revé. She was quiet and composed, but he knew his wife well enough—she'd been blindsided by the news.

Walsh quickly told Hartman that he'd been reassured the discovery had nothing to do with Adam. And in any case, the news only underscored the importance of their appearance on the show. There were terrible things that were going on all the time, and no one was hearing about them. It was vitally important to get the word out quickly, everywhere, when a child went missing.

By the time the segment was over, Revé seemed to have put aside the disturbing news Hartman had divulged, and John was relieved that his sister Jane and a few others were there to help. "I have to run up to the room to make a couple of calls," he told them, as the car delivered them back to the St. Moritz. He promised to meet them just down the street at the Plaza for something to eat in just a few minutes.

Back in his room, John checked for messages and was relieved to find there were none. Still, he could not shake the ominous feeling that the 6:00 a.m. call had instilled in him. A child's head found severed and floating in a canal. Unthinkable. Surely such a thing could not have happened to his Adam. Besides, the voice on the other end of the telephone line had told him not to worry. But how long could he live with such uncertainty? One moment he was composed, the next he found himself fighting to draw a breath.

He glanced at his watch—11:35 a.m.—and that was when the phone rang again. "Give it to me straight," he told the caller. And that is what he got. *Hollywood Sun-Tattler* reporter Charlie Brennan, who'd accompanied John and Revé on their trip to New York, was in the room and later described Walsh as he hung up the phone: "A man with a large part of his heart now stolen."

Revé Walsh was sitting with her sister-in-law at the bar of the Plaza Hotel when a young man with a carefully masked expression came to whisper something in Jane's ear. Jane's expression did not waver, but in Revé's mind, all the pieces fell immediately into place.

All Jane would say was that John was waiting for her back at the hotel. But Revé knew. No one had to tell her. She was Adam's mother.

On the way back to the St. Moritz, it was Revé who squeezed Jane's hand and told her it would be all right. And when John opened the door to their room and said simply, "Our baby's dead," Revé could only reach out for his waiting arms and hold on and tell him that yes, she knew.

Shortly after noon on Tuesday, and at the urging of Hollywood authorities, medical examiner Cox phoned Dr. Ron Wright, his counterpart in Ft. Lauderdale, to pass along the results of his preliminary examination. As chief medical examiner in the county where the investigation of Adam's disappearance was centered, Wright was the natural choice to complete the autopsy. Accordingly, Cox had the remains packed in ice and handed them over to Ronald Young, one of the Hollywood detectives present at Cox's exam, who quickly boarded a helicopter for Broward County.

By 4:00 p.m., Dr. Wright had begun his own examination, quickly determining that the brain matter inside the skull had liquefied, which suggested that death had occurred at least ten days or more prior to discovery. Among other findings, Wright reported that the victim had received repeated blows to the face and had suffered a fractured nose. Given the presence of burst blood vessels in the eyes, Wright theorized that the victim had been strangled and, at the time of the decapitation, was likely dead. He noted the likely cause of death as "asphyxiation," which put a slightly finer point on medical examiner Cox's preliminary notation of "homicide."

As to the decapitation itself, Wright said that it had taken place with the victim lying facedown, that the assailant had been right-handed, that the person had employed a machete or cleaver with a blade five inches or more in length, and would necessarily have needed two hands on the weapon's handle in order to exert the required force.

Meanwhile, search and dive teams had been dispatched to the canal where Adam's head had been discovered, but the failure to find the slightest bit of evidence led authorities to believe that the crime had taken place elsewhere, with the head discarded in the canal at a later time. Law enforcement officials in four neighboring counties searched other canals and fields for the body. Florida Highway Patrol officers combed both sides of Florida's Turnpike between Miami and Orlando looking for clothing or other clues, and game wardens in the vast swampy regions west of the turnpike redoubled their own efforts.

By Wednesday, the story was front-page news across South Florida: "Adam Walsh Found Dead—Discovered in Vero Canal." "Sixteen Days of Agony Grow into Horrid, Tragic Climax." "As Parents Pleaded, Police Suspected the Worst." Broward County medical examiner Wright told the Associated Press that indeed Adam had been dead for at least ten days before his head was found, and Hollywood supervisor of detectives Hynds warned that a dangerous psychopath was on the loose: "No one else could have done it," Hynds said.

The Walshes returned to South Florida on Tuesday evening and, after spending the following day fending off an onslaught from the media, held a private wake for their son at a local funeral home. On Saturday, Adam's funeral took place at St. Maurice's Catholic Church in Hollywood, with more than one thousand people in attendance.

Father Michael Conboy, John Walsh's cousin and a pastor at an upstate New York parish, delivered the eulogy. "We'll see you again, Cooter," Conboy said. "We promise."

The words were spoken as John, wearing a gray suit and tie, and Revé, in a muted print dress and dark-banded straw hat, stood somberly by an empty coffin. Adam's remains were being held by police. It was a necessary step, authorities explained. Should there be a confession, they would then be able to match the statement against the evidence.

Also in accordance with standard police procedure, Hollywood PD stationed a photographer to take surveillance photos of the attendees. It was not unknown for a stranger to turn up among the mourners of a loved one, and sometimes that stranger—drawn by the stir—turned out to be the reason for it all. Or to put it another way, sometimes the cops plain got lucky.

It was in this way, then, that the search for a missing little boy was transformed to a search for the person responsible for his death. The former undertaking, however grueling, had been fueled in part by a certain measure of hopefulness; but success in the latter would depend much more on grim resolve. In the end, it would turn out to be an extraordinarily long and arduous undertaking, and where luck figured in, almost all of it was bad.

CHAPTER FOUR

Through the Boneyard

Q: I know it's been four years . . .

A: Yeah, sometimes I can't keep it all straight in my mind.

Q: If I show you some pictures, maybe it'll help you remember.

A: Maybe.

Q: How about this one looking down into the culvert where we found the body. Do you remember stopping and throwing her down into the culvert?

A: Not really.

Q: How about this one? It's a little closer. You can see she's wearing only orange socks.

A: Yeah, I remember, now.

Q: But you don't remember what you did with the rest of her clothes?

A: Lots of times I'd just take the clothes and drive a piece and throw them down on the road a little ways from the body. Other times I'd leave them right there. I just don't remember about this one.

—OTTIS TOOLE TO DETECTIVES, JACKSONVILLE COUNTY JAIL, DECEMBER 28, 1983

HOLLYWOOD, FLORIDA—AUGUST 13, 1981

The day after the news of Adam's death broke, Hollywood detectives received a report from Dr. Mark Reisner, a psychologist sometimes employed by the Los Angeles Police Department, who offered an unsolicited profile of the type of individual "capable of abducting, murdering and decapitating Adam Walsh." According to Reisner, who based his report on a match of the known details of the case against data compiled on known psychopathic behavior, Adam's killer was almost certainly male, somewhere between nineteen and thirty-five, though most probably in his early twenties.

Because such behavior is not generally interracial in nature, Reisner theorized that the perpetrator was either Caucasian or Latin. The nature of the crime also indicated the possession of a "borderline" psychopathic/psychotic personality with a powerful homosexual conflict ultimately expressed in rage and violence. Although the person was very likely a loner, liked by few, he would nonetheless be motivated to brag about the actions he had taken in order to validate his sense of self-worth. However, Reisner said, it was unlikely that he would exhibit any sense of remorse or guilt, or offer a formal confession to the abduction or murder.

The individual would likely have gained little formal education, Reisner noted, and probably came from a lower socioeconomic background, with a work history involving manual labor and jobs requiring minimal skills. Because such an individual would not have progressed in any meaningful social or psychological way himself, he would be likely to identify with and be attracted to children. He might even have sought work that placed him in the company of children, with whom he could more easily develop bonds than with adults, either male or female.

Almost certainly, Reisner said, this individual had abducted or attempted to abduct other children in the past. And Reisner was equally certain that he had sexually assaulted other children and had very likely been arrested and imprisoned for such acts. Perhaps most distressing was one of Reisner's final observations, that the decapitation and disposal of the head indicated that there had been sexual contact with the boy—the perpetrator ridding himself of the principal locus of the shame, as it were.

While all this might have proven of interest to investigators, there was little that matched up with any of the individuals in the known orbit of the Walsh family's lives. Certainly, Reisner's profile dovetailed with Lieutenant Hynd's statement that only a psychopath could have done what was done to Adam, but as to the identity of that individual or suggestions as to how he might be found, there was not much to go on.

On Tuesday, August 18, lead detective Hoffman called Revé Walsh to Hollywood PD headquarters, where he and partner Hickman led her through a painstaking re-creation of her activities on the day that Adam disappeared. Her account was virtually identical to that which she had provided before, however, leaving the detectives stymied. By August 27, the baffled department issued a statement to the press that the investigation had been scaled back to three detectives. As Detective Hoffman explained, "It can't go on forever. The manpower is needed in other places."

On August 28, Hoffman met with Adam Walsh's first-grade teacher, Christine Bernard, who assured the detective that Adam was a good student, but a shy and somewhat timid boy who had never wandered off during recess or school outings. Following that interview, Hoffman returned to the Sears store to interview the clerk who had waited on Revé Walsh the day of Adam's disappearance. The clerk recalled Revé, obviously, and remembered her returning in distress to the lamp department looking for Adam, but she had nothing useful to add. On the following day, a UP story carried a statement that seemed provocative enough: an investigator with the Broward County medical examiner's office told reporters that they knew what kind of weapon had been used to decapitate Adam Walsh but were keeping the information secret so that they could discount the claims of "wackos who want to claim responsibility."

There appeared to be no surplus of such wackos lining up, however. Hollywood PD public information officer Fred Barbetta admitted to reporters that the investigation seemed to have hit a dead end. "We have nothing to go on," he said. "Nothing whatsoever."

The only solid lead that had come their way—the supposed sighting of Adam being dragged into a blue Ford van—had resulted in nothing but frustration for officers and area drivers alike. Police had checked a list of nearly seven thousand such vehicles sold in South Florida over the past three years, Barbetta said, but nothing had come of it. Though twenty-five detectives had originally been assigned to the case, only Hoffman and Hickman now remained, and scarcely a month had gone by.

On September 2, Detective Hoffman for the first time interviewed Sears security guard Kathy Shaffer, the first person at the store to whom Revé had gone for help when she discovered Adam missing. Though Shaffer had told Revé that she had not seen her son that day, her story to Detective Hoffman was somewhat different. She said that in fact she had witnessed a bit of a disturbance at the Atari PlayStation display at around 12:30 on the day of the disappearance. Two white male children and two black male children appeared to be arguing over the game, and as she approached them to see what was going on, one of the black kids slapped one of the white kids, a child whom she judged to be ten or so. One of the black children spoke impertinently to Shaffer, she said, and she told them all to leave the store.

The two black children left via the south doors, Shaffer told Hoffman, and the two white children left through the north doors. When the detective asked her to describe the second white child, Shaffer said that he was probably about seven, and had been wearing green shorts and a white shirt. At that point, Hoffman produced several photographs of Adam and asked if that was the boy she was talking about. Shaffer studied the photographs and then glanced up at Hoffman. She simply was not sure, she told him, and with that, Hoffman concluded their interview.

Two days later, on September 4, Hoffman's partner Hickman reinterviewed Marilyn Pottenberg, mother of the young boy who reported seeing Adam being dragged into "a blue van." With Mrs. Pottenberg and her son Timothy on that day was Timothy's grandmother Carolyn Hudson, and the two women pieced together the details of their shopping trip to Sears on the day of the abduction. They had arrived at the store about 11:45 a.m., they recalled, and left to have lunch at about 12:35 p.m. As they were leaving the store, Hudson recalls, they heard the page for a missing child. They all had lunch together, and at about 1:25, nearly an hour later, as they were walking through the parking lot toward their car, Timothy witnessed the incident with "the blue van."

If Hickman sighed as he recorded the details given him by Mrs. Pottenberg and her mother, he doesn't say so in his notes. But the information he'd just been given was the death knell for the "blue van" theory. Who knows what Timothy Pottenberg had actually seen that day? But it certainly wasn't Adam Walsh being dragged into a van, not almost an hour after his mother had begun her frantic search for him. "It appears that the incident that Timothy Pottenberg witnessed is unrelated to the Adam Walsh abduction," Hickman concluded.

With that lead gone, Hollywood PD was reduced to grasping at straws. Joe Matthews was asked to schedule a polygraph examination with Revé Walsh, to confirm that her unwavering account of Adam's disappearance could be trusted, and Mat-

thews arranged it for Thursday, September 10, at police headquarters.

At about nine on the morning of September 10, as Matthews
traveled down Flamingo Road in western Broward County, on
his way to meet with Revé, he found himself stuck behind a
sedan traveling maybe fifteen miles an hour. Matthews pulled
into the opposite lane to pass, but realized that the wise-guy
driver on his right had suddenly sped up. Worse yet, a dump
truck was now approaching from the opposite direction, and
the driver he was trying to pass showed no signs of letting him
by. Trapped now, Matthews floored his Plymouth and managed
to squeeze past, only an instant before the roaring dump truck
could pulverize him.

A bullet dodged, he was thinking, but then the real night-
mare began.

What happened next was a blur. His wheels dropped off
the pavement, digging into the gravel shoulder, and in the next
instant the Plymouth was airborne. To anyone watching, it
would have seemed like a spectacular scene from a car chase in
an action film. The Plymouth soared out over the broad drainage canal that paralleled the highway, twisted over, then pan-
caked top-down onto the water's surface.

The impact rendered Matthews momentarily unconscious.
When he came to, he found himself under several feet of water,
still behind the wheel, the Plymouth sinking steadily toward
the canal's muddy bottom. People and their vehicles ended up
in these canals on an almost daily basis, and helicopter shots of
bystanders gaping as cars and vans—often bearing their unfortunate passengers—were winched out were a staple of South Florida television news. Matthews had seen it a hundred times and
had always marveled at the spectacular misfortune of the victims.

He'd rather go head-on into a bridge piling than sink to a
watery grave, but somehow he had ended up in just that place,

and goddamn Napoleon Bonaparte Broward anyway for thinking he had the right to drain the Everglades just so he could line
his pockets. . . .

It's the sort of thinking that passes in a millisecond during
a crash. In the next moment, Matthews had already forgotten
about bad luck and greed, one hand groping for the door lever,
the other flailing about for the precious possession beside him.
He snatched his polygraph instrument by its case handle, managed to wrench his door open, then kicked himself free of the
sinking car and burst to the surface of the murky water, gasping.
Already, there was a highway patrolman clambering down the
steep bank to help him out.

The cop took the case and helped Matthews up the rocky,
debris-laden slope. At the top he regarded Matthews for a
moment, then reached into the trunk of his cruiser and handed
him a towel. "You better hold this on your head until the ambu-
lance gets here," he said.

Matthews stared back at the cop, uncomprehending. "Why
would I need to do that?"

"Just hold it right here," the cop said, pressing the towel to
Matthews's head.

At the hospital, several hundred stitches to his laid-open
skull later, Matthews gradually came to realize how badly he'd
been hurt. Furthermore, he recalled, he'd been on his way to
an important appointment, and managed to convince his doctors that he had to make a phone call. Only after he'd spoken to
someone at Hollywood PD, then managed to reach his brother
to tell him what had happened, did he give in to the doctors and
the sedatives.

When he woke the next day, there was something nagging
at Matthews, but he was still groggy from the concussion he'd
suffered, and a severely dislocated shoulder was causing him
immense pain. He simply couldn't put his finger on what was
gnawing at him.

Not until he was released and on his way home several days later did he remember once again the polygraph exam that he had scheduled with Revé Walsh. The moment he made his way through the door of his house, he called Jack Hoffman at Hollywood PD. "I'm sorry about the exam, but I had a pretty bad accident—," Matthews began, but Hoffman cut him off.

"Yeah, we heard," the detective said. "Don't worry. We got somebody else to do it."

"Really?" Matthews said, taken aback. Matthews wasn't even sure how Hoffman knew he'd been hurt, for he had no recollection of making the call to Hollywood PD from the hospital. And while he couldn't blame Hoffman for going ahead without him, it was still a bit disconcerting—it would have been better for consistency's sake to have the same person conducting all the polygraph exams. What Hoffman said next, however, took him completely by surprise.

"Fact is, I'm glad you called," Hoffman continued. "I wanted to let you know we won't be needing you any longer."

Matthews felt his jaw sag as Hoffman continued. The investigation was winding down, the detective explained. If the need for any other testing arose, the department could take care of it themselves. Matthews could go on back to Miami Beach.

Matthews stared at the phone, as the connection broke, incensed at Hoffman and dismayed at the prospects for the investigation. From the beginning, he had pegged Hoffman as a turf-protecting blowhard if there ever was one, but he had dealt with those types before. What was truly disheartening was the response he'd received from Lieutenant Hynds when he'd tried to point out how the investigation seemed to be going awry.

From the moment that Hynds had put him off, he'd sensed that he was battling a prevailing current of face-saving at Hollywood PD, but what could he do besides perform the job he'd been called in for and hope that his results would have some effect? And, he supposed, his efforts had achieved something. If not for his work, it was possible that a hapless Jimmy Campbell could be in custody right now, desperately trying to proclaim his innocence.

There was plenty on his own plate. He had a full-time job in Miami Beach, and he was being called in as an outside polygraph expert on a regular basis by other agencies as well, including Canada's Crown Counsel, the equivalent to the office of the U.S. attorney general. Also, there was his thriving technical school, the Southern Institute of Polygraph, to manage. In the end, Matthews could only wish Hollywood PD well, offer his help on the Walsh case at any time, and, for the time being, anyway, go back to work.

As Hoffman had suggested to Matthews, it seemed the beginning of the end of any serious search for Adam's killer at Hollywood PD. When Revé Walsh showed up for her scheduled examination with Matthews, she was questioned briefly about her activities on the day that Adam was taken. She was told that her polygraph would have to be rescheduled, and on the following Monday, September 14, an examiner from the Broward County State Attorney's Office conducted the exam. Once again, Revé recounted the events of the day that her son disappeared, and the examiner confirmed that she had passed—there were no signs of deception anywhere in her account.

A few days later, detectives returned to the Sears store to reinterview the employees who had been working the day of Adam's kidnapping, but the results were fruitless. On September 22, there was a brief flurry of excitement when a St. Lucie County Sheriff's Department detective phoned Hoffman to relay a tip that a Fort Pierce woman named Mary Green was involved in the kidnapping of Adam Walsh. According to the tipster, Green had knowledge as to who had actually killed the boy.

It took Hoffman and Hickman a few days, but on September 30, the two traveled to Fort Pierce in St. Lucie County, just south of the spot where Adam's severed head was pulled from the canal. They spoke with St. Lucie County detectives and then interviewed Mary Green and her live-in lover J. A. Childress, whom local authorities identified as the source of the tip.

Green admitted to the detectives that she was a chronic alcoholic—in fact she had spent a couple of nights in the Fort Pierce detox center shortly before the time of Adam's disappearance. Like everyone else, she had heard all about the crime, but she certainly had no involvement in the matter, nor did she know anyone who did. She explained to Hoffman and Hickman that Childress, the man who had turned her in, was also a drunk and prone to all sorts of deception. He was upset with her at the time, and simply decided to tell people she'd been involved in the kidnapping.

Though by now it seemed a waste of time, Hoffman and Hickman arranged for the St. Lucie County Sheriff's Department to administer a polygraph examination to Green. When the examiner was finished, what already seemed apparent to the detectives was confirmed. Mary Green might be a hapless loser, but she had nothing to do with the kidnapping and murder of Adam Walsh.

It was as if the trip to St. Lucie County had sapped the last energies of the Hollywood PD. An internal supplemental report dated October 5, 1981, gave a terse, if somewhat inelegant, statement of the obvious: "As of this date this agency has not received any substantial leads that would implicate anyone to the crime."

Nine days later Detectives Hoffman and Hickman, acting on a tip, interviewed a man named Charles Elchwartzle, the owner of a blue Ford van, but, as it turned out, being in possession of such a vehicle in South Florida at the time was Elchwartzle's only misstep. On October 22, Hoffman and Hickman called in Jimmy Campbell to cover "areas possibly not covered in the previous interview . . . conducted by Mr. Joe Matthews," but that came to nothing as well. For all intents and purposes, and less than two months after the incident, the active investigation of the abduction and murder of Adam Walsh was at a standstill.

JACKSONVILLE, FLORIDA—JULY 28, 1981

When Ottis Toole returned to Jacksonville following his late July 1981 foray into South Florida, his life resumed without a hitch. He returned the Cadillac he had "borrowed" from the Reaves Roofing compound without anyone having noticed it missing. And though his brother Howard and his sister-in-law Georgia had tried to file charges against Ottis for the theft of their pickup truck that was abandoned in Delaware, the Florida state attorney's office found the case too shaky to prosecute.

With his mother's house a charred ruin, Toole needed a new place to live, so he rented a room in a blue-collar rooming house owned by a woman named Betty Goodyear. Toole then reconnected with his erstwhile wife, Rita, and convinced her to move in with him on July 31.

At about 4:00 p.m. the following day, Rita—twenty-four years Toole's senior—glanced out the window of their room to see a familiar-looking man striding up the sidewalk. "Hey, looks like your brother Howard's here," Rita said, turning. But Ottis was in full flight out the back door.

Howard was about to knock, but when he heard the back door bang, he realized it would be a waste of time. He vaulted off the porch and lit out after Ottis, who was running down Market Street for all he was worth. Ottis made it as far as the entrance to a Little Champ convenience store on the corner before his brother caught up with him.

"Someone's going to shoot me," Ottis cried to the clerk as he burst through the door.

"Go ahead and call the cops," Howard added as he ran in on Ottis's heels. He snatched Ottis by the collar and began slapping him. "This son of a bitch stole my truck."

The encounter might have given Howard Toole some minor satisfaction, but as the cops who arrived to quell the disturbance soon pointed out, there were no grounds upon which they could take Ottis into custody. For his part, Ottis had no interest in pressing assault charges against his brother, and the matter ended for the time being with Howard skulking off and Ottis figuring he'd taken his rightful lumps.

In the days that followed, Toole got by doing yard work for Goodyear at her various properties and helped out as best he could in her office, though the fact that he could not read well limited his usefulness there. He also found employment at the modest parish of the Church of God on Ramona Boulevard, where pastor Cecil Wiggins paid him $17.50 for lawn maintenance one day late in August and another $22.75 on the next.

In the meantime, Betty Goodyear's son James Redwine had returned home from some kicking around in Miami of his own, and he and Ottis were soon hanging out together, sometimes cruising the streets in an older-model Cadillac. One evening Toole showed Redwine a .22-caliber pistol that he pulled from under the seat of the Caddy. He told Redwine he was thinking of using the pistol to kill a couple of drifters who had been hanging around a local park. Redwine, who had also seen a large wooden-handled knife under the seat of the Caddy, didn't know if Ottis was serious about killing anyone, but he did see him fire a shot over the head of one of Goodyear's tenants shortly thereafter.

"What was that all about?" Redwine asked Toole as the tenant hightailed it in terror down the street.

"The guy just pissed me off," Ottis said.

Early in October, with the car theft charges dropped, Ottis Toole's former lover Henry Lee Lucas was finally released by Pikeville, Maryland, authorities. Lucas made his way back to Jacksonville, and before long found Ottis and was able to explain where he'd been all this time. Lucas had not abandoned Ottis for his niece Frieda. The separation was just bad luck, and once he'd been thrown in jail, there was no way for him to get in touch.

As to Frieda and nephew Frank, they were now in foster care somewhere in Polk County, down by Tampa. The children's mother had died of a drug overdose that might have been a suicide, and they'd spent a few weeks in the custody of their stepfather, A. J. Carr, until Frieda told Child Protective Services that Carr was physically abusing her. When a polygraph exam confirmed Frieda's story, Health Rehabilitation Services had stepped in to take custody of the children. All grim news by most standards, but in the world of Ottis Toole and Henry Lee Lucas, it was just the ordinary stuff of life.

Ottis was happy to know that Lucas had not forsaken him, of course. Things had not worked out so well between him and Rita, and before long he and Lucas had moved into another of Betty Goodyear's rooming houses. He and Lucas worked together for Reaves Roofing for one day right before Christmas, and then Ottis managed to get Goodyear to hire Lucas as a fellow maintenance worker. Indeed, five months after they'd split up and Toole had gone to South Florida on his little fling, things seemed to be working out for the two of them.

There was a troubling incident at one of Goodyear's properties right after the New Year, however. At about ten o'clock on the night of January 4, 1982, a fire broke out in one of the bedrooms of a house she owned at 117 East Second Street, near downtown Jacksonville. When firefighters responded, they found sixty-five-year-old George Sonnenberg unconscious in the room next to the vacant quarters where the fire had broken out, second- and third-degree burns covering most of his body. Another tenant had suffered burns to his hands while trying to escape through a blazing door, and a third had broken his leg jumping from an upstairs window. Sonnenberg lingered in the hospital for a week before dying on January 11. Fire marshals ruled it an accident.

About the same time, James Redwine, Betty Goodyear's son, overheard Ottis Toole and Henry Lee Lucas cooking up a plan that seemed sure to land them in serious trouble. They'd discovered the whereabouts of "Becky" Powell, now living with foster parents in Auburndale, a small town about halfway between Tampa and Orlando, two or three hours from where they sat. "Me and Henry Lee'll go on down to Auburndale," Ottis explained to Redwine, "and we'll bring Becky on back."

But what if the foster parents she was living with objected? Redwine wondered.

Toole smiled at Henry Lee before he answered. "What do you think, you dumbass? Anyone tries to stop us, we'll just kill 'em."

Redwine tried to talk the pair out of the plan, but they were resolute. As Toole explained to Redwine, he and Henry Lee had pulled off far more difficult things in the past. A few days later, as they were about to get in Ottis's car and head out for Auburndale, the front door of their rooming house on East Seventh Street flew open, and Redwine heard a female voice shouting, "Uncle Ottis! Henry Lee!"

It was fourteen-year-old Frieda "Becky" Powell with her arms outstretched, overjoyed to see Uncle Ottis and Henry Lee again.

To Redwine it seemed a miracle, but authorities in Auburndale were well aware of Frieda's history with Ottis Toole and Henry Lee Lucas, and it was not long before investigators were nosing around Betty Goodyear's office, wondering if anyone had seen a young woman matching Frieda's description.

If Toole wasn't sure what to do next, Frieda and Henry Lee had no difficulty making their decision. According to Redwine the pair had been gone from Jacksonville for two days before Toole realized that they had skipped out on him once again.

Toole, whose only real loves in life were his mother, his niece, and Henry Lee, took it hard. He paced his room for days, muttering to himself, and then, after buying a white-on-white two-door Cadillac from Spencer's Motors in Jacksonville, he disappeared.

Toole spent some time out west, made a few brief acquaintances in Louisiana, then finally turned up again in Jacksonville, where he was arrested on September 22, 1982, for driving without a valid driver's license. On November 1, he was arrested again by sheriff's deputies on the same charge, giving his address as 217 East Third Street and the name of his employer as Betty Goodyear.

Toole was through with wandering. He rekindled his relationship with Goodyear's son James Redwine and picked up his threadbare existence in Jacksonville where he'd left it a year before, though still without Lucas and "Becky" at his side. It is hard to say how long he might have carried on as it appeared he always had, just one more figure on the margins of life, managing somehow to stay afloat.

But the truth beneath the surface of Toole's dismal existence was far darker than anyone might have suspected. *Rotten teeth, unkempt hair, rank breath, and filthy clothes*—check! *Borderline intelligence, a bad attitude, poor coping skills*—on the mark. *Friends*— none. *Acquaintances*—few. *Skills*—nonexistent. *Prospects*—nil.

All dismal enough, perhaps, but what Toole had hiding in the wings made those attributes seem the stuff of a Disney hero in comparison. And if he hadn't finally had a little truly bad luck, the horror-show side of Ottis Toole might never have been known.

JACKSONVILLE, FLORIDA—MAY 31, 1983

Until the passage of the Uniform Holidays Bill in 1968, Memorial Day was always celebrated on May 30, a time set aside to honor U.S. men and women who died while engaged in military service. As John Logan, the commander in chief of the Grand Army of the Republic, wrote in his 1868 general order, the purpose of "Decoration Day," as it was originally known, was to fly the flag and strew graves with garlands in proud memory of all those heroes who had "made their breasts a barricade between our country and its foe."

Over time, Memorial Day has become a somewhat trivialized occasion, its luster dimmed by a series of unpopular wars over the past half century and its date now shifting year by year to coincide with the last Monday in May. Perhaps a weary workforce and school population now welcome a three-day weekend as an unofficial kickoff to the summer season, but surely the holiday achieves little to instill the sense of honor, duty, and sacrifice it was designed for.

Certainly there was no such apparent effect on James Redwine, Ottis Toole's sometime companion, and pal Charles Hammock, two juveniles picked up by police the afternoon following the holiday's observance in Jacksonville in 1983. That morning, Redwine and Hammock had expressed their own holiday passions by setting fire to an unoccupied house at 1203 Hubbard Street.

Tipped off by an informant, police tracked down the pair, who quickly admitted setting fire to both the Hubbard Street house and another unoccupied house in the same neighborhood of Springfield a week earlier. However, Redwine told officers, they had help in these arsons. A man named Ottis Toole, an erstwhile boarder in his mother's various rooming houses, had convinced them that burning down houses could be great fun, and they had gone along.

Accordingly, officers set out looking for Toole, who offered no resistance when they finally picked him up the following Monday, June 6. In fact, Toole not only confessed to the two arsons in question but told police that he had set dozens of fires in Jacksonville over the past twenty years, most of them in vacant buildings. He rode along with officers through a series of downtrodden neighborhoods, identifying thirty-six such sites where arson had been suspected, including his mother's house at 708 Day Street. He'd been setting fires since he was nine, he told police, doing it "to keep blacks out of the neighborhood" and also because it turned him on sexually.

During a court-ordered psychological examination, Toole told Dr. Ernest Miller that setting fires allowed him to "fantasize sex," and that he would characteristically watch the blazes from a distance and masturbate. He told the doctor that he was a homosexual, but claimed that while he enjoyed the company of children, he had never consummated a sexual relationship with a child. He also told the doctor that he'd been suffering seizures from the time in his childhood when he'd been struck in the head with a rock. He'd been taking Dilantin for years, he said, and was accustomed to drinking a little whiskey each night— "about half a pint"—plus several six-packs.

He told Miller that he had been suffering from depression for more than two years since the death of his mother and admitted that the overdose of pills that had landed him in the hospital in Newport News was in fact a suicide attempt. "At times he fancies he hears voices saying he should kill himself and 'go to rest,'" Miller wrote, adding that Toole was unclear as to whether the voices came from his own mind or from the devil.

While Toole told the doctor that he thought his memory was "poor" and that he "had trouble thinking," Miller adjudged that his basic cognitive functions were intact and that he exhibited only minor memory problems related to immediate recall. "Can tell time and is of average native intelligence," Miller said. "Is able to register, store, and retrieve data fairly well."

The doctor's clinical impression was that Toole exhibited borderline character disorder and that while he was a "severely disturbed man," he was nonetheless competent to stand trial. Meanwhile, Miller recommended that Toole receive treatment for "psychosexual conflicts, pyromania and alcoholism-drug dependency."

While Toole received no formal treatment for his problems, he was awarded a speedy trial where he was summarily convicted of the two May arsons he confessed to in his Springfield neighborhood. He received a fifteen-year sentence for one fire and a five-year sentence for the second, with the terms to run consecutively. On Thursday, August 11, 1983, he was received at the Union Correctional Institution at Raiford, Florida. At the age of thirty-six, and with a lifetime of bad news behind him, the tide of Ottis Toole's fortunes had finally begun to turn.

At the same time that Toole arrived at Raiford, his former partner Henry Lee Lucas was facing serious difficulties of his own in Texas, where he and Becky Powell had gone when they'd fled Jacksonville back in 1982. Lucas had been arrested in Stoneberg, a hamlet northwest of Fort Worth, near the Oklahoma border, on June 11, 1983, suspected in the murder of a woman named Catherine Powell. Powell had been discovered in her rural home outside Tyler, Texas, the previous summer, sexually abused and shot once in the head. In addition, Lucas had been questioned by Ouachita Parish, Louisiana, detective Jay Via about a series of unsolved murders in the county seat of Monroe and elsewhere in the area.

Finally, Lucas began to crack. He admitted that he had killed Catherine Powell the previous August, and he also said that he had killed Ottis Toole's niece Becky, then fifteen, in Denton, Texas, a few days later. Lucas would eventually claim responsibility for more than two hundred murders, though he also told police that he had been assisted in several of the crimes by a man from Jacksonville, Florida, named Ottis Toole. While authorities were uncertain as to just how much credit to give these claims, police with dead-end cases from around the South were soon on their way to Texas to speak with Lucas.

One such detective was Buddy Terry, from the Jacksonville Sheriff's Office homicide unit. On Thursday, August 11, during an interview with Terry, Henry Lee Lucas confessed to the murder of eight women in Jacksonville between 1979 and 1981.

Lucas also recounted another crime to Terry, one that involved Ottis Toole.

He'd been with Toole when he set fire to one of Betty Goodyear's rooming houses, Lucas told Terry. Toole was upset with several of the men who lived in that particular house because they would not respond to his sexual advances, Lucas said. While Lucas watched, Toole took a can of gasoline from the trunk of his car, made his way into a vacant back bedroom of the house, doused the room with the fuel, and lit it with a match.

Lucas told Terry that the two of them drove around the block several times, watching as the flames built, firemen responded, and residents leaped from windows. Lucas said that they also watched as EMS technicians dragged resident George Sonnenberg to the front porch and worked desperately to revive him. From Toole's point of view, Lucas assured Terry, things could simply not have turned out better.

JACKSONVILLE, FLORIDA—AUGUST 30, 1983

Following his interview with Henry Lee Lucas in Texas, Detective Terry returned to Jacksonville and made arrangements with Florida prison authorities to interview Ottis Toole at Raiford. Understandably, Terry was eager to learn whether Toole had in fact been complicit in the various crimes as Lucas claimed, or whether the convicted arsonist might simply be a convenient scapegoat for a guilty man to use in easing his own burden.

On August 30, 1983, Terry met with Toole at the prison's Reception and Medical Center. There, Toole confirmed that he had known Lucas since 1979 and that he had in fact been in love with him. He and Lucas had shared a homosexual relationship, Toole said, and the two of them had traveled together to several parts of the country.

As to the rooming house fire, Toole told Detective Terry that not everything that Lucas had said was true. For instance, Toole wanted Terry to know that he had not doused that vacant bedroom with gasoline before setting it ablaze . . . given his experience in starting fires, he explained, there was no need for such trouble. He had set the fire, sure, but to get it going he had simply torn the cover off a foam mattress and set that highly flammable substance ablaze with a match. And while he was aware that several men lived in the building, he had no idea that anyone, including the unfortunate George Sonnenberg, was home at the time. It was simply Sonnenberg's tough luck.

So if Toole hadn't set out with the intention of harming Sonnenberg, Terry wondered, then why had he set the fire in the first place? The question brought a guileless smile to Toole's face. Setting fires just made him feel good, he told Terry. He guessed he'd set a couple hundred of them around Jacksonville over the past few years.

Detective Terry nodded, finished up his notes, and gave Toole a smile of his own. "You're under arrest for arson—," he began, but Toole simply shrugged.

"I'm already here for that," he said, indicating their spartan surroundings.

"—and for the murder of George Sonnenberg," Terry concluded. The fool's luck that Ottis Toole had enjoyed all his life had finally run its course.

Nine days later, on Thursday, September 8, 1983, Toole was indicted in Jacksonville on charges of murder and arson, and on September 13 he was transferred from Raiford to the Duval County Jail to await trial. It is hard to know if Toole felt anything similar to the apprehension or fear that most individuals might experience at such heightening of circumstance, but judging from the conversations he had with some of his cellmates and other detectives drawn to interview him in his new quarters, it does not seem that he was guarded or fearful.

He seemed happy to discover that among his fellow prisoners in the Duval County lockup were two old friends from his days in the early 1980s at Reaves Roofing, Bobby Lee Jones and James Collins, a man who also used the alias of Julius Wilkes. Toole chatted freely with Jones and Collins/Wilkes about the circumstances that had finally led him to jail, and when a Brevard County detective named Steve Kendrick showed up to interview him about an unsolved homicide that had taken place in Cocoa Beach, some two and a half hours to the south, Toole was even more forthcoming.

During the interview, which took place on Monday, October 10, 1983, Toole readily confessed to Kendrick that he had probably committed or taken part in at least sixty-five murders, though he didn't have any recollection of the Cocoa Beach case that Kendrick had come to talk about. After a half hour or so, Kendrick sensed that he was getting nothing useful regarding his own case out of Toole and turned his tape recorder off. As the detective was packing up to leave the interview room, some switch seemed to flip inside the man who had just a few moments before admitted to killing scores of people.

According to Kendrick, Toole suddenly straightened in his chair and looked up at him intently. "You're from Fort Lauderdale, right?"

"No." Kendrick shook his head. It occurred to him that Toole had confused Brevard County with Broward County, two hours farther south along the coast. But being an able cop, Kendrick was not about to let it drop. "Were you expecting someone from Fort Lauderdale?" he asked Toole.

Toole nodded.

"You get into something in Fort Lauderdale?" the detective prompted.

"Yeah, I did," Toole said.

Given that the man in front of him had readily identified himself as a serial killer, Kendrick might not have thought too much of the exchange, were it not for the sudden shift in Toole's behavior. He was gripping the sides of his chair tightly now, shifting uneasily from side to side, his gaze dropping abruptly from Kendrick's to the floor and back again. As his case notes make clear, Kendrick sensed that he had stumbled onto something big: "Reporting agent felt that for a man to admit involvement in sixty five (65) murders, but get upset about Ft. Lauderdale, it had to be something appalling."

Kendrick sat back down across from Toole and folded his hands in front of him. "Why don't you tell me about it?" the detective said. And Toole began to do just that.

He had found a little boy at a Sears store, Toole said, and told the boy that he had some candy and wanted to talk to him and convinced him to get in his Cadillac out in the parking lot. Toole told Kendrick that he was intending to take the boy back to Jacksonville and raise him as his own son, but it all changed when this Adam started crying and saying he wanted to get out of the car. The boy's behavior made him mad, Toole explained, and so he hit him in the face to shut him up. And then he turned off the highway onto a dirt road that had a fork at the end of it. And that was where he murdered this Adam and cut off his head and threw it into a pond somewhere along the side of the road.

In hindsight, one might wonder why such a statement did not mark the end of the hunt for the killer of Adam Walsh then and there. True, Detective Kendrick was from another jurisdiction and was only vaguely familiar with the case, and there would understandably be a bit of time for sorting out just what Ottis Toole was talking about . . . but surely, one might think, a speedy resolution of the matter was at hand. As the old saw goes, however, that is the trouble with assumptions. In truth, the trouble was just getting under way.

When Kendrick left the room after his second interview with Toole, he was a man on a mission. He found Detective Buddy Terry in his office and quickly shared the news. "He's talking about killing a child down in Broward County," Kendrick told Terry. "He says he cut him up and left the body in two different places. This is all out of the clear blue sky."

Terry remembers the moment well, though at the time he was not familiar with any child-killing case in South Florida (if nothing else, Terry's obliviousness speaks volumes about how times have changed). Still, based on Kendrick's certainty that Toole was confessing to a gruesome crime that he had in fact committed, he began calling various agencies in Broward County.

"I finally got hold of the Hollywood Police Department," Terry recalls, "and they told me that it sounded like the Adam Walsh case." Terry had no idea what Hollywood was talking about, but once it had been explained to him, he hurried to Kendrick with the news.

The following morning, October 11, Kendrick reached someone in the homicide division at Hollywood PD and gave a brief account of what he'd come across. "I identified myself as an investigator for the Brevard County Sheriff's Office," he says, "and said that I had just interviewed an individual pertaining to a homicide I was investigating. During the interview with the individual, he said a number of things that led me to believe that he is in fact the one who killed Adam Walsh."

Whomever Kendrick spoke to took the information and said that someone would be back in touch immediately. But "immediately" seemed to have a relative meaning. "Probably a week after that," Kendrick says, "I got a call from someone and we spoke briefly about my conversation with Ottis Toole about Adam. I don't believe I had any additional contact with them [the Hollywood PD] after that. I think I only spoke to them once."

With notification having been made to the Hollywood PD, there was nothing more for Detectives Kendrick or Terry to do regarding the Adam Walsh case. Kendrick returned to his office in Brevard County, and Terry went off to Louisiana to confer with authorities there pertaining to Henry Lee Lucas and his own investigation of the murder of George Sonnenberg.

As a result of the information shared during Terry's trip to Monroe, three detectives from Ouachita Parish, Louisiana, traveled back to Jacksonville with him to interview Toole regarding the murder of sixteen-year-old Sherry Alford in Monroe. On Tuesday, October 18, 1983, Detective Jay Via, who'd been among the first to question Henry Lee Lucas following his arrest, began his pre-interview conversation with Ottis Toole while Toole was eating his lunch.

Via casually asked Toole when he was going to start talking about all the blacks that Henry Lee Lucas claimed the two of them had killed. Toole broke off from eating to smile his Alfred E. Neuman–like smile. Surely Via understood why he wasn't about to start talking about that subject, Toole told the detective. The population of the Duval County Jail was about 90 percent black. How long did Via think Toole would last if he started bragging about killing "brothers"?

Via nodded in appreciation of Toole's wisdom. But he'd also heard some rumors that Toole had killed a bunch of kids during his travels across the country, he said. Kid killers weren't very popular in prison either. Were those rumors true? Via wondered.

At that, Via recalls, Toole's manner suddenly changed. He stopped in mid-bite and put down his chicken leg. "You talking about the kid that got his head cut off around West Palm Beach, Florida?" Toole said, guardedly.

Via checked his watch, noting that it was 3:20 in the afternoon. Toole had become a different person, instantaneously. For the first time, he made direct eye contact with Via and inquired again in a somber voice whether or not he was talking about the "kid" he had killed in South Florida.

"What kid are you talking about?" Via asked.

Toole pulled his knees up to his chest and began to weep. It was the "kid" he got from the Sears store, he explained.

Via was genuinely puzzled. He'd just been baiting Toole, and he'd certainly heard nothing of any child murder case in Florida—in fact, his conversations with Detective Terry of Jacksonville had been confined to the Alford case connecting Toole and Henry Lee Lucas. "I don't know what you're talking about," Via told Toole.

By this time, Toole was racked with sobs. He thought Via wanted to know about the kid he'd grabbed from the Sears store, the one whose head he'd cut off, Toole said.

At that point, Via went to the door of the interview room and called to Buddy Terry, who was standing down the hallway talking with Lieutenant Joe Cummings of the Monroe Police Department, who had come over with Via to interview Toole. "You better come in here," Via told Terry and Cummings. "He's just confessed to killing a child in South Florida."

While Terry quickly realized what Toole must have been talking to Via about, there was no point in getting into a discussion with him at the moment. He simply followed Via and Cummings back into the interview room and listened as Via asked Toole to explain exactly what he was referring to.

Toole replied that he had traveled to South Florida in a black-over-white Cadillac to find a "kid" to keep for his own. After driving around for some time, he spotted a mall parking lot, pulled in, and saw a young white boy standing outside a Sears store. Toole told the officers that he forced the child into his Cadillac, pulled out of the lot, and ended up on a highway. When the child would not stop screaming and crying, Toole said, he backhanded him in the face with a closed fist and then struck him again in the stomach, at which point the child slumped down in the seat, unconscious.

Toole was relieved that the child had stopped making noise, but it was not long before he began to think that he had actually killed the child and that he would have to dispose of the body. He traveled some distance on the "freeway," Toole said, exiting a couple of times before he ended up in a remote swampy area.

He parked, took the child out of the car, and laid him facedown over a log. He took a long-bladed knife—maybe a machete—from the trunk of the Cadillac and went back to where he had left the boy . . . and cut off his head.

It took several blows to accomplish the decapitation, Toole said, and after that, he used the blade to dismember the rest of the body and scatter it about the swamp. As he described his actions to Via, Terry, and Cummings, Toole took care to illustrate how he'd used his knuckles to backhand the boy in the face and his closed fist to hit him in the stomach. He also pantomimed removing the child from the seat of the Cadillac and laying him gently against a log.

Crying now, he told the detectives how he decided to keep the child's head at first, tossing it onto the backseat floorboard of the Cadillac. After he had driven a bit, he began to think better of this notion, however, and he pulled over to toss the decapitated head into a drainage ditch or canal of some kind. And after that, Toole said, he drove back to Jacksonville.

At the conclusion of the statement, the three detectives stepped out into the hallway, and it was only then that Buddy Terry told Via and Cummings that it sounded to him like Toole had just repeated—albeit in far more grisly detail—a confession he'd made the previous week, the killing of a child named Adam Walsh, who had been abducted from a Sears store two summers previously. Adam's head had been found floating in a canal a couple of weeks after his disappearance, Terry explained, but his body had never been found, and the killer was still on the loose.

Via shook his head and glanced back through the window of the interview room, where a shaken Toole still sat. He'd never heard of the case, Via told Terry. But whatever terrible things had happened, it sure seemed as if they'd found the party responsible.

It seemed that way to Buddy Terry, too. But both he and Via were reasonable men. And what developed with Toole from that point on would have little to do with reason.

JACKSONVILLE, FLORIDA—OCTOBER 19, 1983

According to a Hollywood PD supplemental report, eight days went by before Lieutenant Hynds passed along word to lead case detective Jack Hoffman that Buddy Terry of the Jacksonville Sheriff's Office had called with information pertaining to the disappearance and murder of Adam Walsh. Hoffman notes that he returned Terry's call at 3:10 p.m. on Wednesday, October 19, and by 9:00 p.m., he and his partner Hickman were in Jacksonville to interview Ottis Toole.

When they arrived, Terry advised the two that Toole was just finishing up another interview with Detective Via, from Louisiana. Via was the investigator who had extracted the most specific information from Toole, he explained, and they would likely want to confer with him before talking with Toole themselves. Yes, they did want to talk to Via, Hoffman told Terry, and with that, the two Hollywood detectives sat tight-lipped until Via came out of the interview room and Terry made introductions around.

It didn't take Hoffman long to set the tone for their interchange. He fixed Via with his disdainful stare, then delivered a jaw-dropping accusation. "So you're the one who's been feeding Toole details of my investigation?"

Via stared at the pair across from him, incredulous. "I don't know what you're talking about," Via managed finally, glancing at Terry to make sure he hadn't misheard. "I was interviewing Ottis Toole about a murder in Ouachita Parish, Louisiana, when, out of nowhere, he started talking about killing some 'kid' in South Florida."

Via had the distinct impression that nothing he was saying mattered in the slightest to Hoffman, but still he continued. "I got Detective Terry in the room along with my colleague Joe Cummings from Monroe, and asked this Toole to take us through his story from the beginning. When he was finished, I still didn't know who he was talking about. We left Toole in the interview room and went out in the hall to talk, and that's when Detective Terry told me that it sounded like Toole was talking about killing Adam Walsh. That's the first time in my life I even heard the name."

Hoffman glanced at Terry then, as if he had just spotted someone else to blame for meddling in his investigation. "I'm going to need a written report on this," he said to Via, skepticism saturating his tone.

"You can read my notes any time you want to," Via said. "Furthermore, I don't appreciate your attitude, my friend. I'm trying to do you a favor, and you come in here insinuating I'm leaking information to some douchebag like Ottis Toole? Where the hell would I even get it?"

Apart from another sidelong glance at Terry, there was no response. "Can we have him now?" Hoffman said, waving toward the interview room.

"He's all yours," Terry said. "You won't mind if I sit in, though, will you?"

The look Hoffman gave Terry told him that Hoffman very much minded, but there was little the Hollywood detective could do to keep Terry out. "He's your prisoner," Hoffman told Terry tersely, and the three moved inside the interview room with Toole.

Hoffman introduced himself and his partner Hickman and told Toole that they were from the Hollywood, Florida, Police Department. He offered a standard rights form for Toole to sign, but Toole waved it away. He understood his rights, he told Hoffman, and he understood that he was waiving his right to have an attorney present during the questioning that was about to take place. He didn't read all that well, he told Hoffman, indicating the form on the table before him. He'd only gone through the seventh grade, but he understood the English language well enough and he understood exactly what they were saying about his rights.

With that established, Hoffman asked Toole to give him a statement about what he claimed he'd done down in South Florida, and Toole readily agreed. It was a couple of years ago, he began, when he and his partner Henry Lee Lucas drove down to Fort Lauderdale in a 1973 black-over-white Cadillac that Toole had purchased from a woman in Jacksonville named Faye McNett. Buddy Terry lifted an eyebrow as he heard the mention of Lucas in the matter for the first time, but he said nothing.

Toole explained to Hoffman and Hickman that he had been depressed over the death of his mother that May, and that he and Lucas had been traveling around the country, as far as Texas and California, with his niece and nephew Frieda and Frank Powell. He told Hoffman that he and Lucas had returned to Jacksonville some time in June, and that before they set out on the trip to South Florida, he'd taken a Pennsylvania license tag from a car on the street and switched the plate on the Caddy.

The two of them had snatched a kid from outside a Sears store in a shopping mall, he told Hoffman, who then asked how Toole could be sure it was a Sears. Toole looked at Hoffman as if he were the barely functioning individual in the room. " 'Cause I know a Sears when I see a Sears," he said, as if explaining it to an idiot. He didn't remember actually going inside the Sears, though he may have, he told Hoffman. He was just window shopping and remembered having passed a wig shop when he saw the boy.

As to the time of the abduction, however, Toole responded in a way that was typical of his tenuous grasp of matters that most take for granted. "It would have to have been . . . ah . . . the afternoon, afternoon, afternoon. I call afternoon around noontime and that."

There'd been trouble with the boy in the car, Toole continued, and he'd had to slap and punch him to get him to quiet down. Eventually, he and Lucas had pulled off the turnpike, and Lucas had killed the boy by decapitating him "with an 18-inch bayonet" while Toole held Adam down on his stomach. He said Lucas had to hit the kid three or four times to get his head cut off. After that, they chopped the boy up and threw his body parts out the window along the turnpike. They'd kept the head for a while longer because Lucas wanted to have sex with it, Toole said.

As to why he was making this confession, Toole told the detectives that he wanted to get it out of his mind.

Hoffman next showed Toole the photo of Adam that the family had reproduced on the missing person's flyer, but Toole wasn't sure that it was the same boy that he and Lucas took. When Hoffman showed Toole a second photo in which Adam's hair was wet from swimming, Toole nodded. He believed that the second photo did resemble the boy he killed, he said.

With that, Detectives Hoffman and Hickman concluded their interview and left the room, leaving Detective Terry and Ottis Toole alone.

"Why are you jerking them around?" Terry asked Toole, his arms folded.

"What are you talking about?" Toole replied.

"You know as well as I do that Henry Lee Lucas was in jail in Maryland when all this happened. What are you trying to pull?"

Toole looked away and stared at the wall for a few moments. Finally he turned back to Terry. Yes, he'd lied about Lucas being involved. "Tell them detectives I want to talk to them again," he said to Terry, who shook his head and went to look for Hoffman and Hickman.

It was well past midnight when the two detectives from Hollywood came back into the interview room and Toole announced that he hadn't explained things exactly right the first time around and would like to correct his statement. Hoffman gave Terry a skeptical glance, but nonetheless he and Hoffman sat down and began to take a second recorded statement from Toole.

The biggest thing he had to correct was that Henry Lee Lucas hadn't been involved in the crime, Toole told them. Then he set out to explain how things had really happened. Early in July of 1981, he and Lucas had borrowed Toole's brother's 1972 Ford pickup, supposedly to haul some scrap iron to the Jacksonville dump and sell it. In truth, Toole and Lucas lit out of Jacksonville immediately, accompanied by Toole's niece Frieda Powell, thirteen at the time, and his nephew Frank Powell, twelve. They'd abandoned the truck in Maryland about a week later, and on the fifteenth of July, Toole's sister-in-law Georgia reported the truck stolen to the Jacksonville sheriff. Toole had gotten separated from Lucas and his niece and nephew and, after a brief hospital stay, had returned to Florida by himself. Meantime, Lucas had been arrested by Delaware police on charges of vehicular theft and remained in jail there well into October.

Toole had traveled to South Florida alone, he told Hoffman and Hickman, and ran into Adam Walsh coming out of the Hollywood Sears store on the west side of the building. He enticed the boy into his Cadillac with the promise of candy and toys, then quickly rolled up the windows and locked the doors. Though the engine on the Cadillac had been giving him a little trouble ("It wasn't runnin' right. It would just roll off"), he got it started and pulled out of the parking lot, with Adam now asking about the toys and the candy. It took him about ten minutes to get from the store parking lot to Florida's Turnpike, Toole said, and by the time he went through the tollbooth to get a ticket, he had to start slapping and hitting the boy to get him to quiet down.

"The kid was getting on my nerves," Toole said. "I hit him quite a bit of times in the car. I think I did knock him out. I'm pretty sure that I knocked that kid out."

The rest of his account matched closely with what Toole had already told Detective Kendrick from Brevard County and Detective Via from Louisiana. He pulled off the turnpike onto a dirt road to kill the child. The child was unconscious when he carried him from the car and laid him facedown on the ground. And it took him four or five blows to sever the child's head.

"He was unconscious, so I didn't have a hard time chopping his head off," Toole said. "I laid him facedown and I did it."

Hoffman glanced up at Toole and asked whether he was right-handed or left-handed.

"Right-handed," Toole answered.

"And you said you kept the head for a while," Hoffman continued. "Just where in the car did you put it?"

Toole shrugged. "I say I switched it different times. I had it in the back one time on the floorboard and I ended up putting it in the front floorboard."

After the decapitation, Toole said that he dismembered and scattered the body parts, then got back onto the turnpike and drove another ten minutes or so northward before he began to think better of keeping the head. When he spotted a bridge railing up ahead, he told Hoffman, "I stopped the car and got out and I threw the head over in the canal."

How about the boy's clothes? Hoffman asked. "Oh his clothes were in the car," Tool said. While he was stopped, he used the clothes to wipe up some of the blood off the seat and then tossed the clothes out. Or maybe he had thrown the clothes away in a Dumpster in one of the roadside rest stops, Toole said, for that is what he remembered doing with his own blood-soaked clothes. "I threw them in the Dumpster."

And all this blood on his clothes had come from the child? Hoffman wanted to be sure.

Not only on his clothes but on his shoes as well, Toole assured the detective. "I threw my shoes away too and put on another pair."

He'd then driven on back to Jacksonville and junked the car at a yard on Holloway Avenue, Toole said, and that was pretty much the end of that story.

But why had he lied to them and implicated Henry Lee Lucas in his first statement? Hoffman wanted to know. "Because I figured I could tie him up in it and get even with his ass," Toole said.

"And you also said that Henry Lee got a blow job from the head," Hoffman continued, looking up from his notes. "Was that really *you* that got the blow job from the head?"

Toole shook his head at the question. "No," he said, dismissively, "I didn't even fuck it."

Hoffman then withdrew a third photograph of Adam and laid it beside the other two he'd already shown Toole. Was this the boy he was talking about? the detective asked. Toole studied the third photograph briefly, then glanced at Hoffman, "The other pictures, the other pictures look more like him than that one does," Toole said, but still there seemed no doubt in his mind. "Yes, I'd say. Yes, that's him."

It was almost two in the morning by the time Hoffman and Hickman wound up their second interview with Toole. "If we take you back down to South Florida with us, can you show us the places you've been talking about. This Sears store, the place where you decapitated the child, and where you threw his head in the canal?"

"I guess so," Toole said.

"We'll let you know," Hoffman said, and with that the interview was finished.

Once again, it might seem to any sentient observer that every element was in hand for a swift delivery of justice, or as swift as one is permitted in a system as full of checks and balances as our own. An individual with a history of violent behavior has made three unbidden confessions of murder to law officers from three different jurisdictions, providing details obviously known previously only to the medical examiners and the detectives in charge of the case. Surely justice was about to be dispensed. How could it possibly not be?

JACKSONVILLE, FLORIDA—OCTOBER 21, 1983

In the early hours following his second conversation with Toole, Detective Hoffman—whether or not he was miffed that his theory about Jimmy Campbell had been discredited, or simply that someone other than he and his partner Hickman had found Ottis Toole and extracted a confession from him—went quickly to work securing an order from a Duval County circuit judge allowing the two of them and Detective Terry to transport Toole to Hollywood for the purposes of identifying the purported crime scenes he had described. Meanwhile, Toole returned to his cell in the county lockup, where he began to pace and mutter, waking his cellmate James Collins.

What was the matter? Collins asked. He was trying to get some sleep.

Toole glanced around the cell nervously, then leaned close. What did Collins suppose other inmates would do to someone who had murdered children? Toole wondered, his voice low. Collins wasn't sure what might happen, but he did think that Toole was unusually agitated.

Toole went on to explain to Collins that the cops had found the head of this kid he'd killed, and that now they wanted him to go down to Fort Lauderdale and help them find the body. "I just hope it ain't there," Toole said, and then he went back to his pacing and muttering. Collins never told anyone whether he actually did get back to sleep that night. Ordinary people might have had great difficulty doing so. But if men believed everything they heard in prison, there'd be precious little sleep enjoyed there.

At nine on Friday morning, Toole was escorted by Detectives Hoffman and Terry from the Duval County Jail and flown by private plane to the North Perry Airport in Pembroke Pines, not far from Hollywood. They were met at about eleven thirty by two other detectives from Hollywood PD and driven by van to the nearby sprawling Broward Mall, which contained a Sears store.

This was definitely not the place, Toole said, as they pulled into the huge lot. The lot outside the store where he'd taken the boy was much smaller, and the mall had been a single-story structure, not a two-story like this one.

From the Broward Mall, they drove next to a Sears store that sat just off Federal Highway in Fort Lauderdale, but again, Toole shook his head. This was not the place.

Detective Larry Hoisington of the Hollywood PD, who been assigned to drive the team, was behind the wheel. Hoisington next drove to I-95 and piloted them the few miles south toward Hollywood. As they pulled off the exit ramp at Hollywood Boulevard, Toole gazed intently out the van windows. "This looks like the road I got off on," he told the detectives. As they passed the train station that abuts the boulevard there, Toole noted that the area looked familiar to him. "I think the store is up there," he said, pointing to the right.

Hoisington glanced in the rearview mirror to be sure which way Toole was directing them. Owing to his various deficiencies, Toole never used such words as *left* or *right*, *north* or *south*, *east* or *west*—just hand motions and phrases like "over there" and "down that way." Hoisington followed Toole's gesture and, a few blocks farther, pulled the van off Hollywood Boulevard and into the lot on the east side of the Sears store. He circled the store to the north, then turned along its west facade, where the garden shop was located. "This is it," Toole said, pointing. "This is where I picked up the kid."

Hoffman glanced around at his colleagues, then noted the time on his watch. He directed Hoisington to drive the few hundred yards to Hollywood PD for lunch before they started out for the turnpike.

After lunch, however, Toole asked if they could take one more look at the Sears lot, just so he could be sure. Hoisington took them back to the north entrance, where the catalog store was located, and parked the van. After a few moments, Toole nodded again. This was the place, he was more than sure of it. He pointed to a nearby bus bench located in the lot beneath an overhang. He'd been standing right there when he saw the boy come walking out of the doors by the garden department.

He repeated his story of luring Adam into the Cadillac with the promises of toys and candy and then showed the officers where he pulled out of the lot and made a right turn on Hollywood Boulevard, heading west toward Florida's Turnpike. It took about ten minutes, Toole told them, recalling there was a "sharp bend" in the road somewhere along the way. When Hoisington took them around a traffic circle on Hollywood Boulevard, Toole glanced out at a school located there and confirmed that this was the road he remembered driving on.

To test Toole, Hoisington decided that he purposely would not exit the roundabout where Hollywood Boulevard continued west toward the turnpike. Instead, he continued on toward the south exit of the roundabout. Toole laughed at that. "I did the same thing you just did," he told Hoisington. "You were supposed to turn back there." Hoisington glanced at Hoffman, but if he expected any recognition of his cleverness, none was forthcoming.

"Take the right fucking turn, will you?" Hoffman growled.

At the northbound turnpike entrance Hoisington brought down the van window to take a toll ticket; Toole said that he remembered doing the same thing the day he had Adam in his car. As they passed through the second toll plaza on the route north, Toole told the detectives it was where he'd pulled over to "quiet the kid down." Adam had been crying for his mother, Toole explained, and he had to beat him until he was unconscious to get him to stop.

By 3:30 p.m., as they clicked past mile marker 126 on the turnpike, well over an hour north of Hollywood, the van whisked beneath an overpass, and Toole pointed out the window toward the side of the road. "Hey, this is where I got off at," he called.

Hoisington pulled the van to the shoulder of the turnpike and, just as Toole had when he overshot the nearly hidden exit, backed cautiously to the service road leading to a desolate construction staging area. "You can pull off into there," Toole said, pointing. "This is where I stopped and killed the kid."

Hoffman told Toole to direct them to the place where he'd left Adam's body, and a shackled, handcuffed Toole gave it his best, even though he told them his memory was a little hazy—he'd been pretty intoxicated at the time, he said. He thought there was a fork in the road, to be quite honest, but there were no turnoffs to be found. Just a straight shot down the service road through the pine barrens to a spot where the road petered out at a guardrail blocking the road. "It was over in there someplace," Toole said, and a dubious Hoffman led his men, along with Detective Terry, out for an inspection of the area.

While Hoffman and the others tramped about the desolate woods, Hoisington and Toole sat alone inside the van. Hoisington had been ordered by Hoffman not to speak with Toole—"You're here for one reason, to drive the goddamned van, okay?"—and he was not about to start trouble. But Toole seemed agitated now, and the longer they sat together, the more restless he became.

"I killed a lot of people," he blurted to Hoisington suddenly. "But of all I did, I wisht I hadn't killed that little kid."

Toole indicated the area where the others were walking with a nod of his head. Hoisington followed Toole's gesture, but said nothing.

"It was right here," Toole said, tears welling in his eyes. "I took him out of the car and carried him yonder in the woods, and I cut off his head with a machete I always carried." He went on to explain how he'd dragged the body into the brush and covered it with leaves. He came back to the spot where he'd left Adam's head and took it back to the car and tossed it on the floor behind the driver's seat.

Hoisington knew that Toole was a suspect in the murder of Adam Walsh, of course, but he had no idea of the details of Toole's confessions. Everything that Toole was recounting to him sounded like the stuff of a nightmare.

"Why did you keep the head?" Hoisington heard himself asking.

Toole glanced at him as if he were explaining why you'd duck under cover when it started to rain. He'd already sodomized Adam's body, he told Hoisington. "I was going to have sex with the head later on."

As a cop, Hoisington had heard his fair share, but Toole's offhand declaration was enough to make his stomach heave. With great relief he saw an obviously irritated Hoffman leading his group back toward the van.

"We can't see anything over there," Hoffman grumbled as he climbed in, waving vaguely toward the tangle of vines and underbrush on the far side of the guardrail. He slapped at a mosquito on his neck, one of a cloud that followed him through the opened door. It had been more than two years, the hot and frustrated detectives reasoned, as they piled back into the van. A jungle could spring up around here in that amount of time. Heavy equipment would have to be brought in.

Meantime, Hoffman declared, Toole could show them where he'd disposed of the head. Sure, Toole assured them. It wasn't far, no more than ten minutes from where they were parked.

Hoisington piloted them back down the rocky trail, then waited for a break in the traffic to pull back on the highway. It wasn't like they'd pulled off into a paved rest area where there was some nicely banked reentry road. The very maneuver to regain the highway in a sluggish nine-passenger van was not without risk. Some hopped-up kid in a fast car comes up too quickly behind them, they'd all be toast. And all because of a scumbag like Toole? What a way to go.

Still, Hoisington managed it without incident, and had hardly got them back up to cruising speed when Toole called out again, this time near mile marker 130. The group exited the van at roadside this time, and Toole directed them a few yards eastward to the bank of a nearby canal, where a wooden dock jutted out over the water. He'd walked out onto the dock there and thrown the head into the water, Toole said.

Detective Hoffman, who was well aware that they were standing near the spot where Adam's head had been discovered by fishermen more than two years previously, said nothing to his colleagues. It was after 6:00 p.m. by this time, and Toole said he was hungry and wondered if there was anything to eat. Detective Hoisington handed Toole one of the sandwiches they'd brought along, but another detective swatted it out of Toole's hand.

"You don't need to do this guy any favors," Hoffman told Hoisington. "He's just jerking us around."

Toole glanced at the sandwich that had landed in the dirt. "Fuck you," he said to Hoffman.

"No," Hoffman replied. "Fuck *you*."

At that point, they all got into the van and drove home.

Back at Hollywood PD, Hoffman took another recorded statement from Ottis Toole in which he yet again formally confessed to the murder of Adam Walsh, and provided a detailed account of the circumstances under which he had committed the act. Toole broke into tears several times during this statement, claiming that he liked the little boy and had only wanted to take him home to raise him to be his own child. He had to kill Adam, though, because he realized the boy was very smart and could probably identify him as his kidnapper. When asked why this, of all the killings he had confessed to, bothered him so much, Toole said, "Because that was the youngest person I ever killed."

While that interview was taking place, Detective Hoisington ran into deputy chief Leroy Hessler in a hallway. "So how'd it go?" Hessler asked.

Hoisington hesitated but decided he should give the chief an honest answer. This was a pretty important matter, and he wasn't so sure things were running as they should. He explained to Hessler that he was surprised that Toole was cooperating at all, given Hoffman's treatment of the man, and also shared with Hessler some of the details that Toole had told him about the crime when Hoffman was out of earshot. Hessler listened patiently, then asked Hoisington if there was some point to all this.

Hoisington hesitated. He wasn't assigned as an investigator to this case, as Hessler well knew, but he was a detective, after all. "I just thought maybe I should write a supplemental report, or at least give Detective Hoffman a formal statement for his files," Hoisington said, still taken by Toole's offhand ghoulishness. "If what Toole told me independently corroborates or contradicts something he's said elsewhere, that might be useful."

Hessler stared at Hoisington for a moment. "You understand that this is Detective Hoffman's case, right?"

"Yes sir," Hoisington responded.

"Then you go talk to Hoffman about all this," Hessler said and walked away.

Hoisington made an effort to do what Hessler ordered, but by the time Hoffman and his partner Hickman had finished with Toole, it was past ten thirty at night. When Hoisington caught Hoffman coming out of the interview room, the lead detective warned him to make it quick. Chief Martin had already called a press conference for eleven, and was waiting on Hoffman in his office.

Hoisington had hardly begun his explanation when Hoffman cut him off. "I thought I told you not to talk to that asshole," he said, pointing inside the interview room where Toole still sat.

"He was talking to *me*," Hoisington protested, "and some of those things he said—"

Hoffman held up a hand impatiently. "I heard you. I'll include it in my report," he said; then he hurried down the hall to confer with Martin.

At 11:00 p.m. during a hastily arranged press conference, Hollywood chief of police Sam Martin made the momentous announcement. They had found the man who killed Adam Walsh, and on Monday, Ottis Toole would be officially charged with the crime.

Toole was a confessed serial killer, Martin told reporters, though of the thirty-five to fifty murders he had committed, Adam's was the only one over which he had expressed any regret. "Listening to him talk about the things he's done makes Charles Manson sound like Tom Sawyer or Huck Finn," Martin said. And Assistant Chief Hessler added his own opinion that Toole's stories were "grisly and heinous beyond belief." But as to the murder of Adam Walsh, Hessler said, there could be no doubt. "There are certain details only he could know. He did it."

Hessler assured reporters that his detectives had been grilling Toole ten to twenty hours a day for two days solid, and that he had finally broken down earlier Friday evening. As to the confessions that Toole had made to Detective Kendrick on October 10 and to Detectives Via and Terry on October 18, Hessler was curiously—or not so curiously—silent. As far as the outside world was concerned, then, Jack Hoffman and the Hollywood PD had cracked this case without assistance.

Indeed, Martin assured those gathered, they had finally found their man. Ottis Toole, already convicted of another crime in Jacksonville, would be returned to that city this night or the following morning, but soon he would face justice for the murder of Adam Walsh.

Any reasonable individual would have been inclined to take Martin's assertions as fact. An unhinged psychopath, finally snagged by a system through whose cracks he had tumbled for most of his miscreant's life, had confessed details of a heinous crime only he could have known. It might have been a shame for the murdered boy's family that so much time had passed, and it might be galling if it was learned that his apprehension was almost accidental, and perhaps it was annoying that a public defender would have to be engaged at the taxpayers' expense, along with a costly trial to be followed—were a death penalty handed down—by any number of appeals based on what would be surely specious ground . . .

But despite all that, a grievous wrong could now be righted, and some shred of society's order might be restored.

HOLLYWOOD, FLORIDA—OCTOBER 22, 1983
The news of the break in the case was trumpeted across the region on Saturday, and any viewer, listener, or reader who caught it might have assumed that though it had been two long and agonizing years for John and Revé Walsh, the grieving parents were about to see justice done. John Walsh's stirring response upon being given the news was replayed again and again on network and local outlets: "Just give me three minutes alone in a room with this guy." Finally, it seemed, the long-suffering parents would find some measure of relief.

However, it was not necessarily the call of Chief Martin or Leroy Hessler as to whether or not Ottis Toole would in fact be charged. It is true that a police officer can arrest and charge a suspect at a crime scene or in the course of an investigation during which a suspect makes a confession. Following such an arrest there is an arraignment, normally held within twenty-four hours, at which the suspect pleads guilty or not guilty, where bail is set or denied, and at which a public defender is appointed if necessary. In most jurisdictions, the state attorney then has a set period of time—twenty-one days in Florida—in which to file formal charges or drop the case. In fact, it is not unusual for a case initiated as an arrest to be dropped or negotiated, owing to something overlooked or unknown during the relatively hasty process of arrest.

In this instance, however, Toole was already in custody for other crimes, and there was no risk of him fleeing—and thus no reason for immediate arrest. Accordingly, the department took the alternative route toward charging a suspect: that of seeking a warrant for the suspect's arrest on new charges from the state attorney for Broward County.

In most cases, a state attorney asks that as much evidence as possible be presented before issuing an arrest warrant, for obvious reasons. No reputable prosecutor wants to be involved in harassing innocent citizens, for one thing; but also, the more ironclad the evidence presented, the easier it is for a successful prosecution to be brought. It was common knowledge among police agencies in Dade County during Janet Reno's tenure as head of the state attorney's office that unless an arresting agency presented its case in fail-safe terms, no warrant would be forthcoming. As a result, Reno compiled a sterling record as a prosecutor, one that eventually vaulted her into the office of U.S. attorney general.

In the case of Ottis Toole, a prosecutor in Broward state attorney Michael Satz's office advised Hollywood PD that the case would be bolstered considerably if physical evidence were obtained that placed Toole at the scene of the crime, or at least confirmed his presence in South Florida during the time that the crime took place.

If Hoffman and Hickman had done a more meticulous job of documenting the information revealed by Toole in his confessions to Detectives Kendrick and Via, and if they had presented the results of their own investigation in a way that made it seem they were independently corroborating what only the killer could have known about the crime, perhaps Satz would not have asked for more. But because Hoffman had not even mentioned the fact of the previous confessions, claiming that he had "broken" Toole after hours of relentless grilling, the state attorney's request for corroborating physical evidence was not out of the ordinary.

For most who heard Chief Martin or Leroy Hessler trumpet the news of an impending charge on radio and television, however, all the fine points of arrests versus warrants were the stuff of "inside baseball." What most ordinary citizens believed was that a suspect had confessed to the killing of Adam Walsh, and he would soon be tried and convicted and fried in the electric chair—good riddance to bad rubbish, on to better news ahead.

One of those watching as the news concerning Ottis Toole was broadcast across South Florida was Bill Mistler, the man who had been on his way into Sears to pick up some supplies for a camping trip on that fateful day when he had seen a neatly dressed young boy go off into the parking lot with a disreputable-looking man who seemed all wrong for him. When Mistler heard the news anchor's eager pronouncement that at long last a break had come in the Adam Walsh case, he glanced up at the television with an interest that soon grew into astonishment. As Chief Martin named the suspect in the case and a picture of Ottis Toole filled the screen, Mistler jumped straight from his bed.

At that moment, certainty filled his mind. The face he was staring at was that of the down-and-outer who'd led the young boy away from the Sears store that day. He had in fact witnessed the kidnapping of Adam Walsh, Mistler thought, a kind of awe filling him.

As other images connected with the story swirled across the screen, Mistler could do nothing but gape, his mind whirling. He thought about calling Hollywood police on the spot, to recount to them what he'd seen that day, but then he hesitated. As a teenager Mistler had spent a year in prison for his ill-advised participation in a robbery. He had put that all behind him, and he was now a respected businessman, the owner of a successful pest control company.

If he came forward and his name and face ended up in the newspapers or on television, who was to say some malcontent wouldn't call in to dredge up his past mistakes? Besides, the cops made it sound like they had Toole dead to rights. There must have been other witnesses who'd seen what happened at Sears that day and had identified the kidnapper. Why else would there be all the hullabaloo? Finally, and though it pained him a bit to do so, Mistler convinced himself to let it go. His help wasn't needed. Justice had prevailed.

Mistler switched off his television and lay back down to stare quietly up at his ceiling. And finally, he fell asleep.

The following Sunday morning, lead detective Hoffman was quoted by the Associated Press as saying that his men had not yet verified that Toole was in the area the day that Adam Walsh had been abducted, but that nonetheless the suspect knew details of the murder that only the killer could have known. Hoffman was not at liberty to discuss the evidence that the department had shared with the state attorney's office, but he was confident that they had plenty to base a case on.

And, moreover, if Bill Mistler did not come forward to place Ottis Toole in South Florida at the time of the kidnapping, there was at least one other person who did. Arlene Mayer, the woman who had taken her daughter Heidi to Kmart for some household supplies less than forty-eight hours before Adam Walsh went missing, was having coffee at her kitchen table on Sunday morning after Chief Martin's announcement, the newspaper trumpeting the news laid out beside her. She was about to take a sip when Heidi walked into the room and stopped dead.

"Mom—" She pointed at the picture on the front page. "That's *him*."

Arlene stared up at her daughter, who was already beginning to cry. "That's the man who tried to get me that night in the Kmart."

Arlene looked down at the photograph of Ottis Toole emblazoned there, then shook her head, fighting the chill that began to envelop her. "Now, Heidi, are you sure . . . ?"

"I wouldn't say it if I wasn't sure," Heidi said, her voice rising to a near shriek. "That's the man who tried to get me!"

Arlene Mayer rose to comfort her daughter, and when she finally had Heidi calmed down, she picked up the phone and dialed the Hollywood police.

Shortly after 5:00 p.m. on Monday, Detectives Hoffman and Hickman conducted a formal interview with Heidi, who recounted her memory of the visit to Kmart the night she was accosted. Following the completion of her statement, the detectives presented her with a photo lineup to see if she recognized anyone.

"That's him," Heidi said, pointing without hesitation at a photograph of Toole. "There's that big gap between his two front teeth."

Following their interview with Heidi, Hoffman and Hickman then interviewed Arlene, who independently selected Toole's photo out of the array they presented her. She told the detectives that following the confrontation between Toole and her daughter, she'd found a Kmart security guard to walk them to her car, and that the big white car that both she and her daughter had seen the man get out of was still sitting in the lot at the time. Furthermore, she told Hoffman, she had driven straight home and called Hollywood PD to report the incident, though the detective couldn't locate any record of that call.

Meanwhile, an intensive search for the rest of Adam's remains was under way at the spot near mile marker 126 on Florida's Turnpike, where Toole told detectives he'd left the body. Detectives from Hollywood PD had discovered from the lessee of the property, Sergeant James Carter of the St. Lucie County Sheriff's Office, that the guardrail fence that had stopped their progress on the service road the day they'd first visited the area with Toole had been in place for only ten months.

Carter took them down the faint trail on the other side of the fence to show them that there was indeed a fork in the road, one branch that ran about a mile east to a grazing pasture, the other heading south to a shallow valley where Carter maintained a trailer park. At least that much seemed promising. The day he'd been out here with Toole, the man seemed incapable of any reliable memory.

Meantime, Hollywood PD had called in the Florida Department of Law Enforcement, an agency far more experienced and better equipped to conduct the kind of search at hand. FDLE technicians used steel probes to examine the ground on the north side of the fork in the road, where Toole had claimed he'd left the body. In turn, the FDLE was assisted by specialists from the Florida Department of Agriculture, who surveyed the entire area with a special ground-penetrating radar unit. By late Wednesday, the team had identified seven locations just beyond the fence and north of the road as having unidentified objects buried beneath the ground. Because it was nearly dark, they decided to wait until morning to begin the actual digging.

Detective Hoffman had flown back to Jacksonville, in search of evidence that would prove Toole had been in South Florida at the time of Adam's abduction. In discussing his movements in late July of 1981, Toole had told Hoffman that following his release from the hospital in Newport News, he received a check for $78 from the local Salvation Army to pay for a bus ticket back to Jacksonville. Hollywood detectives followed up, speaking to a Mrs. Hall in that Newport News agency. After a bit of rummaging about, Hall confirmed that in fact a check in the amount of $71.93, payable to the Greyhound Bus Corporation, had been given to someone named Ottis Toole by her agency on Friday, July 24, 1981. That was the amount the bus company had quoted for a one-way fare from Newport News to Jacksonville, she said.

When he arrived in Jacksonville, Hoffman met his counterpart Buddy Terry, who took him directly to the Duval County Jail, where Toole was being held. Terry was buoyed by the fact that a local judge had just declared Toole competent to stand trial in the boarding house arson that killed George Sonnenberg, but Hoffman couldn't have cared less. He couldn't wait to get to the county lockup, where he took Toole through another recounting of his movements in late July of 1981.

Toole told Hoffman that he'd taken the check from the Newport News Salvation Army and walked directly to the nearby bus station, where he'd had to wait for a couple of hours. He said it was "nighttime" when he finally boarded a bus bound for Jacksonville, and that he was not sure when he arrived back in the North Florida city, though bus schedules suggest it would have had to have been sometime early Saturday morning.

Nor was Toole exactly sure what he'd done the moment he stepped down from the air-conditioned bus into the cloying summer heat. Maybe he'd walked to Reaves Roofing to see if they might need him to work that day, or maybe he went instead to the residence of a Nancy Jackson over on Iona Street, where his wife Rita was staying at the time.

Probably he had gone to work and stayed in Jacksonville "a pretty good while," he told Hoffman that evening, because he was broke, and his wife was getting tired of staying with this Jackson woman and wanted him to get them a place of their own. Everything was a little hazy in his mind, Toole said, but he did remember that he rented himself and Rita a place in one of Betty Goodyear's rooming houses on East Second Street, and that is where his brother Howard came to beat him up for stealing his truck.

Hoffman left the matter of the chronology of Toole's movements aside for a moment and returned to the details of the kidnapping and murder. When Hoffman asked what Toole had done with the machete and the shovel he'd used to bury the body, Toole told Hoffman that he had been wondering about that himself. With his mother's house all burned up, he couldn't have hidden those items there, now could he?

So what *had* he done with them? Hoffman wanted to know. And that is when Toole delivered a thunderbolt. "That's why I'm trying to give you all these statements," he told Hoffman. "I'm not really sure that I really *did* kill Adam Walsh."

Hoffman took a deep breath. So Toole was now saying that he had stayed in Jacksonville to work after he got back on Saturday, July 25? He was broke and had to make some money before he took his trip to South Florida. Did Toole realize that Adam had been taken from that Sears store in Hollywood on Monday, scarcely two days later?

Toole blinked, apparently trying to rack his thoughts into something resembling logical order. "So the only thing, if I really didn't kill Adam Walsh, I would have to have been working the Monday, on the twenty-seventh?" he said to Hoffman.

Hoffman leaned back in his chair. "That's the long and short of it," he said. "We'll check the company's records. If you were working on July twenty-seventh, then everything you've told us about the murder is a load of BS."

At this point, Buddy Terry could hold himself back no longer. Without asking Hoffman, he leaned across the table toward Toole.

"Ottis," Terry interjected, "are you lying today? Are you sure you didn't kill Adam Walsh? Now, come on now, let's don't do it this way. Look at me. Look at me, Ottis."

But Toole wouldn't look at Terry. "My mind ain't gonna take much more of this shit," he mumbled; then he began to cry.

"Just tell me the truth," Terry said quietly, "that's all I want to know."

Through his sobs, Toole shook his head. "No, I didn't kill Adam Walsh."

Terry ventured a glance at Hoffman, who wore his characteristic scowl of disgust, then turned back to Toole. "Are you sure, or are you not sure?"

Toole was still staring down at the interview table. "I'm sure I didn't," he said.

"How are you sure?" Terry persisted. "What makes you sure you didn't kill Adam Walsh?"

Toole finally looked up at Terry, his voice plaintive. "Because if I was really sure, I could come up with his body," he said.

Hoffman broke in then, demanding to know where Toole had come up with all the details he'd been giving them about the crime.

"*I made it all up*," Toole said in an anguished voice, and then he began to cry again.

It was enough for Hoffman. He glanced at his watch and saw that it was 10:30 in the evening. They'd been listening to Toole ramble on for forty-five minutes, and they were just going in circles. He snapped his notebook shut and stood to leave the interview room. Terry, however, stayed behind with Toole.

For the next ten minutes, while Toole wailed in misery, Terry sat patiently, making the occasional reassuring sound, gradually calming the prisoner down. Finally, Toole stopped sobbing and appeared to pull himself together.

"You okay now?" Terry asked. He glanced at his watch. It had been exactly twelve minutes since Hoffman left the room.

Toole nodded. "I need to talk to that guy again," Toole said. Terry glanced toward the door through which Hoffman had departed.

"Detective Hoffman?"

Toole nodded again.

"And why do you need to talk to him?" Terry inquired, carefully.

"Because I wasn't telling the truth just now," Toole said. "About not killing Adam Walsh."

Terry nodded. "I'll just go get him, then."

In his *fifth* interview regarding the abduction and murder of Adam Walsh, recorded shortly after Terry brought Hoffman back to the interview room that night, Toole spoke calmly and in an assured tone of voice, adding details to his account that he had not included in any of his previous statements. He told of walking directly from the Jacksonville Greyhound station to the yard of the roofing company where he knew the Cadillac he'd given back to Faye McNett was stored. He used the keys he'd kept to get inside the fence and took the car, driving to the burned-out site of his mother's home. From under what was left of the front porch, he dug up the can he'd used as a bank and pocketed the $300 or so that was there, then went down to the gas station on the corner, filled the tank, and got on I-95, headed south toward Miami.

"I had everything right in the car," he told Hoffman. "I had all kinds of tools, a shovel, a machete underneath the seat."

As to his encounter with the child outside the store, Toole was even more forthcoming. "He told me his name was Adam, that his mom was in the store shopping. He told me he liked baseball, that he was playing on some kind of Little League team," Toole recalled. He liked talking to the boy, and it was then that he decided that he was going to take him and raise him for himself.

As to the moments when his plans began to fall apart, Toole was appallingly graphic. "He was crying more and getting a little bit louder. And so that's when I really did slap the daylights out of him. I slapped him pretty . . . pretty darn hard. I slapped him dead in the face. Dead across the eyes."

But it seemed not to be enough. "He kept getting a little bit wilder and I hit him real hard in his stomach and that would take the wind out of him. And I did punch him in the eyes a couple times . . . more . . . more than a couple of times."

Finally, Toole said, "I really hit him hard in the stomach. I grabbed onto his throat and started choking him, with both hands. He was unconscious. He never . . . never gained consciousness."

Toole took the detectives back through his account of finding a place to pull off the turnpike, of stopping the Cadillac at the fork he'd mentioned in the service road, and of carrying Adam's body out. "I pulled the bayonet out from underneath the seat," he said, repeating the use of that term for the weapon before he began once again to refer to it as a "machete." And then Toole said, "Well, I done chopped him down. I chopped his head off. I had to come down real hard."

After it was done, Toole said, "I pulled his shirt off, wrapped his head up in it and put it in the car." When he finally decided that he should get rid of Adam's head, he had been driving no more than five or ten minutes. That is when he spotted the canal and the wooden bridge and pulled over and threw the head into the water. He stood and watched to be sure it would sink, and then he turned and got back into the Cadillac. He drove to the next rest plaza, and pulled in beside the entrance to a gas station restroom, where he went in "to clean up and all . . . got all this blood off me."

He filled his tank then and drove back to Jacksonville to the site of his mother's burned-out house, where he parked and slept in the car through the night. In the morning, he woke and cleaned up the car and his tools, and that was pretty much that.

Detective Hoffman noted that it was 11:41 p.m. when he asked Toole his final question of the evening. Just why was it that Toole had lied to him earlier about not having killed Adam Walsh? Hoffman wanted to know.

Toole shrugged. "I couldn't get my head together," he told the detective, as if that ought to explain everything.

While it was surely a blow to Hoffman that Toole had briefly recanted his confession, a more experienced homicide investigator might have reassured the Hollywood detective that this was not out of the ordinary. According to Toole's own words, the killing of "that little boy" was the worst thing that he had ever done. And while it is not out of the ordinary for a guilty person to confess in order to find some peace, neither is it unusual for that same person to later recant. The reasons are many: fear of reprisal, a wave of psychological denial that one has actually done the worst thing possible, and on and on. Furthermore, if one were looking for the model of rational behavior, you wouldn't be searching among convicted killers in the first place. The fact remained that Ottis Toole had confessed to this killing on multiple occasions, citing details that only someone who'd been present could have known.

But Hoffman had not joined the Hollywood Police Department until late in 1975, and he served as a uniform patrolman for nearly three years before he was transferred to the Criminal Investigations Division as a detective. When he took over the investigation of the Adam Walsh case, he had less than three years of time in grade as an investigator, and no experience at all with a case of such magnitude and difficulty. If his reputation as a know-it-all was merited, such an individual would be especially prone to second-guessing himself in his heart of hearts.

Furthermore, one might wonder why on earth the detective did not take this opportunity to question Toole as to whether or not he'd had an encounter with a young girl in a Kmart during his foray to Hollywood back in 1981. After all, only two days before, Hoffman had listened to Arlene Mayer and her daughter Heidi describe their frightening evening in minute detail and witnessed them independently identify Toole's photograph as the man they had seen. Had Toole verified the encounter—which had not been reported anywhere—it would have placed Toole in Hollywood at the time of Adam's murder and in all likelihood put the matter to rest.

VERO BEACH, FLORIDA—OCTOBER 27, 1983

The following Thursday morning, Judge Trowbridge of the Nineteenth Judicial Circuit of Florida, which includes Indian River County, where the crime was presumed to have occurred, ordered the appointment of a temporary public defender for Toole. Before a local defender could be appointed, however, Elton H. Schwartz, an attorney practicing in Miami, drawn by the publicity inherent in the case, offered his services to Toole free of charge. Subsequently, the court—now absolved of any expense in the matter—approved the arrangement.

While that was going on, Detective Hoffman set out on his rounds about Jacksonville, trying to substantiate the details of Toole's story. First, Hoffman tracked down Faye McNett, who in fact recalled selling a 1971 Cadillac to Toole. It was a white car, with a black vinyl top, a four-door, McNett said, and while Toole wanted it badly, he didn't have enough money to pay for it. He gave her a few dollars down, she recalls, and agreed to have her take $20 or $25 a week out of his paycheck until the balance was satisfied. Ultimately, he told her he couldn't keep up the payments and would have to return the car, which she then kept in the roofing company's compound.

If he had an extra set of keys to the car and was prone to "borrowing" it, she hadn't known about it, but sure, she supposed it was possible. Lots of people had keys to the yard fence, McNett said. That was just how it was.

After he spoke with McNett, Hoffman interviewed John

Reaves Jr., owner of Southeast Color Coat and the son of John Reaves Sr., owner of Reaves Roofing, where Toole had also worked occasionally. The last day Toole had received any pay for either company was June 4, 1981, Reaves said after a check of his records. Furthermore, Reaves did remember getting a phone call from the Salvation Army in Newport News, Virginia. They'd wanted to confirm that Toole did have a job to return to in Jacksonville, and Reaves had vouched for him. Toole had never actually come back to work at either his company or his father's, though, Reaves Jr. said. As to whether or not Toole had a set of keys to the company compound where McNett's Cadillac was kept, Reaves thought it was possible—one of Toole's responsibilities was to let employees and their trucks in and out of the gate.

Meantime, just off Florida's Turnpike at mile marker 126 in Indian River County, FDLE technicians were using a front-end loader to excavate the area where their scans had indicated buried objects were to be found. The machine scraped off four inches of earth at a time in all seven spots, down to a depth of two feet, but no clothing or remains were found.

Also that afternoon, Hoffman received a call from a Detective Steve Upkirk of the Oklahoma City Police Department. Based on statements made by Henry Lee Lucas and Ottis Toole, his department had concluded that Toole was likely responsible for somewhere between four and six unsolved homicides in his jurisdiction, Upkirk said. In addition, there were other unsolved cases in other Oklahoma jurisdictions that Toole was probably responsible for as well. It wasn't necessarily information that would help Hoffman in his own investigation, but it did seem to confirm that Ottis Toole was a very bad person indeed. With him in prison, the world was surely a better place.

On the following morning, Friday, October 28, Hoffman's boss, Hollywood chief of police Sam Martin, found a letter from an attorney's office in Miami waiting for him when he came to work. It was a notice from Elton Schwartz, Toole's newly appointed public defender, advising Martin that forthwith his men were to cease interviewing his client, unless Schwartz was present.

At the same time, Hoffman was at the offices of Southeast Color Coat in Jacksonville, where clerk Ilene Knight dug out records to show that Ottis Toole had been employed by the company from 1976 through June 4, 1981. She did find that Toole had returned for work at the company after that, but it was only for a single day, in December of 1981. Toole had not worked for the company since, Knight was certain.

Next, Hoffman tracked down Georgia Toole, Ottis's sister-in-law, who confirmed that she had in fact tried to have him arrested for stealing her pickup truck, just as the sheriff's records showed. She also told Hoffman where he could find Norvella "Rita" Toole, Ottis's wife. Rita told Hoffman that she had married Toole on January 14, 1977, and that in fact they were still married to that day. "But," she told Hoffman, "he was always running me off, and I couldn't figure it out, and one day I got thinking, I said, well, what would a man tell his wife to leave all the time for, unless there's something wrong?"

Rita told Hoffman that she was away from Ottis so much that there wasn't really a lot she could tell him. "The only thing, Ottis was good to me, and that's all I know, he never mistreated me. He never beat me, he always called me baby, and I was kinda shocked when I heard all this."

Following his interview with Rita, Hoffman met briefly with Vernon Toole, Ottis's brother, and then with Mack Caulder, a foreman for the roofing company, but obtained little of use from either. A bit after 3:00 p.m. that Friday, Hoffman interviewed John Reaves Sr., the owner of Reaves Roofing. He confirmed that Toole had worked for him at times and was responsible for cleaning the compound and had access to the company gas pump and keys. He also told Hoffman that owing to a number of thefts on company property, he had all the locks changed back in 1982, some time after Toole had left his employment. Reaves remembered that Faye McNett had sold her Cadillac to Toole, and he assured Hoffman that indeed his company kept a number of tools on the property, including crowbars, shovels, and the like.

When Hoffman asked if they had any machetes, Reaves thought about it. "I believe we got one or two of them too," he said. "It had a wood handle, I'd say about 10 or 12 inches, but I don't remember seeing it lately." At the conclusion of their interview, Reaves Sr. took Hoffman out to the company tool shed to look around for the machete, but they had no luck.

For all his work in Jacksonville, Hoffman had developed little of value. On the one hand, he had ruled out any possibility that Toole had been working for his old employers on Monday, July 27, 1981, the day that Adam was abducted, but on the other, he had found no one who could place Ottis Toole in any specific location—particularly Hollywood—between July 26 and July 30. This makes the failure to corroborate Toole's encounter with Heidi Mayer all the more confounding.

In any case, while Hoffman had been busy with his interviews, Buddy Terry had set to work on actually finding the Cadillac that Toole claimed he had used during the abduction and murder, and which Faye McNett had long since sold. Terry finally tracked the then-twelve-year-old vehicle to an outfit called Wells Brothers Used Cars, at 4334 Brentwood Avenue in Jacksonville, and found that indeed it was a black-over-white four-door model with a black leatherlike interior, a black dashboard, black carpeting, and power window and door locks that could be controlled by a master panel in the driver's armrest.

On Monday, October 31, technicians from the Florida Department of Law Enforcement were dispatched to pick up the Cadillac from the Wells Brothers lot and take it to the FDLE crime lab on Platen Road in Jacksonville, where it was to be examined for fingerprints, blood, and fibers. That same day, public defender Schwartz met with his client for the first time, and on Tuesday the attorney announced to reporters in Tallahassee that Ottis Toole now claimed that he did not murder Adam Walsh or anyone else. "Ottis Toole has denied every one of the crimes he's confessed to," Schwartz somewhat predictably said. Asked to comment, Hollywood chief of police Martin told the Associated Press that he felt his department still had a prime suspect in the case.

On that same Tuesday, Detectives Hoffman and Hickman were still in Jacksonville, interviewing Howard Toole, Ottis's brother, at a halfway house. Yes, Howard told the detectives, when he found out that Ottis was back in Jacksonville on August 1, 1981, he had gone to Betty Goodyear's rooming house to confront his brother about the theft of the pickup, and in fact he had chased him down to the nearby mini-mart, where he caught Ottis and slapped him around.

But as far as Ottis having keys to the Reaves Roofing compound or driving a 1971 black-over-white Cadillac, Howard claimed to have no knowledge. Nor did he know that Ottis had been hospitalized in Newport News. It was not unusual for Ottis to take off for weeks at a time without notifying him or anyone else in the family, Howard told Hoffman.

On Wednesday, November 2, 1983, FDLE technicians began their processing of the 1971 Cadillac that Ottis said he'd been driving when he kidnapped and killed Adam Walsh. Five rolls of film were used in photographing the interior and exterior of the vehicle, and the carpets were removed to be treated with luminol, a substance that glows when it comes in contact with blood.

In addition, the car was vacuumed and hair samples retained. Following all that, the vehicle was turned over to technicians in the latent prints section for processing. The various samples were sent off to the department's microanalysis section in Tallahassee and its serology lab in Jacksonville, while the photographs were retained by FDLE's Jacksonville office.

On the same day, Detective Hoffman spoke with Spencer Bennett, of Spencer Motors, at 1401 North Main Street in Jacksonville. Bennett claimed to have known Toole since he was seventeen and also said that he had sold him a two-door white Cadillac in 1982. That car had ended up with Ottis's brother Howard, Bennett said, because—once again—Ottis couldn't keep up the payments. Bennett described Toole as a quiet, meek individual. And if he was in fact a homosexual, Bennett said, it was news to him.

Hoffman then asked Bennett if he knew if Ottis ever carried a knife or machete around with him. Bennett told Hoffman that in fact he had found a machete in one of his vehicles a while back, though he didn't remember exactly when or which car he'd found it in. He rummaged around in a closet and finally produced a machete with a wooden handle wrapped in black electrician's tape, and housed in a green canvas sheath. The blade was rusty and had what looked like tar smeared on it. Hoffman was welcome to it, Bennett said.

Hoffman took the machete and traveled to the offices of Reaves Roofing, where he showed it to John Reaves Sr. Reaves glanced at the machete, but said it didn't look familiar. For whatever reason, Hoffman didn't bother to show the blade either to John Reaves Jr. at Southeast Color Coat or to company foreman Mack Caulder, both of whom worked more closely with Toole. While he was at the offices, however, Hoffman did take a statement from Helen Reaves, who told him that she had heard from a neighbor, Catherine Butler, that back in 1982 quite often a white car would turn up at the company gates after everyone had gone home. Whoever was in that white car would enter and leave the compound at will, Butler told Mrs. Reaves.

From Reaves Roofing, Hoffman drove back to Wells Brothers Used Cars to check on the provenance of the 1971 black-over-white Cadillac that FDLE was now processing. The records were spotty, but it appeared that they'd had the car since some time in the summer of 1982. They'd sold the car to a person named Ronald Williams on December 31 of that year, for $1569.75, but Williams had defaulted on the payments, and they'd had to repossess it. The Wells Brothers had had the car to themselves again until Detective Terry showed up and the FDLE came to take it away.

If all this seemed less than consequential, Hoffman had something of a more interesting conversation that evening at the Duval County Jail, where he interviewed Bobby Lee Jones, who not only had worked with Toole at Reaves Roofing and Southeast Color Coat, but had recently shared a cell with Toole for about a month.

In the days that the two of them had worked together, Jones told Hoffman, he knew that Toole had what he described as an "18-inch butcher knife" with a wooden handle under the driver's seat of his car. Toole's car was a white '72 Cadillac with a dent in the right side of the rear bumper, Jones said. He remembered the dent clearly because he had put it there. "I ran into the back of him," Jones said. "I never said anything about it, but I remember that dent."

Jones said that Toole always carried a big ring of keys when he was working for the company and would often disappear from work for several days. He'd show up and explain that he'd been partying, Jones said, though Toole also claimed that he burned down houses for money.

As to their recent time together in the Duval County Jail, Jones told Hoffman that Toole had told him all about the kidnapping and murder of Adam Walsh. He said that Toole talked about driving up and talking to the boy and making friends with him, and then for some reason starting to beat him up and cutting him apart with a big knife. "I told him to shut up and lay down," Jones said.

Following his conversation with Jones, Hoffman then interviewed James Collins, aka Julius Riley Wilkes, the other cellmate who had also worked with Toole at Southeast Color Coat.

According to Collins, it was common knowledge that Toole was gay. Collins related an on-the-job incident at Southeast Color Coat where another worker was making deprecating remarks to Toole about his lover Henry Lee Lucas. According to Collins, Toole didn't say much, but simply walked off the job abruptly. A few minutes later, Toole returned to work in his Cadillac with a shotgun under his arm. He approached the man who had been making fun of Lucas and pointed the barrel of the shotgun in the man's face. "Just keep on talking and I'll blow your brains out," Collins reported Toole as saying.

When Hoffman asked Collins to describe the car that Toole was driving that day, he replied that it was either white or black, one of the two. In any case, Collins thought it looked like the Cadillac that was on the news just the other day. It was toward the end of this interview that Collins divulged the recent conversations he'd had with Toole in their cell about the fact that he was leaving jail to help the cops in Fort Lauderdale look for the body of a child he'd killed down there, and his fears as to what other inmates might do to a fellow convict known to have murdered children.

On the following morning, Thursday, November 3, Hoffman drove the forty miles to Raiford, where he interviewed a man named James Michael Poole, who'd shared a cell with Ottis Toole in the Butler Transient Unit back in July. Poole told Hoffman that Toole had made various strange statements about being in the "child repossession business." Another time, he told Poole that he had "taken" his own son from Broward County and that somewhere on their way back to Jacksonville he had just dropped the boy off along the highway. Poole thought that odd because the boy was supposedly only seven or eight years old, but then again, people did strange things—especially the kind of people you meet in jail.

While at Raiford, Detective Hoffman also spoke with Boyd Earl Gilbert, another cellmate of Toole's in the Butler Transient

Unit. Gilbert told Hoffman that the two of them had met on August 31, some two months previously, and that at that time, Toole claimed that up until the time of his imprisonment, he had been earning a living burning down buildings for people who wanted to collect the insurance. Unfortunately, there'd been an old man sleeping in the last place he burned down, and the guy died.

During that same conversation, Gilbert said, Toole also told him that he had murdered a little kid down around West Palm Beach, the son of a policeman. Though it might seem a puzzling claim, it is quite possible that Toole had confused the adult-sized boat captain's hat Adam was wearing when he was taken with the similarly styled patrolman's dress cap worn by most South Florida cops at the time. In any case, if Gilbert was being truthful, it meant that Toole was talking openly about his involvement in the killing of Adam Walsh for more than a month before he'd made his first formal confession to Detective Kendrick of Brevard County on October 10.

As Hoffman was conducting these interviews at Raiford, Buddy Terry took the machete that Hoffman had picked up at Bennett Motors to the FDLE offices in Jacksonville to have it tested for blood. Technicians had already identified eight different areas of carpet and padding from the floorboards of Toole's Cadillac to test for blood as well.

Terry was hopeful that something would come of the tests, of course, but his mind kept wandering to what awaited him at his next stop. A call had come into his office the previous evening from Ottis Toole, something Terry was hardly expecting, given the public pronouncements of his newly appointed attorney.

Toole had said that he needed to speak with Terry right away. He was upset with this lawyer from Miami who'd come up to talk with him. According to Toole's message, the guy was actually trying to get him to say he wasn't guilty of the murder of Adam Walsh.

JACKSONVILLE, FLORIDA—NOVEMBER 3, 1983

Ottis Toole's seventh recorded statement to police regarding the murder of Adam Walsh began shortly after noon on November 3 with a preamble from Detective Terry. "I came to the county jail to talk to you because you contacted Detective Ron Carool and told him that you wanted me to come over and talk to you," Terry said. "Is that correct?"

It was indeed correct, Toole assured him. "The lawyer I had from Miami and the lawyer I got in Jacksonville told me that I don't have to talk with you at all," Toole said, "but I still want to talk to you. And the detective is trying to get me to say I ain't guilty on the Adam Walsh case."

Terry looked at Toole closely. "The detective, or the attorney?" he asked.

"I mean the attorney," Toole answered. "I really know myself that I really did kill Adam Walsh but the lawyer I got from Miami, he's trying to tell me I didn't kill Adam Walsh."

Though it was frustrating, Detective Terry told Toole that he was sorry, but they could go no further. They couldn't talk about Adam Walsh anymore, not without Toole's attorney present. Whether he liked it or not, Toole had a lawyer now. They could talk about other things, Terry said, but their private conversations about Adam Walsh were at an end.

That same afternoon, Detective Hoffman drove from Raiford another three and a half hours south to a State of Florida foster care facility in Lakeland, Florida, where he interviewed Frank Powell, Ottis Toole's nephew and brother of Frieda "Becky" Powell. Young Frank told Hoffman that he had not seen Ottis Toole since they all were separated one night on their way up to Maryland back in July 1981.

He told Hoffman that he often rode around Jacksonville with his uncle and that he had been with him on several visits to Reaves Roofing and Southeast Color Coat, when Ottis used keys on his ring to unlock the gates so that he could fire up the tar kettles and such. And Frank also remembered that Ottis kept a leather-sheathed hunting knife under the front seat of his black-over-white Cadillac. He'd had the car in 1980 and '81, Frank said, and had used it even after he'd had to give it back to Mrs. McNett.

All the information seemed to confirm that Toole in fact had access to a car that he could have used to drive to Miami, one with a resemblance to a car seen in the vicinity of the abduction of Adam Walsh. Also, it seemed that Toole probably had kept a sizable bladed weapon of some sort under the seat of that car. But aside from the reported sighting of Toole by a woman and her daughter in a Hollywood Kmart a day or two before Adam's disappearance and Toole's apparently wobbly confessions to the crime, Hoffman had still not come up with the solid evidence he was after. He thanked young Powell for his help and began the long drive back to Jacksonville.

Early on Friday morning, as Toole was being escorted by Detective Terry toward an interview room in the Duval County Jail, where yet another team of out-of-state homicide detectives were waiting to interview him regarding a set of unsolved cases, Toole glanced down the hallway to see Detectives Hoffman and Hickman conversing with each other, and he called out to them. He'd remembered this church where he used to work back in 1981. It was out off Lane Avenue, near I-10, Toole told them, near a Days Inn. Maybe they could track it down and find out exactly what days he was working, Toole told the detectives.

Detective Terry suspected that Toole's attorney wouldn't be happy with his client's offer of such information, but since Toole had initiated the conversation, it did not violate counsel's dictates that no interview be scheduled independently. Certainly, Terry made no move to intervene. Hoffman and Hickman made a note of Toole's information and told him they'd look into it.

First, though, the two Hollywood detectives followed up with Betty Goodyear, to see if they could confirm the date when

Toole had moved into one of her houses with his erstwhile wife Rita. As was the case with employment records, any piece of evidence that would place Toole in Jacksonville on July 27, 1981, would render all of his statements regarding Adam Walsh null and void.

But Goodyear insisted that if she did nothing else, she kept accurate records. She produced a pair of receipt books for the period in question, the first of which showed that she had rented a room to Ottis Toole on July 31, 1981. She also showed them another book with a copy of a receipt made out to V. Toole on August 7. Toole did have a brother named Vernon, but as to why his name was in her book, Goodyear did not know.

From there, Hoffman and Hickman traveled to University Hospital, where Ottis's wife Rita was a patient. When they asked her about Betty Goodyear's records, Rita cleared the mystery up quickly. She'd moved out of living with Ottis shortly after they'd reunited there at the end of July, and moved in with his brother Vernon for a week. Since he paid the rent, that's why his name was on the receipt. As for her time together with Ottis during that period, it began the day she moved into the Goodyear Apartments on July 31. She'd been staying with a woman named Nancy Jackson for seven or eight months before that, and she hadn't seen Ottis at all during that time.

The two detectives left University Hospital to follow up on Toole's recollection that he had done some work for a church around the time of Adam Walsh's murder. After some digging, they finally found a Church of God next to a Days Inn just south of I-10, about fifteen minutes west of downtown. The church's pastor, Reverend Cecil Wiggins, didn't recall anyone named Toole ever working for him, but, prodded by the detectives, he agreed to consult his records. Somewhat to his surprise, the good reverend discovered that the church had in fact paid Toole for lawn maintenance work on two separate occasions in 1981: $17.50 on August 27, and $22.75 on August 28.

Hoffman and Hickman could only stare at each other. After all their digging, they had been able to place Ottis Toole in Jacksonville on July 25, when he'd arrived from Virginia on a Greyhound bus. And they knew that he was back again on July 31, when he'd rented a room for himself and his wife from Betty Goodyear. But as to where he was during the time in between, and especially on the afternoon and evening of July 27, when Adam Walsh was kidnapped and murdered, they had only the sighting reported by Heidi and Arlene Mayer and the word of Toole to go on.

Given the amount of time that Hoffman had spent in Jacksonville talking to Toole's family and associates, it might seem in hindsight that he was more intent on proving that Toole was in that city on July 27 and thus could not possibly have committed the murder of Adam Walsh than he was with trying to find evidence placing Toole in South Florida at the time. Perhaps Hoffman was simply following the line of least resistance in interviewing individuals who knew Toole and might exonerate him; but it is puzzling, at the very least, why Hoffman or his team did not expend a greater effort on trying to place Toole at the scene of the crime: broadcasting appeals to witnesses in local media, for instance, or canvasing the ranks of Sears shoppers.

Possibly it seemed easier to Hoffman to track down and talk to people who knew Toole than to search for needles in the haystacks of South Florida; possibly, given his relative inexperience with crimes of such magnitude, he was simply out of his depth as an investigator; or possibly he simply believed Toole was lying when he said that he had kidnapped and murdered Adam Walsh. Were this his reasoning, though, he had committed the cardinal sin of an investigator—allowing his subjective feelings to interfere with his work. And whatever his reasoning, it seems odd that Hoffman was spending most of his time and effort trying to prove that the person who had confessed to the crime did not do it instead of the other way around.

In any case, and out of leads in Jacksonville for the time being, Hoffman and Hickman returned to Hollywood to await the results of the various tests being performed by the FDLE labs. On the following Wednesday, November 9, Hollywood police chief Sam Martin called Hoffman in to share the report that the FDLE had finally sent him. The eight sections of carpet and padding from the front and rear floorboards of the Cadillac had been treated with luminol to indicate the presence of blood, the report noted, and areas of strongly persistent luminescence were observed on the portion of carpet taken from the driver's-side floor, the carpet from the left rear floorboard, and on the padding beneath the carpet on the left rear floorboard. While it would have taken a considerable quantity of blood to soak through the carpet and into the padding itself, the report stated that—given the amount of time that had passed (and the limitations of DNA technology at the time)—there was an "insufficient" amount of blood present for further testing.

As to the machete that Hoffman had confiscated at Bennett Motors, chemical tests on the blade edge also demonstrated that traces of blood were present, but once again, the quantity found was insufficient to allow for further testing. While such results may seem maddeningly inconclusive to a present-day audience conditioned by the mind-boggling feats achieved by *CSI* investigators on contemporary television, those were the unequivocal findings of the most sophisticated crime technicians working in Florida law enforcement at the time.

Tests for blood on the canvas sheath of the machete were also inconclusive, the report added. And as for other debris found on the blade and sheath, that would be examined by FDLE's microanalysis section in Tallahassee. Five rolls of film had been taken to document the various forensic procedures performed on the Cadillac, the report noted, though the disposition of that film was not made clear.

The thought of setting science aside for the moment and simply showing the machete to the several people who had reported seeing Ottis Toole in possession of such a weapon might have occurred to almost anyone at that point. After all, Hoffman had gone to the trouble of taking it to *one* of Toole's employers for the purposes of identification. But if Chief Martin or Detective Hoffman or anyone else at HPD thought of such a low-tech undertaking, there is no indication of it.

WILLIAMSON COUNTY, TEXAS—NOVEMBER 12, 1983

In November 1983, two days before what would have been the celebration of Adam Walsh's ninth birthday, Henry Lee Lucas wrote from his jail cell in Texas to his former lover and partner in crime, Ottis Toole. He wasn't sure if word had reached Toole yet, but Lucas wanted him to know that he had confessed to the murder of Toole's niece, Becky Powell. Lucas hadn't written sooner regarding the matter, he explained, because he didn't want to "hurt" Toole.

Despite the fact that he had killed her, Lucas assured Toole that Becky had been his life: "I loved her more than anything else," he said, and then, having dispensed with that matter, went on to ask Toole for help in piecing together the details of the many crimes they had committed together, "so we can get the [w]hole thing out in the open." Lucas had not yet implicated Toole in anything, he said, but he had found considerable peace in coming clean, and he was writing now to find out if Toole as well might be willing to talk about their various misdeeds.

On Monday, November 14, Lucas followed up with a phone call, one that was being tape-recorded by the Texas Rangers, a fact that Lucas passed along to Toole at the beginning of their conversation. Certainly the warning did not deter Toole from being forthright.

"Remember that one time I said I wanted me some ribs?" Toole asked Lucas. "Did that make me a cannibal?"

"You wasn't a cannibal," Lucas assured him. "It's the force of the devil, something forced on us that we can't change. There's no denying what we become," he added. "We know what we are."

Toole seemed quick to pick up on Lucas's theme. "Remember how I liked to pour some blood out of them?"

Once again, Lucas—whose first murder victim was his own mother, in 1960—seemed compassionate and reasoned. "Ottis, you and I have something people look on as an animal. There's no way of changing what we done, but we can stop it and not allow other people to become what we have. And the only way to do that is by honesty."

Apparently Lucas had achieved some sense of salvation by baring his soul to investigators about his many misdeeds (quite a few of them fanciful, as it turned out), and it seemed as if his words had some effect on Toole. The following day, Tuesday, November 15, Toole was interviewed by Calcasieu Parish chief of detectives Donny Fittz about the murder of twenty-year-old Catherine Martin back in 1982, near Lake Charles, Louisiana. She'd been stabbed sixteen times with a screwdriver. Yeah, he had done it, Toole said. And his account of the crime reflected that he saw nothing unusual in his choice of weapons. If you had a hammer, you'd use a hammer. If there was a knife, use a knife. What was so different between a knife and a screwdriver anyway?

As he was winding up his interview with Toole, Fittz casually tossed out something he'd heard in the hallway.

"We understand you say you really didn't kill Adam Walsh," Fittz said to Toole, who seemed surprised by the statement.

"Oh no, I killed him too, there's no doubt about that," Toole replied. "It was like the kid, he wouldn't shut up. I was driving him in the car. I slapped him. I hit him several times."

Fittz gave an interview to reporters concerning his own investigation of the murder of Catherine Martin, but thought enough of what he'd heard from Toole about the Walsh case to pass that information along as well. Thus, in a story published on November 23 in the *Fort Lauderdale Sun-Sentinel*, the public was assured once again by Toole that he was the man responsible.

Meanwhile, Detective Hoffman had returned to Jacksonville yet again, looking for something that would pin down Toole's whereabouts between July 25 and July 31, 1981. On Thursday morning, November 17, Hoffman went to the Jacksonville Sheriff's Office homicide unit to meet with Buddy Terry. Toole was in the unit as well on this day, being interviewed by detectives from agencies near Houston and others from Colorado.

The door to the interview room was open, and when Toole glanced up to see Hoffman walking by, he called out after the detective. "Hey, Jack," he said, "I need to speak with you."

Hoffman grudgingly stopped to acknowledge Toole. "So where's Detective Hickman?" Toole wanted to know.

Hoffman glanced at his two colleagues. "He's back in Hollywood," Hoffman said to Toole. "This is Lieutenant Smith and Sergeant Standley," he added. "And neither one of them believe a thing you've said about Adam Walsh."

Toole had already complained to detectives Kendrick from Brevard County and Via from Louisiana that he didn't like the way that Hoffman treated him. Hoffman had called him a "retard" and an "asshole" on several occasions the day they were out there by Florida's Turnpike looking for the body, Toole said, and that "really pissed him off."

"I know I'm an asshole," Toole told Kendrick earlier. "And I am a retard." But if the Hollywood cops thought they were so smart, then let them go find Adam's body themselves, that's what he'd decided.

Thus, it is not difficult to imagine what Toole thought of the three Hollywood cops glowering at him from the hallway. Hoffman would later note in his log that Toole seemed quite upset, in fact.

"You want me to go on national TV and state that I killed Adam Walsh?" Toole called angrily to Hoffman. But despite the fact that he had no other leads in the case of a lifetime, Hoffman apparently felt he'd already been sufficiently played the fool by Ottis Toole. He simply shrugged and led the other officers away down the hall.

That day, Hoffman looked at medical records supplied by jailors that indicated that since his arrival, Toole had been receiving 50 milligrams of Benadryl at bedtime, presumably to help him fall asleep, along with regular dosages of Meladril, an herbal supplement sometimes used in the treatment of herpes. Though medical records showed that he had been diagnosed as having suffered convulsions from grand mal epilepsy some fifteen years previously, Toole was taking no epilepsy medication at Duval County. Little of import there, it seemed.

On the following day, Hoffman interviewed Toole's stepfather, Robert Harley, who told the detective that he had married Toole's mother Sarah in 1957, when Toole was ten. He told Hoffman of the thefts that occurred from his home after Toole's mother died and of his suspicions that Toole and Henry Lee Lucas were responsible for those, as well as for the fire that destroyed the house on June 23, 1981.

At the same time, other detectives from Hollywood were at the Lake Butler facility, interviewing James Redwine, Betty Goodyear's troubled son, who had fallen in with Toole after his return to Jacksonville from a treatment center in Miami. Redwine, serving time for arsons he committed along with Toole, said that while Toole often acted meek and timid, he could fly into rages, especially if he had a weapon available.

Redwine described a few such incidents for the detectives and also confirmed that he had seen Toole in possession of a large knife with a brown wooden handle. However, Redwine said, he was not going to submit to a sworn statement about any of this. He did not want to get involved in the investigation, period.

On Saturday, Hoffman and his cohorts, Smith and Standley, were back in the homicide unit at the Jacksonville Sheriff's Office. Once again, Toole spotted him passing the open interview room and called out after him. Hoffman ignored Toole, but Buddy Terry caught up with him and explained that Toole was being insistent. "Just go see what he wants," Terry urged.

Hoffman may not have cared what Ottis Toole wanted, but he was on Terry's turf and needed some element of cooperation if he was going to accomplish anything in Jacksonville. Thus, he walked into the interview room and informed Toole brusquely that he, Toole, was being represented by public defender Elton Schwartz and that Schwartz did not want Toole talking to any investigators without his attorney present.

To Toole, none of it mattered. "I do not want to be represented by anyone," he told Hoffman. "I want to speak to you about Adam Walsh, and I do not want to be represented by any attorney."

Hoffman glanced about the room, where any number of fellow law officers stood watching, waiting for his call. Certainly, Toole seemed well aware of his rights, and this was anything but a coercive situation, as cops from several different jurisdictions could testify. He was stymied in his own investigation; what was the harm of hearing Toole out? Suppressing something of a sigh, Hoffman sat down and began to take the *eighth* statement offered by Ottis Toole concerning the murder of Adam Walsh.

Toole began by telling Hoffman that essentially everything he had confessed to concerning the murder was correct, from the time of his arrival in South Florida and the abduction of Adam Walsh from the Sears Mall in Hollywood until his arrival at mile marker 126 on Florida's Turnpike and the subsequent decapitation. But the part about burying Adam's body in that same location was not exactly right, Toole said.

"Everything I told you about the killing, about the chopping, all that's true," Toole told Hoffman. As to Adam's torso, though, "I wrapped him in some blankets and put him in the trunk."

Following his brief stop to dispose of the head in the canal, Toole said, he drove on to Jacksonville, arriving in the evening hours at 708 Day Avenue, where the remains of his mother's gutted house still stood. At that time, Toole said, he took Adam's body out of the trunk and carried it around to the backyard and placed it in a gutted-out refrigerator that he had used as a kind of incinerator in the past. He'd start a fire and toss in coils of coated wire to burn the insulation off and expose the copper, he explained, which he could then sell at junkyards around town.

In this instance, however, his aim was quite different. After he'd gotten Adam's torso inside the refrigerator, Toole heaped on some pieces of wood and doused it all with gasoline. He lit the fire then, hoping to cremate the body, but to his disappointment, the fire went out fairly rapidly. Some of the skin on the body had turned black and crumbly, but it was not in any way completely burned. So he did what he had to do: he heaped on more wood, poured on more gasoline, and set the blaze going again.

After he was finally satisfied with the results, Ottis tried to push the gutted refrigerator on its side, so he could dump the remains onto a blanket he had spread out. But the refrigerator was heavy to begin with, and with all the debris and ash that now filled the insides, Toole couldn't budge it. So he went back to the Cadillac, found a shovel, and used that to scoop out the remains onto the blanket.

He gathered up the blanket and its contents, wrestled the bundle to the Cadillac, and managed to heave it up and into the trunk. He was about to slam the lid down when something occurred to him: What if there were hot ashes still lurking in that mess somewhere? They could smolder for hours and eventually start a blaze in his trunk. Toole might not be smart, but he knew about fire.

He also knew that no one had bothered to turn off the water at the ruined house and so he went to fetch the hose that still dangled from a spigot outside. He opened the faucet and doused the trunk and its contents until he was sure that no embers could have survived.

By then it was late, and Toole, who'd had himself a full day, was tired. He slammed the lid of the trunk, climbed into the Cadillac, and slept there through the night. In the morning he rose to clean off his machete and his shovel, and then hid the tools under a still-standing portion of the ruined house.

After that, he drove the Cadillac to the city of Jacksonville's northernmost dump, where he backed up to a muddy area and tossed the water-soaked bundle out. Satisfied that the wadded blanket looked no different from any other bundle of discarded goods in the vast wasteland, he was about to get back into the car when it struck him that the sodden carpeting of the trunk might now contain traces of blood, so he pulled that up from the floorboards of the trunk and tossed it out into the dump as well. That night, long after he knew all the employees would be gone, Toole returned the Cadillac to the yard of Reaves Roofing.

And whatever happened to that machete he had used? Hoffman wanted to know. Toole wasn't sure what he had done with the blade, finally, he told Hoffman. It could have ended up over at Spencer's Motors in Jacksonville, though. He'd left a lot of his stuff in paper bags over there at one time or another.

Hoffman's notes do not indicate whether or not his heart quickened at this chance comment of Toole's, but if it did not, one would surely wonder why. Finally, after all the fruitless searching, Ottis Toole had unknowingly suggested that Hoffman was in possession of a piece of evidence that would directly link the killer to the crime.

Asked to describe this machete further, Toole told Hoffman that it was in a green canvas holster that kept the blade covered, and that he had wrapped tape on the wooden handle, "to keep from getting blisters from chopping." It seemed a perfect match to the machete that Hoffman had confiscated at Bennett Motors: the handle had been taped, the grips were wooden, the blade was housed in a green canvas sheath, and one of the substances on the blade looked very much like tar, indicating its use by someone involved in the roofing trade.

Hoffman next asked Toole where he had stayed between the time he took the Cadillac back to the roofing company on the evening of July 28 and the afternoon of July 31, when he moved into one of Betty Goodyear's houses with Rita. Toole wasn't too sure. He might have slept in a portion of his mother's house that still had its roof, or he might have slept in one or another of the parks in the area.

Hoffman concluded the interview at 11:08 that morning, asking Toole to explain why he had lied before about burying Adam's body down near mile marker 126 on Florida's Turnpike. Toole didn't say anything about the sandwich that Hoffman had slapped out of his hands the day he'd led detectives to the site where he'd decapitated Adam. Nor did he mention that it pissed him off mightily that Hoffman had called him an asshole and a retard on numerous occasions.

Yes, he had told Hoffman that he cut off Adam's head and buried his body nearby on that day, he admitted, but there was a very simple explanation: "I was just fucking around with the police department," he said.

SATURDAY, NOVEMBER 19, 1983

Following that interview with Toole and a break for lunch, Hoffman and his fellow officers from Hollywood tracked down David Gillyard, who'd worked as sales manager for Wells Brothers Used Cars, starting in November 1982. He remembered taking in the 1971 black-over-white Cadillac, Gillyard told the detectives, and recalled very clearly that there was no carpeting in its trunk. Rather than go to the expense of paying for new carpet for such an old vehicle, he had ordered one of his lot men to simply "paint splatter" the trunk to give it some appearance of finish for sale.

After they'd spoken to Gillyard, the detectives went back to Faye McNett, just wondering, they said, if the Cadillac she'd sold to Ottis Toole had carpeting in its trunk. Indeed it did, McNett told them. What kind of a question was that, anyway?

On Sunday, Hoffman, accompanied by Lieutenant Smith and Sergeant Stanley, took a drive to the North Jacksonville dump, where they took photographs of the area—with more than two years of trash heaped on the site since Toole said he had disposed of the body there, it seemed little else could be done.

Early Monday morning, seeking further corroboration of what Toole had told them, the detectives spoke with the Jacksonville Fire Department arson specialist who had investigated the burning of Toole's mother's house at 708 Day Avenue in June of 1981. The lot had been leveled back on December 10, 1982, by an outfit called Realco Wrecking. But as to what had and had not remained standing after the fire, there were numerous photographs in the files, Captain Hinkley said. The Hollywood detectives were welcome to them.

At about nine thirty that morning, Hoffman interviewed Robert L. Hammond, who owned Hammond's Grocery at 700 Day Avenue, next door to Toole's mother's house. Yes, he knew both Toole and Henry Lee Lucas, Hammond told the officers, and he well remembered the day that Toole's mother's house burned down.

He had also observed that Toole stayed at the house on several occasions after the fire, and he had often seen Toole digging up and burying various articles of trash in the backyard. Toole eked out a living by collecting junk, Hammond said, and often stored various items he'd found in his mother's yard. He brought back discarded refrigerators, then hacked them apart for the aluminum he could sell at salvage yards. And he also used the gutted refrigerators as incinerators where he burned the insulation off wiring to expose the salable copper underneath. Hammond's mother Sarah was present at the interview, and she too told Hoffman that she had seen Ottis Toole back at his mother's house after the June 23 fire.

Hoffman next spoke with a man named Charles Lee Hardaman, who claimed to have known Toole for about three years. The two of them would ride around picking up junk like refrigerators, stoves, and furniture, and then bring it back to 708 Day Avenue, where they'd break it apart for whatever salvageable materials might be obtained—and yes, he had also seen Toole use the carcasses of refrigerators as incinerators.

When Hoffman asked if he ever knew Toole to carry weapons, Hardaman confirmed that there was a shotgun around sometimes. And how about any large knives? Hoffman wanted to know.

"I never seen him with knives," Hardaman said first, but then corrected himself. "Well, he had one like they used in the old days."

Just how large a knife was this? Hoffman asked.

"I don't know," Hardaman said. "I saw it," he added, holding his hands a foot or more apart. Then he raised his thumb and forefinger, with perhaps a two-inch gap between them. "A blade about this wide."

"What kind of case?" Hoffman asked.

"A steel case."

"What color?"

Hardaman shrugged. "Rust," he said, going on to explain to Hoffman that it was the kind of knife that you could fix onto a gun barrel.

"A bayonet?" Hoffman asked.

"Yeah," Hardaman said.

In his first confession to Hoffman, Toole had begun his description of the decapitation by saying he'd used a bayonet. But Hoffman had responded by saying, "Like a machete?" and Toole had subsequently followed the detective's lead in referring to the weapon he'd used as a machete. It could have been a simple misstatement, given the limitations of Toole's intelligence, but then again, the matter was certainly worth pursuing.

"When did you see that knife?" Hoffman asked.

Hardaman gave him a look. "Well, it was mine," he finally admitted. "I left it there at the house and told him to sharpen it."

"And he kept it? Never returned it to you?"

"Right," Hardaman said.

"When did you give it to him?" Hoffman next asked.

Hardaman thought. "It was when his momma was living, that much I know."

"So that would have been before May 1981?"

"Yeah," Hardaman said.

Following the conversation with Hardaman, Hoffman drove with Smith and Standley to Daytona Beach, about two hours south, where they met briefly with William O. Toole, another of Ottis's brothers. William refused to speak with them in any detail about Ottis, however, and the trio drove home to Hollywood that evening.

It was on Wednesday of that week that the *Fort Lauderdale Sun-Sentinel* ran the story in which Louisiana detective Donny Fittz told reporters that Ottis Toole had confessed to the killing of Adam Walsh during an unrelated interview. When reporters called Hollywood PD for a comment on Fittz's allegations, public information officer Tony Alderson dismissed it as nothing new. "We believed Toole the first time," Alderson said.

Meantime, the FDLE lab in Jacksonville had concluded its examination of Toole's Cadillac for Adam's fingerprints. Alas, no latent prints of any value had been found.

Almost a week went by without any significant developments, though the treatment center in Hialeah where Betty Goodyear's son John Redwine had stayed prior to meeting Toole did confirm to Hollywood PD that Redwine had gone on vacation from the facility on July 24, 1981, and had boarded a bus bound for Jacksonville at nine that morning. Conceivably, Redwine could have been helpful in placing Toole's whereabouts if Hoffman could find him.

On Wednesday, November 30, 1983, Detective Hoffman reached a clerk named Filiore in the Jacksonville Water Department, who confirmed that water service to the home of Toole's mother at 708 Day Avenue had in fact been disconnected for nonpayment, but not until September 9, 1981. "This information was needed in order to verify a part of Ottis Toole's confession in which he indicated that he used the hose in the rear of his mother's residence to wash out the 1971 Cadillac trunk area in which there was trace evidence of blood," Hoffman wrote in his notes, adding that the information did corroborate Toole's claim that there was water available to him on the date in question.

Later that day, Hoffman phoned Dennis Bedwell, supervisor of the City of Jacksonville Sanitation Department. Since Toole had claimed that he disposed of the body of Adam Walsh in the North Jacksonville dump on the morning of July 28, 1981, Hoffman needed Bedwell to provide the names of the employees who were on duty between the time of that facility's opening and, say, 3:00 p.m. Bedwell checked his records and came up with a couple of names and phone numbers for Hoffman, but there is no indication that the detective ever spoke to either employee or searched sanitation department records (or those of other landfill operations) for any information that might have confirmed a visit by Toole at the time he claimed to have been there.

The following day, Thursday, December 1, Hoffman took the machete he'd found at Bennett Motors to the Metro Dade Police Department crime lab with a request that technicians perform tool marking tests on the weapon. Though the blood tests were inconclusive, Hoffman hoped that the striations found on the spinal column at the base of Adam Walsh's skull could be matched to the blade.

The Broward County medical examiner's office had also found a couple of embedded "paint chips" during their further cleanup of Adam's skull, and Hoffman brought the fragments along for Metro Dade's analysis as well. If the chips could be identified as paint or other materials traceable to the 1971 Cadillac, that too might serve as evidence linking Toole to the crime.

The following Tuesday, December 6, Hoffman and Lieutenant Smith traveled to the Williamson County Jail near Austin, Texas, where Henry Lee Lucas was being held, hoping that Lucas might be able to implicate Toole in the killing of Adam Walsh. Lucas told Hoffman and Smith that it was quite possible that Toole could have been responsible for such a crime, for he and Toole had traveled various parts of the United States together at one time or another and had committed any number of murders both independently and as a team. However, as to this particular crime, Lucas said he had no knowledge of it whatsoever.

On that Friday, Hoffman received more disheartening news, this from the Miami Dade crime lab, advising that their "best efforts to date" had not been able to produce a positive identification of the tool markings on Adam's vertebrae as having been made by the machete he'd submitted. Analyst Bob Hart had "worked the evidence with great vigor," Metro Dade crime lab commander Edward Whittaker assured Hoffman, but all the physical factors combined appeared to be leading to no positive identification.

As to the "white fragments," or paint chips, that Hoffman had submitted, those were still being analyzed. Though the chips did not appear to be composed of automotive paint, the report said, they had obviously come from *something*, and the fracture patterns observed at the edges of these chips were deemed very likely sufficient to permit an absolutely positive ID if whatever material they had broken from could be recovered. Thus, "the questioned vehicle should be searched with extreme care for such material and if found, for any defect or break in any surface."

A few days later, however, on December 14, lab commander Whittaker called to inform Hoffman that in fact the examination of the machete against the markings on the vertebrae had come up negative. They were still trying to identify what the white fragments he'd submitted might have come from, Whittaker said, and they would let him know the moment any information was available. There exists no record in the case file that Hoffman ever contacted the FDLE crime lab regarding a search within the Cadillac for any object from which the chips might have derived.

On Thursday, December 22, FDLE got in touch with Hoffman to report that no fibers from the vacuum sweepings from the front or rear seat carpets of the Cadillac had matched fibers from the machete's canvas sheath. On the following Tuesday, December 27, FDLE technician Glen Abate traveled to the then-vacant lot at 708 Day Street and began to dig in what had been the rear yard, searching for evidence that the body of Adam Walsh might have been placed there. At one spot, about a foot below the surface, Abate uncovered a pair of light green shorts and advised Buddy Terry of the Jacksonville Sheriff's Office of his findings.

Since Revé Walsh had told detectives of dressing her son in a pair of light green shorts on the morning of July 27, 1981, Terry thought it a significant discovery. He called Detective Hoffman in Hollywood to let him know, and had the shorts placed in an evidence locker until he could pick them up.

New Year's Day of 1984 dawned with Hoffman back in Jacksonville, still trying to trace Toole's movements at the time of the crime. On January 4, he met with Timothy Harold Jones, the clerk who was behind the counter of the Little Champ store the day that Ottis Toole burst in, screaming that someone was going to shoot him. The clerk also recalled that, moments later, Howard Toole followed Ottis in and proceeded to slap him around. That all had taken place on August 1, 1981, Jones said, though he also stated that he remembered selling Ottis a pack of cigarettes and a can of beer "one or two days" prior to the fight—which would have meant July 30 or 31, if Jones's memory was accurate.

Meantime, Lieutenant Smith checked the various distances between the Jacksonville Greyhound bus station and the places Toole might have walked to upon his arrival on July 25. It was 3.6 miles from the station to his mother's home at 708 Day, and 7.8 miles to the Reaves Roofing lot from which he claimed to have taken the Cadillac—a hour's walk to one, two hours to the other.

At 8:00 a.m. on Thursday, January 5, Hoffman arrived at the former site of the home at 708 Day Street, along with Lieutenant Smith and two other detectives from Hollywood PD. Also present were Detective Terry, three technicians from the FDLE crime investigation unit, and a representative of the Jacksonville Public Works Department. They were convened to excavate the property in a systematic search for evidence.

Using a front-end loader with an eight-foot-wide bucket, the team employed the standard method for excavating crime scenes, dragging the property two inches at a pass, until they had reached depths anywhere from four to six feet. About two hours into the search, as they dug in the northwest section of the lot, the machine unearthed bone fragments that resembled a section of a human pelvis. Three hours later, in a different section of the lot, two other unidentifiable bones were uncovered. And at about 3:30 p.m., in a third quadrant of the lot, a left-footed yellow rubber "zori," or flip-flop, in a small child's size, was found. All of the items were duly cataloged by FDLE crime scene technician Abate and turned over to Detective Terry.

While Hoffman stayed behind to watch over the rest of the search, Terry and Lieutenant Smith hurried to the Duval County medical examiner's office with the bone fragments. Whatever hopes they had, however, were soon dashed. These were the remains of some type of animal, the ME said. No chance they had come from a human.

On Friday, Hoffman spoke with Yvonne Grant, the manager of the Little Champ where Howard Toole committed his battery on his brother Ottis. That day was August 1, 1981, Grant confirmed, and like her employee Timothy Jones, she remembered that Ottis Toole had in fact been in her store previously, only a day—or at most, two days—prior to the incident.

The entire period from October 1983, when Toole made his first confession to the murder of Adam Walsh, to the following January 1984, during which Toole made at least seven more confessions to the crime, must have seemed very much a time of "one step forward, two steps back" for Detective Hoffman and the Hollywood PD. After two years with essentially nothing, a man already convicted of another senseless murder and implicated in dozens of others around the country had come forward to claim responsibility for the abduction and murder of Adam Walsh.

Yet despite the repeated confessions and the offering up of detail of the crime that it seemed only the killer could have carried with him, Hoffman could find no evidence linking Toole directly to the crime. It must have been a period of intense frustration for Hoffman, and one senses from a pattern of dogged, repetitive inquiries down the same oft-tracked trails a desperation in his actions.

But whatever degree of frustration Hoffman may have felt or whatever adjective one might employ to describe the tenor of his investigation, it seemed that he was weary of whatever Ottis Toole had brought to the table. As evidence, consider what happened next.

JACKSONVILLE, FLORIDA—JANUARY 6, 1984

Though there is no indication as to who called for the meeting between Detective Jack Hoffman and Ottis Toole on the first Friday of the new year of 1984, there is certainly no reason for Hoffman to have requested it. He already had seven sworn statements from Toole confessing to the killing of Adam Walsh, and, if Hollywood PIO Tony Alderson is to be believed, most every-one at Hollywood PD "believed Toole from the beginning."

In any case, at 9:56 on Friday morning, January 6, Hoffman, accompanied by fellow Hollywood PD detectives Smith, Naylon, and Banks, entered the interview room at the Jacksonville Sheriff's Office, and once again sat down with Ottis Toole.

"What is the reason that you are giving us this statement regarding Adam Walsh?" Hoffman began.

Toole fumbled a bit, but he seemed clear enough, ultimately. "Ah, I didn't, ah, I didn't kill Adam Walsh."

Hoffman glanced at his fellow officers, then back at Toole. "You didn't kill Adam Walsh?"

Toole shook his head. "No."

Hoffman's next question had an odd ring to it. Instead of asking Toole who or what had motivated him to call them in to say such a thing, Hoffman took more of a petulant tack. "Then why have you stuck with your confession all these months, from the first time I met you?" Hoffman asked. "Can you tell me why you stuck to your story all this time?"

Though there may seem a certain relevance to the question, it also seems that Hoffman had been prepared for what he was going to hear during the interview. In any case, Toole managed an answer for the detective, lame as it may have sounded:

"Ah, I was trying to hang Henry Lucas at first, but I found out he was in jail."

Another interviewer might have pointed out to Toole that he had known for months that Lucas was in jail, and then gone to work on Toole, trying to determine just who had drawn up the scenario for the present morning's meeting. But Hoffman did none of those things, and by 10:06, ten minutes after it had begun, the lead detective on the case signaled to his associates that the interview was over.

Hoffman then asked Buddy Terry to hand over the green shorts and yellow rubber zori that had been recovered during the excavation of the property where Toole's mother's house had stood, and Terry complied. Hoffman took the shorts and flip-flop back to Hollywood with him that evening, and placed them in the PD evidence room, where—rather than being shown to John and Revé Walsh for purposes of identification—the items inexplicably remained unexamined for more than thirteen years.

For all intents and purposes, Jack Hoffman's investigation of Ottis Toole as a suspect in the murder of Adam Walsh was over. For whatever reason—his innate distrust of Toole, his inability to let go of Jimmy Campbell as a suspect, or simply a natural inclination to step away from a frustating task—Jack Hoffman had finished with Ottis Toole.

Shortly thereafter, the last vestiges of Detective Hoffman's investigation of Toole were wrapped up without fanfare: in late January, the Tallahassee lab reported that hairs found in Toole's Cadillac—vacuumed from the seats, headrest, and carpet— did not belong to Adam Walsh. Subsequently, according to an FDLE memo, all the evidentiary items examined by both the Tallahassee and Jacksonville labs were returned either to the Hollywood PD by registered mail or directly to Detective Terry of the Jacksonville Sheriff's Office.

Ottis Toole's difficulties with the law were scarcely over, to be sure. Just two weeks later, at the end of a three-day conference in Monroe, Louisiana, hosted by the Ouachita Parish Homicide Task Force, law enforcement officers from nineteen states issued a joint announcement that Henry Lee Lucas and Ottis Toole had been positively linked to 81 murders out of the 150 or more that they claimed to have committed.

During his various interviews with those agents, Toole explained that quite often, after Henry Lee had sex with some of the female victims, he would turn them over to Toole to be killed. Toole, inflamed with anger and jealousy, was only too happy to comply. A number of the victims had suffered extensively, with multiple stab wounds and deep—though not fatal—cuts along the arms, thighs, and lower legs. Several had been disemboweled, and a number had been doused with diesel fuel—stolen by Lucas and Toole during erstwhile stints on roofing crews—then set afire.

In Jacksonville, Buddy Terry had enjoyed far more success with his own investigation of the arson case in which Toole had caused the death of Betty Goodyear's tenant George Sonnenberg. Toole went to trial on those charges in late April and somewhat predictably testified that he did not in fact set the fire that he had on numerous occasions previously confessed to. The defense introduced Dr. Eduardo Sanchez, a psychiatrist, who testified that Toole was a pyromaniac, his intelligence on the borderline of retardation. He was childlike and impulsive, Dr. Sanchez said, subject to bouts of "overwhelming tension" that had to be relieved. "Setting fires is one of the ways he does it," Sanchez said, and in such terms it might sound almost rational.

Whatever the jury thought of Dr. Sanchez's explanations, they seemed far more compelled by the evidence presented. On Friday, May 11, that body took thirty-five minutes to reach its verdict: Ottis Toole was guilty of the arson murder of George Sonnenberg, and the recommended penalty was death.

As he was being led from the courtroom, a furious Toole whirled on Detective Terry, who had supplied much of the evidence during the trial. "Friends don't testify against friends," Toole shouted at Terry. "I'm going to fuck you."

Toole, who had been formally charged with nine other murders in Texas, Colorado, and Louisiana by that time, was sentenced to death for the murder of Sonnenberg and was finally

transferred back into the State of Florida prison system at Lake
Butler on May 18, 1984. Shortly after his arrival at Lake Butler,
Toole granted an interview to *Jacksonville Times-Union* reporter
Mickie Valente, during which he repeated his confession to the
murder of Adam Walsh.

He took Valente through the details of the abduction, explaining once again that he had done it to "keep him for myself," and
the decapitation—"I put both hands on it [the machete] and I
chopped his head off." And he included the information that
he had given Hoffman about what he had actually done with
Adam's body, though he had a grisly coda to add.

He had taken the body back to Jacksonville and stuffed him
into a discarded "icebox" on his mother's property, Toole told
Valente. And then he said, "I took that machete and I cut out
some of his side and I ate some of it." And following that, he
burned the corpse and tossed the remains into a Jacksonville
city dump on the following day. As to the specter of execution
for his current conviction, Toole told the reporter that he was
not really concerned. "It might not really happen," he said. "You
can always appeal, for years and years."

Only three days after that sensational story appeared, on May
24, 1984, the FDLE returned the principal piece of evidence in
the case—Toole's Cadillac—to the Jacksonville Sheriff's Office.
There had been no word from Hoffman or the Hollywood PD in
the wake of Toole's sordid public confession, and with no hold
placed on the car as evidence, it was subsequently sold by the
sheriff's office to a used car dealer. A St. Augustine resident
named Sirree Safwat bought the vehicle, despite his complaint
that it lacked carpeting on the floorboards and trunk. Less than
a year later, after the car began to exhibit serious engine problems, Safwat said, he sold it to a junk dealer as scrap for $50.

On October 18, 1984, Detective Hoffman granted an interview with the *Florida Today* newspaper in Cocoa. In it, he told
the reporter unequivocally that Ottis Toole was no longer con-

sidered a suspect in the murder of Adam Walsh. "He was a suspect until we were able to put holes in his story," Hoffman told a reporter, though he did not say what those "holes" were. "His confession only vaguely matched" the actual details of the killing, Hoffman claimed. An aide to Broward County state attorney Michael Satz said that his office concurred, though he also made it clear that the call was entirely Hoffman's: "Hollywood police apparently saw fit to say that Toole is no longer suspected and we're just agreeing," press aide Dave Casey offered.

When Buddy Terry heard the news, he was not surprised. As far as he could tell, Hoffman had never really taken Toole seriously. He believed that Hoffman had missed an opportunity to nail Toole for the Walsh murder, but at least Toole was in prison, Terry thought, and facing execution. Clearly, he would have to put the rest out of his mind.

Which he might have done, were it not for the astounding news that Terry soon was to receive from his superiors. Hoffman, it seemed, was not quite finished with Ottis Toole and the Adam Walsh case, after all. He had filed a complaint with Duval County authorities that Terry had supplied Toole with case file information that Toole used to concoct his confession. Terry had done this, Hoffman alleged, because the Jacksonville detective and Toole had formed a secret agreement to write a book based on Toole's sensational confession.

Terry, who hadn't even heard of Adam Walsh the first time he overheard Toole confessing the crime to Brevard County detective Steve Kendrick, was dumbfounded by Hoffman's allegations. Still, while the matter was investigated, he was to be transferred out of the robbery and homicide unit where he had served as a detective for more than twelve years, back to the uniform patrol division, assigned to the graveyard for wayward detectives, otherwise known as the Communications Center.

CHAPTER FIVE

As Evil Does

Q: Tell me about some of the weapons you've used to kill your victims.

A: I've used jack handles, two by fours, shovels, axes. Run them over with a car. Strangled them with stockings, skip ropes, phone cords. You name it.

Q: And shot them?

A: Oh yeah, shot 'em. Sure. In the head. In the chest. In the back. In the stomach.

Q: And sometimes in the top of the head . . .

A: . . . sometimes, if somebody's been going down on you. You have to be careful there, though.

Q: And this is with a handgun?

A: Usually. A .22, a .25, a .357 magnum. But sometimes a shotgun. And I've used a rifle, too.

Q: Is there any weapon you never used?

A: I never used an ice pick. That would have been good, though. I wish I would have used an ice pick, just once.

—OTTIS TOOLE TO TEXAS RANGERS,
MARCH 24, 1984

HOLLYWOOD, FLORIDA—NOVEMBER 14, 1984

Given the train wreck that the investigation of Ottis Toole had become, the November Wednesday that would have marked the celebration of Adam Walsh's tenth birthday instead seemed to serve as a milestone of frustration. A year or so before, it appeared that his killer had been found, and while it would not bring their son back, John and Revé Walsh might have found a certain kind of relief had Toole been charged and tried. At the very least, some sense of justice might have prevailed, some semblance of the possibility of order restored to their world.

The Walshes were certainly not the first parents to be visited by such predation and calamity. As they soon found out in the aftermath of their loss, thousands of families around the country had suffered similar tragedies and had been similarly frustrated in their ability to find help from local law enforcement agencies and the justice system. Children went off to corner stores, or out in backyards to play, and they simply never came back. Or sometimes were brought back in body bags.

In most cases, stricken parents could do little but grieve, but more than a few took the time to share their sadness and their frustration in letters to the Walshes. None of the aggrieved parents who had suffered the disappearance or murder of a child had any idea exactly what to do, but many sent checks to the Walshes urging them to use the money any way they saw fit.

And then, in September 1981, less than two months following Adam's murder, the Walshes received a call from the office of Florida senator Paula Hawkins, who had tried unsuccessfully to get the FBI involved in the search for Adam at the outset. Senator Hawkins had joined the push on Capitol Hill to pass legislation that would require the federal government to maintain a centralized database on missing children and those who had been found dead but unidentified.

It seemed ludicrous to supporters of the bill, the Missing Children Act, that you could report your stolen car—or horse—

to the FBI and have that agency spring immediately into action, while a child could disappear without so much as an eye blink from federal crime fighters. Outrage over the 1932 Lindbergh baby kidnapping had resulted in the passage of the Federal Kidnapping Act (the so-called Lindbergh Law), making it a federal offense to transport a victim across a state line or use the mail to send a ransom note. Ostensibly, the act gave the FBI the authority to pursue kidnapping cases, but the agency had maintained a long-standing reluctance to interfere with local police in such matters. It often made for bad politics, for one thing; for another, most kidnapping cases turned out to be the result of messy, interfamilial wrangling; and for yet another, they were reluctant to create more work for themselves. The official FBI line was that "local agencies have more mobile manpower," necessary to efficiently pursue kidnappings.

Indeed, though Walsh had pleaded with the FBI to get involved in the initial search for Adam, and the agency pledged its support, records show that no such action was ever taken. The message that was passed down was this: If it got to the point where Hollywood PD was searching for a suspect somewhere out of state, then the feds would be happy to lend a hand. Otherwise, the local cops were on their own.

Though the prospects for passage of the proposed legislation were dim, a staffer for Senator Hawkins wanted the Walshes to go to Washington to lobby on behalf of the bill, and though it was a mission they would have to carry out at their own expense, they were more than happy to do so. At the very least, it was a way to vent some of the frustration they had felt from the outset of Adam's disappearance.

It did not take the Walshes long to sense the enormous weight of indifference they were confronting, however. As even newly elected presidents have learned, trying to correct the conduct of business as usual in the federal bureaucracy is like trying to nudge an ocean liner off its path by standing on a rubber raft and pressing on the liner's hull with your bare hands as it speeds by. But, fueled by their outrage and sense of injustice and buoyed by the support of so many strangers around the country, they had already formed their own nonprofit agency, the Adam Walsh Outreach Center for Missing Children, and they now threw themselves wholeheartedly into lobbying Congress on the Missing Children Act.

In October 1982 the effort, which had been joined by a number of prominent politicians, including Henry Hyde, Paul Simon, Arlen Specter, and even staunch FBI supporter Strom Thurmond, paid off with the act's passage—and though it simply provided for the establishment of separate categories for missing children and the unidentified dead in the FBI's national database, the legislation marked the first time in history that missing children, runaways, child prostitution, family abductions, and a host of associated ills were formally recognized as matters that impacted an entire nation.

For nearly two years following, John Walsh balanced his work for Paradise Grand Hotels and his efforts on behalf of the Walsh Outreach Center and various legislative efforts around the country. *Adam*, a made-for-television movie based on the case, had aired on October 10, 1983, just as Ottis Toole was making his first confession to Brevard County detective Steve Kendrick. Though one of Toole's cellmates later told investigators that they had turned the movie off that night and watched a football game instead, in other parts of the republic the film was well received, critically and popularly. Forty million viewers watched as a roll call of photographs of fifty-five missing children played at the end of the film, and thousands of calls flooded the 1-800 number provided. As a result, thirteen of those fifty-five missing children were reunited with their families.

The Walshes, realizing the limitations of the Missing Children Act, next turned their attention to the establishment of a national version of their own nonprofit, a center where parents of missing and abducted children could go for practical help. Limited in effect as it was, the passage of the Missing Children Act had nonetheless broken the political logjam that impeded progress on such issues, and even President Ronald Reagan threw his support behind the establishment of a National Center for Missing and Exploited Children. Finally, on June 13, 1984, the center was opened, in the form of a private organization, funded at the outset by a $3.3 million grant from the U.S. Department of Justice. The only hitch was that John Walsh had to agree to serve on the center's board of directors, which in turn meant that he would have to leave his job with Paradise Grand.

In some ways it was a difficult decision. Revé had given birth to a daughter, Meghan, in July 1982, and in 1984 she was pregnant again. John's pay would be a fraction of what he was making in the hotel business, but there was no fighting the tide. The Walshes had in fact helped accomplish the impossible—and once you had pushed against the hull of a massive ocean liner and felt it wobble from its intended course, you couldn't simply stop.

There was great satisfaction for both John and Revé Walsh in what they had accomplished, but even though their work in Florida and Washington had helped other parents regain their children and see that persons who had committed such crimes received their just deserts, it did not ease the ache that filled them every time they thought of Adam. It did not matter that other children had come along. It did not matter that time had passed, and that life had brought them many blessings. Their firstborn was gone forever, and his killer remained unidentified. And despite their suspicions that Ottis Toole was responsible, the police certainly didn't seem to think so. For all the Walshes knew, then, the person responsible was still out there somewhere, and was killing still.

Adam's eleventh birthday, November 14, 1985, came and went with no word from the police, and as the years piled up and no progress was reported, the prospects that a break in the case would ever come dimmed. In January 1986, Hollywood police chief Sam Martin retired, and though insiders presumed that Leroy Hessler—prominently involved in the Adam Walsh investigation—would be his replacement, city commissioners were troubled by reports of rampant favoritism in matters of promotion, transfer, and assignment within the department. Instead of going along with Hessler, they appointed Richard Witt, a twenty-seven-year veteran of the City of Miami Police Department, to take Martin's place.

If the Walshes thought it would mean anything in terms of progress on the case, however, they would be sadly disappointed. Witt had plenty to attend to without diverting his department's resources down what was to him a dead-end road, and thus Adam's twelfth birthday passed with no word, as did his thirteenth in 1987.

Then there arrived some news from a quarter the Walshes could scarcely have envisioned. A letter dated October 4, 1988, began:

Dear Walsh,
My name is Ottis Toole. I'm the person who snatched, raped, murdered, and cut up the little prick teaser, Adam Walsh and dumped his smelly ass into the canal. You know the story but you don't know where his bones are. I do.

Now you are a rich fucker, money you made from the dead body of that little kid. OK, he was a sweet little piece of ass! I want to make a deal with you. Here's my deal. You pay me money and I'll tell you where the bones are so you can get him buried all decent and Christian.

Elsewhere in this despicable letter to John Walsh, Toole explained that he wanted $5,000 right away as "good faith money" and Walsh's signed promise of $45,000 more once Toole had shown him Adam's bones. Toole closed by telling Walsh that Adam had been crying for his mother as he sodomized him.

"If you send the police after me before we make a deal then you don't get no bones and what's left of Adam's hot pussy can rot," Toole warned. "Tell the cops and you don't get shit."

"Tell the cops," of course, is exactly what John Walsh did. He immediately gave the letter, signed by Ottis E. Toole—in script that precisely matched Toole's signature on various prison forms—to Detective Hoffman at Hollywood PD. Walsh had become aware that Hoffman was unwilling to believe that Toole was Adam's murderer—it had gotten back to Walsh that Hoffman thought Toole was simply trying to draw attention to himself by claiming responsibility. And while Walsh was willing to accede to Hoffman's claims that there was no physical evidence linking Toole to the crime, he was sure that this blood-boiling message would reignite the detective's interest.

Walsh was wrong—Hoffman simply filed the letter away. As it turns out, it was not the only letter that Toole sent out at the time. On the same day, he had also written an extortion note to Sears, explaining that he had cut a deal with a magazine to tell the story of how he had kidnapped, raped, and murdered Adam Walsh, and now, he said, he was threatening to tell the world how easy it was to abduct and assault children at their stores. "I do my shopping for juicy little kiddies at Sears," he said in his missive to the company. But for a "fast check," Toole said, he was willing to omit any direct mention of the chain in his magazine account. "See you soon," he closed. "Bring money."

On the following day, Toole sent off another letter to the *Orlando Sentinel*: "Someone told my ear that a big paper" like theirs might pay a "nice amount" for his personal account of the murder of Adam Walsh. And maybe once he told the story, people would leave him alone about it, Toole explained. But there were conditions: "No cops, no lawyers. Just me and a reporter. Please make me your cash offer promptly."

For its part, the *Sentinel* summarily forwarded the letter from Toole to Detective Hoffman. "Probably not anything new to you, but here it is for what it's worth," reporter Sean Holton said, before adding, "Let me know if anything comes of it."

Toole sent a similar letter to the *National Enquirer*, which prompted reporter Charlie Montgomery to place a call directly to Jack Hoffman. His paper wasn't about to offer Toole any money, Montgomery said, but it was his intention to write Toole back and ask what new details he might be willing to supply. If he got anything interesting in response, he would let Hoffman know. Meantime, he reminded Hoffman, he would very much appreciate hearing should anything new turn up in the case. More than seven years had passed since Adam's death, and five since Ottis Toole had first confessed, and still, it seemed, the case exerted its great power over the collective psyche of the country.

By October 12, having received no offers from any of the major outlets he'd written, Toole was drafting "To whom it may concern" appeals, trying to find anyone who might be willing to pay him for his story. "Dear Editor," began one such. "My name is Ottis E. Toole. I am the one who kidnapped, raped, murdered and hacked to pieces the boy Adam Walsh in 1981. I also murdered 3 women and a man up around Holmes County, Florida." Toole went on to explain that he had already written to the sheriffs of both Broward County and Holmes County, a rural enclave in a part of the Florida Panhandle often referred to as L.A. or "Lower Alabama," claiming that he was ready to confess to the aforementioned five murders. Furthermore, Toole said, he had decided to invite one member of the media to sit in on the confessions to ensure that police did not abuse him in the process. "If your paper is interested then let me know," Toole said in closing.

Copies of this letter and the one that had been sent to Sears were forwarded to Hoffman without apparent effect, but another letter sent to Broward County sheriff Nick Navarro finally prompted some action. In this missive Gerald Schaffer, a fellow inmate of Ottis Toole's at Florida State Prison, explained that he was actually writing on behalf of Toole, owing to Toole's difficulties in reading and writing. However, Sheriff Navarro should have no doubt: Toole was responsible for the murder of Adam Walsh and for other unidentified murders in Broward County, and he was willing to admit formally to his involvement.

There were conditions, said Schaffer, a former Martin County sheriff's deputy serving two life terms for the murder of two teenage girls. He was to be present during all interviews with Toole; the interviews were to be of short duration; and both Schaffer and Toole wished to be relocated to the Broward County Jail. It may have seemed a presumptuous offer, but if most of the other letters that Schaffer wrote on Toole's behalf were dismissed, this one received significantly more attention.

MONDAY, OCTOBER 17, 1988

Shortly after Navarro's office heard from Toole, on October 17, 1988, Captain Walter Laun, the commander of the Broward County Sheriff's Office criminal investigations unit, summoned Detective Sergeant Richard Scheff, supervisor of the homicide unit, to a meeting where he handed over a copy of the letter they had received.

Laun instructed Scheff to take one of his men up to the Florida State Prison to meet with Schaffer and Toole and try to assess whether there was any validity to the claims. Because Laun was aware of Toole's history of recanting his confessions, he wanted Scheff to try to extract some detail or form of evidence that would lend credence to Toole's assertions.

Two days later, on October 19, Scheff and Detective Sergeant Fantigrassi made the five-and-a-half-hour drive north to Florida State Prison, the state's maximum security facility. "Starke," as it is sometimes referred to, for its proximity to that aptly named town, houses the inmates considered to be the most dangerous in the system. It is also the location of the death-row cell blocks, and while lethal injection would become the standard method of execution in 2000, at the time of Scheff and Fantigrassi's visit, it was still "Old Sparky," the electric chair, that held the preeminent place of prominence at Starke.

Scheff and Fantigrassi first met with Gerald Schaffer, who told the detectives that he had become acquainted with Toole while both were incarcerated there, and that at present he was functioning as Ottis Toole's legal representative. Furthermore, Schaffer told them, he was interested in claiming the various reward monies still outstanding for the clearing of the Adam Walsh case.

Toole had admitted to abducting and killing Adam Walsh, Schaffer said, and to dismembering the body, partially devouring it, and discarding what was left in a canal. Toole was willing to formally confess to the killing and appear before a grand jury in the matter. Toole also had told Schaffer about numerous other slayings he had committed in Broward County, in the vicinity of U.S. 27 and south of State Road 84, but at present Schaffer was unable to provide specific detail about those cases.

That was all well and good, Scheff told Schaffer, but neither he nor Toole would be taken out of Starke on any pretext until such time as they provided verifiable, independent evidence that could be used to support Toole's claims. Schaffer seemed to have anticipated this demand. Without hesitation he pointed to a matter that no investigator had seized on in the seven years that had passed since the murder. Toole had told him that he'd used *two* weapons to cut Adam up, Schaffer said: a machete *and* a bayonet.

In his first confession to Hoffman, Toole had made passing reference to using a bayonet, but Hoffman began referring to the weapon as a "machete," and Toole apparently began to follow the detective's lead in subsequent references. In any case, the possibility of Toole's use of two weapons had never been pursued. Even the claim of erstwhile companion Charles Lee Hardaman that he had given Toole a bayonet prior to the time of Adam's murder apparently elicited little interest. But Schaffer's claim would seem to have changed all that. Whatever had led to the confusion, Toole would be able to provide a more detailed description of both items, Schaffer assured the Broward County detectives.

Accordingly, on the following day, October 20, 1988, Detectives Scheff and Fantigrassi met with Schaffer and Ottis Toole. Scheff recited the Miranda warning to Toole, who assured the detectives that he was well aware of his rights and was happy to waive them. Then Toole got quickly to the point, repeating his confession to the killing of Adam Walsh and stating that he was willing to testify to the matter in court. He had used a "straight knife" with a black plastic handle as well as a bayonet to kill and dismember the boy, he said, adding that the knife (presumably the machete) had been in the possession of Jacksonville authorities since shortly after his arrest, when it was taken from his car. The bayonet, Toole said, belonged to his sister Vinetta Syphurs, and was part of a display mounted on the living room wall of her home in Bostwick, Florida, about forty miles southeast of the interview room where they were sitting.

The detectives then pressed Toole to tell them where he had disposed of the body, and Toole told them that he had tossed various parts into the same canal where he had disposed of the head. The canal paralleled the turnpike for a ten-mile stretch or so, Toole said, and every so often he would pull to the side of the road and rid himself of another piece of the corpse. He couldn't recall anything memorable about any of the places he had stopped, save that little wooden bridge where he had thrown the head into the water.

At times, Toole seemed to need help from Schaffer in formulating certain of his answers, the detectives noted, leaving them uncertain as to whether or not Schaffer had been coaching Toole in this undertaking from the outset. In the end, the only new information that Toole had provided was that pertaining to the bayonet. But on the other hand, all they needed was one piece of physical evidence to tie Toole to the crime, so off the two went to find Vinetta Syphurs.

It took about an hour to drive to Bostwick, a remote, unincorporated community just west of the broad St. John's River several miles south of Jacksonville. It is the sort of place one works hard to get to, a sparsely populated expanse of piney forest and scrub that has changed little since that part of the continent was formed, perhaps the perfect place to be if you wanted to keep your distance from a relative like Ottis Toole.

When they got to Bostwick, the detectives made their way to the local post office, where a clerk checked the records. Vinetta Syphurs had indeed once resided at 2942 Cedar Creek Road, he told them, but she had moved a while back and had left no forwarding address. Scheff and Fantigrassi drove to the address the clerk had given them and knocked on the door of the modest house they found. A woman named Violet Fleck answered. She had never heard of anyone named Syphurs, she told them.

Scheff and Fantigrassi weren't particularly daunted by the response. Most cop work consists of exactly what they were doing. You knock on doors, you ask questions. One day someone behind the screen will have the right answer, or so you hope.

Across the street, at 2941 Cedar Creek Road, Charles B. Council answered their knock and told them that there had in fact been a Rodney and Vinetta Syphurs living opposite him, but they'd moved out about a year earlier. He had no idea where they might have gone. Scheff and Fantigrassi thanked Council for his help and moved along.

It wasn't all that unusual—in the dimension of American life through which they were moving, and often moved as cops—to trail after individuals whose existences seemed as transitory as those of tribal huntsmen or migrating birds. Yes, there was the America where people left forwarding addresses, and kept in touch with old friends and neighbors, and were as easy to find as a schoolhouse or a bank branch. But when you were looking for criminals, or the associates of criminals, or the families from which they'd sprung, you often found yourself traveling through such a netherworld as this in Bostwick, where identity and even existence often seemed as tangible as smoke.

From the Council residence, Scheff and Fantigrassi traveled southward ten miles or so to Palatka, population 10,000 and the seat of Putnam County. At the offices of the tax assessor, they learned that the property at 2942 Cedar Creek Road in Bostwick had been purchased by Violet Fleck, with whom they'd talked earlier in the day. She and her husband David had bought it from a Ralph Nelson Green of Jacksonville.

Armed with this information, the two detectives then visited the Putnam County clerk's office, where they discovered a record of Green's eviction of Rodney and Vinetta Syphurs from his property on Cedar Creek Road in 1987. And as it turned out, Mr. Green had employed the services of a Jacksonville attorney in the matter, one Wesley Wallace, Esq.

Detective Scheff got Wallace on the phone and explained who they were looking for. Finally, it appeared, he had knocked on the right door. Wallace happened to know that the Syphurs were now living with Vinetta's daughter, who was married to a man named Greg Bishop. And if Wallace was not mistaken, the Bishops had a place in Orange Park, in Clay County, just south of sprawling Jacksonville.

Scheff accordingly called the Clay County sheriff, who in turn located Greg Bishop, who dutifully called Detective Scheff as requested. He listened to Scheff and promised to have his mother-in-law call right back. Thus, following such a trail of crumbs, did Scheff and Fantigrassi finally find the woman with whom they wished to speak.

Perhaps it is not the glamorous stuff of series television, but this is the way detectives work, the real ones, the dedicated ones. There are those who weary of such deadening chores, of course. They let things slide. They get tired of traipsing through the rat warrens and the pine barrens after the smoke people. They never find the right door.

At approximately nine on the evening of October 20, Scheff and Fantigrassi, accompanied by Lieutenant Redmond of the Clay County Sheriff's Office, finally sat down with Vinetta and Rodney Syphurs. Mrs. Syphurs told the detectives that she had purchased an antique bayonet in 1979 and had mounted it as a decoration on the wall above her mantel. If her brother Ottis, or anyone else, had removed it for any period of time, she would have certainly noticed its absence. When the detectives asked if they could take a look at the bayonet, Mrs. Syphurs paused.

All this fuss over Ottis had resulted in an unbelievable amount of hounding of her and Rodney by the press, she told the detectives. That is why the two of them had moved in with her daughter, to get away from it all. It had all happened rather suddenly, she explained—omitting any mention of eviction proceedings—and quite a bit of their personal property was still stored in boxes. But she would find the bayonet, Mrs. Syphurs assured them, and as soon as she did, she would bring it to Lieutenant Redmond's office.

The following day, Scheff and Fantigrassi went to the Jacksonville Sheriff's Office to check on the machete. There they discovered that Detective Terry had in fact turned over such a weapon to the FDLE for testing, but that the department's labs had not been able to tie it definitively to Toole or the crime. Also that day, and somewhat to Detective Scheff's surprise, Vinetta Syphurs actually showed up at the Clay County Sheriff's Office with the bayonet in hand. Scheff arranged to have it sent to the Broward County Sheriff's Office crime lab, where it would be tested for blood and the blade compared to markings on the base of Adam Walsh's severed head.

Though the recovery of the bayonet from Mrs. Syphurs constituted the sum of the efforts of Broward County detectives in their pursuit of physical evidence and their interview with

Toole, Sergeant Scheff concluded his report on the matter with the observation, "No review of this matter would be complete without a thorough understanding of the background of Ottis Toole's original confession in the Adam Walsh case." Scheff went on to reiterate that many of the confessions to other killings made by Henry Lee Lucas and Ottis Toole had not been substantiated (there was no mention of the eighty-plus murders that *had* been attributed to the pair).

And while Scheff went on to point out that Toole was presently imprisoned "in reference to a Duval County murder," he did not mention that Detective Terry had carried out the investigation upon which that conviction was obtained. However, Scheff did take the time to reiterate the details of the complaint that Jack Hoffman had lodged against Terry.

"Apparently believing that he could enrich himself," said Scheff, "Terry entered into an arrangement with Ottis Toole in regards to book and movie rights to Ottis Toole's life story. Detective Terry then provided Ottis Toole with confidential information he had obtained from the Hollywood Police Department."

According to Scheff's report, Terry then contacted Hollywood PD to let them know that Toole had confessed to the killing of Adam Walsh. "Detectives from the Hollywood Police Department . . . invested one year in the investigation before uncovering Detective Terry's actions," Scheff continued, and finished by noting, "Ottis Toole's statements were dismissed, and Detective Terry was removed from the Homicide Unit."

It was proof, said Scheff, "of the ease with which Toole, a brain-damaged and troubled man, can be manipulated by others. Ottis Toole now appears to be under the influence of Gerald Schaffer who may be using Toole for his own purposes." As to the exact nature of the purposes of Schaffer—a convict with an IQ of 130, suspected in the deaths of thirty-four women in three states—Scheff was not clear.

Scheff's conclusions might carry weight, save for the fact

that at the time he compiled his report, only three days had passed since his interview with Toole. The analysis of possible new evidence in the case—i.e., the bayonet he had obtained from Vinetta Syphurs—had not even begun, and the complaint against Detective Terry, the man whose work had put Toole on death row in the first place, remained an unsubstantiated claim made by one of Scheff's fellow investigators working just down the road from the Broward County Sheriff's Office. There is no evidence that Hoffman himself pressured Scheff to include his uncalled-for coda, but at the very least, its presence in the report carries something of the scent of home cooking.

About a month passed before D. P. Hughes, chief investigator for the Broward County medical examiner's office, passed along to the Metro Dade crime lab the weapon that Scheff had taken from Vinetta Syphurs. The knife was described as a Japanese army bayonet, with wood grips and a fifteen-and-a-half-inch blade, held in a sheath, and Hughes asked that since the Dade crime lab had already performed a comparative analysis against the machete that Hoffman and Terry had provided, they be the ones to compare the bayonet against the markings made at the base of Adam's skull.

It took Robert Hart, the same forensics specialist who had performed the earlier analysis on the machete, nearly three months to get back to Hughes, and when he did, on February 14, 1989, the news was once again inconclusive. "Although the class characteristics are consistent [with the marks on the skull]," Hart said, "insufficient similarities are present to determine if this bayonet was the weapon used to inflict the injuries."

While it might have been disheartening news, it does not explain why Hoffman did not, at the very least, carry the bayonet to Jacksonville and simply ask Charles Hardaman if it was the same bayonet he had once given Ottis Toole to sharpen. Had Hardaman been able to identify the weapon, it would have corroborated yet another aspect of Toole's story.

HOLLYWOOD, FLORIDA—NOVEMBER 14, 1988

While Broward County detectives pursued their leads, Adam Walsh's fourteenth birthday came and went, marking the passage of more than seven years without significant progress in the case. On December 6, 1988, something of a milestone was reached when FBI deputy director Alan Burgess made it known that the case of Adam Walsh had finally been entered into the new nationwide database known as VICAP, the Violent Crime Apprehension Program.

The program had come into existence in 1985, and had developed in large part due to the work of former LAPD captain Pierce Brooks, who was involved in the investigation of the notorious "Onion Field" killing of a Los Angeles police officer in 1963, an incident later popularized in a Joseph Wambaugh best seller. Brooks was among the first to apply formal statistical analysis to determine patterns in violent crime and to theorize that psychologists might be able to provide useful profiles of the type of individual responsible for a violent crime or a series of such crimes. At the very least, if details of unsolved crimes were shared in a national computerized database available to police departments everywhere, the likelihood of apprehending "pattern" or "repeat" killers would surely be increased.

In 1983, John Walsh had been asked to testify before an Arlen Specter–chaired Senate Judiciary subcommittee looking into the efficacy of such an undertaking, and as he recalls, it was the sort of thing that people assumed was already in place. The truth was, however, that in the early 1980s the very concept of "national computer database" was something of an exercise in wishful thinking. At the time such notions as e-mail and the Internet were for most Americans only fantasy. A certain amount of information on unsolved crimes was shared between jurisdictions via teletype and snail-mail-carried bulletins, but the notion that anyone, anywhere, was paying much attention to what clattered off those machines or piled up in the mailroom, or was investing the time to catalog, file, and analyze the data on hundreds and thousands of violent crimes all across the country, was simply laughable.

But by this point, Walsh was well versed in the psychology of the Ted Bundys and the John Wayne Gacys of the world, and he had become increasingly convinced that it was such an individual who was responsible for Adam's death. He was more than happy to appear on behalf of the initiative. There was also a great deal of support for such a database within the FBI itself, where behavioral sciences unit special agent Robert Ressler had advanced the practice of profiling repeat rapists and killers through the 1970s. Ressler, generally credited with coining the term *serial killer*, played a key role in the eventual formation of VICAP, advocating it as an invaluable tool to a local agency when and if a nomadic predator came calling.

In 1985, the program was approved by the Department of Justice, and FBI-VICAP become the national repository for violent crimes, collating data on homicides, sexual assaults, missing persons, and unidentified human remains. Comprehensive case information concerning crimes anywhere in the country would thenceforward be submitted to FBI-VICAP, maintained in a comprehensive database and automatically compared to all other cases to identify similarities. The program also provided for a staff of agents trained specifically to analyze data and provide profiles where evidence suggested repeat and nomadic offenders might be at work, especially those involving abduction; those apparently random, motiveless, or sexually oriented; or those known or thought to be part of a series.

If such a program had been in place in 1981, would the actions of Henry Lee Lucas and Ottis Toole have landed them a place on VICAP's most-wanted list or prevented Adam's abduction and murder? John and Revé Walsh had no idea, but at least the fact that such a program was now in place and that the details of their son's case were thus operative gave them some sense of a shred of order restored, some vague assurance that Adam had not died in vain.

So far as progress on the case went, however, there was none forthcoming, and Adam's fifteenth birthday, in November 1989, passed uneventfully.

There was something of an ironic footnote deriving from the brief partnership of jailhouse lawyer Gerard Schaffer and Ottis Toole in 1990, however, when news came that a federal appeals court had dismissed Schaffer's complaint that his public defender had deliberately botched his court case to make sure he would stay in jail. In his complaint, Schaffer pointed to the fact that immediately after his conviction on murder charges, his attorney had married Schaffer's ex-wife, Theresa. Schaffer's attorney happened to be a public defender by the name of Elton Schwartz, the same man who had represented Ottis Toole back in 1984. Schwartz, apparently passionate on behalf of the rights of accused serial killers, had taken on Schaffer's case in the wake of his involvement with Toole.

And then, in early November 1990, twelve days before Adam's sixteenth birthday, an event took place that would almost by accident draw Joe Matthews back into the orbit of this story and eventually change the course of the investigation. At first, the event might have seemed without any bearing on what had befallen the Walshes, but that is the thing about cause and effect in all effective narrative. What might seem an unimportant or "butterfly" moment at the outset is one thing; but once a profound conclusion is reached, it is a simple matter to trace backward through all the possible turning points where a different decision might have been made. In this way, the investigator comes to a simple realization: in the story at hand, things couldn't have turned out any other way.

On November 2, 1990, Detective Sergeant Joe Matthews was called in from vacation by his superiors at Miami Beach PD to investigate a particularly heinous crime. The body of an unidentified three-year-old boy had been found discarded beneath a hedge that surrounded a home in one of the Beach's most exclusive residential neighborhoods. The emaciated child, weighing 18 pounds, with weeks-old Pampers duct-taped to his body, had died from multiple fractures to the skull, leading the Dade County medical examiner to call it the worst case of child neglect, abuse, and torture that he had ever witnessed.

It was not by accident that Matthews had been summoned. In the more than nine years that had passed since he'd rejoined his colleagues at Beach PD, he had continued to rack up accolades for his work as a polygraph examiner, interrogations expert, and homicide investigator. In 1987, during a period of civil unrest and racial rioting in Miami, German national Dieter Reichmann stopped a Miami Beach policeman and pointed to the body of his girlfriend in the seat beside him. While driving the streets of downtown Miami, Reichmann claimed, an unidentified black male had approached his car, then shot and killed his German girlfriend as part of a botched robbery attempt.

Matthews was placed in charge of the charged investigation, while an outraged community demanded justice, if not ultimately a lynching. From the outset, however, Matthews spotted various minor inconsistencies in Reichmann's story, and following forty to fifty hours of interviews and his usual persistent digging, Matthews discovered that Reichmann had taken out $2 million in German insurance policies on his girlfriend's life. It was fuel for a reconsideration of everything, and eventually Matthews had assembled a substantial amount of circumstantial evidence implicating Reichmann as the killer.

However, Janet Reno, Dade County state attorney at the time, advised Matthews that she deemed his evidence insufficient for the issuance of a warrant. Though Reichmann was arrested and tried on a federal weapons charge, he was found not guilty. He was ordered to be released from custody and allowed to return to his native country. As Matthews was escorting Reichmann to the property room to reclaim his personal effects, including a number of items that Matthews considered potential evidence in his murder investigation, the grinning German turned to tap him on the cheek with his palm. "Ah, my friend Matthews," Reichmann said in condescension, "you'll have to try harder next time, eh?"

At which point Matthews responded by pulling a pair of handcuffs from his belt and snapping them onto Reichmann's wrists. "Ah my friend Reichmann," Matthews said. "You are under arrest for first-degree murder."

Matthews's actions astounded Reichmann, of course, and they infuriated Janet Reno as well, for she wanted no part of a case that she considered dicey. Fortunately for Matthews and for the legal system, however, several on Reno's staff were convinced that Reichmann was guilty, and the case was prosecuted vigorously.

Ultimately, Reichmann was convicted of the murder and sentenced to death—even though the perpetrator had never confessed, the firearm used was never recovered, no witnesses ever appeared, and the exact location of the murder was never determined. The Florida Supreme Court reviewed Reichmann's case twice, but upheld the conviction. No wonder, then, that with no apparent leads, his superiors wanted Matthews on the case of the three-year-old discarded under a hedge off North Bay Road like so much garbage.

But even Matthews was having difficulties with this new case. No one had seen anything, and without an identification of the victim, it was difficult even to know where to begin an investigation. During a canvasing of the neighborhood where the child was discovered, he found himself talking to a little girl who knew very little about the crime save that it had terrified her and that the little boy had been found wearing only a T-shirt with lollipops printed on it.

"Poor baby Lollipops," the little girl told Matthews. "I hope you catch who did it."

He hoped he'd catch who killed "Baby Lollipops" too, Matthews told the little girl, and even if he had little by way of leads, he now had a name that seemed to galvanize the interest of the public in the case. On Monday, November 26, 1990, almost two weeks after Adam's sixteenth birthday, Joe Matthews called the producers of the television show *America's Most Wanted*, asking how he might get details of the "Baby Lollipops" case aired, in order to help identify the child.

Matthews was well aware that John Walsh was the host of the program, the brainchild of media mogul Rupert Murdoch's Fox Television Network. The show had begun its run in February 1988, the second piece of original programming produced by the network after *21 Jump Street*, which starred a then-unknown actor named Johnny Depp. *America's Most Wanted* was devoted to the dramatization of various violent crimes around the country and the apprehension of the persons responsible.

It was the first in what would become a landslide of "reality" shows, and it was a smash hit from the beginning, despite the fact that Walsh was initially anything but a polished performer. But as a result of his obvious sincerity, his status as a victim of violent crime, and his well-known work as a champion of the victimized everywhere, he had grown into the role of citizen crime fighter. By the time that Joe Matthews made his phone call, Walsh had hit his stride. The show had resulted in thousands of tips and the capture of more than a hundred criminals who had evaded justice previously.

Still, as a staffer explained to Matthews, their show was focused on the capture of wanted fugitives, not on the identification of a victim. Rather than argue that the one generally was the first step leading to the other, Matthews talked the staffer into connecting him with John Walsh's administrative assistant. He briefly explained the purpose of his call and made a simple request: just tell Mr. Walsh what he was asking, and that it was the same Detective Matthews who had conducted the polygraph examination for the Hollywood police when his son Adam was abducted.

The assistant did as Matthews asked, and the results were

exactly what the detective hoped for. Three days later, Thursday, November 29, 1990, John Walsh and his film crew were on their way to Miami Beach, where they filmed an *AMW* segment devoted to the crime and seeking the public's help in making the true identity of "Baby Lollipops" known.

After the filming, Matthews and Walsh spent some time together along Government Cut at the south end of Miami Beach, where the *AMW* motor home, Walsh's traveling office, had been parked. The two sat in a pair of lawn chairs, watching the sun descend and the glittering ocean liners dock and sail, discussing the handling of Adam's case over the past nine years.

It wasn't that the rank-and-file detectives didn't care or were totally incompetent, Matthews assured Walsh, it was just that from the beginning the department seemed overwhelmed by the task before it. Furthermore, there seemed to be no supervision emanating from Jack Hoffman, the lead detective on the case. As Matthews recalled the helter-skelter comings and goings of well-meaning detectives and the flutterings of their unfiled scraps of paper, Walsh nodded glumly. He'd been in the detective's bullpen one day, too. He'd seen one guy writing down information on a matchbook cover.

There was that, Matthews said, and there was also the fact of Jack Hoffman's personality. Hoffman, he thought, always seemed on "send," never on "receive." To Matthews, the effective way to get help, and information, was to present yourself with some humility—"Hey, I need a hand here, can you help out?" To Matthews it was a far more effective approach than the one that went, "Don't bother telling me anything. I know it all already."

Until that evening, Walsh had not realized that Matthews had been on loan to the Hollywood PD from Miami Beach at the time, and he was more than interested in Matthews's critique of the shoddy procedures he had witnessed there. Nor had he ever heard another piece of news that Matthews passed along. Years ago, Hollywood PD had officially cleared Jimmy Campbell of any involvement in the case, Matthews told him. It was a welcome surprise to Walsh, even though he had never really suspected Jimmy. But he also wondered why the Hollywood PD had never passed along word that they had exonerated his old friend. In fact, Walsh told Matthews, he had never heard any news unbidden from Hollywood PD.

To Matthews it was quite a surprise to hear that Hollywood police had not informed the Walshes that Campbell had been cleared. For John Walsh, it might be important enough—validation that a person he considered a friend was innocent. But imagine what a burden would be lifted from Revé. She had lived with enough guilt for simply having left Adam alone for a few moments. To have it confirmed that Campbell was in no way responsible would have been more than a courtesy. It simply seemed insensitive in the extreme that Hoffman had not bothered to share such information with the Walshes.

Matthews could only shake his head. The fact was, he was not surprised by anything that smacked of Hoffman's unwillingness to part with Jimmy Campbell as his prime suspect. He didn't say anything more to Walsh about the matter, but simply commiserated with him over the frustrations he'd experienced over the years, and asked that his sympathies be extended to Revé as well.

He did tell Walsh that he wished he had been allowed to stay on the case originally, for it was his professional opinion that the Hollywood PD was simply too ill equipped, and the lead detective assigned to the case too inexperienced, for a proper investigation. Furthermore, so far as the viability of a case against Ottis Toole, Matthews had been involved in other successful murder prosecutions where far less evidence was at hand. In his estimation, the Hollywood PD seemed unnecessarily obsessed with the need for physical evidence linking Toole to the crime scene. Given the circumstantial evidence that had come to light, they already had more than what they needed to present the case to a prosecutor.

Walsh heard Matthews out, but at that point, he was still reluctant to divorce himself entirely from the system, though he did share his own feelings that Hoffman and Hickman were less than stellar investigators. Shortly after Adam had gone missing, Walsh told Matthews, Detective Hickman had taken him aside for some private counsel. Hickman handed over a religious pamphlet that invited Walsh to become "born again." Hickman took Walsh's arm and explained. "I know how you feel," he said. "But if you'd take Jesus as your savior, your son will return."

He didn't know what to say to the detective at the time, Walsh told Matthews, but on a number of occasions since he had wondered if it was Jesus or the Hollywood PD he should have been counting on. He had lost sleep on many a night owing to his frustrations with the lack of progress in the case, but to repudiate the police department that he and Revé had placed their trust in for ten years was a difficult leap. He thanked Matthews for all his good work and expressed his hope that the segment they had just filmed would lead to a break in the Baby Lollipops case, and the two parted amicably.

Walsh needn't have worried. On Saturday, December 1, the Baby Lollipops segment aired, and a tip came in, identifying the murdered child as Lazaro Figueroa, his mother a thirty-year-old Cuban immigrant named Ana Cardona, and her lover as a woman named Olivia Gonzalez. Eventually, Cardona confessed to Matthews that she had left her seriously injured son to die in the bushes that night.

While an autopsy determined that young Lazaro's skull had been crushed by repeated blows from a baseball bat, Cardona claimed that the abuse of young Lazaro was begun by her lover, Gonzalez, with whom she had begun an affair following the murder of the victim's father. Owing to depression stemming from an abusive upbringing in Cuba and a dependency on cocaine that she had developed in the United States, she had lacked the courage to defend her child, Cardona claimed, and eventually joined her companion in starving, abusing, and beating Lazaro.

Though Cardona would ultimately plead not guilty to the crime, her lover turned state's evidence and testified against her. In the end, Olivia Gonzalez received a forty-year sentence. Anna Cardona was sentenced to death.

As a result of his work on the case, Joe Matthews was named Police Officer of the Year by the Dade County Association of Chiefs of Police in 1991.

MIAMI, FLORIDA—JUNE 26, 1991

Both Matthews and Walsh were gratified by what had come of their collaboration in the Baby Lollipops case, but neither could be happy with the continued lack of progress in the investigation of Adam's murder. And then, some six months after the break in the Baby Lollipops case, there came—seemingly by accident—an interesting development.

On June 26, 1991, the *Miami Herald* ran an article on the retirement of Major J. B. Smith of the Hollywood Police Department. Smith had been a cop at the agency for twenty-one years, the story noted, and was a sergeant in the robbery and homicide unit, assisting in the investigation of the disappearance and murder of Adam Walsh in 1981.

Smith spoke to the writer at some length about the still-unsolved case, adding, "Ottis Toole was probably the most complete investigation we've ever done to prove somebody didn't do it."

If the department had in fact unearthed any evidence to prove that Ottis Toole had not committed the crime, he did not share it, and the reporter—who apparently was content to believe that Toole had been "proven" innocent—did not inquire further. One person was dumbfounded by J. B. Smith's comments, however.

In Hollywood, Bill Mistler read, then carefully reread the

story, just to be sure he understood correctly. Back in 1983, when Ottis Toole was identified as the prime suspect in the abduction and murder of Adam Walsh, Mistler had wavered about coming forward to tell police what he had seen outside the Hollywood Sears store that day. But from the tenor of the stories he read at the time of the announcement, Mistler assumed that his testimony was unnecessary. Furthermore, until he read Detective Smith's comments that day in 1991, he thought that Ottis Toole had been charged and that the matter had been concluded.

Mistler, who'd been carrying a burden of guilt for almost ten years, got up from his chair and went into the kitchen where his wife was fixing dinner. Did she know that Ottis Toole had never been charged with the murder of Adam Walsh? he asked, brandishing the newspaper. She didn't, she told him, then listened as he recapped the details of what he'd read.

"What do you think I ought to do?" Mistler asked his wife when he'd finished.

She couldn't tell him what to do, she answered. But did he remember how scared they'd been the day their own son had wandered off for half an hour during a camping excursion?

Mistler remembered very well how he felt, and the recollections were enough to send him finally to the telephone, where he did what he'd been meaning to do for a long, long time. When he finally got through to Hollywood PD, an operator transferred him to Jack Hoffman, still the lead detective on the case. Mistler told Hoffman who he was, and then gave a brief account of what he had seen in the parking lot outside the Sears store that day. "I'm telling you, I saw Ottis Toole kidnap Adam Walsh," he said.

Hoffman waited for Mistler to finish, then thanked him for the call. It had been ten years since the incident, and here was some guy out of nowhere claiming he'd seen it all? Hoffman explained that he was a little busy right now, getting ready to go on vacation. If Mistler didn't mind, why not get back to him in a couple of weeks, and they'd take it up again?

Mistler, who'd just battled past any number of fears and uncertainties to make the call, stared at the phone in disbelief as Hoffman hung up. The detective hadn't even asked for his phone number or his address. He wasn't even sure the guy had caught his name.

Still, Mistler had made up his mind. He'd felt better about himself from the moment he'd picked up the phone and began to dial the police. And so, at about noon on Monday, July 22, Mistler called again. "I'm the guy who saw Ottis Toole take Adam Walsh from the curb outside the Sears store that day and put him inside a car," Mistler reminded Hoffman. He'd had no reason to believe he was witnessing a kidnapping at the time, for the child showed no signs of resistance or alarm. He simply assumed it was a family member taking the child home.

Mistler also explained to Hoffman that in 1983, when Hollywood PD announced that Toole was the chief suspect, he believed that Toole had in fact been charged with the crime and that the matter had been dispensed with. It was not until he stumbled upon the article concerning Major Smith's retirement, Mistler said, that he'd realized the case was still unsolved. Hoffman listened to it all, and when Mistler was finished, the detective scheduled a meeting at department offices for the following Monday.

On Sunday, July 28, the *Miami Herald* ran a ten-year anniversary piece on Adam's murder and included an interview with Jack Hoffman during which he told a reporter that he still hadn't "totally eliminated" Ottis Toole as a suspect. Whether or not it was Mistler's phone call that had reawakened his interest in Toole is difficult to say. Nothing of note had been added to his case file since the day in late October 1984 when Hoffman assured reporters that Toole had been unequivocally eliminated as a suspect.

In any case, on Monday, July 29, 1991, Bill Mistler appeared as scheduled at the offices of Hollywood PD, where he met with Detective Hoffman to make a voluntary sworn statement. Mistler broke into tears on two different occasions during the interview, explaining that he felt tremendous guilt for not having reacted differently to what he witnessed that day outside Sears. If he had approached Toole, or if he had summoned security or called police, he might have prevented Adam's death. Make no mistake about it, Mistler said. It was Ottis Toole he had seen leading Adam Walsh away from the Sears store that day, and he had lived and relived every moment in his mind ever since.

He arrived at the Sears lot via the northwest corner entrance near the garden shop, he told Hoffman. He was waiting for an older woman to park her car when he first saw Toole, driving past him in his Cadillac, headed the opposite direction. He recollected that the car was in good condition, other than what looked like rust stains from well water and a sizable dent in the right rear bumper. It was bearing a Florida license plate, and there were what appeared to be a number of gardening tools in the backseat.

Mistler said that he saw Toole stop his car in the opposite driving lane, get out of the driver's door, and walk around the car toward the curb. He remembered that Toole appeared to be checking out his surroundings, glancing left and right, and that the two actually locked eyes for a few seconds. Toole was an odd-looking type, he said, around six feet tall, with a wandering eye and reddish brown hair. He was dressed shabbily, his T-shirt filthy—hardly the picture of the typical suburban Sears shopper.

Mistler said that he watched as Toole approached the curb outside the entrance to Sears, where a small boy—maybe five years old—was standing. Because he was so caught up in Toole's idiosyncratic appearance, Mistler said, he didn't pay as much attention as he might have to exactly how the child was dressed, though he thought he remembered that the boy was wearing a hat.

Mistler said that Toole knelt down in front of the boy and began to talk to him. On the sidewalk nearby, he recalled, was a woman with a boy of fourteen or so, apparently searching for something in her purse. To Mistler, there was something wrong with what he was seeing. Toole and the boy with whom he was talking simply did not seem to belong together, if for no other reason than the comparative condition of their clothing, a guy off the streets talking to a kid who obviously came from a suburban home.

"I made the wrong call," Mistler said. "I kept looking for Adam to give me some sort of a signal . . ." But it never came.

Mistler watched in his rearview mirror as Toole took Adam by the arm, but he saw no signs of resistance there. The two walked past the front of the Cadillac, with Toole talking to Adam all the while. Toole opened the driver's door to the Cadillac, and Adam crawled in and across the front seat. By this point, Mistler noted that the parking space he was waiting for had finally been vacated.

He parked his truck, got out, and walked toward the curb. He glanced at the spot where the Cadillac had been stopped, but by then it was gone.

Mistler picked up a few items for the family's camping trip, but inevitably he hadn't managed to get everything everyone wanted. At 3:00 p.m. or so, he was back at the Sears store, accompanied by his wife and his nine-year-old son. Shortly after they entered, they noted a woman and a man involved in a heated discussion with "a fat security guard." Mistler's son nudged him and said that he knew the man and the woman. They were the parents of Adam Walsh, a kid his son knew from the playground at school. Mistler didn't think much of it at the time.

Later, as they were shopping for the things Mistler had forgotten, they heard an announcement on the store's PA system, paging Adam Walsh. But again, Mistler did not connect the announcement with what he had witnessed in the parking lot more than two hours earlier. They simply picked up the things they needed, Mistler explained, and then they took their trip.

When they got back the following Sunday, one of his son's friends came by the house and told them all about Adam's abduction, Mistler said. At the time, he reminded his wife that they had seen Mrs. Walsh in the Sears store the previous Monday—that is why she had appeared so upset. Still, Mistler said, it did not occur to him to connect what he had witnessed in the parking lot earlier that day to Adam's disappearance.

In fact, Mistler told Hoffman, it was not until a month to six weeks later, when he returned to Sears on yet another shopping trip, that a news story came on the radio and it suddenly hit him. He might in fact have witnessed Adam's abduction. He actually turned his truck toward the nearby headquarters of the Hollywood PD right then and there, Mistler said, but that was the point at which the news was all about the search for the "blue van" that someone had seen Adam being pulled into. The story he'd been listening to closed on news of the search for that van at that very moment, Mistler said, and he decided that perhaps what he had to offer wasn't that useful after all.

As to why he hadn't come forward in 1983, when Ottis Toole's picture was splashed across television and newspapers as the prime suspect in the case, Mistler told Hoffman that he thought other witnesses had come forward, or they wouldn't have named Toole as the man responsible. Hoffman listened to Mistler's account, then asked him if he would agree to take a polygraph exam and undergo hypnosis to see if those procedures would corroborate the truth of what he was claiming all these years later.

Mistler agreed without hesitation and returned to police headquarters the following day for the polygraph. While no record of the exam itself remains in the case file, a supplemental report filed by Detective Hoffman notes that the results of Mistler's polygraph were "inconclusive."

Three days later, on Friday, August 2, 1991, Mistler again reported to Hollywood PD, this time to be placed under hypnosis by a doctor attached to the Broward County Sheriff's Office psychological services unit. However, during the prehypnosis interview, Mistler again became so upset regarding his recollections of the day that the physician adjudged him unfit to be hypnotized at the time. Instead, detectives drove him back to the west parking lot of the Sears Mall in hopes that revisiting the scene might jog Mistler's memory as to what Adam had been wearing on the day of the kidnapping. But Mistler could simply not recall those details.

Finally, on Monday, September 2, Mistler returned again to police headquarters, where this time he successfully underwent hypnosis. During the session, he was able to recall that Toole had rotten, greenish teeth, a two-week beard, strange eyes, and was wearing dark pants and brown shoes. As far as Adam's clothing went, Mistler said that the child was wearing a baseball hat.

Mistler, of course, was interested in what effects his decision to come forward would have on the long-stymied case. If the cops had not received proof that Toole had committed the crime, they now had an eyewitness who could give them exactly what they needed. Furthermore, during his initial interview with Hoffman, when he'd first begun to detail the sighting of Toole in the Cadillac that day at the Sears store, Hoffman suddenly snapped alert. He'd been listening idly to Mistler's account of the day, cleaning his nails with a pocketknife. But at the mention of the Cadillac, Hoffman sat upright, making eye contact with Mistler for the first time.

"Nobody knows about that Cadillac," Hoffman told Mistler, then left the room to get photographs of the car for Mistler to identify.

When Hoffman originally asked Mistler to submit to a polygraph and to undergo hypnosis, he assumed that it meant that the cops were excited and interested in what he had to tell them.

But Mistler began to worry the day of his second hypnosis session, when he ventured to ask Hoffman what was going to happen with Toole now. Hoffman glanced away, Mistler says.

"I don't know," the detective said. "I don't think this is going anywhere."

Stunned, Mistler asked him what he meant.

Hoffman shrugged. "Well, the mother doesn't want to go into court and listen to all the gory details about what happened to her child. And Ottis is already convicted of another murder . . ." The detective trailed off.

At that point, Mistler had the chilling sensation that his decision to come forward meant absolutely nothing to the lead investigator in the case, but he went ahead with his session nonetheless. How could he not?

A few days later, he called Hoffman to check on how he'd done. If the polygraph exam and the hypnosis supported his account of what he had seen, then surely the cops would go after Toole for the killing, he reasoned.

"So how's it going with the case?" Mistler asked when Hoffman came on the line.

There was a pause, and the sounds of paper being shuffled in the background. "Ah, well," Hoffman said, "I went up and talked to Ottis, and Ottis assured me he didn't do it. He told me, 'Why would I lie to ya, Jack, I'd tell ya if I killed this kid.' "

Mistler had to take a deep breath. "Let me get this straight," he said to Hoffman. "You give me a polygraph exam, you hypnotize me twice, you interview me four times, and you go up and have a little chat with this psycho and you believe him and not me?"

When Hoffman didn't respond, something occurred to Mistler. "Look, tell me the truth, tell me what's going on. If the Walshes don't want to go through with this, that's one thing, but at least you have to tell me you told them about what I saw."

"Oh, yeah," Hoffman said. "I told the parents."

The offhand tone in which he said it so angered Mistler that he hung up the phone and turned to his wife to explain what it was all about. "He's lying," Mistler told her. "He never said anything to the Walshes. I'm gonna go over there to the PD and make him look me in the eye and tell me the same lie."

But Mistler's wife had the last word on that score. "I don't think that's such a good idea," she said.

Upon reflection, Mistler decided she was right. Instead of confronting Hoffman, he placed a call to the FBI, asking to speak with the agent assigned to work with the Hollywood police on the Adam Walsh case. After some delay, he was transferred to a Mrs. Grey or a Mrs. White—"some kind of color," Mistler recalls—who asked him again why he was calling. Mistler explained that he had witnessed the abduction of Adam Walsh by Ottis Toole and that though he had come forward to Hollywood police, he was worried that Detective Hoffman was not taking him seriously.

The person to whom Mistler spoke took down the information and said that someone would get back to him, but no call ever came. To Mistler it meant that perhaps what Hoffman said about the Walshes wanting to bury the case was true. They must have been told that he had come forward, Mistler reasoned, or the FBI would have called him back. "So it's okay," he told himself. He'd done everything he could. "It's over. It's done."

TALLAHASSEE, FLORIDA—AUGUST 14, 1991

At the same time the drama between Bill Mistler, Jack Hoffman, and the FBI was playing out, Joe Matthews was in Tallahassee conducting a three-day seminar on investigative interviewing and interrogation techniques for the University of North Florida's Institute for Police Technology and Management. Matthews's coinstructor was a retired FBI agent named Bill Haggerty who had been involved in the investigation of the Adam Walsh case at the time Ottis Toole had first come forward with his confession back in 1983.

After the first night of classes concluded, Matthews and Haggerty were relaxing over a drink when the Walsh case came up. While Matthews had maintained an interest in the investigation, there was really little he could do—he was a homicide cop working for another police department.

Sears video game display and west exit doors where Adam was escorted out of the store on July 27, 1981. *Hollywood Police Department evidence file*

Adam Walsh in the captain's hat he was wearing the day he was abducted. *Courtesy John and Revé Walsh*

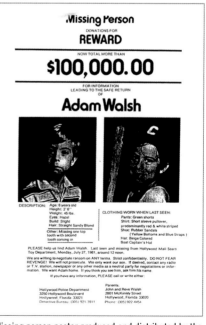

Missing person poster produced and distributed by the Walshes. *Courtesy Broward County Medical Examiner. Photograph by Gerlinde Photography/Michael Hopkins*

Hollywood Police Department detective Jack Hoffman,
original lead investigator on the Adam Walsh case.
Courtesy Hollywood Historical Society

Detective Ron Hickman, Hoffman's partner. *Courtesy
Hollywood Historical Society*

Sam D. Martin, Hollywood chief of police at the time of
Adam's abduction. Martin served as chief from 1974 to
1986. *Courtesy Hollywood Historical Society*

John and Revé Walsh, on their way to *Good Morning America,* on August 10, two weeks after Adam's disappearance. *Courtesy Hollywood Historical Society*

The grieving Walshes at Adam's memorial service, August 15, 1981. *Courtesy Hollywood Historical Society*

Ottis Toole, gap-toothed and with a wandering eye, shortly after he gave his first confession to police.
Hollywood Police Department evidence file

Clown drawing signed by Ottis Toole and given to niece Sarah Patterson during a prison visit in December 1995.
Courtesy Joe Matthews

Detail of extortion letter sent to John Walsh by Ottis Toole, October 4, 1988 (see text on page 152).
Hollywood Police Department evidence file

Canal beside the Florida Turnpike near Vero Beach where Adam's severed head was found.
Hollywood Police Department evidence file

Ottis Toole's Cadillac (with dented rear bumper) used in the abduction of Adam Walsh.
Florida Department of Law Enforcement evidence file

Aerial view of the turnpike service road west of Vero Beach where Ottis Toole admitted dismembering Adam Walsh.
Hollywood Police Department evidence file

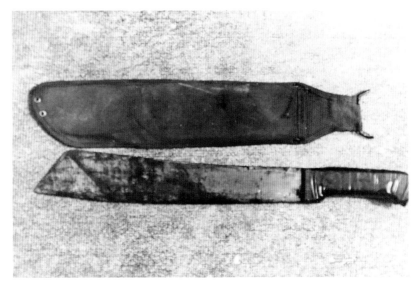

Machete believed to have been used in the dismemberment of Adam Walsh's body.
Hollywood Police Department evidence file

Luminol enhanced photograph of machete handle indicating presence of blood.
Florida Department of Law Enforcement evidence file

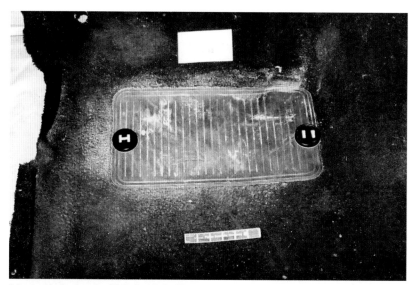

Driver's-side floorboards of Ottis Toole's Cadillac.
Florida Department of Law Enforcement evidence file

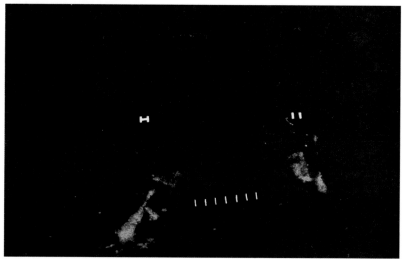

Luminol enhanced photograph of driver's floorboards indicating bloody footprints.
Florida Department of Law Enforcement evidence file

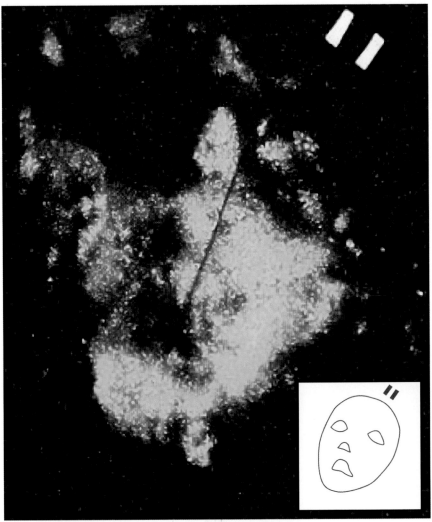

Luminol enhanced photograph of Cadillac's rear floorboard carpeting with imprint of bloodied face. *Florida Department of Law Enforcement evidence file*

Inset showing outline of face in luminol.

Matthews was intrigued to know what the Bureau's take on the matter had been—the Feds might not have wanted to get directly involved for various political and practical reasons, but that didn't mean they hadn't provided peripheral consultation. And indeed the agency had, the retired agent assured Matthews. In fact, when Ottis Toole surfaced as a suspect back in 1983, Haggerty told Matthews that he had eliminated Toole as a suspect almost immediately.

"Oh yeah," Matthews said, curious. "Why was that?"

The agent leaned forward, his face a sage mask. "Think about it," he said to Matthews. "A guy takes a bus ride all the way from Virginia to Jacksonville, maybe sixteen, eighteen, twenty hours. No way he's going to get in a car and drive another five or six hours all the way to Miami or Fort Lauderdale and spend the night hustling gays."

Matthews stared back at his federal counterpart, not sure if he wanted to start up with the guy. After all, they had a couple more days together. What was to be gained? But was this the kind of thinking upon which an FBI agent had based his investigation of the Adam Walsh case?

As Matthews saw it, Ottis Toole was the kind of guy who slept on park benches and on plastic bags in mulch piles. On a good night, he'd get blasted and sleep in his car. A twenty-hour ride on a plush reclining seat in an air-conditioned bus would be like a stay in the Ritz-Carlton to Toole.

Besides, what on earth had such off-the-wall suppositions to do with whether or not Ottis Toole had committed the crime he said he had? Matthews could only hope that the guy sitting across from him had not been the lead FBI investigator on the case.

Matthews was well aware that no one had ever conducted a proper investigative interview with Toole—after all, he was in Tallahassee to explain the very concept. All that Toole had ever provided were statements. For the most part Toole talked, and instead of asking questions, detectives simply listened, taking notes, following the agenda set by the suspect. It was the opposite of effective investigative interviewing in Matthews's book, but with Toole that is what had happened.

What's worse, Toole had never been polygraphed, not once. On a number of occasions he said he killed Adam Walsh, a couple other times he said he didn't. It seemed to leave a lot of people in law enforcement guessing: On which days had he been deceptive?

But you didn't have to guess, Matthews reminded himself, shaking his head at the smug agent sitting across the table. There was this scientific instrument called a polygraph that could help you learn the truth, and when he got back to South Florida, he would give it one last shot to see if he could put it to use on Ottis Toole.

Late that month, motivated by nothing more than his sense of duty and an innate desire to do the right thing, Matthews drove to the headquarters of Hollywood police, where he met with Captain Gil Frazier, who was then in charge of the Criminal Investigations Division. Matthews pointed out his concerns over the handling of Ottis Toole as a suspect and made a simple request of Frazier: let Matthews conduct a formal investigative interview of the type that had never been performed on the suspect. "What do you have to lose?" he asked.

Frazier thought about it for a moment, then nodded. Matthews was right; why not give it a shot? As Matthews looked on, the captain got Detective Hoffman on the phone. He wanted Hoffman and Matthews to travel to Starke, Frazier said, where Matthews would interview Toole about the Walsh case. Hoffman acknowledged his superior's order and suggested that Matthews give him a call in a day or two to arrange a date.

Things couldn't have gone more smoothly, Matthews thought, until he began trying to set a date with Hoffman. He left several phone messages for the lead detective, all of which were ignored. Finally, Matthews drove back to Hollywood PD headquarters and confronted Hoffman at his desk. When were they going to go interview Toole? Matthews wanted to know. "Soon," Hoffman assured him, but right now he was busy with a million things. He'd get back to Matthews as soon as he possibly could.

Matthews was frustrated, certainly, but since he wasn't signing Hoffman's paycheck, there was little he could do. Without the detective in charge of the case, Matthews had no access to Toole.

Toole, meantime, was convicted in late September of three more homicides in Florida's Jackson County, a rural enclave bordering Alabama and Georgia, and had returned to Starke with yet another life sentence tacked onto his list. Other jurisdictions seemed happy to investigate, charge, and convict Toole of murders he had confessed to, Matthews thought. What was the problem at Hollywood? Why on earth wouldn't you want to do anything you could to try and solve this case?

On October 16, 1991, Matthews was back in Tallahassee, team-teaching another course with Bill Haggerty, the retired FBI agent whose misguided notions had provoked him into making his request of Captain Frazier at Hollywood PD a couple of months before. During a break, Haggerty mentioned to Matthews that he might not be in class the following day— he'd promised to drive the two hours to Starke to help out on a case.

No problem, Matthews assured his counterpart. He could handle the class on his own. But just what was it that was calling the agent away?

Oh, just a pain in the ass, really, Haggerty replied. He'd received a call from Jack Hoffman down at Hollywood PD. Hoffman's boss wanted Hoffman to reinterview Ottis Toole for some reason, and Hoffman had asked Haggerty to accompany him. "Big waste of time, if you ask me," the agent told Matthews, "but hey, I'm always ready to lend a hand."

Matthews listened, then excused himself to make a phone call. When he reached Hollywood PD, he asked to speak with Gil Frazier. He couldn't believe what Hoffman was trying to pull, Matthews thought. But Frazier would put a stop to it. The captain had been 100 percent in support of his request, Matthews was certain of it.

Abruptly the connection went through, and Matthews took a breath, about to launch into the summary of what he had learned. "Captain Frazier is on vacation," an assistant's voice said before he got a word out. "He'll be gone for the next six weeks." Matthews replaced the phone and leaned back in his chair, releasing a pent-up breath. Unless everything he knew about cops was wrong, Matthews told himself, Hoffman had simply waited for his boss to go on vacation, then purposefully ignored his order to have Matthews interview Toole. Apparently, Hoffman was bound and determined to make sure nothing ever moved forward on this investigation.

"Told you so," Matthews's fellow instructor reported when he returned from Starke the following afternoon. He explained to Matthews that Toole had informed them that he hadn't been involved in the Walsh kidnapping back in July 1981. He'd returned to Jacksonville from Virginia and had not left. As to why he'd told some people otherwise back in 1983, Toole said it was "for his own personal gain." He got taken out of jail for a while, ate real food, got to smoke cigarettes.

He'd also been approached by another inmate, a guy named Gerald Schaffer who wanted to write a book about the killings that Toole and Henry Lee Lucas had been involved in. Schaffer was working with some author, Toole said, and this guy would funnel monthly payments to them both if Toole would sign over the rights to his story. That sounded fine and dandy to Toole, but, he claimed, he had told Schaffer at the time that he didn't kill Adam Walsh. Toole omitted any reference to the letters that Schaffer had helped him write in 1988, as well as any mention of such details as the bayonet that he and Schaffer had dangled before the Broward County investigators at the time.

Toole told Hoffman there wasn't any reason for him to be withholding information at this time, not when he was already facing multiple life sentences. Hoffman, without bothering to bring up the fact that there might be several reasons for an incarcerated felon not to confess to the abuse and murder of a six-year-old child, took Toole's word on the matter. "Based on the interview with Ottis Toole," he wrote in summary, "it is this detective's opinion that Ottis Toole was being truthful and sincere about his noninvolvement in the Adam Walsh homicide."

And Haggerty, the retired agent who had witnessed this most recent exchange between Hoffman and Toole, agreed, or so he told Matthews that afternoon when he returned from Starke. "Ottis is telling the truth."

"Oh yeah?" said Matthews, who could hold his tongue no longer. "Would that have been today he was telling the truth, or the twenty-one other times when he said he did it?"

For Matthews, it wasn't an accusation, but an honest question. The two of them were in Tallahassee to instruct other detectives in proper investigative methods. Matthews believed that it was vital to understand the difference between listening passively to a statement and a proactive investigative interview, where the questioner, not the subject, controls the agenda. Left to his own devices, a suspect might change his story concerning a crime for any number of reasons.

Jack Hoffman had not found physical evidence that tied Toole to the crime, but there was a mountain of circumstantial evidence that did, and Hoffman had certainly not found any evidence that excluded him from the crime. In the end, it seemed to Matthew, he had simply "decided" that Toole was not involved.

Matthews, on the other hand, felt certain that if Toole were properly interviewed and his responses subjected to polygraph examination, the question of his involvement could be determined once and for all. Not to have done so in all this time seemed simply unfathomable.

Which begged the question as to why Hoffman seemed so dead set against allowing Matthews access to Toole. If Matthews discovered that Toole was in fact being deceptive when he spoke of matters related to the crime, it would only support what Hoffman had apparently chosen to believe long ago. But if Matthews found good reason to believe that Toole was being truthful when he spoke of killing Adam Walsh, it would mean the virtual ruin of a detective who had been unable to make any headway on the most celebrated crime his department had ever encountered. He had staked his career on his steadfast refusal to arrest the only viable suspect who had surfaced during his ten-plus years of investigation, and he still had his job. Why on earth take any chances? Meantime, Adam Walsh's seventeenth birthday passed in November 1991 without further progress on the case.

As evidence that he was still on the job and willing to pursue any lead, Detective Hoffman at the request of John Walsh traveled to Madison, Wisconsin, in the late summer of 1992, where he interviewed Jeffrey Dahmer, who had been arrested for a series of gruesome murders the previous year. While most of the seventeen killings Dahmer was charged with took place between 1987 and 1991, he had taken his first victim in 1977. Some of his victims were as young as fourteen, and many had been spectacularly tortured, abused, and dismembered. Moreover, when he'd been discharged from the army for alcoholism in 1981, Dahmer had spent some time in Miami Beach. It seemed, at the very least, a lead worth pursuing.

Accordingly, Hoffman interviewed Dahmer in his Wisconsin prison on August 13, 1992. At that time, Dahmer assured Hoffman that he was not involved in the abduction and murder of Adam Walsh. No polygraph examination was administered to Dahmer regarding the case. Hoffman returned to South Florida, advised John Walsh as to what he had found, and recorded the information in the case file, where it would reside as the only record of note for the next two years.

Adam Walsh's eighteenth and nineteenth birthdays passed in 1992 and 1993, and nothing new had turned up to suggest who might have taken his life. Still, if the calendar pages seemed to be flipping with no apparent concern for the answer to that question, the steady beat of those tsunami-causing butterfly wings continued.

In 1994, there was something of a startling development within the Hollywood Police Department, where a new command staff was assigned to take over the Criminal Investigations Division. Major Brian Maher and Lieutenant Debbie Futch were placed in charge, and one of the first things they agreed upon was the transfer of Jack Hoffman out of their arena. Hoffman was sent summarily to the Patrol Division as a uniform cop.

As part of her own skills improvement program, Lieutenant Futch attended a homicide investigation seminar being conducted at Broward Community College by Harry O'Reilly, a retired NYPD homicide detective and a well-respected instructor in death investigation technique. Futch told O'Reilly of her own frustration with her department's failure to progress with the Adam Walsh case, and O'Reilly had a quick suggestion: "Why don't you call Joe Matthews over at Miami Beach PD?"

O'Reilly knew and respected Matthews and had heard him talk about the various miscues in the Walsh case on more than one occasion. He was sure that Matthews would welcome the opportunity to involve himself formally, and he assured Futch that there was no better investigator in South Florida to aid in the investigation.

Lieutenant Futch told her boss Maher about the conversation, and Maher thought it was an excellent way to restore credibility to the investigative division. They called Matthews and asked if he'd be willing to consult with their department if they reopened the investigation of the Adam Walsh case. It was a welcome overture to Matthews, who was grappling with grief over the recent death of his father Al, following a fall and a forty-day stay in an intensive care unit.

The opportunity to busy himself in pursuit of a case he'd always been passionate about promised a way to displace a portion of his misery, and he agreed without hesitation. Then–chief of Hollywood police Dick Witt made the request of Miami Beach Police that Matthews be formally assigned, and the deal was done.

Detective Mark Smith—who in 1981, as a rookie cop seated behind the wheel of a patrol car, had assured John Walsh that he and every one of his fellow officers were doing everything they could to find his son—had been assigned to oversee a new cold case squad at Hollywood PD, and among the first he was assigned to reopen was that of the murder of Adam Walsh.

As ordered, Smith met with Matthews to discuss a game plan for how the homicide would best be investigated. From the outset, however, Matthews had his concerns. Smith seemed much more protective of his department's image than Maher and Futch had been, and while he made many of the case files available to Matthews, he held back certain reports and memos that he assured Matthews were inconsequential.

To Matthews, nothing was inconsequential, especially files that might shed light on mistakes and oversights made early on in the investigation, but there was little he could do about it. He set aside his doubts and discussed with Smith the interviews that should be conducted and the evidence that could be reexamined, especially in light of the newly advanced DNA testing now available.

Smith assured Matthews that he would pass along a summary of their recommendations to his superiors and that as soon as he got approval, they would move forward. To Matthews, it sounded good. Just possibly, a new era was about to dawn at Hollywood PD where the Adam Walsh case was concerned. Though he doubted that he and Smith would ever become bosom buddies, he judged that at least he would be working with a competent, hardworking cop. Quite understandably, he looked forward to the day when he could report to John and Revé Walsh that at last significant progress was being made in finding the killer of their son.

On Monday, August 15, 1994, Detective Smith composed a memo to deputy chief Mike Ignasiak outlining what he thought could be done to revive the Walsh case. In his memo, however, he noted that "due to the amount of time since the incident, it would be virtually impossible to set out and try to establish new suspects or motives," an odd position for a cold case investigator to take, given that the aim of such undertakings is to consider the possibility of new suspects or motives.

Smith also suggested in his memo that one thing that they might do was to conduct a follow-up inspection of the area around mile marker 126 on Florida's Turnpike to try and determine why that might have been selected as a place for the killer to dispose of Adam's head, though he doesn't make clear exactly what significance he attributed to that question. More important, Smith recommended to his superiors that "a re-interview" be scheduled with Ottis Toole, "to either eliminate him as a suspect or reaffirm his involvement." This was necessary, Smith said, because it seemed that the "original investigators" believed that Toole was confessing for publicity reasons and had been furnished confidential case file information by "an overzealous Jacksonville detective."

Despite Hoffman's reluctance to pursue the matter, Smith said, "Toole has not been successfully eliminated as a suspect in the case," and he recommended that Miami Beach detective sergeant Joe Matthews be involved in the interview of Toole. "Mr. Matthews has agreed to accompany this agency in an interview with Toole free of charge," Smith explained, before adding something of a curious addendum. "Although he may have ulterior motives for his willingness to assist, I feel Matthews is a resource that could be beneficial to this investigation."

As it turned out, Matthews would not view this memo until ten years after it was written, and when he did see it, he found it mystifying, to say the least. For one thing, the very notion of compensation for his involvement was ludicrous—he was in the paid employ of the Miami Beach Police Department, and he had been assigned to work with Hollywood PD at the latter's own request. Furthermore, he was not "Mr." Matthews, but "Detective Sergeant Matthews"—a small point, but police protocol is unwavering when it comes to distinguishing ordinary civilians from officers in formal correspondence of any kind.

Most troubling to Matthews was the offhand mention of "ulterior motives." To Matthews, it smacked of Jack Hoffman's accusation that Buddy Terry had signed a book contract with Ottis Toole, an unfounded charge that not only besmirched a good cop's career but hobbled the Walsh investigation.

Of course, he could give credit to Hollywood PD for reopening the investigation, but he could only view Smith's comments as symptomatic of an entire department's unspoken wish that the case simply go away, once and for all.

In order to understand what makes Matthews tick, it may be worth a brief return to the detective's early days as a beat cop on the Miami Beach force. Matthews had joined the force in 1967, shortly after his twenty-first birthday, following a chance encounter with a cop during a stint as a security guard at the Miami Beach Convention Center. Why be busting your ass for a buck and a quarter an hour? the cop asked. Matthews seemed like a smart kid. There was a shortage in the department. If he passed the test, the cop told him, he could be knocking down $500 a month.

It seemed like a fortune at the time, and Matthews decided to follow the advice. He took the entrance exam, placed second among applicants, and soon was enrolled in the Dade County Police Academy.

From the first, there were indications that Matthews was not going to be your ordinary cop. His outspoken nature and willingness to question his superiors earned him respect in some quarters, but not everyone appreciated his candor. One morning during training, he returned from class to his locker to find it yawning open, his holster dangling inside, his department-issued pistol missing. Though losing your weapon was just about the worst offense a cadet could commit, Matthews knew there was no avoiding the matter. He marched himself to the training sergeant's office and made his report.

He'd left his locker on "day-lock," he explained to Sergeant, meaning he'd closed his locker, spun the dial, then clicked in the first number of the combination and the second, leaving the dial a few spots shy of the third. It was the sort of thing many cadets did, for there was little time allotted between training sessions, and being late for roll call too often could mean washing out of the program. You'd hurry back to your locker, move the dial a few notches, grab what you needed, and hurry off.

His supervisor might have been aware of the practice, but it didn't mean he condoned it. "You lost your fucking firearm?" the sergeant bellowed. "Do you know who cleans those locker rooms? The fucking jailhouse trusties. If you don't come up with that pistol, we're going to have to empty every cell and strip-search every inmate." With that, he snatched up the phone and asked for Major Sandstrom, chief of the Dade County Corrections Department, to explain the situation. "Yes, that's M-a-t-t-h-e-w-s," he told Sandstrom. "No, not from Dade County. From Miami Beach."

After a bit more consultation with his colleague, Grant hung up the phone and turned back. "Do you know what a colossal pain in the ass this is going to be? We'll wait a few hours. Go find your goddamn gun. If you come up with it, we'll save a hell of a lot of trouble. And if you don't—" The sergeant broke off, shaking his head. Matthews had little doubt as to what the consequences would be.

Following lunch, the forty-man cadet class was once again assembled before the training sergeant, who wanted to make an announcement before they got back to their regularly scheduled business for the afternoon. Grant proceeded then to give the cadre a detailed account of Matthews's profound screwup, and called for him to stand. Matthews rose, ramrod-straight, ready for the worst. "Have you found your firearm yet?" the sergeant demanded.

Matthews felt every eye in the room upon him. Many of his fellow cadets were squirming, well aware that there but for the grace of God they might be. "No sir," Matthews responded, "but I have identified a suspect, sir."

Grant shared a sadist's smile with the others in the room. "Oh yeah?" he said. "And who might that be?"

"It's *you*, sir," Matthews responded.

There was a momentary silence, then a murmur swept the room. The sergeant's face contorted. "Me? What the fuck are you talking about?"

"I went to Major Sandstrom's office during our lunch hour, sir. He told me he hadn't received any call from you regarding any missing pistol. He didn't have any idea what I was talking about."

"Are you calling me a liar?" Grant said, rising from his seat.

"I'd like permission to interview you, sir. You've been instructing us on interviewing suspects, and I think you took my pistol to teach me a lesson. I'd like to ask if you, or anyone at your direction, might have gone to the locker room this morning and removed my pistol from my locker."

By this point the sergeant's face was an apoplectic mask. "Shut the fuck up and sit down, Matthews," he said.

If he had harbored any suspicion that all of this had been something of a training exercise, the spittle flying from Grant's lips convinced Matthews otherwise. Sometimes discretion was the better part of valor, he decided.

On the way out of the room after class was dismissed, one of his fellow cadets gave him a consoling pat on the shoulder. "You've done it this time, Matthews," he said. "You're out of here for sure."

Matthews shrugged. "Maybe you're right," he said. "But I do know one thing. That bastard took my gun."

His fellow cadet could only shake his head, and the two hurried off to class. Later that afternoon, Matthews returned to open his locker. Sure enough, his pistol had been replaced.

It is one of many stories reflecting Matthews's refusal to be cowed by blowhards, but it is surely not the only one. Shortly after he'd graduated from the academy and joined the ranks of beat cops at Miami Beach PD, Matthews turned up at morning roll call to hear a pronouncement: there had been too many complaints from high rollers in big cars and the owners of delivery companies with drivers trying to navigate the clogged streets of the densely populated island. Every officer was to make the ticketing of double-parked cars a priority.

Not a problem, Matthews thought, and set out upon his rounds for the day. He had scarcely turned the corner of Lincoln Road onto Alton when he saw a big Buick pull up beside a car parked in front of Alfie's, a mega-sized Miami version of a New York City candy store *cum* newsstand. The driver got out of the Buick, gave Matthews an uninterested glance, and then strolled casually into the store. It might have been a brazen enough action, parking your barge of a sedan in a busy traffic lane while a cop approached—but on top of everything else, there were empty parking places both in front of and behind the car the guy had parked beside.

Matthews shook his head and made his own way into the store. There he found the guy from the sedan at the counter, engaged in earnest conversation with the owner. "Excuse me, sir," Matthews called. "You're double-parked outside. You'll have to move your car."

The guy kept on talking, ignoring him.

Matthews joined him at the counter, holding up his ticket book. "You're double-parked," he repeated. "If you don't move, I'll have to write you a ticket."

Alfie the proprietor gave Matthews a doubtful look from behind the counter, but said nothing. The guy at the counter turned, gave Matthews a snicker, then turned back and resumed his conversation with Alfie.

"Okay by me," Matthews said. "I'll be outside writing tickets," he went on. "And I'll still be writing them until you come out there and move your car."

He left the store and walked to the back of the car to check the plate number. Having never issued a citation for double parking, he had to consult his statute book to find the proper code, and that took him a few moments. He had completed that citation and was at work on a second—for obstructing traffic—when the door to Alfie's finally opened and the guy came out, a look of disbelief on his face.

"What do you think you're doing?" the guy said.

"Exactly what I told you I'd be doing," Matthews said. He finished the second citation and tore a copy out of his book. He thrust the two tickets at the guy, who rolled his eyes and brushed past him.

As the guy got into his car and slammed the door, Matthews approached, lifted the wiper on the driver's side of the windshield, and snapped the two tickets under the rubber blade. The driver's-side window rolled down, and the guy thrust his face through the opening. "You don't know who you're screwing with, do you?" he demanded.

By the point Matthews had had enough. He bent close enough to smell the guy's boozer breath. "You don't know who *you're* screwing with, do you?"

The guy's eyes widened in surprise momentarily. "Fuck you," he said finally, then floored the Buick's accelerator and sped away.

"Fuck *you*," Matthews called after him. He noted that Alfie had come out onto the sidewalk to witness the scene. The proprietor gave Matthews a baleful look, then went back inside. Matthews shrugged and went on about his day.

Before dismissal at the following morning's roll call, the patrol sergeant reiterated the need for them all to be vigilant about ticketing double-parkers, and then, as everyone was filing out, called Matthews to his desk. "Captain Webb wants to see you," the sergeant said.

When Matthews asked the sergeant if he knew what it was about, the sergeant gave him a look. "I think I'll let the captain explain. Just get your ass down there."

Accordingly, Matthews made his way to the patrol commander's office. As Matthews stood nervously at attention, Webb gave him the once-over, then tented his fingers and finally began.

"Since when did you start issuing parking tickets to police officers?" Webb inquired.

Matthews was genuinely perplexed. "I don't know what you mean, sir. I wouldn't do anything like that."

"Then why did you write Captain Henry Dworkin, who happens to be commander of the detective bureau, two parking tickets yesterday? One for double-parking and another for obstructing traffic?"

Matthews stared at the tickets Captain Webb had produced, a feeling of dread washing over him. "Uh . . . I had no idea he was a police officer, sir."

His supervisor stared at him. "Well, you made one hell of a mistake, Matthews."

"Yes sir," Matthews said.

"And you need to take care of these tickets," his supervisor added.

Matthews nodded. "I'll do that, sir."

"Good," his supervisor said, giving him a weary look. "Go to it. And try to keep your head out of your ass from now on, will you?"

By the time he made his way down the hallway from the squad room, Matthews's shock had abated, and resentment had begun to take its place. Why hadn't Dworkin just said he was a cop in the first place? Why be such a dick about it?

Anyway, he thought, his supervisor had told him to take care of the matter, and so he would. He'd go right to Captain Dworkin's office and do whatever it took.

At his knock on Dworkin's door, a voice issued, inviting him in. Matthews entered to find the guy he'd given the tickets sitting behind a desk. "What are you doing here?" Dworkin said, the instant he saw who it was.

"I just wanted to talk to you about those tickets—," Matthews began.

Dworkin stared as if a leper was about to climb into his lap. "Get the fuck out of my office and don't you ever come back," he said.

"Yes sir," Matthews said, and turned on his heel.

As he was making his way down the hallway in the aftermath, he heard a voice calling after him. "Hey, Matthews."

What now? he thought, as he turned to see Detective Walter Philbin stepping out of a doorway, beckoning toward him. Philbin was a lieutenant of detectives, a tall, muscular guy with plenty of swagger and the look of a ladies' man. He was a big drinker and a high-stakes gambler, but he had connections inside the department and on the streets as well. His was a legendary presence in the department's detective bureau.

"I just wanted to say you got some balls, kid. Telling Dworkin he doesn't know who he's fucking with. That's classic." Philbin laughed and clapped him on the shoulder.

Matthews stared back in some concern. "How'd you hear about that?" He glanced down the hall toward the office he'd just left. "Did Dworkin tell you?"

"Hell, no," Philbin said, waving his hand. "The guy's a total asshole. Nobody talks to him. Alfie told me what happened. He said he never saw anything like it."

Philbin was about to duck back into his office, then stopped. "By the way, go see Esther down in the traffic division. She'll tell you how to make those tickets go away."

It might have been the end of the matter, and just one more story about Joe Matthews and how his penchant for doing the right thing seemed always to land him in trouble, except for one thing. It was not long after that encounter that Chief Pomerance asked Walter Philbin to put together a task force that would do whatever was necessary to bring down the crime rate on Miami Beach.

Pomerance and Philbin were in agreement as to the kind of officers needed for such an assignment. There'd be some ticklish situations dealing with hardened criminals who'd prefer to take their chances on justice in a shootout as opposed to a courtroom, and you'd need to be able to trust your partners to stand up, during and after tough situations like those.

Accordingly, Philbin primarily chose men whom he'd known for years. Experienced and able cops, those savvy enough to understand when justice had to be dispensed with on the spot, and how to keep their mouths shut afterward. Given his dictum that you couldn't trust a man you couldn't drink with, Philbin would probably have added incipient alcoholism to his list of qualifications as well. But there was rigor in such work, and the need for a certain amount of young blood too.

It was in that way, then, that Joe Matthews found himself plucked from the ranks of the beat cops to become part of a task force that one day would be dispatched to a stakeout at the Shoreham Hotel and from there to any number of other incidents that would propel him upward through the ranks. From task force, to detective bureau, to sergeant. From homicide investigator, to polygraph expert, to Dade County Cop of the Year, and ultimately to involvement with the kidnapping and murder of Adam Walsh. Flap, flap, flap.

HOLLYWOOD, FLORIDA—AUGUST 16, 1994

Despite his "reservations" about the motives of Joe Matthews, Detective Smith proceeded with his work on the Adam Walsh case, albeit at a deliberate pace. He met with Harry O'Reilly, the retired NYPD homicide detective who had put the department back in touch with Matthews, and Smith and O'Reilly traveled to the spot off Florida's Turnpike where Toole originally said he'd disposed of Adam's head and body, to determine whether or not O'Reilly thought it might be worth conducting a second concerted search for remains. O'Reilly doubted that there was anything to be accomplished by such an undertaking, but he did return from the trip with a real concern: he called Joe Matthews to tell him about the foray, wondering why Smith had not asked Matthews to join them, a point at which Matthews realized that whatever might eventuate from his collaboration with Smith, the two were certainly not functioning as true partners.

Not until the following January did Smith take his next significant step, telephoning John Walsh to seek approval to get a DNA baseline sample using Adam's mandible as a source. A few days later, Smith wrote a memo to his superiors indicating that it had been suggested that he send hair samples from the victim, along with the bloody machete and bloodstained sheath and a sample of the carpet taken from the Cadillac, for DNA comparison testing.

Smith then called the FDLE, looking for the carpet samples that they had tested a dozen years before. But those had been sent back to the Jacksonville Sheriff's Office long ago, Smith was told, and accordingly, on January 17, 1995, he drove to Jacksonville to search the sheriff's evidence room for the carpet samples and try and discover the whereabouts of the vehicle itself.

What he discovered was disheartening, to say the least. Records showed that the Cadillac's floorboard carpets and the seven squares tested for blood had been received by the sheriff's property room on May 24, 1984, signed for with the initial "J." Whether the J stood for Jack Hoffman or Jacksonville, no one could say. Whatever had happened to the carpet samples once they arrived at the Jacksonville Sheriff's Office, only one thing was certain: eleven years later, they were nowhere to be found.

As for the car itself, Smith learned, it was sold to a dealer at auction, purchased by a man from St. Augustine, then—when it finally stopped running a half-dozen years or more before—towed to a junkyard and scrapped. Smith, distressed at such sloppy handling of key evidence in the case, filed a complaint with the FDLE, but it went nowhere.

As for the machete and its sheath, those items remained in the possession of the Hollywood PD, and Smith forwarded them for testing. Once again, the results were not what he or Matthews hoped for. Though testing on those items performed by FDLE serologist James Pollack in 1983 had confirmed the presence of small amounts of blood, the laboratory to which they were sent for DNA testing in 1995 could find no blood anywhere. "As a result of that, no additional comparisons were made," the technician advised.

While that scarcely qualified as good news, Matthews moved forward. Following ten months of effort, he was finally able to arrange an interview with Ottis Toole, scheduled for June 20, 1995. Though by this time Toole had adopted a newly stated policy that he would not grant any interviews to law enforcement officials investigating specific homicides, Matthews was able to convince him to make something of an exception.

Matthews had arranged for Toole's prison counselor to identify him in his role as a clinical research associate from Nova Southeastern University and a police detective from Miami Beach, not Hollywood, all of which was true. Toole was told that he was simply one of many convicted murderers to be interviewed by Matthews, who was conducting a study of the phenomenon of serial killing. After some consideration, Toole agreed to talk, and the interview was set to be conducted in the prison library without the use of handcuffs or restraints, so that it might seem more like a bit of academic inquiry than an interrogation.

Though it had taken some time, Matthews was champing at the bit. After years of frustration, he would finally have the chance to fix the lens of reason upon the only viable suspect in the murder of Adam Walsh.

On Father's Day, Sunday, June 18, two days before the interview was scheduled, Matthews called Detective Smith to make sure all was in order for the trip to Starke. There was an awkward pause when Smith realized who was on the other end of the line.

"Hasn't anyone called you?" he asked Matthews.

"About what?" Matthews asked, wary.

"Well . . . ," Smith fumbled, "actually Chief Witt wants me to take this juvenile division detective Navarro along to conduct the interview instead of you."

To Matthews, it seemed as if he were reliving a familiar nightmare. "You can't be serious," he told Smith.

"Look, Joe," said Smith. "I'm sorry. This was not my call. I hope you know that."

Matthews knew nothing, really, except that it had to be some giant mistake. Chief Witt had gone to Matthews's own superiors to negotiate an interagency agreement. Hollywood PD had come to *him*, not the other way around.

Since it was Sunday, however, there was no way to contact

Witt, and Matthews could only stew until Monday morning, when he called the chief, hoping to clear up the misunderstanding. When the two finally spoke, Witt quickly explained that there was nothing to explain. He thanked Sergeant Matthews for all his help and was grateful to Miami Beach PD for making him available, but, said Witt, for reasons having to do with any possible future court proceedings, he wanted Toole's confession obtained by his own personnel.

Matthews could not believe what he was hearing. So now Hollywood PD believed that Toole was guilty, but they wanted to make sure they got all the credit for making the case? He reminded Chief Witt that he had asked for Matthews's assistance, and that Matthews had been working alongside Detective Smith for more than a year, preparing for the opportunity to interview Toole at last.

How about this? Matthews suggested. I'll conduct the interview, and even if we get a confession out of Toole, you won't have to include me in the report. Just use the names of your guys, Smith and Navarro. Whoever you want.

Witt allowed that Matthews was being very generous, but he had made his decision. His own men would conduct the interview with Toole, and that was the long and short of it.

By this time Matthews was ready to lose it. "Just tell me the truth, Dick. What the fuck is really going on over there?" he blurted.

There was a moment of silence on the other end. And then Witt hung up.

Matthews sat back in his chair, literally sick at what had transpired. He'd been jerked around before, plenty of times, but never like this. A long time ago he'd become resigned to the fact that Jack Hoffman wanted no part of his involvement in the investigation, but he could chalk that up to one individual's insecurities, no matter how frustrating and tragic the consequences. But now the chief of the department was chasing Matthews off the case. And for what earthly reason?

Was it because they really thought Toole was guilty and wanted all the credit for themselves? Or was there a darker explanation? he wondered. Could it possibly be that the last thing Hollywood PD wanted was to find that Ottis Toole had been guilty all along?

Hey, the kid's been dead fifteen years, his old man's a celebrity now, the guy who claims he did it is locked up for life—why try to fix what isn't really broken and make yourself look bad in the process? Matthews shook his head at the very thought.

Matthews would never be able to answer his questions with certainty, but certain things that happened in the lee of his dismissal from the case for a third time have their implications. Late in the afternoon of the same day he spoke with Chief Witt, Matthews returned to the offices of the homicide unit, intending to pick up where he'd left off the day before on a troubling matter that had nothing to do with the Adam Walsh case.

A female police officer had filed a lawsuit against the police department for allowing a hostile work environment and, as a result of that lawsuit, had been transferred from uniform patrol to the detective bureau. Soon after her arrival, she'd complained that her new fellow officers were playing demeaning pranks and tampering with the personal effects on her desk while she was out of the office, spilling coffee on her favorite pink desk pads, placing her animal statuettes in coital positions, and the like. To Matthews, it seemed pretty trivial stuff on both sides, and he scarcely paid any attention to it.

But then, after being called in to investigate a homicide during the early-morning hours on Sunday, Matthews had returned to his office and was leaning back in his chair, trying to clarify what needed to be done regarding the crime scene he'd just left. It was then that he noticed something odd about one of the ceiling panels next to the air-conditioning vent directly overhead. He asked one of his junior detectives to place a chair on his desk and check it out.

The kid, who'd worked for the CIA out of college, took a look behind the A/C grate, and told Matthews he'd found a video surveillance camera there, trained on the complaining officer's desk but encompassing the entire room.

Matthews notified his immediate supervisor and called in the department's crime techs to remove and process the camera. Though he could not be certain, the fact that the camera bore the logo of a private security firm suggested that the transferred female officer had taken it upon herself to try and collect evidence against those moving her statues around and writing derisive notes on her desk blotter.

Whoever was responsible for hiding this camera, though, and whatever the reason, Matthews wanted the matter settled. They were a crimes-against-persons squad, with all sorts of sensitive information being discussed in that room. You couldn't have someone recording what went on there, willy-nilly, no matter how many times you found your turtle statuettes humping each other.

At least getting to the bottom of who had put that camera up there would take his mind off the fiasco with the aborted Ottis Toole interview, he thought. But such thoughts didn't last long.

He hadn't even sat down in his chair that Monday afternoon when he noticed a memo placed prominently on his desk. Something to do with the camera investigation already? he wondered. He picked up the sheet and began to read it, disbelief filling him as he digested the words. It was a notice from Patricia Schneider, the major in charge of the detective bureau. Effective immediately, a few months shy of his retirement date after twenty-nine years with the department, Matthews was being transferred back to uniform patrol duty.

Matthews couldn't believe his eyes. When he went into the office of his commanding officer for an explanation, she shrugged. It was within her power to transfer at will—she didn't have to explain anything to him.

But no one got transferred without cause, Matthews protested, the sick feeling in his stomach now an icy cannonball. Only if you screwed up big-time. Or couldn't get along with your superiors. It was the unwritten rule within any department. What was going on here? Everyone knew Matthews was the go-to investigator in the department, and he was the supervisor of the crimes against persons unit. And he got along fine with those above and below him. She knew that.

The major shrugged. She wasn't so sure. She had heard he couldn't get along very well with Dick Witt over at Hollywood PD.

Matthews was stunned. Less than six hours since he'd spoken with Witt, and already he was being torpedoed? He left the major's office without another word and made his way to the office of the chief. Matthews had known Richard Barretto for a long time, and while they weren't necessarily pals, they got along just fine. Matthews showed Barretto the memo from his supervisor, and Barretto handed it back to him.

"So?" he asked Matthews.

"So?" Matthews repeated. "What the hell is going on here? Is Dick Witt the chief of this department, or are you? I just talked with the major. She let the cat out of the bag. I give Dick Witt a little grief, and suddenly I'm being transferred back into uniform?"

Barretto stared evenly back at Matthews. "Dick Witt doesn't have anything to do with your transfer. You interfered with a sexual harassment investigation being conducted by our internal affairs division. That's why you're being transferred."

Matthews shook his head in puzzlement. "What the hell are you talking about?"

"That camera you had removed from the office was placed there by IA."

Matthews was dumbfounded by Barretto's revelation. "It was a departmental surveillance camera? You mean internal affairs took all that turtle statue shit seriously? That's still no reason for me to be transferred."

Barretto folded his hands and leaned across his desk. "I'm the *acting* chief," he told Matthews. "And I would like to become *the* chief. The major wants you transferred, and I can't undermine my command staff by issuing counterorders. It's as simple as that."

Matthews started to protest yet again, but what was the point? He'd simply done what any other detective who'd found a spy camera in his office would have done. All that was just a smoke screen.

He stood up and walked out of Barretto's office while the acting chief was prattling on, reminding him that he had just a few months left to retirement, and that he probably had that much leave time accrued. Matthews could in effect retire right now, no worries about uniform duty . . .

Sure, Matthews was thinking. But all he could think about was what had happened to Buddy Terry in Jacksonville. Terry was a well-respected, hardworking detective who had gotten crosswise with Hollywood PD trying to make headway on the Adam Walsh case, and look what had happened to him. Now— and Matthews was certain of it—he had made the same mistake.

When he came home that evening, Ginny met him at the door excited, waving a sheaf of photos. Joe had missed the opening of Cristina's dance recital the day before because he'd been held up at work, but that was no problem—she had these great pictures of their daughter coming out on stage. When she suddenly saw the expression on Joe's face, she stopped.

She took a closer look at what was in the box. Pictures from his office—a dozen years of the kids growing up—one of his father, who'd been so proud of his detective son, and framed commendations. When she heard Joe's account, she was stunned. That's the thanks he got for caring about a case an entire police department had botched? Finally, she took a deep breath and said, "Joe, things happen for a reason. Your family loves you. I love you. It's going to be fine."

When his brother Pete, also a Miami Beach detective sergeant and supervisor of the department's crimes against property unit, heard what had happened, he demanded a transfer back to uniform patrol as well. "You don't need to do that," Matthews protested to his brother, but Pete was having none of it. It was all bullshit, and everyone knew it.

Sure enough, when Matthews turned up at roll call on his first day back in uniform, the entire shift stood to give him a lengthy ovation. They all knew it wasn't much, but it was the very least they could do.

RAIFORD, FLORIDA—JUNE 27, 1995

On Tuesday of the following week, Detective Smith did in fact travel to Raiford, Florida, with Detective Navarro, where they sought to interview Ottis Toole at the Union Correctional Institution. "Toole had no initial response to the introduction," wrote Smith in his report, "until he was informed of the purpose of the interview." Once he realized that the two were there to question him in regard to his involvement in the abduction and murder of Adam Walsh, Toole became "disturbed," Smith said, "and stated that he had no involvement in this case or any other cases, including the ones of which he was convicted."

Adam Walsh's twenty-first birthday passed later that year, and then, less than a month later, on Tuesday, December 5, convicted serial killer Gerald Schaffer, former cellmate and erstwhile legal adviser of Ottis Toole, was found dead in his cell at Starke, stabbed several times in the eye, his throat slit. In an interview with the *Palm Beach Post*, Schaffer's mother and sister said to reporters that he had told them that he was about to cooperate with detectives on the Adam Walsh case. He had agreed to testify in an upcoming proceeding, he confided to them, and explained that he hoped to gain early parole as a result. That explained why he'd been killed, the women told reporters.

If the bits and pieces of the case against Ottis Toole already seemed to be dissolving, what happened in early 1996 appeared to be the death knell for the matter altogether. In early May 1995, the *Mobile Press-Register* had filed a request under the Freedom of Information Act, asking that the contents of the Hollywood Police Department file on Adam Walsh be made public.

As often happens in any missing child case, there had always been a certain amount of innuendo involving the parents. There was the scandal involving Revé's short-lived affair with Jimmy Campbell, and the bizarre suggestion made by Hoffman's partner Hickman that God would bring Adam back if Walsh would only repent for his misdeeds.

Also, as armchair theorists warmed to their work over the long history of the failed investigation, the notion was kicked around that John Walsh had become involved with the mob as a result of his work with an international hotel chain. He'd either screwed up some drug deal—or, more charitably, refused to partake in one—and the killing of Adam was payback.

The real reason that the case had failed to progress, such thinking went, was that Walsh had himself obstructed the investigation and pressured the Hollywood police to drag their feet. Conspiracy theorists everywhere were licking their chops at having the case files laid bare—all the dirt could finally be revealed. And what ace reporter would not dream of being the hero who finally revealed what police couldn't or wouldn't prove in this case of cases? In any event, and whatever they hoped to discover as a result, three other newspapers—the *Fort Lauderdale Sun-Sentinel*, the *Palm Beach Post*, and the *Miami Herald*—joined the *Mobile Press-Register* in its suit.

Walsh was dismayed at the prospect, for he knew what opening police files would mean to any serious ongoing investigation. Accordingly, he went directly to Chief Witt to press for assurances that the department would fight the request. Meantime, Walsh suggested, during a May 15 meeting at which Joe Matthews and Mark Smith were present, that perhaps Witt could issue a statement that suggested how ridiculous the rumors were that tied him to the Mafia. Witt seemed a bit befuddled at the request, however. As Joe Matthews and Walsh stared expectantly at Witt, the chief answered by saying that in his opinion anyone who frequented a certain well-known Fort Lauderdale restaurant for lunch—as Walsh did—"must have something to do with the Mafia."

"With friends like Dick Witt," Matthews told Walsh on the way out the door, "you don't need any enemies."

And then in December, the Walshes received more disturbing news from Hollywood police, when Mark Smith called to check on something. John Walsh listened patiently to a rambling preamble before finally asking the detective to get to the point.

"Well," Smith said, "they did show you these green shorts and that sandal they found back in 1984, didn't they?"

Walsh assured Smith that he had no idea what he was talking about, and Smith finally explained. An FDLE team had dug up the items on Ottis Toole's property in Jacksonville, Smith told him. The shorts and a child's yellow flip-flop had been sent to Hollywood PD, where they'd been in the evidence room ever since.

Walsh, as might be expected, went ballistic at the news. The "Missing" posters that were issued in the wake of Adam's disappearance had described him as wearing green shorts and yellow flip-flops. Now Smith was saying that the detective in charge of the case had discovered such items on the property of the only serious suspect who had ever been identified and had not called him in to see if they belonged to Adam? How could such behavior be explained?

Smith, obviously, could not explain it, but he did arrange a meeting at which the Walshes could view the items. It took nearly a month, but finally, on January 16, 1996, John and Revé

Walsh met with Detective Smith and Chief Witt in a conference room at Hollywood PD. Chief Witt began the meeting
with a long-winded preamble in which he proclaimed the untir-
ing efforts of his department to solve the case. No effort had
been spared, the chief said, no tip had been ignored. Finally, he
paused, holding up a large evidence envelope, and gave Revé a
glance meant to be solicitous.

"Would you and John like to take a minute?" he asked.

Revé stared back, doubfounded. *Good lord*, she thought—
they'd already been kept waiting for fifteen years.

"Just show us what you've got," John said.

Witt seemed taken aback by Walsh's tone, but he broke off to
open up the envelope with a flourish. Revé took one look at the
muddy shorts and the tiny shoe that was barely bigger than one
an infant might wear and shook her head quickly. No way had
these items come from Adam. "They're not his," she told John.

The collective disappointment in the room was palpable.
Once again, it seemed, Ottis Toole had slipped from a snare.

Despite the letdown, Detective Smith did his best to put
a positive spin on matters for the Walshes. He and Sergeant
Matthews had made very real progress on the cold case investigation, he insisted. He mentioned the fact that Sears security
guard Kathy Shaffer had finally admitted sending Adam outside the store through the door where Toole claimed he'd picked
the child up. And he also pointed to the significance of the fact
that when Toole made his first confession, no news report had
mentioned the site near mile marker 126 where Toole later took
detectives. As further corroboration that he knew details that
had never been reported in the press, Toole had spoken several times of driving no more than ten minutes farther north
on the turnpike before disposing of the head in the canal. As
Smith pointed out, the spot where fishermen had discovered the
remains was four miles north, at mile marker 130—ten minutes
was just how long it would take to turn around on that deserted

service road, make your way back to the turnpike, and drive to the spot where Adam's head had been found.

Smith then turned his attention to Witt. All these details that Toole had dropped into his multiple confessions were unknown to anyone outside the circle of law enforcement. If they were divulged publicly, however, that evidence would become readily available to any deranged soul who wanted to claim responsibility for the crime. Anyone could say, "Actually it was me who pulled off there at mile marker 130 and tossed that head in the canal." Surely, Smith said, Witt understood the importance of standing up against the request to open the files.

Witt nodded, tenting his fingers thoughtfully. "I suppose you could look it that way," he said, "but I think it is just as likely that opening up the case files would put pressure on Toole to break down and confess."

Though no one in the room had the temerity to point out that Toole had already broken down and confessed on several occasions, one thing seemed clear: even though no ruling on the matter had been issued, Witt had already decided to release the files. As the meeting was winding down, in fact, Witt made the offhanded remark that he already had aides working to transfer the materials onto microfilm, all ten thousand pages of it.

In the aftermath of this disclosure, an angry Walsh went immediately to Michael Satz, head of the Broward County State Attorney's Office, to plead that Satz intervene. If the state attorney announced imminent plans to bring a suspect to trial, then it would be a good bet no judge would allow potential evidence to be revealed in public. Walsh begged Satz to review the case file, and asked for an explanation why no one in all this time had been willing to prosecute a case against Ottis Toole.

What Satz had to say in response floored Walsh. There was a simple reason why the case had not gone forward, Satz said. Since the day in 1983 when Chief Martin of the Hollywood Police Department had announced that Ottis Toole was their prime suspect in the case, not a shred of evidence had been presented to Satz's office. In fact, the HPD hadn't shared its full case file on the investigation until just five days ago, Satz said.

Walsh shook his head in disbelief. And what did Satz think about the extortion letter in that file—the one that Toole had sent to him, offering to lead Walsh to where Adam's body had been buried for $50,000? Satz had no idea what Walsh was referring to—there was no such letter in the file that had recently been presented to him.

When Walsh showed Satz the letter that described his son as crying for his mother as Toole had sodomized him, the state attorney was stunned. He set the letter aside and stood to apologize to Walsh. Of course his office had been insistent that Hoffman and his team present evidence linking Toole to the crime back in the 1980s, but what he had just read was all a competent attorney needed, Satz said.

"I could get a jury conviction on the strength of this letter alone," he told Walsh.

Furthermore, he said, his office *would* intervene immediately to prevent the opening of the case files to the media on the grounds that a prosecution against Ottis Toole was now imminent, and that opening the evidence to the public would compromise the prosecution's ability to prove its case against Toole.

On February 16, 1996, a hearing was set on the matter, with Revé Walsh present to add a personal plea. But Judge Moe would not allow her to speak—he wanted no appeals to emotion in his court, he explained. And then, after listening to brief presentations by both sides, he issued his order. The case file would be released.

With every detail known to investigators—including all crime scene photos—now a part of the public record, the possibility of ever corroborating any future confession against matters known only to police ended.

Yet, whatever hopes the media might have had as to their

own analysis of the case files, they came to very little. There was no "hidden" evidence concerning John Walsh's ties to the Mafia, nor was there any suggestion that he had meddled with the investigation of the Hollywood police in any way, though the spectacular lack of progress might well have warranted it.

There was a brief flurry of indignation when reporters realized that key evidence—the bloody carpet samples taken from Toole's Cadillac, as well as the car itself—had been lost. As to that matter, the Jacksonville Sheriff's Office was quick to deflect responsibility onto the Hollywood PD. No evidentiary hold had been placed upon the car by the principal investigators, the sheriff's office said, so they were only following proper procedure in returning the car to its owner, Wells Brothers Used Cars. As far as the carpet samples were concerned, the sheriff admitted having destroyed them, but again, that was normal procedure for dealing with what were reclassified as "non-evidentiary materials"—since the original testing was inconclusive, no one had seen any point in keeping them. As to what had become of the sections of the floor carpets that had not been tested, no one could be sure . . . perhaps only the mysterious "J" who signed for them could say.

Whatever the validity of the various claims and counterclaims of the agencies involved, anyone who read the various accounts published in the wake of the release of the case files could be forgiven for assuming that the matter was finished. Propriety and impropriety of procedures aside, it simply looked as if police would never find out who had kidnapped and murdered Adam Walsh.

And yet, even with Hollywood PD apparently at a standstill and Joe Matthews retired from Miami Beach PD, there was still desultory work on the case. In September, investigator Philip Mundy of the Broward County State Attorney's Office took the sworn statement of Bobby Lee Jones, a former cellmate of Toole's in the Duval County Jail, who claimed to have worked with Ottis Toole at Reaves Roofing in 1982. In late July of that year, Jones said, Toole began to talk to him about various crimes he had committed, including the killing of a little boy. Jones recalled Toole telling him he'd lured the child into his car, and had intended to take him home and "be his father." But it had not worked out, Jones said. Toole told him he'd cut the boy's head off and tossed it into a creek, then cut up the body and burned it.

Jones's statement might have had greater impact were it not for the inconsistency suggested by the dates he gave Mundy. Company records indicate that the last day of Toole's employment at Reaves Roofing was June 4, 1981, several weeks before the killing. Furthermore, he drew only one day's pay from Southeast Color Coat in December.

Of course, fourteen or fifteen years had passed, and Jones might have been mistaken about exactly when he'd heard all this from Toole. The conversation could have taken place when they were incarcerated together in 1983. And there was no doubt that many details of Toole's confession had been recounted by the media when the case files had been opened earlier that year. Still, if Jones was being truthful—if he'd heard about it from Toole at work in December 1982, or simply as they chatted on the streets or in a bar—it would mean that Toole had begun talking to others about killing Adam Walsh long before he first admitted it to police in 1983.

Meanwhile, John Walsh had decided to take matters into his own hands, even if it was a stinging blow that led him to do so. In May 1996, as he was on his way to a Washington, D.C., gathering of missing children who had been reunited with their families as a result of *America's Most Wanted*, Walsh received an unexpected call on his car phone. He didn't have to bother coming to New York next week to talk about next year's episodes, a spokesman explained. After eight years, the Fox network had abruptly decided to cancel the show. He'd be kept on contract as a consultant and producer, but the decision was final: *America's Most Wanted* was finished.

Though stunned at the news, Walsh had little choice in the matter. And after it had finally sunk in, he realized that the appropriate way to close the program was with an episode on the one case they had never featured: that of Adam Walsh.

The program, which ran on September 21, 1996, was put together by John Turchin, a reporter for WSVN, Channel 7, the Fox affiliate in Miami, and was based on information and tips gathered by Joe Matthews and Mark Smith, the detective with whom Matthews had worked the cold case investigation at Hollywood PD. Turchin interviewed Sears security guard Kathy Shaffer, who spoke candidly for the first time about her role in the incident back in 1981. She'd just started the job, she told Turchin, and when she realized that big trouble had indeed unfolded on that day, she was overwhelmed. While she had said otherwise, shortly after Revé Walsh showed her the pictures of her son she realized that Adam had in fact been in the store that day. It was also true that she had made him leave, along with all the other kids who were causing a fuss at the video game display. But she hadn't wanted to admit it—after all, if she hadn't sent him outside, he might still be alive.

Turchin also brought up the fact that the cops had recovered the car that was thought to have been used to abduct Adam, but sadly, it had been scrapped. And he pointed out that the cops had seized bloodstained carpeting from that car, as well—also lost, unfortunately.

Turchin also interviewed William Mistler, who recounted testimony that he had provided to the Hollywood police five years previously: he had seen a scruffy-looking man leading a little boy to a white Cadillac parked outside a Sears store on July 27, 1981. Mistler identified the boy as Adam Walsh, and the man who'd kidnapped him as Ottis Toole. The program concluded with some footage the Walshes had stumbled across by accident a few weeks before: six-year-old Adam Walsh in his baseball uniform, full of life, mugging at the camera, swinging his bat, getting a hit, rounding the bases. The stuff of which heartbreak is made.

Shortly after the show aired, Walsh received a call from Peter Roth, president of the Fox Entertainment Group. Hundreds of thousands of letters had been pouring in. Fifty-five members of Congress had complained, as had thirty-seven governors and every attorney general in the fifty states. The FBI had written as well. The network had reconsidered, Roth told Walsh. *America's Most Wanted*—the show that had resulted in the capture of some four hundred fugitives, including eleven on the FBI's "Most Wanted" list, the show that had recovered twenty missing children and led to the apprehension of scores of child molesters—was going to remain on the air.

WASHINGTON, D.C.—SEPTEMBER 23, 1996
John Walsh was heartened by the news from Fox, and he was proud of the way the program on Adam had turned out. How could anyone who had seen it doubt what had really happened? he thought. He and Revé had not yet found closure in a court of law, perhaps, but this was damned close. And as for bringing Ottis Toole to justice, he had plans for that as well.

He'd received word from sources that Ottis Toole had been diagnosed with hepatitis and AIDS by prison doctors at Lake Butler. Toole knew he was dying, Walsh was told, and it was suggested that the convict might be willing to talk to the right person. Walsh, who knew of the calamitous outcome of Mark Smith's visit to Toole the previous year, thought he had the "right person" for the task in the person of Joe Matthews, who had retired from Miami Beach PD in the spring and had volunteered to help Walsh on the case in any way he possibly could.

And by this point, Walsh had formed a substantial network

of friends in law enforcement, including the FBI and the FDLE. He was going to stop mincing around and use some of his influence to get Joe Matthews in to talk with Ottis Toole, once and for all. If Matthews could get a deathbed confession out of Toole, then he and Revé could rest with that, Walsh thought. Certainly, the prospect was worth using every favor he might call in.

Word that *America's Most Wanted* would live on was not the only news that arrived in the wake of the September 21 program featuring Adam's case. A number of tips were phoned in that suggested that Walsh and Joe Matthews were right about the killer's identity.

While Matthews followed up most of the leads at Walsh's request, one tip bypassed *AMW* entirely and went straight to the Hollywood PD: the caller's name was Mary Hagan, she told police, and though she now resided in a retirement community in upstate Florida, she had been living in Hollywood not far from the Walshes at the time of Adam's murder. She had seen things inside the Sears store that day he disappeared, she explained, and hadn't realized until she'd seen that TV segment on Adam that police still hadn't caught the killer. Perhaps what she had to tell them would help.

Phil Mundy, the investigator for the Broward County State Attorney's Office, followed up with Hagan, seventy-six at the time. She told him that on the morning of July 27, 1981, she had noticed an ad for a lamp sale at Sears, and decided to go have a look. She entered the store through the garden department entrance and passed the video game display, where several kids were gathered, including Adam, whom she recognized from the neighborhood. Also standing there talking with the boys, said Hagan, was a "rancid-smelling" man who seemed out of place to her. He was filthy, and she could smell him—"overpowering, like beer and onions"—from several feet away.

The guy had to step out of her way so she could get past,

Hagan said, and when he did, he smiled at her, a goofy-looking expression that exposed a big gap in his front teeth. She hurried on past, she said, and checked out the lamp section, where she couldn't find anything she liked. There wasn't a clerk around—only one customer, an attractive younger woman who seemed to be waiting on something—so Hagan decided to leave. As she passed the video display on the way out, she noted that it was deserted.

She explained to Mundy that she had thought about coming forward when she later learned what had happened to Adam, but wasn't sure what good it would do. By that time, there was all that news about people who'd seen Adam being dragged into a "blue van," so what she had seen didn't seem all that important. "Leave it alone," her husband Lou told her. "Let the police do their job."

And she assumed that is just what happened, she told Mundy, until she watched the episode of *America's Most Wanted* and saw the picture of Ottis Toole displayed on-screen. Oh my God, she thought, You mean he's still alive—they never got him?

To Mundy, Hagan's story was provocative. True, she might have pieced together much of what she'd told him from various reports. But there was one thing that had never been included in any account of Toole's involvement with the crime, and that was his terrible, overpowering body odor. No one who had ever been in Toole's presence for a moment failed to mention just how bad the guy smelled—as if there was something rotting inside him, bursting to get out.

Another particularly provocative call came directly to the *AMW* hotline, from a young woman named Sarah Patterson, the individual listed as "next of kin" on prison records. Patterson was the recipient of Toole's few personal effects: his prison-issued Bible, some letters, and a few photographs.

In years past, she'd also received a lot more from Toole,

though most of it was an unwelcome legacy. As she explained to Joe Matthews, she was Ottis Toole's niece, the older sister of Frieda "Becky" Powell, who had been murdered by Henry Lee Lucas.

After her mother's death, she had been raised by her grandmother and by Ottis Toole, if "raising" was what you could call it. Uncle Ottis, as Sarah called him, favored her younger sister, treating Becky like a daughter and Sarah "more like a friend," though a curious friendship it seemed.

He taught her to drink and smoke dope and they partied hard together. "By the time I was ten, I was a whore," Sarah told Matthews, "and I still am a whore. Back then, Uncle Ottis would turn me out to his friends for $10. He'd watch me fuck them and give them head and beat off while I was doing it."

She never had sex with Ottis, however, because he was as queer as anyone could be, she explained. He shaved his legs, wore stockings, panties, and a bra. He dressed in drag, got shots "for boobs," Sarah said, and wore a wig. That was the way he liked to dress "when he hustled other fags," she said.

He could get mad, Sarah recalled, but he had a good side, too. Even if he only had enough money for one six-pack, he was always willing to share it. And when she got married at age seventeen, Ottis came to the wedding dressed as her bridesmaid.

As to the matter of Adam Walsh, Sarah had some pertinent information for Matthews. Some time around Christmas in 1995, she heard that Ottis was pretty sick and went to see him in prison. During that visit, she said, she asked him directly, "Uncle Ottis, are you the one that killed Adam Walsh?"

"Yeah," he told Sarah. "I killed the little boy. And I always felt kinda bad about it, too." As to why he hadn't confessed to authorities, he told her that he had talked enough about the murder of Adam Walsh and he just didn't want to talk about it anymore.

When Matthews asked Sarah if she believed it, Sarah gave a

bitter laugh. She had no doubt about it. "I know my uncle too well," she said.

The *AMW* segment also resulted in a call from a young South Florida man named Joel Cockerman. Cockerman explained that until he had seen the show, he did not realize it—but he was calling now to report that he had actually witnessed the kidnapping of Adam Walsh.

As he later explained to Joe Matthews, Cockerman, eight at the time, was in the Sears store and was the other boy playing Asteroids with Adam Walsh when the trouble started with the kids who wanted to take the controllers away. When the security guard heard the commotion, she kicked them all out of the store, Cockerman said. Shortly after they made their way outside, Cockerman's mother came and picked up him and his sister, Mia, nine at the time. Cockerman told his mother that he wanted to stay with his little friend until his parents came for him. In all likelihood, it is Cockerman and his mother and sister whom Bill Mistler had witnessed standing on the sidewalk when he viewed the same scene from his vehicle.

But his mother said it wasn't necessary for them to wait. "Look," she told Cockerman, "his dad is there now." She pointed to where a disheveled-looking man was leading Adam from the curb and into the parking lot. When they saw the photograph of Ottis Toole flash on the screen, during the *AMW* segment, Cockerman's sister clapped her hand to her mouth. "That's him," she told Cockerman. "He had more hair then, but that's him."

Neither Cockerman nor his sister had reported the incident before. They simply did not realize the importance of what they had witnessed until the program aired.

All of this seemed to Walsh and Matthews like fuel that might possibly reignite the investigation, until *AMW* producers fielded yet another call on the Monday following the segment. Just how stupid were they? a caller wanted to know. When asked what he was talking about, the caller passed along what no one at *AMW* had realized until that moment. "Ottis Toole is dead and already in the ground at Raiford Prison, down there in Florida."

As it happened, Barry Gemelli, the health services administrator at the Union Correctional Institution, had been in his office at the prison infirmary one day the previous week, completing the paperwork necessary for the transfer of patient Ottis Toole to the nearby hospital unit at Lake Butler, when he got a summons from an aide. Ottis Toole had taken a sudden turn for the worse. The aide thought Gemelli ought to have a look.

Gemelli hurried to find Toole raving in his bed, begging God to forgive the many bad things he had done in his life. Gemelli had witnessed such scenes before—he knew there were no atheists in foxholes, and it was his experience that even the most hardened of criminals find salvation as the end approaches. But Toole caught Gemelli's attention when he began to tell God about the worst thing he'd ever done. He had killed that little boy named Adam Walsh down in Broward County, Toole said, and he was very, very sorry that he did it.

After Toole had been stabilized and was transferred to the hospital unit, Gemelli notified the prison's investigative unit of what he heard Toole say about killing Adam Walsh, and a report of the matter was entered into prison files. Though Joe Matthews had urged Mark Smith to make his own foray to Lake Butler in the hopes of obtaining a deathbed confession, Smith never followed through. As far as deathbed confessions, what Gemelli heard that day would have to suffice.

On September 15, 1996, Ottis Ellwood Toole, a three-times convicted killer, died of cirrhosis of the liver at the age of forty-nine, in Lake Butler Prison Hospital. His body was unclaimed, and four days later—unbeknownst to John and Revé Walsh, Joe

Matthews, or anyone at *America's Most Wanted*—Toole was buried, in a cloth-covered casket, on prison grounds.

John Walsh was stunned by the news. Over the years, one piece of evidence after another that might have helped link Toole to the crime had somehow disappeared, and now even the perpetrator himself was no more. Some might have theorized that Toole's death would have marked the end of the matter once and for all. The guy who did it is dead. What's left?

Justice, John and Revé Walsh might have answered. And the right of any victim for the chance to know what had happened. An end to the feeling of helplessness. An end to the rage over the actions of a police force that had bungled this investigation from the beginning and now seemed intent on forgetting that the murder of Adam Walsh had ever happened.

Furthermore, the Walshes had spent fifteen years dedicating their lives to the cause of victimized children and their parents everywhere. To simply throw up their hands in the pursuit of justice for their own child's death would make a mockery of everything they'd been fighting for.

In this light, and though it might seem strange to say so, his own death might be the most provocative action a killer could take to elude responsibility for his crime. One can imagine Toole leering from his grave, "You'll never catch me now."

And were those who had pursued him for so many years any less driven, that imagined taunt might have proven true.

Even though the man himself had died, the evil that he had wrought had a way of living on. Not quite a week after Toole was buried, on September 25, 1996, an Associated Press reporter published an interview with Henry Lee Lucas in which Lucas told the writer that he was certain that Toole was responsible for the killing—he had seen blood all over the car after Toole used it. Lucas also said that a couple of months after Adam's death, he and Toole were back in South Florida one day when Ottis decided to drive him over to the Sears Mall and show him where he had picked "that kid" up. At that time, Lucas said, Toole took him through a step-by-step re-creation of the abduction and the killing.

From his cell in Texas, Lucas told a reporter that he had actually seen Adam's body in the shallow grave where Toole had buried it. "He kicked it uncovered and showed it to me," Lucas said. "I got sick about it. I said, 'Let's get the hell out of here.' I left. I never heard no more about it until '83."

That interview, startling as it was, prompted no action from law enforcement despite what seemed a compelling offer from Lucas. "If they want to talk to me and take me down there, I'll show them where it's at," he said. He described the burial site as being located in an isolated area off a freeway. "We got to an old foundation in there, either a barn or a house. There was nothing there, just a foundation. There was an old oak tree or pine tree and that's where the body was at."

At the time, Hollywood spokesperson Todd DeAngelis told reporters, "None of it is news to us," but there is no mention of Lucas's claims anywhere in the case file. Furthermore, it would mark the last significant public mention of the case for a very long time.

In fact, were it not for the simple axiom that the truth has a way of making itself known when someone wants to find it badly enough, the case of Adam Walsh—its files laid bare for anyone to see, the only suspect of substance to have surfaced in fifteen years now dead—might have also been laid to rest forever.

CHAPTER SIX

Thunder from Heaven

Q: So you admit that you're a cannibal?

A: I have eaten some parts of them. And the skin.

Q: Did you eat them raw?

A: Oh no. You can't eat that without cooking it. Are you
crazy?

—OTTIS TOOLE, WITH TEXAS RANGERS,
MARCH 24, 1984

HOLLYWOOD, FLORIDA—OCTOBER 1, 1996

In early 1996, following an acrimonious investigation into irregularities in the department's hiring practices, Hollywood police chief Richard Witt was fired by city manager Sam Finz. "Just say I'm leaving due to health reasons," was Witt's parting shot. "The city manager is sick of me."

Finz appointed deputy chief Mike Ignasiak as interim chief while a national search was conducted for a permanent replacement for Witt. On October 1, the city hired Rick Stone, a veteran cop from Dallas who had recently retired as a chief with the Wichita, Kansas, PD.

Soon after Stone came on board, in early February 1997, former chief Sam Martin died of a heart attack, and in the story that accompanied that news was a reminder of how profound the impact of one case had been: "Although his 11-year tenure as chief was marked by rapid modernization and a raising of educational standards on the force," the *Herald* reporter noted, "it was marred by a still-unsolved crime that shocked and horrified the nation: the kidnapping and murder of Adam Walsh."

Nor was Chief Stone immune from reminders that his department had failed in the matter. In September 1997, stung by charges of "laziness, stupidity and arrogance" against his department made by John Walsh in his own recently published chronicle of the case, *Tears of Rage*, Stone told reporters, "I'd like to go back and start from scratch, but none of us can do that." While he would not acknowledge that the department had made mistakes in the investigation of the case, he did assert that with contemporary technology and the "professional team I have today, it's possible things could have turned out much differently."

Stone refused to address specific blunders Walsh pointed out in the investigation of the crime, choosing instead to focus on the fact that nothing could have saved Adam's life: "The FBI didn't kill Mr. Walsh's son," Stone said. "The media didn't kill Mr. Walsh's son. And the Hollywood Police Department didn't kill Mr. Walsh's son." While true, it might have sounded a bit callous of the new chief, who was quoted in closing, "I've spoken with the few people who are still here who worked the case, and they feel they bent over backward to help the Walshes and investigate this case."

Undeniably, "bending over backwards" and "doing one's best" are admirable traits, but when it comes to assessing the quality of the investigation of a murder case, questions of capability are more germane. In any case, Stone would not last much longer at the top in Hollywood. He may have gotten along well with his own superiors, but before another year had passed he had begun to clash with the police union, and in late 1998 he was dismissed.

At that point, Finz approached Broward sheriff Ken Jenne for interim help, and Jenne assigned Major Al Lamberti as temporary chief while commissioners launched another search. Finally, in July 1999, they were successful in luring James Scarberry, assistant chief for the city of Miami Beach, to the position. Scarberry, a twenty-seven-year veteran with a reputation as a "cop's cop," was endorsed by the police union and was capable as an administrator as well.

Nor was Scarberry confronted in any meaningful way regarding the Adam Walsh case, though reminders of its enduring power continued to surface. The March 14, 2001, death of Henry Lee Lucas, serving a life term in a Texas prison, prompted a call to Hollywood PD for a comment on Lucas's onetime role as a suspect in the case, but Detective Sergeant Mark Smith, by then in charge of the department's homicide unit, reminded reporters that Lucas had been in a Maryland jail at the time of Adam's disappearance. When questioned about the status of that investigation, Smith said simply, "It's still an open case."

In July 2001 the *Miami Herald* ran a pair of lengthy articles by staff writer Daniel de Vise concerning the case, concurrent with the twentieth anniversary of Adam's disappearance. The first focused on the impact of the case on the nation's attitudes, rewriting laws and redefining relationships between adults and children. Many tragic child murders had faded from the public consciousness, de Vise wrote, "but Adam Walsh's endures."

That was likely due to the indefatigable John Walsh, de Vise opined, who included in his piece criticism directed at Walsh by some experts. "In some ways, he's taken his personal tragedy and inflicted it upon the nation," a Mount Holyoke College sociologist was quoted as saying. "He's made all kids afraid." Noted pediatrician Benjamin Spock had also criticized the practice of placing the pictures of missing children on milk cartons, said to have begun at Chicago-area Hawthorn Mellody Farms and copied by legions of others across the country, including South Florida's McArthur Dairy. While Spock understood the impetus behind such efforts, he worried that it turned breakfast into a ritual of terror for the young and impressionable.

But others, particularly the parents of children lost and missing, praised Walsh's work in redefining a nation's indifference to a significant problem. As a spokesperson for the National Center for Missing and Exploited Children put it, "Before the Adam Walsh case, it was easier to locate a stolen car than a missing child."

That first piece ended with a reprise of milestones to date in what de Vise referred to as the "missing-children movement," including the FBI database established by the Missing Children Act of 1982, and the 1984 legislation establishing the National Center for Missing and Exploited Children. Also referenced was "Megan's Law" of 1996, named after Megan Kanka, a New Jersey seven-year-old raped and murdered by a child molester who had moved into the neighborhood unbeknownst to residents. That measure required the notification of communities when a freed sex offender moves into a neighborhood.

De Vise also cited the AMBER Alert system, named for Amber Hagerman, a nine-year-old resident of Arlington, Texas, kidnapped while riding a bicycle near her home, her body later discarded in a ditch. It began as a grassroots movement in 1996 and has since been formalized nationwide, with bulletins interrupting radio programming and emblazoned on highway alert displays and elsewhere during the first hours following an abduction. Also mentioned was the Jimmy Ryce Act, the Florida measures named after a young Homestead boy taken and killed by a handyman, allowing law enforcement to publicize the identities of sexual offenders and extend the sentences of the most violent sexual predators.

On July 27, 2001, de Vise's follow-up piece centered on the

status of the long-stalled investigation. De Vise cataloged the emergence and dismissal of various individuals considered as suspects, including the quickly cleared John and Revé Walsh and Jimmy Campbell, who, de Vise pointed out, not only passed his polygraph examinations but also had an alibi. De Vise also rehashed the brief flurry caused in November 1981, when a drifter in a Broward County lockup claimed his cell-mate Edward James had confessed to the crime. As it turned out, however, James, who passed a voice stress analysis test, was proven to be at work the day of the crime.

And in 1995 there were reports in an Alabama newspaper contending that Michael Monahan, the younger son of Walsh's former boss John Monahan, might have murdered Adam Walsh as a favor to his pal Jimmy Campbell. After all, police records showed that just three days after Adam's disappearance, the younger Monahan had slashed through a door of a Broward County home with a machete during a dispute over a stolen skateboard.

But that also came to nothing. Tests on the machete revealed no evidence, and Monahan had an alibi for his whereabouts at the time of Adam's death. Once he passed a polygraph exam, police quickly cleared him as well.

Ottis Toole remained the most likely suspect, de Vise wrote, before adding the familiar saw, "But there is no hard evidence to support it." For his story, de Vise tracked down former Holly-wood police chief Richard Witt, who acknowledged in an inter-view that the department could have done a better job. Focusing on Jimmy Campbell had probably been a mistake, and, given their relative inexperience in such matters, they might have tried harder to get the FBI involved at the outset. "Within the first few months of this case," Witt told de Vise, "it was really screwed up to the point where obtaining a conviction had been compromised."

A companion piece in the *South Florida Sun-Sentinel* (Fort

Lauderdale was replaced in the paper's title in 2000) quoted Hollywood detective Mark Smith as admitting that the case was "probably too big for us at the time," and while he stopped short of criticizing those who had preceded him, he did say, "The investigation was not handled to my satisfaction. Let's just leave it at that." While Smith stoutly proclaimed that he "really believed" that his department would close the case someday, he admitted that he had not interviewed anyone concerning the matter in more than three years. Attempts to solicit comment from former detective Jack Hoffman, still on the force but scheduled for imminent retirement, went unanswered.

In the end, and following a rehash of missed opportunities and dead-end investigations, *Herald* reporter de Vise concluded, "The prospect that it will ever be solved has never looked so dim."

So it had always been at Hollywood PD, it seemed, and so it would remain for most of Chief Scarberry's tenure as well. Despite Detective Smith's upbeat contentions, five more years would pass without further pronouncements on the case, until the *Miami Herald* published yet another milestone story, this one proclaiming the twenty-fifth anniversary of failure, though this time there was a positive coda to add: "25 Years after Crime, a New Federal Law." The piece, mirrored by many in South Florida and around the nation, recounted the grim outline of Adam Walsh's kidnapping and murder, calling it "a crime that would change the nation."

Few parents would ever again leave their children alone or unattended in public places, reporters noted, pointing to such widespread practices as the "Code Adam" alerts broadcast by big-box retailers such as Walmart and Home Depot any time a child is reported lost in their stores.

In addition, laws had changed to help police mobilize and defend on behalf of children, including the new Adam Walsh Child Protection and Safety Act, legislation that President Bush was poised to sign on the twenty-fifth anniversary of the tragic event. The act mandated ten-year prison sentences for sex crimes against persons under the age of eighteen, created a uniform sex offender registry in every state, and outlawed any depiction of sexual abuse of children and its dissemination.

As to the case itself, however, commentators held out little hope for a solution. "The Walshes—and all families of missing children—never get closure," said Bill Fleisher, a Philadelphia forensic scientist and commissioner of the Vidocq Society, a cold case investigative group. Despite the likelihood that their son's murderer would never be found, Fleisher called attention to the good that had come out of personal tragedy. "They are likely the most important advocates that the country has ever had for preventing and solving crimes against children."

Still, there was always reason to hope, some opined. Detective Mark Smith again told reporters of his hopes that someone might come forward one day with information that would allow him to close the case, a prospect echoed by noted criminologist Vernon J. Geberth. "A new witness could come forward," said Geberth, former commander of the NYPD Bronx homicide unit. "A relative of the killer who knows about the crime may want to finally unburden himself."

The Walshes had survived on such hopes for a quarter of a century, of course, and while John had assumed a role as a celebrity crime fighter in his own right, the years in the spotlight had not always been kind. In 1983, just a few weeks shy of the statute of limitations in such matters, the couple had contemplated suing Sears over what they considered shortcomings in store security, including the fact that six-year-old Adam had simply been turned out on the street without so much as a "Where are your parents, little boy?"

However, attorneys for the company countered by saying that if the Walshes sued, they would parade details of Revé's affair with Jimmy Campbell in court and paint her as an unfit mother.

It wasn't really a threat, a Sears attorney told reporters—he was just trying to save the Walshes some embarrassment. Faced with such a prospect, the Walshes dropped the suit.

And in 1999, as if following the statistical mandate that more than half of the couples who lose a child to tragedy will split up (some studies have put the figure as high as 80 percent), Revé filed for divorce from John. However, there were three children still at home at the time—Meghan, then seventeen, Callahan, fifteen, and Hayden, fourteen—and four months later, Revé rescinded her petition. Eventually the couple smoothed over their difficulties and resumed a united place at the forefront of efforts on behalf of missing and exploited children.

As for Joe Matthews, his days following his retirement from Miami Beach PD remained full as well. He joined the faculty of the Center for Psychological Studies at Nova Southeastern University in the 1980s and he continued on there, lecturing on investigative interviewing and clinical polygraph. He also traveled extensively about the United States speaking at universities, police departments, and corporations on behalf of DNA LifePrint, a company formed to offer child safety programs and distribution of an inexpensive home DNA identification kit developed as a result of the difficulty he encountered in identifying "Baby Lollipops." And while he had stepped away from his interest in polygraph services and instruction, he continued as an investigative consultant to law enforcement agencies and the private sector across the United States and in Canada.

In 1999, when John Walsh asked if he might be interested in doing some investigative work for a new "cold case" component for *America's Most Wanted*, Matthews—a detective through and through—jumped at the opportunity. The producers expected that Matthews might present evidence pertaining to various cold cases and let the audience theorize for themselves what might have actually happened, but Matthews took one look at the known elements of the first case suggested to him, one involving the year-old death of a former high school wrestling champion in eastern Pennsylvania, and decided he could do better than what was proposed. After nearly two years of digging, he unearthed evidence proving the involvement of four drug-dealing University of Lock Haven football players in the killing. Having solved the first cold case investigation in the show's history, Matthews secured his career as an on-screen investigator.

From time to time during their association, both Matthews and Walsh would reflect on the one case that had baffled authorities and galled them both, and they each vowed on more than one occasion that one day they would see justice served. In fact, from the time of the airing of the first *AMW* show on Adam in 1996, Matthews had followed up every tip concerning the case submitted to the program, calls that came on the average of two or three a month. The former homicide detective traveled around Florida and as far away as the prisons of Colorado and California in search of viable leads, but nothing panned out.

And Matthews admits that if it hadn't been for the boorish reporter who buttonholed John Walsh in January 2006, just a few months before the signing of the Adam Walsh Child Protection and Safety Act, things might have stayed that way forever.

When Joe Matthews got the call from John Walsh to let him know he was coming to South Florida for an *AMW* shoot in early February 2006 and would like to get together, the detective didn't think too much about it. Matthews was still working regularly as an investigator for the show and simply assumed that Walsh wanted to run an idea for some new investigation past him.

Even when Walsh added that Revé would be with him and that they wanted to talk to him about an important matter, it still didn't register. Most of the time John traveled by himself for the shoots, but since this one was in South Florida, it made sense that Revé would come along, and Matthews, who enjoyed her company, was happy to hear it. Walsh suggested that they meet at the Atlantic Hotel on Ocean Drive in Fort Lauderdale, where the crew would be set up, and Matthews said he'd be there with bells on.

When he walked into the hotel's second-floor conference room on the afternoon of February 20, Matthews found John and Revé waiting, along with Lance Heflin, then executive producer for *AMW*, and Heflin's wife, Jan. John invited Matthews to sit and began to explain why they'd asked him there that afternoon. It was only when Revé put her hand on John's arm and cut in that Matthews began to understand that something out of the ordinary was afoot. In all his years around the Walshes, he'd found that John usually did most of the talking, while Revé listened patiently. She would have her incisive piece to add, to be sure, but it was almost always after John had led the way. As she began to speak on this day, Matthews was still trying to remember the last time he'd seen her interrupt her husband.

"Excuse me, John," Revé said, then cast an apologetic glance at Heflin's wife. "But I'd like this to be a closed meeting. I'm sorry, Jan. It's just that it's a very sensitive matter."

By the time that Heflin's wife had left the room, every cop instinct in Matthews was on alert. Again, John Walsh started his preamble. They'd been up in Washington a few days ago, working the Hill on behalf of the Adam Walsh Child Protection and Safety Act, when he'd been confronted with the question that had plagued him most of his adult life. As always, Walsh said, he realized the futility of trying to explain the million and one screwups involved . . .

Then Revé interrupted again. "Joe," she said, "we've heard the question a hundred times, and we'll hear it again on July 27 when we're back in Washington to watch the president sign the bill—'Why can't you find out who killed your son?' And you know what? I'm sick of it. Do you think I don't *want* to find out?"

There were tears in her eyes by that point, and Matthews stole a glance at John and Heflin, two guys accustomed to riding in the front seat. But they were way, way in the back right now, he thought.

"For twenty-five years, my husband has been pretty much in charge of this matter, protecting me from things. He's shielded me from the awful details, and he's minimized all the incompetence we've had to deal with from the police. He's done it because he loves me and doesn't want me to have to hear horrible things about what happened to our baby, particularly when he worries that they can't be proven. And he hasn't wanted to make me any more angry than I am already when the cops throw up their hands over and over again. But I am here to tell you that all that has come to an end." She glanced at her husband, then turned back to Matthews.

"When I left Adam that day, I told him, 'Honey, I'll be right over there in the lamp department,' and he looked back at me and said, 'I know where you'll be, Mommy.' Those are the last words I ever heard him say. That's the moment I've lived with for twenty-five years, and that is worse than anything some sick son of a bitch could ever say to me."

Revé leaned across the table toward Matthews, who was riveted in his chair. By this point, the tears were streaming down her face. "I've known you a long time, Joe, and I think you're one of the few cops ever involved in Adam's case who knows what the hell he's doing."

Matthews might have mumbled his thanks at that, but Revé held up her hand to stop him. "But it's been twenty-five years," she said, her voice rising, "and nothing has happened. I still don't know who killed my little boy. I want *you* to investigate. I want to know every detail. I want to know who did what and who didn't do what."

She was wiping away tears with the heels of both hands now. "This has nothing to do with the show. For John and me, for our sake as parents, I want you to prove once and for all who killed our son. We *think* we know who did it, but we want you to *prove* it. And we want the cops to clear this case. Until that happens, we won't have peace. It doesn't matter that Ottis Toole is dead. He died without ever being charged, and as far as John and I are concerned that's the same thing as going free. Our baby was murdered, and someone has to be held accountable. That's not too hard to understand, is it?"

She paused, still wiping at her tears, and fixed Matthews with an even gaze. "Joe, will you do this for me?"

At this point, everyone in the room was choked up. John Walsh leaned to comfort his sobbing wife, and Matthews struggled to get his voice under control. He'd spent his whole life trying to bring criminals to justice, and he knew exactly how Revé felt. Her words spoke to the core of his reason for being.

"I'm honored that you'd even ask," he told Revé quietly. He would start immediately. He would investigate as he would were he a police officer assigned to a cold case, and he would bring to the job all that he had in him. He couldn't predict the outcome, of course—no one could—but at least this time there'd be no one there to throw him off the case.

HOLLYWOOD, FLORIDA—FEBRUARY 21, 2006

The resurrection of the Adam Walsh case had never been a matter high on Hollywood police chief James Scarberry's priority list. Still, Scarberry knew that Matthews had put in a good word on his behalf with the Hollywood police union while he was being considered for the job, and he was also well aware of the blemish the high-profile matter had left on the record of his new department. Furthermore, Scarberry knew from his time in Miami Beach that Matthews was an accomplished cop—whatever the public thought, you didn't get to be Officer of the Year by accident. Thus, when Matthews showed up in his office on

February 21, 2006, some five and a half years after he'd taken over the reins in Hollywood, Scarberry knew enough to listen.

He was there for important reasons, Matthews told Scarberry, and then got quickly to the point. Almost twenty-five years had passed since Adam Walsh went missing, and were he still alive, he would have been looking forward to celebrating his thirty-second birthday. Nearly ten years had passed since the record of the failed investigation in his abduction and murder had been made public—effectively putting an end to its investigation—and nearly ten years had passed since the only viable suspect ever identified had died while imprisoned for other killings. There'd been any number of lurid stories concerning the disappearances and deaths of children splashed across the pages of the newspapers of the nation and the region—those of Jimmy Ryce and Shannon Melendi, a young South Florida woman kidnapped and slain by a softball umpire, among them.

There might even be a few people who'd forgotten all about Adam Walsh, just one more unfortunate kid in what had become a long line of them. But Adam Walsh was really the first kid in that line, Matthews pointed out. Before Adam, there really wasn't much attention paid to the problem of missing and endangered children. And now, due in large part to the efforts of Adam's parents, John and Revé Walsh, the issue had become one of the most important priorities of law enforcement and society as a whole.

Yet for all that John and Revé had accomplished, *they* had certainly not forgotten about Adam. Furthermore, as every new day dawned, they thought about the son whom they had so tragically lost, and they were reminded that his killer had yet to be brought to justice. Matthews recounted the recent incident in Washington, where John Walsh was confronted by a reporter who wanted to know if it ever "bothered" him that he had been unable to find the killer of his own son.

If that reporter had any idea what John Walsh had gone

through, Matthews reminded Chief Scarberry, he would have been running for the doorway before he finished his question. It was true that Walsh had heard such things before, and though he had placed his trust in the Hollywood PD for many years, he felt a certain amount of guilt that he hadn't done more to move the investigation forward earlier. He'd even felt bad that the baseless innuendo regarding his lifestyle and his ties to organized crime might have somehow affected the conduct of the case. And certainly there was a point to the reporter's question, offensive as it was. John Walsh had helped to apprehend a lot of bad guys in his time, but the worst one of all had gone scot-free.

"That's why I'm here today," Matthews told Scarberry. He'd been asked by John and Revé Walsh to reopen the case and to conduct a complete, independent investigation to prove once and for all who had kidnapped and murdered their son. And Matthews—who was doing this as a favor to people he cared about, and for the sake of justice—was asking for Scarberry's help. The files had been opened to every reporter under the sun ten years ago, Matthews pointed out, though the motivations of those who wanted them opened were somewhat dubious and their abilities to evaluate what they were looking at just as questionable.

Matthews was an experienced investigator with a single aim in mind: to reexamine files and statements, reevaluate evidence, and reinterview witnesses, and, where new leads presented themselves, to follow them wherever they might go. As Scarberry well knew, Matthews had solved any number of cases thought to be unsolvable before. Surely, said Matthews—who had not come to take no for an answer—it was time to give him his final shot. John and Revé and Adam Walsh deserved that much, at least.

Scarberry heard Matthews out, then sat back in his chair, considering things. He glanced away for a moment, then turned back to Matthews and gave his okay. If Matthews thought he could manage to prove anything after all these years, who was Scarberry or his department to stand in the way?

He would have access to everything in the department's files, Scarberry told him. And he further assured Matthews that now-captain Mark Smith, the detective who had opened the cold case investigation with Matthews back in 1995, would provide whatever help he could. Godspeed and good luck.

The promise of "help" from Mark Smith was a favor that Matthews could have just as well done without, he thought, but at least this time there was no selective withholding of files.

The transfer of all case file documentation, including myriad reports, statements, memos, photos, and interviews—including those filmed and on CD—began the following day, February 22, 2006. Day after day, Matthews (convinced by their disarray that he was the first to do so) combed through the voluminous files, refreshing himself on details, cataloging crucial information and evidence, building for the first time a comprehensive chronology of events and identifying key witnesses who had never been interviewed, or who were never asked the necessary questions in the first place.

On Thursday, February 23, Matthews—backed by a film crew *AMW*'s Lance Heflin had been happy to provide for the purposes of documentation—interviewed retired Hollywood detective Larry Hoisington regarding the things Ottis Toole had told him on October 21, 1981, when Hoisington had been the driver for the team taking Toole around to the various scenes connected to the crime. Hoisington told Matthews that on that day, while Hoffman and others were busy with other things, Toole had given him a complete and independent confession to the crime, the gruesome details of which he recounted for Matthews. Hoisington also recounted Hoffman's treatment of Toole and repeated what he'd told Leroy Hessler year before: "I'm surprised Toole cooperated at all."

Hoisington reiterated his conversation with Deputy Chief Hessler at the time and recounted Hessler's response that Hoisington simply tell Hoffman about it. Matthews pointed to the files, shaking his head. Despite Hoffman's assurances that he would include what Hoisington told him in his report, no such mention of Toole's confession to Hoisington existed there.

On Saturday, February 25, Matthews interviewed Arlene Mayer, who had identified Ottis Toole as the man who accosted her and her daughter Heidi at a Hollywood Kmart store two days prior to Adam's abduction. They both recalled the incident vividly and confirmed that they had identified Toole from a lineup of photographs shown them by Hollywood police. For all the good it did, Matthews thought. Had Hoffman bothered to confirm Toole's encounter with the Mayers when he had the chance, all this could have very likely been concluded back in 1983.

The likely reason why Hollywood police had placed so little credence in what the Mayers had told them had to do with the timing, Matthews understood. Arlene had been sure that their trip to Kmart to place on a Friday or a Saturday night because those were the only nights they ever went shopping. But the fact that her husband wouldn't go into the store with them because he had just gotten off work suggested to detectives that it had very likely been a Friday night when the Mayers had their frightening encounter. That, of course, would have ruled Toole out of the scenario, since he would have been on a bus somewhere between Newport News and Jacksonville at the time.

However, Matthews had since spoken with Susan Schindehette, coauthor of John Walsh's *Tears of Rage*. She'd wondered about that seeming inconsistency, too, she told Matthews, until she asked Wayne Mayer a simple question, one that the detectives never had. Did he ever work at his construction job on Saturdays? "Oh, sure," Wayne told her. "All the time."

The simple questions, Matthews thought to himself, as he finished up his notes on the Mayers. When you forget to ask them during an investigation, that's when things go south.

On the following Tuesday, February 28, Matthews got in touch with prison hospital administrator Barry Gemelli, who confirmed that he had overheard the unsolicited confession to the crime by Ottis Toole as he was lying on his deathbed. The two made arrangements to meet the following week.

In the meantime, Matthews conducted an interview with Kathy Shaffer, the Sears security guard who had ordered Adam Walsh out of the store that day. "His mom showed me two pictures of Adam that day," Shaffer told Matthews, "and I really wasn't sure about the first one. But then she made me look at another one, and I knew right then. I was chilled. One hundred and ten percent, I knew it was him."

But she had lied to Revé that day and said she didn't recognize Adam because she was just seventeen, and she was scared. She thought Revé would get mad at her for throwing Adam out of the store, Shaffer said, and besides, at first she thought he was just some kid wandering around and he was going to turn up just fine without any help from her.

By the time detectives arrived and were beginning to question her, she realized the enormity of what had happened. This child had really, truly disappeared. She couldn't own up to what she had done by then, she said to Matthews. She had started to feel truly responsible for Adam's disappearance. Eventually she came to feel responsible for his death.

"I still do," she told Matthews, tearfully. "Not a day has gone by in twenty-five years that I haven't thought about it. If I had just said, 'Where's your mama?' he might still be here today." She had to pause to gather herself before she could get her last words out, and even then Matthews had to ask her to repeat them. "I pray every night that his mom and dad will forgive me."

Matthews tried to console Shaffer, but he felt like the little Dutch boy his mother used to tell him about, only this wasn't some storybook problem where you could just plug your finger in the leak and wait for help to arrive. Woulda, coulda, shoulda. Once upon a time, what was so terrible about letting your kid play a video game while you walked fifty feet away to buy a frigging lamp? And yet Revé Walsh had been tying herself in knots ever since, thinking *she* was somehow responsible for what had happened. Or how about her husband John, who put the whole idea of going to Sears in her head in the first place—"Hey, honey, we can save a couple of bucks if we just act now"?

Or how about Joe Matthews, for that matter? Maybe if he had simply cold-cocked Jack Hoffman the first time the know-it-all SOB had insulted him, the guy would have ended up in the hospital and somebody else would have taken over the case. Which of course wouldn't have changed anything, really, because Adam Walsh would still have been dead.

The fact is that one person, and one person only, was responsible for what had happened to Adam. One person had taken that little boy and done unspeakable things to him, and Matthews was going to prove who that person was, because, quite frankly, that is the only way he knew how to give meaning to his life.

On Tuesday, March 14, Matthews met with Barry Gemelli, the former health service administrator at the Union Correctional Institution. Gemelli, himself suffering from advanced leukemia, recounted the details of the confession he heard from Toole just before he died, and confirmed that he had followed up with the criminal investigation unit at the facility both verbally and with a follow-up written report. Gemelli told Matthews that Toole seemed well aware that he was dying. He was sad and scared, and there seemed to Gemelli no reason on earth for the man to be lying. He had done something particularly terrible, and he wanted to get it off his chest. As far as Matthews was concerned, Gemelli was only underscoring what Toole had told officers when he originally confessed in 1983: "It was the youngest person I ever killed and I feel bad about it." Even ghouls sometimes feel a pang of conscience, he thought.

And then, on the following day, Wednesday, March 15, Matthews conducted an interview that would cast new light on a matter that had seemed to color Ottis Toole's confessions so profoundly. Despite the fact that Toole had divulged details of the crime that only Hoffman and his fellow detectives could have known at the time, including the place where he had disposed of Adam's head, Hoffman had stuck to his accusations that Detective Buddy Terry had struck a book deal with Toole and was feeding him privileged information.

However, in the course of going back through Toole's movements in Jacksonville, prior to and just after the time of the crime, Matthews had occasion to speak with John Reaves Jr., son of the owner of Reaves Roofing at the time. Yes, he'd verified all those dates pertaining to Ottis Toole's work history at the company, Reaves told Matthews. And he also confirmed that his aunt Faye McNett had sold Toole the Cadillac, later repossessing it when Toole couldn't keep up the payments. For a time, though, Toole had used it as his work vehicle, and usually kept it full of rakes and shovels and other gardening-type tools. Toole didn't like heights, Reaves explained, so he was always doing cleanup and other such work around the job sites.

Maybe he didn't like to climb because of his eyes, Reaves theorized. Toole would be looking at you and suddenly one eye would go floating in another direction, Reaves said, accounting for the odd-looking expression that other witnesses had noted.

All that was interesting enough, but it wasn't until Matthews asked the obvious question that Reaves dropped his own bombshell. Did he have any knowledge of Toole's involvement in the abduction and murder of Adam Walsh? Matthews wanted to know.

Actually, he did, Reaves responded. In fact, Toole had admitted the whole thing to him in great detail, during a visit they'd had in the Duval County Jail. Ottis had told him he'd taken the kid from a store, though he didn't mention Sears. It was down around Miami, somewhere, Reaves remembered Ottis saying, and that while he was driving them back to Jacksonville, the kid wouldn't stop crying. Ottis hit him hard in the stomach, and when the kid starting gasping for air, Ottis said he put his hands around his neck and choked him until he was dead. Then Ottis said he cut his head off and threw it, or the body, into a canal. There was a lot of blood in the Cadillac as a result, Ottis told him.

And why was it that Reaves had not told detectives this back in 1983 when they questioned him? Matthews asked. Well, because they never asked, Reaves replied. He and Ottis had their conversation about the killing a few days after the detectives had called about the dates of Toole's employment, Reaves said, and he'd just never seen the point of calling the cops back on his own.

And besides, there was the matter of the book contract that he and Ottis had worked out, Reaves added.

Really? Matthews replied, blandly, trying to conceal his eagerness. Just what book contract was Reaves talking about?

It took Reaves, who was undergoing treatment for lymph node and prostate cancer, a bit of time to find the document in his files, but finally he came up with a copy for Matthews. Dated October 29, 1983, shortly after Ottis made his first confessions to detectives from four separate jurisdictions (Steve Kendrick of Brevard County, Jay Via from Louisiana, Buddy Terry of Jacksonville, and Jack Hoffman from Hollywood), the agreement gave John Reaves Jr. the exclusive rights to any film and book adaptation of the "life and deeds of Toole." Ottis and Reaves would split any profits fifty-fifty, the contract stipulated, and even if something happened to Toole, his surviving brothers and sisters would reap the rewards. In return for affixing his signature at the end of the document, Toole received an immediate advance against earnings of $10.

So indeed there had been a book contract, Matthews realized. Reaves was just a businessman who'd recognized a good possibility when he'd seen one.

Matthews would never know why Hoffman was so reluctant to pursue Ottis Toole, but if it truly was his belief that Buddy Terry had struck a book deal with the killer, what a shame it was that he'd never taken the trouble to have a follow-up conversation with John Reaves Jr. It would have dispensed with the chief ostensible reason why Hollywood PD and others in law enforcement and the media were so reluctant to believe Toole's account of the killing, and it very possibly could have changed the course of the investigation.

On the following day, March 16, 2006, Matthews interviewed Sarah Patterson, the woman who called *America's Most Wanted* following the 1996 segment on Adam, indentifying herself as Toole's niece and claiming that he had confessed the killing to her. Patterson, the last person to visit Toole in prison before his death, reiterated her account of her uncle's confession during that visit. Nothing had changed in the ten years that had passed, she said. There was no doubt in her mind that he had done exactly what he said he did.

She did not mean to be unfaithful to her uncle, who had always been good to her, but Patterson simply felt that after Ottis's mother died, he lost what tenuous grip he might have had on self-control. "When Grandma Sarah died," Patterson said, "this whole family went to hell."

There were some good moments, however. During his stay with her just prior to her wedding years ago, he had offered to bake a cake for the occasion, but then he'd dropped it right before the reception. Uncle Ottis had spent his last $20 to buy her another, she recalled. But right was right, and the parents of that poor boy down in Hollywood deserved to know the truth.

At the end of her interview with Matthews, Patterson said she wanted him to have something her uncle had given her the last day they'd talked. She handed over a sheet of paper and Matthews found himself studying a multicolored drawing signed by Toole.

It was a clown's face, Patterson said, and a clown's face should make you happy. But this clown's face haunted her. Looking at its dark-circled, bulging eyes and its protruding tongue reminded her of what evil her uncle did by taking the life of Adam Walsh. As much as she had once loved her Uncle Ottis, she now wanted only to forget him.

JACKSONVILLE, FLORIDA—MARCH 17, 2006

The day after his interview with Sarah Patterson, Matthews interviewed retired Jacksonville sheriff's detective Jesse "Buddy" Terry. Terry had known Ottis Toole for nearly twenty years prior to his arrest for the murder of George Sonnenberg, Terry told Matthews. A lot of cops knew Ottis Toole—he had been a fringe dweller in Jacksonville from the time he was a kid. As an adult, Toole—openly gay, and prone to dressing in drag—had been picked up several times for prostitution and various petty offenses, and was a suspected arsonist as well. No one, however, made him for a serial killer until James Redwine, the delinquent son of Toole's landlady, fingered Toole in the arson-murder of George Sonnenberg, and Toole began to talk.

Terry recounted to Matthews the details of the various interviews he had witnessed where Toole confessed to the abduction and murder of Adam Walsh, and went back over the visit he'd made to South Florida, accompanying Toole on his tour of the crime scenes. From the outset, Terry said, he was not sure why Detective Hoffman was so reluctant to view Toole's confession as truthful, for it seemed clear to every other detective who'd been involved that Toole knew things that only Adam's killer could possibly have known.

As to Hoffman's accusations that he had cut a book deal

with Toole, Terry was comforted to hear what Matthews had discovered about the real partners in that undertaking, but he was still indignant. He felt that he'd been used as a scapegoat in the matter, Terry said—there was so much public outcry at the lack of progress in the case that his own department was happy to let Hoffman's claims go unopposed. Though an internal affairs investigation eventually cleared Terry of Hoffman's allegations, and the detective was offered his old job back, the department never issued a formal statement on the matter. To Terry, it seemed that the Jacksonville Sheriff's Office was perfectly willing to have it seem as if he had manufactured Ottis Toole's various confessions out of whole cloth.

Yes, practically speaking, the investigation was in the hands of Jack Hoffman and Hollywood PD, but if his own superiors had been more forceful in refuting Hoffman's trumped-up charges, more attention might have been given to Toole's statements that clearly proved his involvement in the crime.

To that day, there remained no doubt in Terry's mind that Toole was responsible. "He even drew us a little stick-figure diagram of the area where the killing took place and how he stood over Adam with his machete to cut his head off," Terry told Matthews. Hoffman took the diagram away with him, Terry said, but as Matthews discovered, no such drawing had found its way into the case file. Somehow, he was not surprised.

When he had concluded his interview with Detective Terry, Matthews once again pulled out copies of the various interviews that Jack Hoffman had conducted with Toole at the Duval County Jail: the first had taken place just before midnight on Wednesday, October 20, 1983, and during that conversation Toole had described the Cadillac he was driving, the Sears store from which he took Adam, and the force he employed in rendering Adam unconscious. He had used a "bayonet" to decapitate Adam, Toole told Hoffman, and during that interview, he also claimed that Henry Lee Lucas was present during the abduction and killing, and that Lucas had sex with the decapitated head.

In the course of his statement, Toole told Hoffman that he had been "window shopping" in the mall before he made his way to the Sears store and remembered looking at some of the wigs displayed in a nearby shop. Broward County state attorney's investigator Phil Mundy had later ascertained that there was indeed a wig store operating in the Sears Mall at the time of Adam's abduction. It might have seemed an inconsequential detail, but Matthews knew there had been no mention of "wig shops" in any of the press coverage of the case. How could Toole—cross-dresser and wig fancier that he was—have known there was a wig shop in that mall unless he'd been there and seen it with his own eyes?

When Hoffman and his partner Hickman left the room following that first interview, Detective Terry had confronted Toole about his contention that Henry Lee Lucas had taken part in the crime. Toole admitted lying about that and asked to speak with Hoffman and Hickman again to clarify the matter. Shortly after midnight, the Hollywood detectives took their second statement from Toole, during which he once again described using "four or five" blows to sever Adam's head from his body, though in this interview Detective Hoffman began to refer to the weapon as a machete instead of a bayonet. For a second time, then, Matthews noted, Toole had confirmed detailed autopsy findings that had not been made public. And later, when Toole was trying to broker his way out of Raiford, his jailhouse lawyer Gerald Schaefer would tell Broward County investigators that Toole had used *both* a bayonet and a machete in the murder.

Following those statements, on Friday, October 21, Hoffman flew with Toole to South Florida, where Toole guided detectives to the Hollywood Sears store where Adam was taken, and then to the spot near mile marker 126 on Florida's Turnpike where he said he had decapitated and dismembered Adam. Finally, he identified the canal at mile marker 130 as the spot where he disposed of Adam's head. At the time, Matthews noted, the only person in the party who knew Toole had ID'd the very place where fishermen had found the severed head was Jack Hoffman.

It could have been the end of the matter then and there, Matthews thought, but it was not to be. On the following Wednesday, October 26, Hoffman returned to Jacksonville to take a fourth statement from Toole, ostensibly to clarify the suspect's movements from the time he left the hospital in Newport News, Virginia, and his arrival at the Sears store in South Florida shortly thereafter. It was during that fourth statement that Toole broke down and told Hoffman, "I'm not really sure that I really did kill Adam Walsh."

It occurred to Matthews that Hoffman might well have responded by asking Toole how he could have known, for instance, where Adam's head was discarded or how many blows it took to sever his head from his body, but he did not. Instead, Hoffman concluded his interview and walked out, leaving Buddy Terry to calm Toole down.

Not fifteen minutes later, Toole asked Hoffman to return so that he could tell the truth. Indeed, he had committed the crime, he assured Hoffman. He'd simply been upset there a few minutes ago: "I couldn't get my head together," he said. In this fifth statement, Toole went once more through a detailed account of the crime, including a graphic description of his disposal of Adam's head. After he'd driven north for five or ten minutes following the dismemberment, Toole said, he pulled off the turnpike again:

"I seen a little . . . a little bridge down there and I walked down there and I throwed it in, throwed it in the water."

And what happened next? Hoffman wanted to know. He probably meant to ask what Toole did after he threw the head in the water.

But Toole took Hoffman quite literally. The head sank, he said, simply.

There was a pause. "You're positive about that?" Hoffman asked.

"Positive." Toole replied. And shortly thereafter, the interview was concluded.

Matthews tossed the transcript down on his desk, shaking his head. That exchange might as well have been typed in red, with double underlining. If a cop needed any further assurance that Toole had done just what he said he'd done, there it was on the page before him.

"*It sank,*" Matthews repeated. Yes, that's exactly what would have happened. Adam's head would have hit the water and sunk like a stone. If Toole had been making his story up, he'd have probably said something like, "It went floating off," or "It went under for a second and then it bobbed right back up."

Matthews had investigated a murder case once and had known something was wrong from the moment he heard the tape of the 911 call. "Help. I think my husband's dead. He's just floating there facedown in the pool." *Yeah? Not unless he was lying on the bottom for a couple of days first, lady. Dead bodies—and body parts—hit the water and go down like lead. After a couple of days and enough decomposition, gases form in cavities and then gruesome things float to the surface.*

Nor were such oversights the only oddities Matthews found during his examination of Hoffman's records. Along with the failure to include Toole's drawing in the case file and the failure to request that the Walshes come in to identify the items of clothing found during the search of Toole's mother's yard, Matthews discovered another startling inconsistency.

As Matthews worked his way through the case documentation, he eventually came to a mention of the polygraph examination that he had administered to Jimmy Campbell during the early hours of August 8, 1981. Following that examination Matthews had his first conversation with Detective Hoffman regarding his polygraph examination of Campbell. Prior to that conversation, Hoffman had not even known Campbell's name, but within moments, the Hollywood detective was declaring his virtual certainty that Campbell was the perpetrator. And following the heated exchange with Detective Matthews, Hoffman tracked down and interviewed Campbell as to his alibi for the time of the kidnapping.

All that was clear in Matthews's memory. However, as he studied Hoffman's files more carefully, Matthews discovered something dumbfounding: Hoffman had filed a report claiming that he had interviewed Jimmy Campbell on Friday, August 7—*the day before* Matthews had alerted Hoffman to Campbell's very existence. Nor was there mention of the fact that Matthews had already conducted a polygraph examination that cleared Campbell of any guilty knowledge concerning the crime. The report suggested that Hoffman had tracked down Jimmy Campbell on his own, and *then* ordered Matthews to call Campbell in for a polygraph exam the following week.

Furthermore, while Hoffman had assiduously recorded all other interviews he conducted in the course of his investigation, the one with Campbell was not recorded. That was for one simple reason, Matthews theorized: the date recorded on the tape would have determined when the interview actually took place. Most disturbing to Matthews, however, was a supplemental report that Hoffman filed on August 8, where he falsely stated that the results of Matthews's polygraph examination of Campbell were "inconclusive."

To Matthews, all this was evidence that from the beginning Hoffman had seen Jimmy Campbell as the perfect suspect and had set about constructing a scenario where he would seem a supersleuth for having deduced things about the case that no one else had. By switching the dates of his interview with Campbell,

Hoffman made it seem that he had smoked Campbell out, then ordered Matthews to administer a test that incriminated him.

Later that evening, as Matthews made a visit to the unmarked grave site of Toole's mother, a call came from Vinetta Syphurs, Toole's sister and the owner of the Japanese bayonet that Broward County detectives had questioned her about a decade before. Matthews had left a message for her earlier that day that he was hoping to talk with her about the matter.

She was suffering from cancer, Vinetta told Matthews—in fact she was dying. Her husband Rodney had recently died as well, and somehow the timing of Matthews's phone call, after all this time, suggested to her that it was a message from the grave, her Rodney suggesting that she tell police the truth about the things she knew.

She told Matthews that she and Ottis were the closest of all the nine children, especially after their mother died, and that he often confided to her about some of the things he'd done. She had visited Ottis in prison—a fact noted by Toole in one of his letters to John Reaves Jr.—and during that visit he told her, without expressing remorse, that he had murdered Adam Walsh. This confession had so disgusted her that she disowned her brother and refused to visit or correspond afterward. She had lied to Broward detectives when she'd told them she had that bayonet mounted above her mantel, she told Matthews. She wasn't even sure where it had come from or when she got it. It had just been stuck on a shelf somewhere.

If Ottis had taken the bayonet and replaced it some time later on, she would have never known. She'd been trying to protect her brother at the time she spoke to detectives, but when she asked him point-blank and he admitted the killing, she'd been sickened. She wanted Matthews to pass on what she'd told him to the Walshes. She was sorry she had not come forward sooner, but now she felt at peace.

.   .   .

It was a score for Matthews, one more suggestion that the original investigators had been more intent on proving Ottis Toole's innocence than his guilt, but he would have to keep going until he'd picked through the case file from top to bottom and—if possible—found that elusive piece of evidence that had so consumed his predecessors.

On Saturday, March 18, Matthews met with retired Brevard County sheriff deputy Steve Kendrick, the first police officer to whom Toole had confessed. Kendrick took Matthews back through his initial interview with Toole and the chance confusion with Broward County that had set twenty-five years of history into motion.

Thank God the dumb bastard couldn't spell, Kendrick said, or else the whole thing might never have come out. When Matthews reminded him that actually the thing had not yet "come out," Kendrick nodded in commiseration. Still there was not a doubt in his mind. Toole wasn't the kind of guy who would have seen any value in confessing to such an awful thing unbidden. He'd confessed the crime to him twice, offering details that Kendrick realized—once the Hollywood police finally shared their information with him—only the killer could have known at the time.

In the weeks that followed, Matthews continued to pore through the voluminous file, and in late May he began to work back through an analysis of the physical evidence. In 1986, while still with the Miami Beach Police, Matthews had supervised the investigation of a case that stymied detectives until he ordered a tool marking analysis comparing a knife found in possession of a suspect and the wound in the deceased's chest. As a result, the killer was convicted, among the first to be solved by such means.

Accordingly, on Thursday, May 25, he coordinated a reexamination of Adam's skull for tool markings by the Miami Dade crime lab and the Broward County medical examiner's office.

Once again, however, though the markings showed "some similarities," the results were inconclusive.

That same day, Matthews asked that Hollywood Police turn over certain evidence that it appeared they had not yet shared with him: Matthews wanted to examine copies of the photos taken by the FDLE, specifically those of the search and analysis of Ottis Toole's Cadillac. Sergeant Lyle Bean, the Hollywood officer in charge of the file, checked, but then told Matthews that there were no such photos to be found.

Well, Matthews told Bean, FDLE reports indicated that five rolls of film had been shot documenting the search. If in fact the photos were not in Hollywood's files, perhaps Bean would be willing to call the FDLE and find out what had happened to them.

Bean told Matthews he would place the call, and Matthews waited a week to follow up. On June 1, he called back. "They haven't found them yet, but they're still looking," Bean said.

On June 19, Matthews placed yet another call to Bean, asking for an update on the status of those misplaced photographs. The FDLE had told him that no such photos existed in their files, Bean said.

Matthews hung up and sat pondering the situation for a moment. Twenty-three years had passed. Witnesses had died, the likely killer of Adam Walsh had died, and a great deal of evidence had disappeared as well. If the bloody carpet samples had vanished, along with the 4,200-pound automobile from which they'd come, why couldn't five rolls worth of photographs have vaporized as well? Still, Matthews was not the sort to leave stones unturned. If you were a good cop, you turned them all over. And sometimes, if you were lucky, you found exactly what you were looking for.

He reached for the phone then and called the FDLE crime lab himself. He'd have to speak to someone in the photo lab, a voice told him, and Matthews waited patiently while he was transferred. When an attendant answered, he explained that he was simply following up on the request of Sergeant Bean from Hollywood PD. Were they absolutely certain that no copies of the photographs taken of Ottis Toole's Cadillac back in 1983 existed in their files?

There was a pause on the other end. No one in the office seemed to know what Matthews was talking about. There'd been no request for any photos from anyone at Hollywood PD.

Matthews nodded and hung up. He'd played this game before. Except the last time around, the joker on the other side of the table had been a guy named Jack Hoffman.

In the end, Matthews spoke to an FDLE public information officer, Sharon Gogerty, who checked the files in reference to Hollywood PD case #81-56073. Yes, she told Matthews, they had ninety-eight photo negatives pertaining to the processing of suspect Ottis Toole's vehicle.

Well then, Matthews asked, would it be possible for him to obtain copies of the prints? Gogerty paused, then said a surprising thing. There were no prints, she told Matthews. The film had been processed into negatives for the purposes of storage—standard operating procedure at FDLE—but never in twenty-three years had any prints been developed.

Matthews paused. In other words, he asked, no detective has ever requested or looked at the photos taken of Ottis Toole's Cadillac?

"That would seem to be the case," Gogerty replied brightly. "But you can be the first."

On Tuesday, June 27, 2006, an FDLE regional legal adviser, John Kenner, sent ninety-eight photographs copied from lab case file 831043357 to Matthews at *America's Most Wanted*, where staffers in turn forwarded them to his offices in Davie, a few miles northwest of Hollywood. Matthews, who had come in early that Wednesday to work on his report, glanced up as his longtime secretary Mary Alvarez came through his door with a hefty UPS envelope in hand. "Were you expecting something in the overnight?" she asked.

Indeed he was, Matthews assured her. He set his coffee aside and quickly spread out the thick sheaf of three-by-five-inch prints on his desk, trying all the while to keep his expectations under control. He was excited to have unearthed the photographs, but he had suffered his share of setbacks on this case before—in all honesty, it wouldn't have surprised him to find he'd been sent a series of shots of an FDLE employee's birthday party.

This time, though, he'd hit pay dirt. He was looking at the outset for any shots of the rear bumper of the Cadillac. When he quickly found three that depicted the sizable dent described by both William Mistler and Bobby Lee Jones, Toole's coworker from Jacksonville, Matthews nodded with satisfaction. It was confirmation that indeed it was Toole's car that Mistler had seen in the Sears parking lot the day that Adam had been taken.

"Good, good, good" is Matthews' characteristic way of expressing enthusiasm, and that is what he murmured as he turned to see what other treasures might have come his way. There were other shots of the Cadillac's exterior, dashboard, and seats, but he expected nothing of real import there. Of far more interest were a series of dark shots that resembled negatives, dotted here and there by objects that glowed a psychedelic blue.

In fact, these were a set of specially processed shots taken by FDLE crime scene investigators using luminol technology to identify or enhance the presence of blood traces on items of evidence. In this process, ordinary photographs are taken of objects, then chemicals that become luminescent when in contact with blood are applied to those objects, and the photographs taken again. The second series of photos are shot in darkness, with a wide aperture setting and the lens open for a minute or more. The only images that appear are special luminescent markers that orient the viewer and any part of the item where blood residue—invisible to the naked eye—might exist. Anything that retains the presence of blood will show up in a ghostly metallic blue.

Matthews first went about arranging a comparison of a set of photos taken of the front driver's-side floorboards. Given all the disappointments of the past quarter-century, he expected little. But now he sat staring in disbelief at what was laid out before him.

The pictures of the front floorboard carpeting shot in ordinary light showed nothing beyond the ordinary dirt and dings he might expect, except for the presence of the orienting marker the technician had placed along the edge of the carpet. But as Matthews placed the corresponding luminol-enhanced shot alongside the first, he could hear Ottis Toole's reply to Jack Hoffman during his confession of October 20, 1983, ringing in his mind:

> *Hoffman:* Did you get blood all over you from the child?
> *Toole:* I got it on my shoes. I throwed my shoes away too, and I put another pair of shoes on.

So you did, Matthews murmured to himself, so you damned well did. There in the photograph before him glowed a blood-engendered image of a pair of shoeprints firmly planted on the driver's floorboards.

Matthews set those images aside, well aware of the significance of the discovery. At long last, here was physical evidence tying Ottis Toole to the crime.

He set aside the images of the bloody footprints, and turned to another set of prints of the machete that Detective Terry had confiscated from Toole's car-dealer associate in Jacksonville. In one of his confessions, Toole had mentioned wrapping tape around the handle of his machete to keep from getting blisters, and the luminol shot of the machete with its taped-up handle showed nothing.

But in a second image, taken after the tape had been removed from its handle, the wooden grips of the blade glowed from blood as if radioactive. Matthews studied the image, compared the location of the marker in the luminol image with that in the original again, then exhaled deeply and leaned back in his chair. There before him was a photograph of Ottis Toole's machete, taken from his car, its handle soaked in blood.

Matthews turned back to what was left of the photographs, then, riffling through a set taken from the rear floorboards. At first he saw nothing of interest, just some streaky, vague imagery, nothing to compare with that bold set of footprints or that pulsing machete handle; then he stopped himself and looked closer at the photograph in his hand.

He studied the image for a moment, glanced away, then turned to look closely again, not sure whether to trust his eyes. He double-checked the markers to be certain—but indeed he was looking at a shot of the carpet directly behind the driver's seat. The image taken in ordinary light revealed nothing. But as to the luminol-enhanced image . . .

In all his years as a cop, Matthews had never seen anything like it—though having been raised as a Catholic, he was more than familiar with similar images preserved by church fathers over the centuries. What he was looking at chilled him—but there was more to the feeling than that. From this image there emanated reassurance, and a strange kind of peace, and the blessed feeling that twenty-six years of effort had not gone in vain.

Unless he was just finding images in clouds, that is.

He tucked the photographs into a folder and hurried out of his office with a distracted wave for Mary. Once in his car, he paused to dial his old friend Pat Franklin, also a former Miami Beach detective and now a private investigator with his own firm. The two of them often met at a cigar bar far north on Biscayne Boulevard for a smoke and a coffee on the way home from their respective offices, but Joe was an hour or more ahead of the usual curve.

"Something wrong?" Franklin asked when he picked up. He'd recognized who it was from the caller ID. Neither one of them bothered with unnecessary pleasantries anymore.

"You gotta meet me right now," he told Franklin.

"It's a little early," Franklin said.

"I'm not kidding," Matthews said. "I need you to see something."

There was a pause, and some rustling of papers. "Give me fifteen minutes," Franklin said.

When he caught sight of his still-trim friend entering the bar, Matthews felt the urgency rising in him again. He hadn't dared to look at the photograph since he'd left his office.

"Take a look at this," he said, thrusting the folder at Franklin.

Franklin smiled at him quizzically. "Good to see you, too," he said, opening the folder. He glanced at the photo, then looked back at Matthews. "The light's for shit in here." He stepped closer to the window in the front of the place and Matthews tagged along after him.

Franklin studied the photo for a moment and Matthews watched his face. Franklin was well aware of what he was working on, and knew the last detail of every roadblock and frustration he'd encountered over all the years. Finally Franklin closed the folder and handed it back. They'd both learned how to play poker as cops. If Franklin didn't want you to know what he was thinking, you could beat your brains out wondering.

"You weren't going to ask me what I see there, were you?"

Matthews gave him something like a shrug. "I wasn't sure, that's all."

Franklin nodded. He might have smiled, except for the horror of what they'd been looking at.

"The hell of it is, I have to show the Walshes," Matthews said. "But right now, let's have us a cigar."

.   .   .

Throughout the course of his two-year reinvestigation of the case, Joe Matthews met regularly with John and Revé Walsh to update them on his progress, but despite Revé's insistence that he share *everything* with her, he hesitated about showing her and John the images from the machete and the floorboards of Toole's Cadillac. Still, he could scarcely keep such a discovery from them. Furthermore, he needed their corroboration of the results.

Accordingly, he arranged for a meeting in the law offices of Kelly Hancock, John and Revé's attorney and longtime friend. Hancock, a former Broward County prosecutor, had already spoken to Matthews and knew what to expect, but he, too, understood how tough it would be for any parents to view what Matthews had uncovered. While Matthews explained the luminol process and tried to prepare John and Revé for what he was about to show them, Revé cut in. "Let me see the photographs, Joe," she said, her face set.

Matthews hesitated, but finally handed over the packet. Revé studied the photos for a moment—first those of Toole's machete, then his glowing footprints, and then the stunning image taken from the rear floorboards. With her eyes welling, she turned and handed them to John.

John took his own hard look at the photos, lingering over the last, then glanced up at Matthews and nodded briefly. Finally, he turned and wordlessly embraced his anguished wife.

Twenty-seven years of not knowing, Matthews thought, looking on. And now they finally did.

FORT LAUDERDALE, FLORIDA—JULY 14, 2006

As Matthews left Kelly Hancock's law offices that day, he knew well that he had settled the first of the items on the investigation's agenda. If there had ever been a doubt in the minds of

John and Revé Walsh as to what had happened to their son, not a shred now remained.

But still before him was the matter of presenting an investigative file that would convince the Hollywood police to name Ottis Toole as the person responsible. Until the killer was charged—and never mind that he was dead, and no matter how many other slayings he had been convicted of—John and Revé Walsh could never rest.

Especially not after what they'd seen that day. As a law officer and a father of four himself, Matthews understood well the importance of the task that remained. One last bit of business, and then, just maybe, he could rest.

There were several items Matthews wanted to bolster in his report, but one of the first things he did was to place a call to Reaves Roofing in Jacksonville, seeking information on the employment records of Bobby Lee Jones, the man who said he had put the dent in Ottis Toole's bumper and who had told Broward County State Attorney's Office investigator Philip Mundy in 1996 that Toole had confessed the crime to him as early as 1982. When Matthews finally reached family member Alan Reaves at the company offices, Reaves explained that John Reaves Jr. had recently died of cancer. Alan Reaves said that he'd be happy to help, but that no records prior to 1986 were any longer in existence. They had been eaten by termites while in storage, Reaves explained.

Matthews briefly contemplated the fact that even insects seemed to have conspired against him in his pursuit of the investigation, but it was not in his nature to dwell upon disappointment. He simply shook his head and moved on, intent upon building a body of evidence that would compel any law enforcement agency to conclude that a certain individual had committed this crime and that a successful prosecution could be carried out.

Still, events around him were a constant reminder that time

had its own way of imposing a statute of limitations on a case. In July 2007, former Hollywood police chief Dick Witt, who had ordered Matthews off the cold case investigation back in 1996, died in Ormand Beach, where he had retired. And in early November, current Hollywood chief James Scarberry, the man who had authorized opening his department's files to Matthews, retired, hounded by accusations that he had tipped off his command staff that several corrupt Hollywood detectives had been targeted by an FBI sting operation.

Scarberry's departure was no great disappointment to Matthews, for while the chief had posed no impediment to his investigation, he was clearly not greatly interested in the matter either. In fact, as Matthews reviewed the files that had been turned over to him, it became clear that even though every tip that had come to *America's Most Wanted* over the years since the airing of the Adam episode in 1996 had been passed along— leads that Matthews had pursued all the way from Florida to Colorado and points in between—*not one* had ever been pursued by Hollywood PD.

Still, he reminded himself, that was all water under the bridge. The more pressing issue now was the inclination of Scarberry's successor, Chad Wagner, who'd risen through the ranks at Hollywood PD, beginning as a patrolman in 1983 to become assistant chief under Scarberry.

Would Wagner prove to be another in a long line of administrators who would rather the matter were simply buried once and for all, or would he throw the roadblocks up once again? The answer was not long in coming.

In December, Mark Smith of the Hollywood PD, now a captain of detectives at Hollywood PD, called Matthews. By this time Matthews had come across the "ulterior motives" memo Smith had written years before, but Matthews said nothing. Smith was either going to be a help or a hindrance, and bringing up the matter would accomplish nothing.

Smith explained that he was calling on behalf of the newly appointed Chief Wagner, who wondered whether or not Matthews might be able to provide him with an address for John Walsh. Wagner wanted to introduce himself, Smith said, and he also wanted to extend his personal condolences to the Walsh family. Matthews held the phone away from his ear to stare at it for a moment, not sure he had heard correctly.

He gave Smith the address, then went back to work, wondering if he might have imagined the incident. A few days later, however, he got a call from John Walsh, who began by saying, "You're not going to believe this letter I just received . . ." Matthews said nothing, just listened quietly as John Walsh described the contents of the first unsolicited communication that had ever passed from the Hollywood PD to him and his family in more than twenty-six years. Matthews could hear it in Walsh's voice—how much that gesture meant to a still-grieving family.

Then, in late January of the following year, at a reception following a Broward County Police Academy graduation, Dick Brickman, the president of the Broward County Police Benevolent Association, took Matthews by the arm and introduced him to Chief Wagner. Matthews let Wagner know how much his letter meant to the Walsh family, surprising the chief when he mentioned the fact that it was the first such gesture they had ever received from his agency.

Matthews also told Wagner that he was well along on a cold case investigation of the murder of Adam Walsh that had been authorized by Chief Scarberry. Matthews explained that his progress had been delayed by the fact that his ninety-four-year-old mother was now confined to the hospital, where he sometimes took parts of the Walsh case file to work on at her bedside. Still, he looked forward to presenting his report to Chief Wagner soon.

For his part, Wagner seemed glad to hear the news. "I'll read every page," he assured Matthews. They were heartening words, and Wagner seemed sincere enough, Matthews thought, but he had heard a lot of promises in his day.

Still, he continued with work on his report, obsessed with checking every fact, tying up every loose end, reducing his findings to their essence. He prepared a meticulous timeline of the case drawn from the myriad agency reports and supplemental memos, for the first time placing the events and discoveries in order from first to last, and providing a context from which patterns of cause and effect might be discerned.

As an investigator, Matthews was most concerned with the assemblage of evidence. But he also understood that unless he was able to convey those facts in a compelling way, all his hard work was likely to go for naught. He had a natural gift for storytelling and was entirely at ease in front of an audience or a camera, but laying a story out on paper, he soon discovered, was another matter altogether.

On the most basic level, he'd never been the greatest at grammar, and when his mother, Margaret, who'd had a long career as a librarian and was still keen and vibrant despite her years, offered to proofread for him as he went, Matthews was glad to have her help. She had always been interested in the stories he brought home from work, and this was the story of them all.

From time to time, she'd glance up from the pages to offer advice that went beyond matters of the comma splice: "Are you sure you're not being too tough on this fellow here, Joey?" she might ask. And usually, she was right.

One day in March, Matthews arrived at the hospital to find one of his mother's doctors waiting to speak with him outside her room. His mother had a lot of life left, the doctor agreed, but her heartbeat was acting up. She needed a pacemaker implanted, a relatively minor procedure, if any operation could be called minor when the patient was ninety-four.

"You can blame it on my son," Matthews's mother told the

doctor when the pair came into the room to discuss the matter with her. "If you were reading what I've been reading, your heart would be racing, too."

That might be, the doctor allowed, but there was no question in his mind that the operation would make her much more comfortable. They talked it over with Matthews's brother Peter and younger sister Mariann once they arrived, and in the end, the procedure was agreed to.

At first, word from surgery was positive. The operation proceeded without a hitch. Then, suddenly, there were complications. And just as suddenly, on March 18, 2006, his mother was dead, stunning everyone. Michelina Militana "Margaret" Matthews, the daughter of Sicilian immigrants, had led a long and loving life, but if anything, all those years had only suggested to Matthews that somehow she always would be with him.

A few days after the funeral, Matthews forced himself back to his office, where his still-unfinished report lay on his desk. How many people had died in the quarter-century-plus he'd worked on this case? Matthews asked himself. Now even his mother had gone to her grave, with her sticky notes still attached to the pages in front of him.

Another victim of the case, you might call her, he found himself thinking. And when you came right down to it, how much time did he have left? If he croaked, what the hell would happen to all this work then?

With such thoughts in mind, he pinched the bridge of his nose between his forefinger and his thumb, closed his eyes briefly, then took a deep breath and went back to his report.

HOLLYWOOD, FLORIDA—APRIL 30, 2008

On a bright spring afternoon late in April 2008, Joe Matthews appeared at the office of Hollywood police chief Chad Wagner with a thick bound sheaf tucked under his arm. He wished with all his heart that his mother could have looked over his shoulder just once more before he handed the document over, but he had assembled the evidence to the best of his ability, given the writing all he had, and it was time to put up or shut up.

When he handed over the report to Wagner, he stressed the importance of the FDLE crime scene photos he'd had developed for the first time. Wagner was curious as to why such evidence had not been examined before, but Matthews couldn't explain that one. He had had the devil's own time even getting hold of the photos, he told Wagner, explaining that when he'd found them missing from the Hollywood file, he'd had to go to the FDLE himself to find the film and get the prints developed.

Why didn't Sergeant Lyle Bean get these prints added to the department file? Wagner wanted to know. But again, Matthews couldn't answer. Bean had claimed he'd requested the photos several times from the FDLE and was told that the photos did not exist, that's all Matthews knew for sure. He tapped his report. "In the end, we got what we needed."

"That may be so," Wagner said. "But I'll find out why it took so long to get those photos, rest assured of that."

Whatever the upshot of any conversations with Bean regarding the matter, Wagner did not share it with Matthews, though the irony that it took an outsider to accomplish what no detective had in twenty-five years was clearly not lost on the chief. Matthews took the opportunity to point out that while he had gone back through the tool marking test procedures regarding the machete to no avail, DNA testing on that clearly bloodsoaked handle had never been performed. Matthews could not authorize such testing, but the weapon was still in possession of the Hollywood PD, and the chief surely could.

And he would, Wagner assured Matthews. The day following, Matthews got a phone call from Sergeant Lyle Bean. The chief wanted that machete tested for DNA, Bean explained, and he was calling to talk about the matter with Matthews before he sent it out.

So far, Wagner had been as good as his word, Matthews thought. Matthews then explained to Bean that he'd spoken to a forensic geneticist after he'd seen the luminol indications on the wooden handle of the machete. That specialist suggested that the handle be drilled for samples, and not scraped as was normally done, based on the assumption that the blood had soaked into the wood over time. Matthews would never learn whether or not Bean passed his expert's suggestions along, and furthermore, the results seemed to take forever in coming back. It was not until October 14 that Chief Wagner called Matthews to let him know the disappointing findings. The results were, in a word, "inconclusive." Not negative. Not positive. Just, maddeningly, "inconclusive."

All the while, Matthews continued to pore over the files, wondering if he might have missed something that, however small, or seemingly unimportant, might lead him to an unexpected find. He was reviewing the phone and e-mail tips that had come in to *America's Most Wanted* following the airing of the episode on Adam in 1996, when one phone intake sheet caught his eye. On September 21, at 11:10 p.m., a call had come from someone named Wendy Sapp, identifying herself to an operator as a niece of Toole's. The operator had noted, "In 1982 Ottis told caller and relatives that he killed Adam." Matthews racked his brain, trying to remember. He'd talked to Sarah Patterson and to Joel Cockerman at some length, but as to a Wendy Sapp, he was drawing nothing but blanks.

There was certainly nothing in the file to suggest that anyone at Hollywood PD had followed up on this or any of the other tips *AMW* had supplied, but he could certainly talk to her now. He picked up the phone and launched into a series of calls, until finally he found himself talking to one Wendy Sapp Fralick. And, yes, her mother had been previously married to a man named Dickie McHenry, who, she believed, was a cousin of Ottis Toole.

"Uncle Ottis" had often babysat for her and her sisters, Fralick said, and she remembered quite clearly that one night he had told her that he killed Adam Walsh. She was a bit hazy on any details that he might have given, for that was a long time ago. Besides, she told Matthews, she was only eight at the time and didn't truly comprehend the magnitude of his statements.

However, Fralick said, about four years ago she had spent some time with her cousin Erica Toole, the daughter of Howard and Georgia Toole, from whom Ottis had stolen the truck back in June 1981. During that 2004 visit, Fralick brought up the subject of Adam Walsh, and Erica replied that her father Howard, Ottis's brother, had told her that Ottis did in fact murder Adam.

With Fralick's help, Matthews then tracked down her mother Linda, who was by then remarried to a man name Gerald Orand. It was Orand who answered the phone, explaining that his wife was recuperating from a stroke. She had difficulty being understood at times, but she very much wanted to communicate with Matthews, presuming he was who he claimed to be, that is.

After Orand called *America's Most Wanted* to verify Matthews's identity, he got back to the detective, along with his wife Linda. Linda explained a bit of the family tree at the outset of the conversation. She had first been married to a man named Willie Sapp, the father of Wendy. After divorcing Sapp, she married Dickie McHenry, the brother of Georgia Toole, who was married to Ottis's brother Howard.

As to the things that Wendy had told Matthews about Ottis and Adam Walsh, Linda did have a few things she would like to add. On an early winter afternoon in 1981 or 1982, she said, she and Dickie took her kids over to Howard and Georgia's for a visit. Ottis happened to be there that day, and was sitting out in the backyard, drinking beer. While Georgia stayed inside to feed the kids and Howard took a bath, Linda and Dickie went out to the yard to sit with Ottis. He offered them both a beer, she told Matthews, but neither one of them felt like drinking that day, and they declined.

Ottis started talking about how he missed his niece Becky Powell, Linda said. He told them that both he and Henry Lee Lucas liked to fuck her, but Henry Lee had run off with her. After contemplating that dismal fact for a bit, Linda recalls that Ottis then announced to them that it was he who "took" Adam Walsh.

"Who is Adam Walsh?" Linda asked Ottis. She had never heard a thing about the matter at that time.

"The one who's been missing," he responded.

Linda told Matthews that Toole went on to recount how he kidnapped this little boy down in Broward County, fucked him in the butt, cut his head off, cut his body up in pieces, then put the pieces in plastic bags and dumped them. The descriptions were so vivid that Linda stood up and vomited into some nearby bushes.

Ottis watched her wiping her mouth and laughed. "You pregnant or something?" he asked.

"No," she answered. "You make me sick, that's all."

A bit later, Linda said, Ottis offered to take Wendy and her two sisters out for ice cream. "Here's Ottis," she said to Matthews, her outrage palpable still, "who just got through talking about raping Becky Powell and some little boy and then chopping him up in pieces, and he wants to take my kids out for ice cream?"

After that, she made sure her children were never left alone with Ottis Toole. And that is also why Howard and his wife moved up to Georgia soon after, to get away from Ottis. Everyone in the family knew Ottis had killed Adam Walsh, she said. It was simply common knowledge.

Then why on earth had she never told anyone about these

things? Matthews asked. Linda didn't miss a beat. "Because no one ever asked," she said. "You're the first that ever did."

Matthews sat back in his chair and stared at the ceiling for a long time after his conversation with Linda McHenry Orand. Common knowledge among the members of a family that one of their own had kidnapped and killed Adam Walsh. And because no one had ever asked, not one of them stepped forward to tell.

Matthews wrote up a summary of his interviews with Wendy Sapp Fralick and her mother Linda and added them to the list that had been with Chief Wagner for several months now. He also pointed out that the 1996 tip from Sapp had been passed along to the Hollywood PD at the time, just as every tip involving the case had been.

All the while, Matthews couldn't help thinking about Ottis Toole's reply to Linda's question, "Who is Adam Walsh?"

"The one who's been missing," she claimed Toole told her. Not, "The one they found."

Finally, it struck him. If Linda Orand had all her facts straight, if those were indeed Toole's words, then this conversation had taken place *before* Adam's remains had been found, less than two weeks after the killing. Of course Linda wouldn't have heard about "Adam Walsh" all the way up in Jacksonville. At that point, before the fisherman had made their startling discovery, the Walshes were having a difficult time getting anyone outside Dade and Broward Counties to realize their son had been abducted. And there was Ottis Toole sitting in a lawn chair, swigging beer and calmly recounting to his own sister the details of the crime.

Two years before, in a newspaper article commemorating the twenty-fifth anniversary of the crime, criminologist Vernon Geberth had a rhetorical-sounding response for reporters who wanted to know if he believed the Adam Walsh case could ever be solved: "A relative of the killer who knows about the crime may want to finally unburden himself." Or *themselves*, Matthews thought.

The statement might have been only Vernon Geberth's wishful thinking at the time, but Wendy Sapp Fralick and her mother Linda Orand had just become an investigator's wish come true.

Linda McHenry Orand's statement—along with the extortion letter Toole had sent John Walsh and the damning images developed from the FDLE negatives—might have seemed yet another finding upon which a successful prosecution could have been based all by itself, but as Matthews well knew, there is a vast difference between real life and film and television drama, where justice is served up in a moment—one witness breaks down in racking sobs or a single, searing image is produced.

Nowhere had that distinction been made more clear than in the long history of this matter. If it was as simple as dropping one bombshell, then this case would have been closed long ago. Of course, charges are filed readily when an officer catches a perpetrator in the act, or when a suspect is apprehended and confesses. In this instance, however—where a suspect already in custody had confessed to the crime—the state attorney's office asked accordingly that evidence corroborating that confession be presented by police in a form that would suggest any charge as well founded. And no one in law enforcement had ever gone to the trouble of such a submission.

For that reason, Matthews did not for a moment contemplate fashioning a report that did not take into account every shred of evidence that had accumulated concerning the matter. The bombshells would have to take their places in the long chain of evidence, items both great and small. This wasn't a movie, this was life . . . and death.

Accordingly, for two years and nine months Matthews labored on his review of the 10,000-page case file. He reexamined all the taped interviews conducted with Toole and others and conducted his own independent searches, interviews, and analyses of materials pertinent. He found new evidence, and with all the disparate pieces assembled in narrative order for the first time—the many materials upon which this account is based—everything pointed to an inescapable conclusion: Ottis Toole was the man who'd committed the crime.

Certainly, Joe Matthews had long suspected Toole, and it was to his everlasting dismay that he had not been given the opportunity to conduct his own interview with the man and extract and nail down Toole's confession himself. One of the most powerful pieces of evidence that he'd come across in the course of his investigation came from a former Texas Ranger who sent Matthews a videotaped interview conducted with Toole by a former colleague who—shortly after Henry Lee Lucas was arrested—had flown Toole out to that state to try and clear a murder case in their jurisdiction. The interview took place on March 26, 1984, several weeks after Jack Hoffman had accepted Toole's recanting of his various confessions.

During the interview an avuncular Ranger draws Toole out about his typical modus operandi for murder, and Toole rattles on readily—almost cheerfully—about the thrill of shooting old ladies hanging out laundry and garroting unsuspecting drag queens. But when the questioning turns to the case of Adam Walsh, Matthews points out, everything in Toole's demeanor suddenly changes.

"You can see it in his body language," Matthews says, and indeed the signs are apparent to anyone. As Toole (who had offered few specifics in many of the other cases brought up that day) leads the Ranger through the details—the kidnapping and the beating and the effort involved in the decapitation, the wrapping of Adam's head in his shirt and its disposal and the disposal of the body—his shoulders tense and round inward, the cadences of his speech slow, his tone becomes serious, even plaintive, his gaze is suddenly evasive. What Matthews wouldn't have given to be able to climb into the frame and attach Toole to his polygraph instrument!

At one point, when the Ranger interrupts Toole to ask if he

had done anything to Adam's body before he began to burn it, Toole's response is electric. "Oh no," he says, as his eyes roll and his head snaps in emphatic negative.

In place of needles dancing across a polygraph scroll, Matthews had to be content with the reaction of the Ranger. Following the conclusion of Toole's account of eating a few of Adam's ribs before scattering the charred remains, the burly veteran turned away, his disgust scarcely concealed: "Well, that's pretty stout."

As far as his report, Matthews felt that he had done everything he could under the circumstances, and in his opinion, it was far more than enough. His opinion was not the one that mattered any longer, though. He could only wait and see what the response of Chad Wagner might be. If his report was deemed sufficiently convincing, then Wagner might carry it to the Broward state attorney and recommend that Ottis Toole be charged with the crime. But Wagner might not do that, no matter what he thought of the quality of the report.

The new chief seemed a decent man, but he was also the preeminent representative of an entire police force, and—by extension and association—of the governing structure of an entire community. If he swept aside Matthews's report, he would only be doing what many before him had seemingly chosen to do. In weighing the good to be done by naming a killer against the harm it would do to the very institution one was hired to champion, they had all apparently decided in kind: such a blow to the established order could not be justified by the closure it might provide to a family or the vague sense of justice it might provide to the world at large.

In any case, Matthews thought, it was not his call. He could only sit and wait. If Wagner didn't want to proceed on the basis of what he'd presented, maybe there was a way he could get it straight to the state attorney's office himself.

On Friday, November 14, 2008, Adam Walsh's thirty-fourth birthday passed, and, then, six days later, on November 20, Mat-

272 | Bringing Adam Home

thews realized that he would not have to worry about moving things forward himself: Chief Wagner had called a meeting at the Broward County State Attorney's Office.

Present on that day with Wagner were second-in-command state attorney Chuck Morton, assistant chief of Hollywood PD Louis Granteed, Captain Mark Smith, and Hollywood Police legal adviser Joel Cantor. Also present were John and Revé Walsh, their attorney, former Broward prosecutor Kelly Hancock, and Detective Sergeant Joe Matthews.

Wagner had called the meeting to discuss the report compiled by Sergeant Matthews, he explained. Would anyone in the room, Wagner wanted to know, object to the conclusions in the report that Matthews had placed before them? Bits and pieces were familiar to many in the room, and were branded indelibly in the minds of others, but here laid out in Matthews report was the full story:

- Toole's knowledge of crime scene details only the killer could have known
- Dismissal of the theory that a "book contract" tainted Toole's confessions
- Multiple eyewitness identifications of Toole taking Adam from Sears
- Arlene and Heidi Maier's ID of Toole at Kmart the night before Adam was taken
- The damning extortion letter Toole wrote John Walsh offering to lead him to his son's body
- Twenty-five independent confessions to the crime made by Ottis Toole, including that to family member Linda Fralick before Adam's remains were found
- The never-before-seen luminol images of the bloody machete handle and footprints on the carpet of Toole's Cadillac
- And the most damning image of them all . . . which had both haunted and sustained Matthews since the

moment it had wavered into focus on his office desk months before, as powerful to him as the Shroud of Turin:

> Traced in the blue glow of luminol was the outline of a familiar young boy's face, a negative pressed into floorboard carpeting, eye sockets blackened blank cavities, mouth twisted in an oval of pain.

Ottis Toole had told detectives time and again. He'd hacked off Adam's head and decided to keep it for a while. Perhaps he'd had sex with it, perhaps he hadn't. He'd tossed it into the back of his car and driven up the turnpike, before it dawned on him that this might be a bad idea.

Why hadn't the men in charge of the investigation taken Toole at his word? Matthews wondered as he stood among those gathered in the state's attorney's office and stared at the image once again. Why?

Still, as the ancients understood, truth has its implacable force. One of the most haunting of the tales told by the Brothers Grimm is that of the "Singing Flute," in which a craven man kills his younger brother to steal his bounty and buries his body beneath a bridge. Years later, a shepherd discovers a snow-white little bone on the sand beneath the bridge and carves a flute out of it. But when the shepherd begins to play, what issues is not music. Instead it is the voice of the long-dead boy, thanking the shepherd and telling the truth at last. "Ah, friend, thou blowest upon my bone! Long have I lain beside the water; my brother slew me for the boar."

What Joe Matthews had produced—the terrible image which he'd had to show to John and Revé and which everyone in the room around him now viewed as well—was no less powerful in its effect. The glowing blue image pressed into the carpet—the outline of Adam's face, etched in his own blood—was as stark as any fragment of bone; and the cry that issued from his battered lips was as damning an indictment as anyone might ever hear. Poor Adam, friend Joe, the truth singing to the world at last.

Following the summary of Matthews's findings, everyone in the room had the opportunity to respond. As to the image of Adam's face branded into the floorboards of Toole's Cadillac, it was an emotional haymaker, of course, but as he described in his report, Matthews had gone to some lengths to bolster its significance. Shortly after he'd made the discovery, Matthews met with Miami Dade crime lab analyst Detective Thomas Charles to discuss techniques of blood transfer that he might use to duplicate that final image he'd found in the FDLE photographs. As a result of that discussion, Matthews conducted a series of experiments using paint of various consistencies, plastic facial masks, and auto carpeting of the type that was in Toole's Cadillac.

As he detailed, Matthews employed eight different means of transferring paint from saturated plastic face masks onto carpet. And each resulted in the transfer of images to the carpet that were remarkably similar to the one that Matthews had found on the rear floorboards of Toole's car. So far as his research could determine, no crime scene investigator had confirmed such blood evidence previously.

After everyone in the room had delivered their estimations of all that Matthews had presented, Wagner had his mandate, and it was unanimous. All agreed that the investigation of the homicide of Adam Walsh would—pending the final approval of Broward County state attorney Michael Satz—be "exceptionally cleared." Translated, the phrase meant that were Ottis Toole still alive, he would be charged, arrested, prosecuted, and, in all likelihood, convicted of the abduction and murder of Adam Walsh.

Matthews watched on, scarcely able to believe what he was witnessing. For many years, he'd hoped to find a partner, one individual at Hollywood PD who seemed as determined to solve this case as he. In Chad Wagner, it seemed he finally had.

On Wednesday, December 10, Chad Wagner called Joe Matthews with the news. He had just received a letter from the state attorney's office. Michael Satz—the man who had been Broward state attorney in 1981 when Adam disappeared, and who had held the post ever since—had made his call.

Would Matthews like to be the one to let John and Revé Walsh know? And did he mind asking if the Walshes could be present at Hollywood police headquarters on the afternoon of December 16, 2008? Wagner wanted to hold a press conference to announce the decision to the world.

HOLLYWOOD, FLORIDA—DECEMBER 16, 2008

As promised, the press conference Wagner arranged took place at department headquarters the following Tuesday afternoon, with reporters from every major news organization in the United States jostling for space in the crowded training room. More than twenty-seven years had passed since Adam Walsh went missing and was found brutally murdered, and in spite of all the time that had gone by—or perhaps because of it—the case still had the power to mesmerize a nation. This was, after all, an event that had changed how every parent in America viewed the world.

Among the myriad, unkillable pieces of spam that circulate through the Ethernet is one that invites readers of a certain age to "remember when." Popular songs once had melodies, we are reminded, and stores were once closed on Sundays, and "underwear" meant exactly that.

But there are more poignant notes on the list, including an invocation of those innocent summer days when kids blew past a banging screen door with a shouted promise to be "home by dark," and who ever worried about that? Today, of course, such carelessness upon the part of parents is unthinkable, if not vaguely criminal in itself. Perhaps, once upon a time, parents only worried about their kids when they took them to the beach or to the pool, or hiking along some steep path. Now vigilance begins at birth, if not before, and for most the worry never ends.

In his book *Tears of Rage*, John Walsh gave his own account of how the apparently unsolvable case had impacted his life and that of Revé. He said then that though it was terribly painful to revisit such loss, he wanted to do so in hopes that it might help others who had lost children to senseless tragedy. Mostly, he said, he wanted to talk about "how to come to terms with life when you think you're dying of a broken heart."

At that same time, Revé spoke of the helplessness they felt in the aftermath of Adam's disappearance and the subsequent string of failures by law enforcement. "I remember thinking, 'Our son's been murdered, and now *we've* got to be the ones to do something about it?' " she said.

"It was a sad thing for this country that the fight had to be led by two broken-down parents of a murdered child," she added. "But we had to, because no one else was going to do it."

Imagine then, the anticipation of John and Revé Walsh as the chief entered the room and called for order. He was there to announce that the 1981 murder of six-year-old Adam Walsh had been solved, "a day that's long overdue," Wagner said, before adding, "This case could have been closed years ago."

Furthermore, he was not there to brandish news of some "smoking gun" unearthed miraculously after years of fruit-less gumshoe work, he said. Rather, his announcement was the result of the assembly and examination of evidence that had been there all along. "What was there was everything that was in front of our face for years."

His department had been too defensive about its mistakes in the past and could well have arrested the chief suspect for the crime before he died, Wagner said, apologizing to the Walshes for those lapses. But make no mistake about it, were Ottis Toole alive today, he would be arrested and charged with the crime.

And—Wagner was certain—he would have paid for it with his life.

As might be expected, the announcement prompted a barrage of questions from the assembled media. A choked-up John Walsh told reporters that the announcement was a reaffirmation of the fact that Adam didn't die in vain. "For all the other victims who haven't gotten justice," he added, "I say one thing: 'Don't give up hope.' "

When reporters turned to Revé Walsh, she spoke simply and poignantly. "This is a wonderful day, in spite of why we're here. Nothing will bring back our beautiful little boy," she said, "but at least the knowing will close this chapter of our lives."

In that same vein, John Walsh added that while the family would never recover from Adam's death, they could finally move on. Still, he noted, "It's not about closure; it's about justice."

Maybe it was a little of both—closure *and* justice—Joe Matthews thought, as he watched from the wings. As a friend of John and Revé, he understood how important this announcement was— we now know who killed your son, and we should have found out sooner. And as a cop, Matthews also reveled in the fact that a killer had finally gotten his due.

As to the fact that his own name had not been mentioned prominently on this day, that was at his own request. The moment was for the Walshes. His wife Ginny had been in the room as Wagner made his announcement, and as she observed of the family, "It looks as if they're taking their first deep breaths in years."

To Matthews the words rang particularly true. Wagner's pronouncement wasn't going to change the Walshes' lives in an instant—he was reminded of something Revé had once told him when he'd asked her about her grieving:

"It's like you've been in a terrible accident and had your arm amputated," she told him. "After a while, the pain goes away, and eventually you even learn to get along without your arm.

Some days you're sad that you're missing your arm, and some days you're angry about it, and some days you're okay. But, no matter what, no matter how long it's been, you never stop missing your arm."

The simple observation had jolted Matthews at the time. But still, he thought, this day *was* a milestone, a place from which a new journey could begin.

Matthews had overheard Ginny bidding Revé farewell. "I wish you and your family a truly wonderful and Merry Christmas," she said simply.

Revé paused and took her husband's hand. "Thank you," she told Ginny. Her eyes were brimming, but she managed a smile. "This *will* be our first Merry Christmas in twenty-seven years." Even Matthews found himself choked up at that one.

And if anyone present chose to assume that it was Chad Wagner and his men who'd finally put two and two together, that was okay, too. Wagner was, in Matthews's eyes, deserving of plenty of credit. There were surely many of the chief's own men who would have preferred that he simply do as all his predecessors had done. But Chad Wagner was a stand-up cop.

Furthermore, John and Revé Walsh knew how this day had come to be, as did Matthews's own family and all his friends in law enforcement, and that was fine by him. Most important, Matthews felt the presence of his mother in the room, gazing at him with pride, nodding her approval. He'd done his job, banging away at the case for twenty-seven years, and justice had prevailed.

So now, he'd go down to the beach, treat himself to a good cigar, and watch the waves roll in and out. He'd earned it.

As John Walsh made the rounds of the talk shows in the following days, he was quick to point out that were it not for Joe Matthews, he would not be having those conversations, and he reiterated his praise for the retired homicide detective at the close of the year-end episode of *America's Most Wanted*. But even there, it was hardly possible to explain what was really a twenty-seven-year process. Chief Wagner gave hints at the news conference, alluding to the fact that much of the evidence that prompted the closing of the case had been available all along; but he did not go on to add the obvious—"available had anyone competent been in charge of the search and the effort to put a case together."

Furthermore, when Wagner said to reporters, "If you're looking for that magic wand or that hidden document that just appeared, it's not there," his intent was likely to defuse the sort of "Perry Mason" effect engendered by years of exposure to manufactured drama. Still, while neither Wagner nor anyone else wanted any part of a trial by media on that day, one might speculate as to what the effect would have been had he filled a screen with the images of Ottis Toole's bloody footprints glowing on the floorboards of his Cadillac or the rendering of a silent scream from a young boy's severed head.

Along with reminders of how important the Walshes' good works had been—"If people hold their kids a little bit closer in crowded stores these days, thank the Walshes," one writer said—there were also, predictably, a few doubters who surfaced in the wake of Chief Wagner's announcement. A *Miami Herald* story published on December 28, 2008, quoted a Washington criminal profiler as being "appalled" by the decision to close the case without more proof. The story rehashed the reluctance of Hollywood police to charge Toole at the time of his first series of confessions, and also quoted Ron Hickman's 2001 statement to reporter de Vise, "I spent 100 hours with that individual. I'll tell you right now: He didn't do it."

There was "no new evidence" presented, the *Herald* story said, suggesting that either the reporter had not bothered to read the same evidence file that Joe Matthews and Chief Wagner had, or he was simply longing for that "magic wand" that Wag-

ner referred to. The story referenced the various inconsistencies in Toole's own confessions—including his erstwhile claims
that Henry Lee Lucas had taken part, and his varying reports
of where he'd disposed of Adam's body. And it also quoted a
Broward assistant state attorney as saying that while his office
had indeed supported the closing of the case, all the mistakes
made by police would have made a successful prosecution difficult were Toole still alive.

Joe Matthews might have agreed, though he might have also
pointed back to the successful prosecution of Dieter Reichmann, where prosecutors had even less physical evidence and
two dozen fewer confessions on the part of the perpetrator.
While any prosecutor might like to have a videotape of a killer
in the act to carry into court, the truth is that many celebrated
cases have resulted in convictions based almost entirely on circumstantial evidence—from which jurors must *infer* a perpetrator's guilt.

Despite any public perception to the contrary, the U.S.
Supreme Court long ago established the precept that "circumstantial evidence is intrinsically no different from testimonial
[direct] evidence" (*Holland v. United States*, 1954). As any competent prosecutor knows, the distinction between direct testimony and circumstantial evidence has little practical effect
in the presentation or admissibility of evidence in trials. And
while the so-called *CSI* effect might suggest that anything less
than a mountain of forensic evidence tying a killer to the crime
is insufficient, a number of recent studies have shown that
jurors have not changed—even if prosecutors may feel the need
to introduce high-tech data, juries remain as likely to be persuaded by logical argument as anything else.

In another piece published soon after the announcement,
a veteran South Florida columnist expressed his own doubts
about Hollywood PD's willingness to put an end to the matter. He'd been one of the reporters who had trooped to the

multijurisdictional press conference called in Monroe, Louisiana, back in 1983, where authorities were quick to attribute a raft of unsolved killings to Henry Lee Lucas and Ottis Toole. The columnist said that he and his colleagues had been too eager to believe cops back then, when they blamed Lucas and Toole for various crimes that were later attributed to others or which were never successfully prosecuted. Thus, why after all this time believe that police had finally found the killer of Adam Walsh? "It was like a miracle, conjured up with hardly anything in the way of new evidence," the column concluded, ignoring the fact that "old" evidence, even twenty-seven-year-old evidence, becomes "new" when it is finally given a logical context.

Of course, successful prosecutions are always difficult, even when the physical evidence seems ironclad—just ask those who went after O. J. And while one Broward County state attorney may have forecast a difficult time proving the case, another prominent former prosecutor interviewed by a *Sun-Sentinel* reporter weighed in that he had gone to court on several instances with much less.

In fact, FBI findings disclosed just weeks before the press conference, in the case of Caylee Anthony, the two-year-old Orlando girl thought to have been murdered by her mother, Casey, would support Matthews's analysis of the images he had found on the carpets of Toole's car. A September 30, 2008, e-mail from FBI intelligence analyst Karen B. Cowan to a fellow agency employee identified a bodily fluids outline lifted from the trunk liner of Casey Anthony's car using essentially the same methodology. "If you look closely at this photo, there appears to be the outline or silhouette of a child in the fetal position," Cowan wrote. Shortly thereafter, Casey Anthony was arrested and charged with the crime.

And as for "believing," why believe anything, Plato might respond, when the very nature of reality is—like shadows flickering on a cave wall, twice removed from the source—such a subjective matter? Had there been a dozen witnesses present when Ottis Toole carried Adam Walsh from his car, laid him on the ground, and severed his head, there would have been a dozen different accounts as to just what had occurred.

Subjectivity, along with contrariness, is a part of human nature. And when it comes to newspaper adjudications of controversial cases, as the cigar-chomping editor is quick to remind the cub reporter, "Keep the trouble coming. Good news just doesn't sell."

In keeping with that notion, as recently as March 2010, more than fifteen months after the case was cleared by authorities, the *Miami Herald* published a front-page story suggesting that indeed it was Jeffrey Dahmer who had been responsible for the killing, asserting that two new witnesses had come forward claiming to have spotted a disheveled, disturbing-looking man in the vicinity of the Sears store the day that Adam Walsh disappeared. They'd only realized it was Jeffrey Dahmer, they said, after learning of Dahmer's heinous activities a decade later in 1991.

A comparison of the mug shots of preppy-looking Dahmer—who by most accounts long eluded suspicion precisely because he appeared harmless—with those of Ottis Toole suggests the true identity of the frightening individual these new witnesses had actually seen that day in Sears. And most law enforcement officials interviewed for the story scoffed at the notion that Dahmer could have been charged, much less prosecuted, on the basis of such claims.

"The delayed Dahmer identifications certainly add intrigue and mystery to Adam Walsh's tragic death," Chief Assistant State Attorney Chuck Morton wrote in response to the questions of *Herald* reporters at the time. In his eyes, Morton said, such claims might even form the basis for the writing of a murder mystery novel, "but they do not come close to supporting the filing of criminal charges."

As Morton went on to explain, eyewitness identifications

made years after the commission of a crime are among the least
reliable forms of argument in criminal prosecutions. "Such
identifications would have to be corroborated by overwhelmingly credible evidence in order to have 'probable cause' to
prosecute the suspect for that crime—e.g., credible admissions
by the suspect or credible and indisputable physical evidence
that directly links the suspect to the criminal act." Joe Matthews
had finally pieced together such a web of corroborating evidence
against Ottis Toole, one that had been validated by Assistant
Police Chief Mark Smith and others at HPD, Morton pointed
out to reporters. He reiterated his opinion that even though a
successful prosecution of Toole might have been difficult, the
thought of so much as filing charges against Dahmer was out of
the question.

Very little of Morton's response was printed, however, and
soon the *Herald* story had prompted breathless headlines of the
"Bigfoot" variety in various supermarket tabloids, one of which
theorized that Adam Walsh was still alive somewhere, even providing a computer-generated rendition of what he would look
like as an adult so that readers could keep an eye out. Such
stories might seem outlandish, but they are also proof of how
deeply the psyche of the entire nation has been affected by the
Adam Walsh matter and by the time it took for a credible case to
be built. Indeed, unless "old news" is of the caliber of the Kennedy assassination, the paranoia-fostering tabloid press simply
doesn't get involved.

When a rehash of the *Herald* story ran on a local Vero Beach
station at the time, John Walsh turned to Revé and blurted, "For
God's sakes, aren't the ghouls ever going to give up?"

Revé glanced at him. "Maybe not," she said. "But at least
you and I know the truth now."

One of the complaints made by those who have expressed doubt
as to Toole's guilt has to do with his penchant for changing the

details of his story over time. But Joe Matthews sees that as a positive. Were no detail to vary in a killer's various confessions, Matthews points out, *then* you might worry that you were hearing a tale memorized and scripted for some hidden purpose.

"It happens time and again," Matthews explains to students in his classes on interrogation technique: "Stage one, you'll ask the person about the crime and you get total denial. So you talk about other things for a while, and then you come back to the crime again. The second time around, the party might allow as how he knows who did the deed and implicate somebody else. When you circle back for a third time, the guy says, 'Well, actually, I was there, but I was: (a) outside the bedroom where it all happened, (b) just driving the car, (c) didn't realize what was going to take place.' By stage four, you'll get some admission, like 'Well, actually I helped hold her down,' or 'Yeah, maybe I dug the grave.' And by the time you get to stage five, there is no other person involved, and the perpetrator is sitting there telling you he is responsible for every last thing you've been talking about all this time."

From the point at which a confession has been made, all you are likely to get from a perpetrator is damage control, Matthews says. Once a perpetrator realizes that the confession just delivered is a virtual death sentence, why wouldn't he try and reverse the process? Recanting is simply common practice.

As for the incidental details that varied in the various confessions, Toole was not the brightest bulb in the array, and given the additional burden of a lifetime of drug and alcohol abuse, his memory was often in and out of focus. And as for issues such as having implicated Henry Lee Lucas in the crime initially, Toole had a perfectly plausible reason for that. As he himself admitted, he might have been a "retard," but that did not mean he lacked cunning. Were he not street-smart, he could never have survived in the circles where he traveled for nearly as long as he did.

One of the documents that had not come to light before Matthews made his thorough search of the files, in fact, was a report filed by Deputy J. E. Winterbaum of the Duval County Sheriff's Office back in October of 1983, shortly after Toole had initially confessed. As Winterbaum was making a routine check of the cell block, Toole called him close to share a few plans he had in mind once he got out of jail.

"I am going to sue the little boy's father, the one I cut his head off," he advised Winterbaum. "And then I am going to kill him. He [meaning Walsh] is trying to pay me off, and I should have never signed the check."

Given the other documents uncovered by Matthews, it might be theorized that an addled Toole had somehow confused John Walsh with John Reaves Jr., the man who'd paid him big bucks for the rights to his life story. But to Matthews, the explanation is much simpler than that. Just as Toole had explained away a previous inconsistency in his story to an investigator: "I just like fucking with the cops."

In any event, it is hard to fathom that a police agency that had invested twenty-seven years in the hopes that the Adam Walsh case would somehow go away saw much to gain by admitting to the world the embarrassing truth as to "what had been in front of their faces" all those years, other than to see justice served, that is.

For Joe Matthews and John and Revé Walsh, justice has in fact been served in this case, and life goes on. Matthews continues as senior investigator at *America's Most Wanted,* as a contributor at Fox News, as a motivational speaker, and as an investigative consultant to television programmers, media outlets, and the private sector. He regularly tours the United States as chairman of DNA LifePrint, promoting corporate sponsorships of events that provide biometric fingerprinting, digital photographic records, and DNA identification of children to communities.

286 | *Bringing Adam Home*

He often conducts seminars and lectures on homicide investigation, investigative interviewing, and polygraph procedures throughout the United States and Canada.

John Walsh, of course, carries on as executive producer and host of *America's Most Wanted,* the longest-running show in Fox Network history—"The good guys do their thing Sunday through Friday," he likes to say, "but on Saturday night, *I* kick ass." He and Revé also continue their work on behalf of the National Center for Missing and Exploited Children as well as on behalf of any number of national and state initiatives related to the protection of children, a never-ending process. In a recent appearance on *Oprah,* Walsh pointed out that even though Congress passed the Adam Walsh Child Protection Act in 2006, the legislation will as a practical matter cease to have any effect beyond 2010 unless government funding is reauthorized and provided.

And even if legislators are persuaded to authorize the dollars, the mere fact that juvenile sex offenders might register their addresses regularly is no guarantee of anything, as a recent *New York Times* story makes clear. For eighteen years following a rape conviction in California, Phillip Garrido reported his whereabouts to authorities in precise accordance with the schedule demanded of him. But that did not stop him from kidnapping and raping another young woman, fathering two children by her, and holding them all prisoner in the backyard of the home he dutifully kept registered all the while.

It is a chilling reminder that the threat of evil is ever-present and that all the noble deeds and intentions on earth cannot stamp out catastrophe and loss. Broward County medical examiner Dr. Ronald Wright spoke to John Walsh of such matters in the aftermath of the initial investigation, trying to give a grief-stricken parent something to cling to. In his profession, Wright had seen horror stacked on horror, plenty of evidence that there was no shortage of hell right here on earth. As to what had kept him sane in the face of all that he had witnessed, it was a simple sense of purpose. "It *is* that simple, John," Wright said. "There is evil. And there is good."

Once Adam Walsh stepped inside Ottis Toole's Cadillac on that day, almost nothing, it seems, could have saved him. And when that car's heavy door slammed shut, it seemed to mark the end of America's innocence. Can there truly have been a time when audiences believed in *The Brady Bunch*? Was there really a time when a parent could bring a forgotten lunch or book bag to school without passing through security gates and showing photo ID?

Still, the refusal of John and Revé Walsh to submit to such evil and the actions of Joe Matthews in tracing it to its source also remind us that—even in such weary times as these—goodness can prevail.

CAST OF CHARACTERS

LYLE BEAN Hollywood PD detective of little help in obtaining FDLE photos

JIMMY CAMPBELL Walsh family friend, and Hoffman's chief suspect in 1981

JOEL COCKERMAN Boy who was escorted out of the Sears store with Adam

BARRY GEMELLI Union Correctional Institution administrator who heard Toole's deathbed confession

MARY HAGAN Identified Toole in Sears near video game display

KELLY HANCOCK Walsh family attorney and former Broward County prosecutor

ROBERT HARLEY Ottis Toole's stepfather

LEROY HESSLER Hollywood PD deputy chief of police in 1981

RON HICKMAN Hollywood PD detective, Hoffman's partner

JACK HOFFMAN Hollywood PD detective in charge of the Adam Walsh case

LARRY HOISINGTON Hollywood PD detective to whom Toole confessed in 1983

DICK HYNDS Supervisor of detectives for the Hollywood PD in 1981

BOBBY LEE JONES Cellmate and former coworker who dented Toole's Cadillac

STEVE KENDRICK Brevard County homicide detective who took Toole's first confession

HENRY LEE LUCAS Toole's lover, convicted serial killer

SAM MARTIN Hollywood PD chief in 1981; retired 1986

GINNY MATTHEWS Joe Matthews's exceedingly understanding and patient wife

JOE MATTHEWS Twenty-nine years a cop and detective, Miami Beach PD

MAMA MARGARET MATTHEWS Joe's mother

ARLENE MAYER Heidi Mayer's mother, who also identified Toole at Kmart

HEIDI MAYER Twelve-year-old girl Toole attempted to abduct from Kmart

FAYE MCNETT John Reaves Jr.'s aunt, who sold her Cadillac to Toole

WILLIAM MISTLER Pest control company owner who witnessed Adam's abduction

JOHN MONAHAN SR. Hotelier and Walsh family friend

CHUCK MORTON Broward County chief assistant state attorney

PHIL MUNDY Broward County State Attorney's Office investigator

LINDA MCHENRY ORAND Toole's sister-in-law, to whom he confessed in 1981

SARAH PATTERSON Ottis Toole's niece, to whom he confessed while in prison in 1996

FRANK POWELL Ottis Toole's adolescent nephew, brother of Frieda

FRIEDA "BECKY" POWELL Ottis Toole's adolescent niece, lover of Henry Lee Lucas

JOHN REAVES JR. Owner of Southeast Color Coat, Jacksonville

JOHN REAVES SR. Owner of Reaves Roofing, Jacksonville; Toole's employer

JAMES REDWINE Troubled son of Toole's landlord Betty Goodyear

WENDY SAPP Ottis Toole's niece to whom he confessed the murder of Adam

MICHAEL SATZ Elected state attorney for Broward County, 1976–present

JAMES SCARBERRY Hollywood PD chief, 1999–2007

GERALD SCHAFFER Toole's cellmate at Starke, convicted serial killer

ELTON SCHWARTZ Miami attorney who volunteered to defend Toole

KATHY SHAFFER Sears security guard, seventeen years old in 1981

MARK SMITH Detective who conducted Hollywood PD cold case investigation in 1995, and again in 2006

VINETTA SYPHURS Ottis Toole's sister, to whom he confessed while in prison

BUDDY TERRY Homicide detective, Jacksonville Sheriff's Office

HOWARD TOOLE Ottis Toole's brother, from whom he stole a pickup truck

NORVELLA "RITA" TOOLE Ottis Toole's wife

OTTIS ELLWOOD TOOLE Drifter, pedophile, convicted killer

SARAH TOOLE Ottis Toole's mother, who died in May 1981

JAY VIA Ouachita Parish, Louisiana, detective who took Toole's second confession in 1983

CHAD WAGNER Hollywood PD chief, 2007–present

ADAM WALSH (1974–1981) Son of John and Revé Walsh

JOHN WALSH *America's Most Wanted* host and child victims' rights advocate

REVÉ (REE-VAY) WALSH Child victims' rights advocate

RICHARD WITT Martin's successor as chief at Hollywood PD, 1986–96

DR. RONALD WRIGHT Broward County medical examiner